The Power of Protocol

How did the papacy govern European religious life without a proper bureaucracy and the normal resources of a state? From Late Antiquity, papal responses were in demand. The 'apostolic see' took over from Roman emperors the discourse and demeanour of a religious ruler of the Latin world. Over the centuries, it acquired governmental authority analogous to that of a secular state – except that it lacked powers of physical enforcement, a solid financial base (aside from short periods) and a bureaucracy as defined by Max Weber. Through the discipline of applied Diplomatics, which investigates the structures and settings of documents to solve substantive historical problems, *The Power of Protocol* explores how such a demand for papal services was met. It is about the genesis and structure of papal documents – a key to papal history generally – from the Roman empire to after the Council of Trent in the sixteenth century, and is the only book of its kind.

D. L. d'Avray is Professor Emeritus of History at University College London and a Supernumerary Fellow of Jesus College, Oxford. He has published widely on medieval preaching, death and kingship, marriage, rationalities, and the papacy. He has published ten books, the last six with Cambridge, including most recently *Papal Jurisprudence, 385–1234: Social Origins and Medieval Reception of Canon Law* (2022). He has been a Fellow of the British Academy since 2005 and Corresponding Fellow of the Medieval Academy of America since 2016.

The Power of Protocol

Diplomatics and the Dynamics of Papal Government, c. 400–c. 1600

D. L. d'Avray

University College London and Jesus College, Oxford

CAMBRIDGE
UNIVERSITY PRESS

Shaftesbury Road, Cambridge CB2 8EA, United Kingdom

One Liberty Plaza, 20th Floor, New York, NY 10006, USA

477 Williamstown Road, Port Melbourne, VIC 3207, Australia

314–321, 3rd Floor, Plot 3, Splendor Forum, Jasola District Centre, New Delhi – 110025, India

103 Penang Road, #05–06/07, Visioncrest Commercial, Singapore 238467

Cambridge University Press is part of Cambridge University Press & Assessment, a department of the University of Cambridge.

We share the University's mission to contribute to society through the pursuit of education, learning and research at the highest international levels of excellence.

www.cambridge.org
Information on this title: www.cambridge.org/9781009361118

DOI: 10.1017/9781009361156

First published 2023

A catalogue record for this publication is available from the British Library.

A Cataloging-in-Publication data record for this book is available from the Library of Congress.

ISBN 978-1-009-36111-8 Hardback

TO J.C.W.

Contents

Plates

Acknowledgements

Archivio Apostolico Vaticano staff, Benedetta Albani, Bernard Barbiche, Barbara Bombi, British Library Manuscript Room staff, Peter Clarke, Emily Corran, Cecilia Cristellon, Simon Ditchfield, Liz Friend-Smith, Michael Haren (who corrected my errors and suggested the title of the book), Klaus Herbers, Peter Herde, Joshua Hey, Jochen Johrendt, Patrick Lantschner, Ana Paula Lloyd, Werner Maleczek (embodiment of the great Austrian school – I owe more than I can say to his detailed comments), Nelson Minnich, Wolfgang Müller, Jessika Nowak, Sergio Pagano, Miles Pattenden, Ken Pennington, Daniel Ponziani, Kirsi Salonen, John Sabapathy, Benjamin Savill (see copious acknowledgment in footnotes to Chapter 3), Julia Smith, Tom Smith, Ludwig Schmugge, students (inspirational to their teacher) on the UCL 'Manuscripts and Documents' MA course, Ugo Taraborrelli, Julia Walworth, Benedict Wiedemann, Agata Zielinska, and (last but perhaps most) Patrick Zutshi.

Abbreviations

AAV   = Vatican City, Archivio Apostolico Vaticano
ACDF   = Archivio Congregazione della Dottrina della Fede
ANF   = Archives Nationales de France
BAV   = Vatican City, Bibliotheca Apostolica Vaticana
BL   = British Library
J^3 = *Regesta Pontificum Romanorum ... edidit ... P. Jaffé*, ed.
            N. Herbers et al., 3rd edn., 3 vols. to date (Göttingen,
            2016–), i, ed. N. Herbers, M. Schütz, et al. (2016); ii, ed.
            N. Herbers, W. Könighaus, T. Schlauwitz, et al. (2017);
            iii, ed. N. Herbers, J. Werner, and W. Könighaus (2017).
            The number accompanying J^3 is the document number.

            'Old Jaffé' refers to the two preceding editions. The first
            number cited is the document number in the more recent:
            Regesta Pontificum Romanorum ... edidit ... P. Jaffé, ed.
            W. Wattenbach, F. Kaltenbrunner, P. Ewald, and
            S. Loewenfeld, 2nd edn., 2 vols. (Leipzig, 1885–1888).
            The second number cited, in parentheses, refers to *Regesta*
            Pontificum Romanorum, ed. P. Jaffé, 1st edn., 2 vols.
            (Berlin, 1851)
MGH   = Monumenta Germaniae Historica
PL   = electronic Patrologia Latina Database ('Migne'), now
            available through ProQuest
TNA   = The National Archives, Kew, London
★   = see Transcriptions at the end of the volume, at the date
            after the asterisk.

Preface

This book comes from decades of teaching papal Diplomatics with Palaeography to Master's level at UCL to a series of keen and inspiring students. An underlying assumption of that course has been that the admittedly technical discipline of Diplomatics – the study of the structures and genesis of documents – is a key to historical research. That it is especially crucial for understanding papal history is a central argument in this book. I needed to write the book before attempting further studies to explain why individuals and institutions came to the papacy for decisions and privileges. The demand does indeed require explanation, but the complementary problem, addressed here, is to explain how responses were possible on such an enormous scale, given that the papacy lacked a proper 'taxation and salary' system. More than any of my previous books, this one has drawn on the generosity of living experts in the field, as the acknowledgements and footnotes make clear, I hope. The most recent generation of scholars has transformed our understanding of the papacy by the application to concrete historical problems of Diplomatics – 'applied papal Diplomatics' – the niche-orientated title I originally considered for the book. Most of these contributions are papers in journals and collective volumes (the majority in German), so one of my tasks has been to integrate them into a synthesis, since the existing standard syntheses (in Latin, Italian, German and French) treat Diplomatics as an 'auxiliary science' studied separately from substantive historical problems. That is of course a legitimate approach, but the present book is about 'applied' rather than 'pure' Diplomatics. I do follow the example of these 'pure Diplomatics' treatises, however, in extending the field back to Late Antiquity and forward into the early modern period. Thus: the aim has been to explain through the technique of applied Diplomatics how the papacy coped with the governmental burden effectively thrust upon it in the period from c. 400 to c. 1600.

1 Introduction

'Governing the world by writing' is the intriguing title of a recent book about the late antique and medieval papacy. The subtitle reveals it to be about relations with Dalmatia only,[1] but the concept is applicable to the present work, which tries to explain how the papacy governed the world, in its religious aspects at least, by means of documents. The 'power' with which the book is concerned is 'power to' more than 'power over'.[2] 'Protocol' in the title is understood in a sense transferred from the world of computing as 'A (usually standardised) set of rules governing the exchange of data' (Oxford English Dictionary). The implicit analogy with software is not inappropriate, since an argument running through the book will be that cleverly designed systems compensated for the inadequacies of the 'hardware' of papal government – for its lack of a properly financed bureaucratic infrastructure.

The title does not refer to the parts of medieval documents called the 'protocol'[3] by specialists in Dipomatics (called Diplomatic in the U.K.),[4] though that discipline is the key method used in the book. The discipline is devoted to understanding the structure and setting or genesis of documents. It is one of the twin pillars of the training of medieval historians, alongside Palaeography. Diplomatics should really be part of the training not just of medievalists but of anyone using documents for research, as it is a very general methodology. Yet there is no general treatise on Diplomatics in English, and the generally good book-length treatises in other scholarly languages are technical textbooks well

---

[1] S. Gioanni, *Gouverner le monde par l'écrit. L'autorité pontificale en Dalmatie de l'Antiquité tardive à la réforme 'grégorienne'* (Bibliothèque des Écoles Françaises d'Athènes et de Rome, 386; Rome, 2020).

[2] My thanks to Professor John Holmwood for clarifying the distinction in a personal communication. Cf. J. Holmwood and A. Stewart, *Explanation and Social Theory* (Basingstoke, 1991), 118.

[3] Though one of the arguments turns on a part of the protocol (in this narrow sense) called the *arenga*.

[4] *Diplomatique* in French, *Urkundenlehre* in German. I use the U.S. form 'Diplomatics' – as a singular noun – because it reduces the chance of confusion with diplomacy.

insulated from the historical interpretation to which Diplomatics can make crucial contributions.

On specifically papal Diplomatics, R. L. Poole's decent study of the papal Chancery, over a limited period, is over a century old[5] – and it has been a long century full of major highly relevant papers. As noted in the Preface, the excellent book-length treatises in German, Italian and French that focus specifically on papal Diplomatics are rigorously 'pure' and uncontaminated by application to substantive history. They do not try to answer a central historical question about a phenomenon unique in world history, namely, how did the papacy govern the religious life of Europe without the financial and military resources of a secular state?

Letters with 'little power of implementation'[6] poured out from the curia to regions from Norway to Sicily and Poland to Portugal, solicited and accepted, yet the popes had few and risibly weak battalions and for most of the period lacked financial resources commensurate with its authority. 'The medieval Church was a state', according to Frederic William Maitland's famous dictum.[7] But this was a paradox to wake his readers up to its character as a European government. Unlike 'real' states its military powers of enforcement were minimal except where its own modest-sized central Italian state was concerned. Generally speaking, states need the sanction of physical force. The papacy could not deploy the latter outside its own lands.

The small secular state, the 'Lands of St. Peter', gave it independence from other secular states, but the resources of this third-rate principality were required for its own governance: the income from the papal state was not commensurate with government on a European scale, especially in the wake of the eleventh-century 'papal turn', with the intensification of papal involvement in the life of the Church which followed a few decades after it. Again, it is true that the papacy began to raise direct taxes on ecclesiastics, initially for crusades. Such taxes did not solve the problem of paying for government, however: for one thing, kings learned how to cream off the lion's share of papal direct taxes; for another, popes regarded the autonomy of the papal state in central Italy as indispensable for independence (probably an accurate assessment) and had to haemorrhage money to pay for Italian wars, above all against emperors who had

---

[5] R. L. Poole, *Lectures on the History of the Papal Chancery down to the Time of Innocent III* (Cambridge, 1915).

[6] Phrase suggested by Michael Haren.

[7] F. W. Maitland, 'Canon Law in England III. William of Drogheda and the Universal Ordinary', *English Historical Review*, 12 (1897), 625–652 (at 625), reprinted in *idem*, *Roman Canon Law in the Church of England. Six Essays* (London, 1928), 100–131 (at 100).

non-negligible claims to authority in Italy. Furthermore, the cities of the papal states were politically volatile. In the fourteenth century the papacy for a while gave up trying to rule from Rome and moved to the more central Avignon, which belonged to the kingdom of Naples, which was in turn held as a papal fief. In this period papal income was hugely enhanced by taxes on benefices vacated under specified conditions.

Had the papacy been content to remain at Avignon for good, without attempting to reconquer the papal states, a well-funded bureaucracy might have been on the cards. For a while, popes maintained 'the fiction that Rome in a curial sense attended on the pope',[8] and a capacity to design governmental systems was undoubtedly in evidence, as will become clear. The ingenuity was, however, deployed to find substitute systems for proper salaried bureaucracy, which could not be afforded. As the money flowed in from the new sources of revenue, it also flowed out. Separation from Rome was widely felt to be inappropriate, and popes fought expensive wars to re-establish control of the papal states.

To put it crudely, the drain of these wars on papal finances cancelled out the income from benefices. In fact, the papacy never really had a fiscal base capable of supporting a conventional government on a Europe-wide scale, at least under the Ancien Régime. In the Renaissance period and after, it resorted to the expedient of sale of offices. Though this did have some sociological compensations, to be explored in Chapter 5, it was a desperate measure from a rational financial point of view.

Thus the papacy lacked the money to pay either for a proper bureaucracy or for military resources to back up a bureaucracy's authority. Given that, the question of how the papacy coped with a Europe-wide governmental burden is central, and it cannot be answered without the help of Diplomatics. It is what I will call 'Hageneder's question', after the Austrian scholar Othmar Hageneder who posed it more clearly than anyone, and answered it with reference to one class of papal documents,[9] using Diplomatics, an approach the present volume tries to extend to other genres and a longer period. *Mutatis mutandis*, 'Hageneder's question' needs to be asked about Late Antiquity and the earlier Middle Ages too, as also about the post-Schism and post-Trent periods.

---

[8] Again, phrase suggested by Michael Haren.

[9] O. Hageneder, 'Päpstliche Reskripttechnik: Kanonistische Lehre und kuriale Praxis', in M. Bertram (ed.), *Stagnation oder Fortbildung? Aspekte des allgemeinen Kirchenrechts im 14. und 15. Jahrhundert* (Bibliothek des deutschen historischen Instituts zu Rome, 108; Tübingen, 2005) 182–196, at 194: 'wie waren Kirche und Christenheit ohne einen entsprechenden Verwaltungsapparat, der den Urkundenausstoß der Kanzlei auf die Richtigkeit seiner Voraussetzungen und seine Durchsetzung *in partibus* hätte prüfen und überwachen können, zu regieren?'

In Late Antiquity and the first medieval centuries popes issued decrees with the aplomb of Roman emperors but with none of the power the emperors had enjoyed. What kind of power did popes have? Diplomatics can tell us that it was the power of 'responsive' governments, answering rather than initiating, and also that the *prooemia* of the responses were a channel through which the apostolic see poured its image into the minds of those to whom it responded, and of the readers of canon law collections into which their responses were incorporated.

There was again an asymmetry between impact and resources – analogous to the high and late medieval disparity though on a vastly lower quantitative level – from the time of Charlemagne to the generation before the mid-eleventh-century 'papal turn'. Paving the way for the turn was a steady demand for papal documents from the localities. Documents were produced, but sometimes in shockingly poor Latin. Apparently the papacy could not count on scribes and administrators who knew their grammar. Diplomatics can tell us why papal documents did not lose their power to impress. In a nutshell, the answer is that their physical appearance was remarkable and impressive, and the script in which they were written so archaic as to be practically illegible. Much more on all this below.

We need to ask how the papacy was administratively capable of exercising so much power. One answer which may spring to the mind of modernists will not work: fear of spiritual sanctions cannot explain the phenomenon. Such fear did indeed play a part from the late eleventh century on, but it was a result rather than a cause of the growth of papal government. To project back to Late Antiquity or the early Middle Ages the profile and prestige of the high medieval papacy is to put the cart before the horse. So how did the papacy acquire that prestige in the first place? Furthermore, even granted the fear of spiritual sanctions which certainly did count for something eventually, how on earth did the papacy cope with the sheer pressure of business that we can see was thrust upon it?

Elements of the answer are in fact at hand in a plethora of highly specialised monographs and technical articles, mostly by German and Austrian historians.[10] Medieval papal Diplomatics seems to have been a field attractive to Protestant and belief-neutral scholars as well as to Catholics, perhaps because of the appeal of doing research in Rome. Even this impressive German-language scholarship is not, however, brought together within a single book-shaped frame.

---

[10] Important modern Anglophone exceptions include Patrick Zutshi, Barbara Bombi, and Kirsi Salonen. In France, Bernard Barbiche stands out.

A central aim of this book is to make a picture out of these pieces of the puzzle: to synthesise the rich and impressive but scattered scholarship on medieval papal Diplomatics and to show how they cumulatively answer 'Hageneder's question'. I try to do this with regular reference to unpublished original documents which this scholarship can illuminate.

To extend the chronological range of applied Diplomatics is a further aim. Even the rich German-language scholarship on Diplomatics seldom trespasses outside the period between Gregory the Great (c. 600) and the Reformation. For the problem in hand, however, these are not natural limits. As a renowned Marxist historian long ago observed: 'triumphant in late Antiquity, dominant in feudalism, decadent and renascent under capitalism, the Roman Church has survived every other institution – cultural, political, juridical or linguistic – historically coeval with it'.[11] His words about 'the Roman Church' are especially pertinent to the papacy, and the Diplomatics of its documents are part of the explanation. But the explanation has to extend back before and on after the medieval period as traditionally understood (roughly, 500–1500). In an ideal world the analysis would penetrate into contemporary history, but I have let it peter out where my first-hand familiarity with manuscript sources dries up. Any scholar who claimed to be on top of all the sources for papal history for even a much more limited period would be a blatant liar, but I have done serious sampling and transcribing of papal documents into the early modern period.[12]

In summary, as already stated in the Preface: the book tries to show what the technical discipline of papal Diplomatics can contribute to an explanation of how the papacy could meet the demand for its practical authority, from c. 400 to c. 1600.

Diplomatics can supply several keys to the problem of how the papacy ruled so much of Europe's religious life. For one thing, Diplomatics underpins the now generally accepted folk-theorem that the growth of papal government was demand-driven. It is easy to assume that there was an eventually successful then finally self-destructive top-down ideological campaign (an interpretation eloquently articulated though not invented by the late Walter Ullmann). But Diplomatics has shown that this was not the case. It is true that popes did propagate Petrine ideology in their replies, but they seldom initiated communication. Every specialist in high medieval papacy will now tell you that its government was 'responsive'. That works for earlier periods too, as far back as the third century, even.

[11] P. Anderson, *Passages from Antiquity to Feudalism* (London, 1978), 131–132 note 11.
[12] The section on late Antiquity is the shortest because the materials are less plentiful and because I have devoted separate volumes to them: see following note.

In the Church at Rome the idea of office charisma invested in the successor of St. Peter goes back very early. At first it was probably not widely shared, at least as understood in Rome, by other Churches in the Roman empire, but in the West, especially, there was a demand for papal services which could be turned into a belief in the office charisma.

In Late Antiquity the papacy found itself acting as a kind of help-desk in a complex religious world made up of autonomous and often fast evolving sub-systems: the religious year, key rituals like baptism, heresy, penance, celibacy, monasticism, Christological doctrine. There was uncertainty over whether this or that evolution was legitimate, and about the incompatibilities that tended to arise between different sub-systems as they evolved with lives of their own. The first general council, Nicaea 325, resolved a series of uncertainties and became a paradigm for how to do so. General councils could not easily work, however, without an emperor to get the bishops together and keep them focussed on finding solutions. In the late fourth and fifth centuries the collapse of the Western empire left a demand without the means of satisfying it through councils, which had for some decades been meeting that need. Instead, bishops looked to the apostolic see (as what we now called the papacy then called itself), which already had a special standing because it was in the former capital of the empire and claimed succession from the leader of the apostles. This is not to say that the apostolic see had anything like the status it would later acquire. The driving force behind requests for responses was a need felt especially by bishops to resolve the uncertainties that beset them.

The foregoing has been argued elsewhere,[13] but it is only the start of an explanation. Adopting a methodology articulated by another Austrian historian, Heinrich Fichtenau, we need to understand the impact of the *arengae* or *prooemia* to papal documents. When the apostolic see replied to bishops, answering their questions, they prefaced their replies with *arengae*, preambles, that emphasised papal authority. Belief that the bishop of Rome was successor to St. Peter, the leader of the apostles, went back into the mists of time in Rome itself: as A. H. M. Jones put it: '... from an early date the bishops of Rome claimed a pre-eminent position in the church, and ... they claimed it as successors of Peter, the prince of the apostles'.[14] Some papal responses were prefaced with

[13] D. L. d'Avray, *Papal Jurisprudence, c. 400. Sources of the Canon Law Tradition* (Cambridge, 2019), and *idem, Papal Jurisprudence, 385–1234. Social Origins and Medieval Reception* (Cambridge, 2022).
[14] A. H. M. Jones, *The Later Roman Empire, 284–602. A Social, Economic and Administrative Survey*, 3 vols. (with a maps volume) (Oxford, 1964), ii, 887.

strong statements about the apostolic see's authority. These were incorporated into the canon law collections that were put together at the turn of the fifth and sixth centuries, and which circulated widely in the early medieval West. They were also included in the ninth-century 'False Decretals', or 'Pseudo-Isidore', which included many genuine decretals from Late Antiquity. Pseudo-Isidore was widely copied and transmitted these *arengae* to a still wider public. Together with the decretal tradition itself they constitute a causal chain, converging to be sure with other causal chains,[15] that explains the willingness of so many people to respond to the movement known as the 'papal turn', or, more traditionally, the Gregorian Reform. The idea of papal 'office charisma' became more deeply embedded in mentalities, building on a foundation laid, notably, by *arengae* and related ideological content in papal decretals going back centuries: ideological papal *arengae* go back before the fall of the Roman empire in the West.

Not long after that a new kind of document contributed to the growth of papal prestige. By the end of the sixth century, monasteries with large landholdings had become a key part of Christian life. They sought and obtained privileges from kings but also from popes. Those papal privileges were extraordinarily impressive as material objects. They were several metres long, on papyrus (at a time when parchment had become the normal 'support' for writing), and written in strange archaic script, the 'Roman Curiale', that hardly anyone could read other than the scribes themselves. The very aspect of these documents was a source of papal prestige.

In the course of the eleventh century these papyrus privileges were phased out, for reasons to be discussed below. The visual impact of the parchment privileges that replaced them was also exceedingly striking. New forms continued the tradition of documentary manifestation of papal authority.

In the twelfth century more and more workaday documents were required, in response to a snowballing demand for papal judgments and favours underpinned by a now widespread belief in papal office charisma. Twelfth-century English monarchs from Henry II on were

---

[15] E.g. R. McKitterick, *Rome and the Invention of the Papacy: The* Liber pontificalis (Cambridge, 2020) makes a case for the *Liber*, a pope-by-pope history, as a formative influence. (On the *Liber Pontificalis* see now also K. Herbers and M. Simperl, eds., *Das Buch der Päpste – Liber pontificalis. Ein Schlüsseldokument europäischer Geschichte* (Römische Quartalschrift, Supplementband, 67; Freiburg im Breisgau, 2020).) The traditional scholarly 'folk explanation' is that much of Europe was Christianised by Anglo-Saxon missionaries who brought with them a pro-papal tradition going back to the papal missionaries who helped convert England.

experiencing similar demand for their services, but they had a tightly controlled administrative and financial system at their disposal. Counties and sheriffs were part of an integrated royal system, but bishops and dioceses were not integrated into a papal system in anything like the same way, and never would be. In administrative and financial terms there never was a 'medieval Church', but a multitude of more-or-less autonomous systems held together by the Latin language and belief in the apostolic see, alongside demand for the latter's services. The question was, how to meet that demand?

Explaining how that demand was met is, as hinted above, a key contribution of papal Diplomatics. As one cannot sufficiently emphasise, the papacy did not have a bureaucracy funded by monetary taxation, as the English monarchs did (to oversimplify somewhat). For reasons adumbrated above, that possibility was not open to the papacy. Nonetheless, the documentary productivity of the papacy from the later twelfth century on was extraordinary, and technical Diplomatics is the key to understanding how it was managed. It is a complex story but some red threads run through it. The papal court showed great ingenuity in devising systems that minimised the need for thinking at the centre and outsourced the thinking to unpaid *ad hoc* 'honoratiores', able men acting without pay. The administrative costs at the centre were paid for stage by stage, rather than through a 'taxation and salary system' such as underpins the governments of virtually all states today. Finally, ecclesiastical benefices supported absentee officials, something that was regarded as morally dubious by moralisers in the period itself and by its modern historians, though it can be argued that both have imperfectly understood the benefice system and its patchwork uneven character – there was huge variation in the value of benefices – so that some of the moralisation can give place to in-depth explanation. Never assume that people understand their own society!

Here papal Diplomatics merges into straightforward historical interpretation, but for present purposes at least that is a good thing. As a glance at its history shows, 'Diplomatics' started as a technique for detecting forgery, then evolved into a broader study of the structure and setting of documents. The final stage has been the realisation of the symbiotic relation between the 'auxiliary science' and mainstream history. Diplomatics is not a handmaid but integral to historical understanding of the papacy.

As suggested above, Diplomatics ought to be *de rigueur* in the use of any kind of historical document of any period. It identifies the performative efficacy in the world of a document – which often means its legal force. Its history as a discipline dates from the seventeenth century, but papal Diplomatics has a pre-history of acuity on the part of some popes in assessing the authenticity of this or that document.[16]

Given that Diplomatics is a discipline that can be applied to almost any kind of document or historical problem, some delimitation of the remit of the present study may be forgiven. In this and the following chapters the focus will be on papal letters which are 'witnesses to processes of a legal nature', to quote one of the greatest ever specialists in the field, Harry Bresslau.[17] Margaret Meserve has pointed out in the period covered here, after the invention of printing, printed papal documents were not 'published' in the legal sense, even though the papacy made early and frequent use of the new medium. 'Roman printers began to publish the texts of papal decrees quickly enough, but ... a bull ... was still considered officially published only when it was copied out on parchment and posted on a circuit of important doors.'[18] Thus the important story she tells about the papacy and printing lies outside our scope.

The 'legal force' litmus test brings in documents commanding acceptance of a doctrine, but not all the types of source included in the comprehensive definition Leonard Boyle (discussed below). Excluded from the book's remit are records relating to financial administration,[19] and documents which do not attempt to affect what is lawful or unlawful: papal letters conducting what one might call religious diplomacy, and/or to 'admonish, exhort, and console'.[20] Such letters survive throughout the period that concerns us, and from the period well before we get letters with intended legal force. (We have a non-trivial body of letters by

---

[16] L. Schmitz-Kallenberg, in R. Thommen and L. Schmitz-Kallenberg, *Grundriss der Geschichtswissenschaft. Urkundenlehre. II. Papsturkunden* (2nd edition, Berlin, 1913), 56–116, at 57–58; for the history of Diplomatics in general, see the good summary in F. De Lasala and P. Rabikauskas, *Il Documento Medievale e Moderno, Panorama Storico della Diplomatica Generale e Pontificia* (Rome, 2003) (henceforth De Lasala, *Il Documento*), 19–40. For a possible early example, from 371, see U. Reutter, *Damasus, Bischof von Rom (366–384)* (Studien und Texte zu Antike und Christentum, 55; Tübingen, 2009), 348–316, especially 307–308.

[17] 'Urkunden nennen wir ... schriftliche ... aufgezeichnete Erklärungen, die bestimmt sind, als Zeugnisse über Vorgänge rechtlicher Natur zu dienen' (H. Bresslau, *Handbuch der Urkundenlehre für Deutschland und Italien*, i (2nd edition, 1912), 1.

[18] M. Meserve, *Papal Bull. Print, Politics and Propaganda in Renaissance Rome* (Baltimore, MD, 2021), 60. *A fortiori*, communications to individuals or institutions would be on papyrus – in the early Middle Ages – or parchment.

[19] On the setting of these, W. E. Lunt, *Papal Revenues in the Middle Ages*, 2 vols. (New York, 1934, 1965), i, 3–136. For recent research, see W. Maleczek, ed., *Die römische Kurie und das Geld. Von der Mitte des 12. Jahrhunderts bis zum frühen 14 Jahrhundert* (Vorträge und Forschungen, 85; Ostfildern, 2018).

[20] De Lasala, *Il Documento*, 163.

bishops of Rome, Liberius (352–366) and Damasus I (366–384)[21] – both controversial figures in different ways – from the pre-decretal period.) Ordinary letters of this sort can be interpreted with what might be called the 'Diplomatics of common sense', in that these letters are not so different *qua* sources from modern communications by rulers. In an ideal world these classes of sources would have been included, though traditional Diplomatics also tends to marginalise them. On the other hand, the registration, at the centre, of documents with legal force and, where available, the records of discussions that lay behind such documents are included. They certainly help us understand how the papacy ran a world government without the resources of a state.

Chapter 2, 'The History of Papal Diplomatics', traces the evolution of Diplomatics as a discipline.[22] It begins in the seventeenth century, an age of antiquarian scholarship, with an argument between a Jesuit and a Benedictine monk about the genuineness of charters. The Benedictine's seminal treatise *De Re Diplomatica* gave the discipline an identity, the core of which is preserved in treatises on 'pure' Diplomatics, and also specifically on papal Diplomatics, up to the present day. The discipline's boundaries did not remain static, however, and already in the eighteenth century a tradition of applying Diplomatics to substantive historical problems had begun, at the university of Göttingen. In the post-War world the contours of applied Diplomatics as a method were carefully outlined as a method by Fichtenau, of the Institut für Österreichische Geschichtsforschung; and from Othmar Hageneder in the same institute came the question behind this book.

Chapter 3, 'Papal Documents, c. 400–c. 1150', starts from papal letters resolving jurisprudential problems. Like the bulk of later papal letters, their production was demand-driven. Their structure owed much to Roman imperial models. An element of the imperial model was the *arenga*, a preamble which could be a vehicle for propaganda. A study of the *arenga* was one of Fichtenau's key contributions to Diplomatics. In responding to demand for legal solutions, popes took the opportunity to begin with *arengae* which legitimated their claims to authority. Since early papal decretals were transmitted in canon law collections that were widely copied into the eleventh century and beyond, the *arengae* of Late

---

[21] J. T. Shotwell and L. R. Loomis, *The See of Peter* (New York, 1991): context and letters for Liberius: 534–563, 567–568, 590–591, 593–595; context and letters for Damasus: 595–629, 647–648, 673–674, 677–679, 694–696.

[22] Need it be said that this chapter on historiography can only cover a fraction of a field full of fine research? My apologies to all not mentioned: do not assume I have not profited from your work!

Antique decretals help explain the ready acceptance of papal claims in the Gregorian Reform.

While Late Antique decretals were being transmitted to new generations, popes corresponded with kings and emperors, by the mid-to-late eighth century at times in surprisingly faulty Latin, and, furthermore, also around that time a new genre of papal document appeared alongside them: solemn privileges, written on papyrus. These were mostly for monasteries. Not much thought was required to compose them, as beneficiaries brought drafts of the substantive part and a formulary supplied the top and the tail. What exactly these privileges granted is a matter of debate. Since they were written in a script descended from late Roman cursive and hard to read, their import may have been unclear even at the receiving end. In fact this was probably an advantage. The archaic script covered a multitude of sins against Latin grammar and diminished the likelihood of some clever young monk making fun of it. Even just handling one of these privileges would have been a challenge, given their length and the frailty of the papyrus support. That too would have diminished the likelihood of carping criticism of Latin solecisms. And the appearance would have inspired awe, not just because of the strange script but precisely because they were so long physically. With the papal revolution of the eleventh century the late Roman script and the metres-long papyrus format were abandoned, to be replaced by new devices to make the document impressive. What exactly they were granting to monasteries became clearer in the twelfth century.

Chapter 4, 'The Religious Governance of the Latin World, 1150–1378', shows how the papacy tried to meet the mushrooming demand for its documents. In the course of the twelfth century, the type of privilege that had emerged during the papal revolution began to be replaced by a new kind of document, the sort that would become known as a 'letter of grace'. In the late twelfth century, papal documents began to be written in the kind of prose rhythm called the *cursus*. The range of functions for which papal responses were needed stimulated an enlargement of the range of contents of papal documents.

The spectrum of privileges sought expanded. It was letters of grace that met the demand. Demand for benefices was one major category. Only a small proportion of papal registers were registered, and two or more people might receive the same grant, so the curia developed a system of ranked formulae to see which letter had priority.

To ensure the follow-through of grants another category of letters was developed: *litterae executoriae*. In their external features, these resembled 'letters of justice', which appointed judges delegate in the localities, to bring papal justice in the religious sphere to anyone who asked for it. An ingenious system was devised to minimise administrative costs and the need for anyone at the centre to think about a case. A formulary and a remarkable institution called the *Audientia litterarum contradictarum* helped make it work.

The administrative engine behind all this was not a bureaucracy as we understand it: there was no division between home and work, piece-work payment by the client rather than salaries, no line management. Slightly more like a bureaucracy was the Apostolic Penitentiary, which was crystallised institutionally in the thirteenth century and flourished ever afterwards. It dealt with sins too serious for an ordinary priest to absolve, but also with absolutions from excommunication and dispensations. In the fourteenth century, with the papacy based in Avignon, there was a process of rationalisation. Record keeping was less random, and rules to regulate the otherwise unbureaucratic administration were formulated for both Penitentiary and Chancery. High-level letters were handled separately from the quantitatively enormous routine business. The plague of 1348 seems not to have marked a break, but the Schism that started in 1378, shortly after the papacy returned to Rome, would certainly do so.

Chapter 5, 'From Schism to Counter-Reformation, c. 1378–c. 1600' starts with the fall-out from the Schism that lasted a generation from 1378 to 1417. The breakaway cardinals returned to Avignon, taking much of the administration with them (so that the 'Avignon Registers' continued in Avignon while a new series called the 'Lateran Registers'[23] filled the gap in Rome). The departure of so many Chancery scribes was a problem for the Rome-based papacy. To manage, it developed an entirely new kind of document, the brief (*breve*, plural *brevia*) – new that is to the curia but modelled on some secular systems – written by a different set of men, and before long distinguished by humanistic script. From this time on a dual system operated: Chancery and Secretariate. Initially the latter was for high-level letters, but in the later fifteenth century it took on routine business too. The interplay between Chancery letters and briefs written by secretaries in the fifteenth century needs a lot more elucidation as one moves into the post-Trent period.

Another post-Schism innovation was the sale of offices, an apparently absurd system nonetheless soon adopted by secular rulers: but it bound the upper classes of the papal states into the curial system and helped end the hostile relationship that went back to the late eleventh century. In the

---

[23] See H. Diener, 'Die Grossen Registerserien im Vatikanischen Archiv (1378–1523)', *Quellen und Forschungen aus italienischen Archiven und Bibliotheken*, 51 (1971), 305–368, at 321–339.

thirteenth century the papacy had spent a lot of time away from Rome, and in the fourteenth century the *curia* moved to Avignon for a quieter life. In the early modern period residence in Rome was no longer problematic, perhaps because the elites of the papal state were so invested financially in the system.

Arguably more important than any of these developments was the complete reorganisation of papal government after the Council of Trent. By contrast with the excellent scholarship on the medieval and Renaissance papacy, the papal Diplomatics of the post-Trent period is little studied and poorly understood. The last part of the chapter attempts to map out at least sketchily this *terra quasi-incognita*, looking at the changes in the functioning of the Penitentiary, the processes behind the production of letters by the Chancery and of briefs by the secretaries, and at the Congregations of the Council and of the Inquisition. The documentation generated by these two sub-systems on the problem of whether Calvinist baptism was valid (for example) is of a kind that medievalists can only envy.

Chapter 6 looks for lines running through all the centuries covered. One well-known continuity is papal archive keeping. Another, well studied for the central medieval period but important over a much longer span of time, is the use of judges delegate. At the risk of iteration, finally, a salient phenomenon is ingenuity in developing systems capable of meeting demand for papal government.

2   The History of Papal Diplomatics

The Maurists

As a self-aware intellectual system, Diplomatics begins in the seventeenth century.[1] Its history mirrors the development of medieval scholarship generally. The initial breakthrough was the work of a Benedictine monk, Jean Mabillon. His branch of the Benedictine Order, the Maurist Congregation, specialised in scholarship and made considerable contributions to medieval studies. A controversy about forgery launched the new method. A Jesuit, Daniel van Papenbroeck, questioned the authenticity of some early Benedictine documents. He discussed criteria for distinguishing forged from genuine charters ('diplomata'). In his work we see the beginnings of a methodology and the origins of the discipline.[2] Perhaps he did not mind setting the Benedictines straight about purportedly early documents. The Benedictine Mabillon riposted with a treatise on Diplomatics, *De Re Diplomatica* (Paris, 1681), literally 'On the subject of charters', in which he worked out criteria for authenticity on the basis of documents that were unquestionably genuine.[3] (Incidentally he laid the foundations for palaeographical dating at the same time.) He established what was 'common form' for documents in given periods and regions.[4] This technique for distinguishing genuine documents from forged ones would subsequently evolve into the holistic methodology just summarised. There was no special focus on papal documents in Mabillon's great work, but three quarters of a century later the Benedictine Maurists made a second major contribution which did have a special section on papal diplomatic, extremely thorough, probably

---

[1] For the early history of Diplomatics see now M. Dorna, *Mabillon und andere. Die Anfänge der Diplomatik* (Wiesbaden, 2019), especially 32–34, 104.

[2] *Ibid.*, 104–121 brings out van Papenbroeck's originality and importance, which justified emphasis on Mabillon's achievements have tended to leave in the shade.

[3] *Ibid.*, 118 on the Benedictine reaction to van Papenbroeck's critique of Saint-Denis documents.

[4] See *Ibid.*, 122–142, especially 141.

worth closer study than it gets today, but definitely a monument to what applied Diplomatics is not![5]

Papal Diplomatics in a new academic age

By the late eighteenth century the initiative had passed from Benedictine monks. A leader in the field was a Göttingen university professor, Johann Christoph Gatterer, of whom more below. From then on, German and Austrian universities and the Monumenta Germaniae Historica research institute dominated the field, apart from the small but high quality contributions of products of the (quite small) École des Chartes in Paris.[6] From the French and German-Austrian schools, in particular, came traditions of scholarly synthesis of papal Diplomatics (to these we must return), but also of editing, 'calendaring' or summarising long series of papal documents, a tradition which flourishes to this day. The opening of the Vatican Archives in 1881 had an electrifying influence on research on papal documents.[7] The French, Prussian (later, German), and Austrian institutes in Rome were magnets to scholars who liked to combine exciting research with a Roman lifestyle.

On the French side, the École Française de Rome's great series on the papal registers was initiated and carried on at a brisk pace, mostly thanks to scholars trained at the École des Chartes.[8] They provided summaries and, frequently, editions.[9] The French school focussed on the thirteenth century, from the pontificate of Gregory IX (1227–1241), and then on the Avignon popes.

For the (arguably) most important thirteenth-century pope, Innocent III, a full critical edition has been in the hands of the Österreichisches

---

[5] C. F. Toustain and R. P. Tassin, *Nouveau traité de Diplomatique*, 6 vols. (Paris, 1750–1765), tome 5 (Paris, 1762), 78–338; cf. Schmitz-Kallenberg, *Papsturkunden*, 59.

[6] And apart from isolated individuals such as R. L. Poole at Oxford.

[7] O. Chadwick, *Catholicism and History. The Opening of the Vatican Archives* (Cambridge, 1978). For the outpouring of editorial work that followed, see O. Poncet, *Les entreprises éditoriales liées aux archives du Saint-Siège. Histoire et bibliographie (1880–2000)* (Collection de l'École Française de Rome, 318; Rome, 2003). Anyone who looks through this invaluable volume will understand why what follows surveys only a small sample of the work that has been done.

[8] Innocent III's registers are, however, in the hands of a strong team under the aegis of the Austrian Academy of Sciences. In what follows, I give some salient examples of the immense work of calendaring and editing of papal bulls from the late nineteenth century, but for a full list up to the end of the twentieth century see T. Frenz and S. Pagano, *I Documenti Pontifici nel Medioevo e nell'Età Moderna* (Vatican City, 1998), 100–105. An exemplary bibliography of secondary scholarship follows, pp. 106–129.

[9] B. Galland, 'Les publications des registres pontificaux par l'École Française de Rome', *Revue d'historie de l'Église de la France*, 217 (2000), 645–656.

Institut für Geschichtsforschung, that citadel of Diplomatics as a discipline. The original initiative was taken by Leo Santifaller. Since then it has made great progress thanks to scholars like Othmar Hageneder and Werner Maleczek.[10] Between Innocent III's registers and those covered by the École Française de Rome are the registers of Honorius III, for which a proper critical edition is lacking.[11]

German scholarship was complementary: it concentrated on the preceding period, before 1198, when the unbroken series of papal registers begins (also, as we shall see, on the period after the one which the École Française de Rome had made its own). Even without surviving registers, enormous numbers of papal letters survive from the earlier period. At the end of the nineteenth century the academically powerful Paul Fridolin Kehr started a great survey of papal documents up to 1198.[12] The enterprise was meant to culminate in editions of all papal letters before Innocent III. That proved unrealistic, but a huge amount has been achieved. Like the great academic baron – if not emperor – that he was, Kehr divided up the world among project workers, as one of them reported.[13] This was Walter Holtzmann. His assignment was to publish the best text possible of papal bulls with as much context as possible. Volumes whose title begins with *Papsturkunden*, as Holtzmann's does, set out critically to edit all unpublished or inadequately edited texts. Given the state of transmission in England, resulting from the Reformation, he had to work largely from cartularies (volumes of transcriptions of documents made by monasteries and similar institutions).

Another branch of the Kehr tradition[14] includes the word *Pontificia* .... And so: *Italia Pontificia*,[15] *Iberia Pontificia*. These impressive volumes are 'registers': critical summaries of papal documents and references to papal

---

[10] For the history of this great historical enterprise, see W. Maleczek, 'L'Edition autrichienne des registres d'Innocent III', *Mélanges de l'École Française de Rome* 112-1 (200), 259–272.

[11] Maleczek, 'L'Édition autrichienne', 270–272, on the shortcomings of Pressuti's editorial efforts.

[12] For the following I am indebted to W. Maleczek (personal communication).

[13] Cf. W. Holtzmann, *Papsturkunden in England*, i, *Bibliotheken und Archive in London* (Abhandlungen der Akademie der Wissenschaften in Göttingen, Philologisch-historische Klasse, n.s., xxv, 1; Berlin, 1930), 3: '... richtete Paul Kehr an mich die Frage, ob ich nicht an seinem Papstunkundenwerk mitarbeiten wolle. Die Welt sei weggegeben ... nur England und der Orient harre noch der Bearbeitung'.

[14] At the time of writing it is in the sure hands of Klaus Herbers.

[15] See notably K. Herbers and J. Johrendt, eds., *Das Papsttum und das vielgestaltige Italien. Hundert Jahre Italia Pontificia* (Abhandlungen der Akademie der Wissenschaften zu Göttingen, n.s., 5; Berlin, 2009); M. Matheus, 'Das Deutsche Historische Institut (DHI) in Rom und Paul Fridolin Kehrs Papsturkundenwerk', in *ibid.*, 3–12, at 5, gives the background to Kehr's project.

documents, and even actions such as the consecration of a church,[16] arranged country by country. Kehr's approach (which has evolved somewhat since) was revolutionary at the time in that the publications were structured not by the date of issue of documents but by the receivers.[17] This work continues.[18] Other series and standalone volumes calendar papal documents after Kehr's cut-off date,[19] though the mass of material is so large that huge gaps remain.

Another tradition goes back still earlier. A chronological calendar of papal documents was initiated by Philipp Jaffé and his *Regesta Pontificum Romanorum*. This astonishing achievement was published in 1851. A greatly expanded update was produced in 1885 by other scholars: Wilhelm Wattenbach, Ferdinand Kaltenbrunner, Paul Ewald, and Samuel Loewenfeld.[20] A still further expanded third version is currently in progress under the direction of Klaus Herbers.[21] A complementary series is appearing within the framework of another great German series,

---

[16] D. Girgensohn, 'Kehrs Regesta Pontificum Romanorum: Entstehung – wissenschaftlicher Ertrag – organisatorische Schwächen', in Herbers and Johrendt, *Das Papsttum und ... Italien*, 215–257, at 222.

[17] Herbers and Johrendt, *Das Papsttum und ... Italien*, Vorwort, p. VII; Girgensohn, 'Kehrs Regesta'.

[18] Thus, most recently at time of writing, C. Knie, S. Panzram, L. Livorsi, R. Selvaggi, and W. Könighaus, eds., *Iberia Pontificia*, VII, *Hispania Romana et Visigotha* (Göttingen, 2022). Here the receiving region, rather than institution, is the unit; also, contrary to Kehr's original conception (Girgensohn, 'Kehrs Regesta', 220 note 23) canon law sources are important.

[19] There are important volumes in the *Index actorum pontificum romanorum* series published by the Vatican Library, notably B. Barbiche, *Les actes pontificaux originaux des Archives nationales de Paris*, 3 vols. (Vatican City, 1975–1982) and P. Zutshi, *Original Papal Letters in England, 1305–1415* (Index Actorum Romanorum Pontificum / Commision internationale de diplomatique, 5; Vatican City, 1990). For a history of the 'Censimento Bartoloni' project (as it is called after its initiator) see B. Barbiche, 'Le Censimento Bartoloni et ses premiers développements: un nouvel élan pour la diplomatique pontificale', in M. Sohn-Kronthaler and J. Verger, eds., *Europa und Memoria. Festschrift für Andreas Sohn zum 60. Geburtstag* (St. Ottilien, 2019), 227–239. There are also closely related standalone contributions like J. E. Sayers, *Original Papal Documents in England and Wales from the Accession of Pope Innocent III to the Death of Pope Benedict XI (1198–1304)* (Oxford, 1999). B. Schwarz, 'Die Erforschung der mittelalterlichen römischen Kurie von Ludwig Quidde bis heute', in Michael Matheus, ed., *Friedensnobelpreis und historische Grundlagenforschung* (Bibliothek des Deutschen Historischen Instituts in Rom, 124; Rome, 2012), 415–439, 423 note 28, for a list of volumes published when she wrote. The series is still very much alive. Schwarz's own volume, *Regesten der in Niedersachsen und Bremen überlieferten Papsturkunden 1198–1503* (Hanover, 1993) has deliberately distinctive features: it focusses on the reception end, goes into the sixteenth century, is not restricted to original Chancery products (pp. VIII–X) and aims to serve regional and social history rather than Diplomatics; nonetheless, students of applied Diplomatics will learn a lot from pp. XVI–XXVIII.

[20] N. Herbers et al., eds., *Regesta Pontificum Romanorum ... edidit ... P. Jaffé*, 3rd edn., 3 vols. to date (Göttingen, 2016–), i, ed. N. Herbers, M. Schütz, et al. (2016), p. ix.

[21] *Ibid.*: four volumes have appeared to date (summer 2022).

the *Regesta Imperii* founded by Johann Friedrich Böhmer.[22] This too is confined to the period up to 1198, from when Innocent III became pope and papal registers survive.

Somersaulting from 1198 over the period covered by the École Française project, the German school of papal documentary research, as one may well call it, created at the end of the nineteenth century – and still maintains – another great project, the *Repertorium Germanicum*. Its chronological remit is the period from the great Western Schism to the Reformation. It is organised prosopographically. The names of anyone connected with the Holy Roman Empire (generously defined) are listed pontificate by pontificate, with all the documents in the Vatican Archives that give evidence of their activity.[23] It is a valuable tool for Diplomatics once its abbreviations are understood: notably, 'committ. partibus' indicates a commission to judges delegate, on which system much more in subsequent chapters.

Among other national enterprises of the same kind it is worth mentioning the revived *Calendar of Papal Letters Relating to Great Britain and Ireland*, published by the Irish Manuscripts Commission. This took over from an earlier series produced the Public Record Office (now The

---

[22] At present, the easiest way to access a list is via the *Regesta Imperii* opac: http://opac .regesta-imperii.de/lang_en/, *s.v.* 'Papstregesten' (consulted 7 May 2022). Note especially (since even the best websites sometimes disappear): V. Unger, ed., *J. F. Böhmer, Regesta Imperii I. Die Regesten des Kaiserreichs unter den Karolingern 751–918 (926/962), 4. Papstregesten, 800–911. Tl. 3. 872–882* (Vienna, 2013); K. Herbers, ed., *J. F. Böhmer, Regesta Imperii, I: Die Regesten des Kaiserreiches uner den Karolingern 751–918 (926/962), iv, Papstregesten 800–911, t. 2: 844–872, Lieferung 1: 844–858* (Cologne, 1999); K. Herbers, ed., *J. F. Böhmer, Regesta Imperii, I: Die Regesten des Kaiserreiches uner den Karolingern 751–918 (926/962), iv, Papstregesten 800–911, t. 2: 844–872, Lief. 2: 858–867* (Vienna, 2012); H. Zimmermann, ed., *J. F. Böhmer, Regesta Imperii II. Sächsisches Haus 919–1024. 5. Papstregesten, 911–1024* (Vienna, 1998); K. A. Frech, *J. F. Böhmer, Regesta Imperii, III. Salisches Haus 1024–1058. 1. Lieferung: 1024–1046* (Cologne, 2006); K. A. Frech, *J. F. Böhmer, Regesta Imperii III. Salisches Haus 1024–1125. 5. Abt.: Paptregesten 1024–1058. 2 Lieferung: 1046–1058* (Cologne, 2011); K. Baaken and U. Schmidt, eds., *J. F. Böhmer, Regesta Imperii IV: Lothar III. und ältere Staufer, 4. Abteilung: Papstregesten 1124–1198, Teil 4: 1181–1198, Lieferung 1: 1181–1184* (Cologne, 2003); K. Baaken and U. Schmidt, eds., *J. F. Böhmer, Regesta Imperii IV: Lothar III. und ältere Staufer, 4. Abteilung: Papstregesten 1124–1198, Teil 4, Lieferung 2: 1184–1185* (Cologne, 2006); U. Schmidt, ed., *J. F. Böhmer, Regesta Imperii, Regesta Imperii IV. Lothar III und ältere Staufer 1125–1197. 4 Abt.: Papstregesten 1124–1198, Teil 4, Lieferung 3, 1185–1187, Urban III. und Gregor VIII* (Cologne, 2012); U. Schmidt, ed., *J. F. Böhmer, Regesta Imperii, Regesta Imperii IV. Lothar III. und ältere Staufer 1125–1197 4. Abt.: Papstregesten 1124–1198, Teil 4, Lieferung 4: 1187–1191: Clemens III* (Cologne, 2014); U. Schmidt, ed., *J. F. Böhmer, Regesta Imperii IV. Lothar III. und ältere Staufer. 4. Abt.: Papstregesten 1124–1198, Teil 4: 1181–1198, Lieferung 5: 1191–1195, Cölestin III* (Cologne, 2018).

[23] D. L. d'Avray, 'Germany and the Papacy in the Late Middle Ages', *Journal of Ecclesiastical History*, 71 (2020), 362–367, is an introduction to this great series.

National Archives) and published by Her Majesty's Stationery Office.[24] The new series has been on a high scholarly level, and the inaugural volume[25] included invaluable extra features which amount to a 'diplomatic' of the late medieval papal Chancery: an essay by Leonard Boyle on 'The Papal Chancery at the End of the Fifteenth Century',[26] which takes the reader through the *Geschäftsgang* of a letter (its path through the papal administration), and a formulary illustrating fully the common forms that occur again and again in the letters.[27]

Treatises on papal Diplomatics

Boyle's description of the *Geschäftsgang* and the editor's formulary can be situated in a long tradition of analysis of specifically papal Diplomatics going back to the nineteenth century. A notable if compact treatise was devoted specifically to papal Diplomatics by Ludwig Schmitz-Kallenberg,[28] who provided an excellent resumé of earlier research. As well as looking back to medieval attempts to distinguish authentic from forged documents, and tracing the origins of the discipline from Mabillon's *De Re Diplomatica*, he sketched the 'state of research' in his own time, drawing attention to the papal sections of the large scale scholarly syntheses by Arthur Giry[29] (a *chartiste*) in France and Harry Bresslau in Germany.[30]

Bresslau's work in particular wears well even today – the Italian edition of 1998 makes virtually no changes.[31] His long sections on papal Diplomatics remain an essential port of call for anyone working on the topic, and I have had it within easy reach even when I cite more recent studies. Bresslau was closely associated with the Monumenta Germaniae

---

[24] W. H. Bliss et al., eds., *Calendar of Entries in the Papal Registers Relating to Great Britain and Ireland, Papal Letters*, 14 vols. (London, 1893–1933).

[25] M. J. Haren, ed., *Calendar of Entries in the Papal Registers relating to Great Britain and Ireland: Papal Letters*, vol. XV: *Innocent VIII: Lateran Registers 1484–1492* (Dublin, 1978).

[26] *Ibid.*, xv–xxiv   [27] *Ibid.*, xlix–cxxi.

[28] Schmitz-Kallenberg, in Thommen and Schmitz-Kallenberg, *Grundriss*.

[29] A. Giry, *Manuel de diplomatique* (1st edition, Paris, 1894). Continuations of the French *chartiste* tradition were A. de Boüard, *Manuel de Diplomatique française et pontificale*. I, *Diplomatique générale* (Paris, 1929), very interesting for common structures of French royal and papal diplomatic, and O. Guyotjeannin, with J. Pycke and B.-M. Tock, *La Diplomatique médiévale* (Turnhout, 1993), an outstanding and readable introduction to the discipline in general.

[30] H. Bresslau, *Handbuch der Urkundenlehre für Deutschland und Italien*, i (Leipzig, 1889; 2nd edition, Berlin 1912); ii, erste Abteilung (Leipzig, 1915); ii zweite Abteilung, published posthumously by H.-W. Klewitz (Berlin, 1931).

[31] H. Bresslau, *Manuale di Diplomatica per la Germania e l'Italia*, transl. A. M. Voci-Rot (Rome, 1998), pp. X–XI for extremely minor changes made.

Historica institute, which became the gold standard for editorial scholarship in Europe. Among specialists in papal Diplomatics of Schmitz-Kallenberg's own generation, he singles out the publications of Wilhelm Diekamp for special praise, and von Pflugk-Hartung for polite criticism.[32]

Schmitz-Kallenberg's treatise was surely a model for the course on papal Diplomatics which was taught for many years at the Gregorianum University in Rome, and which was crystallised in a textbook by Paulius Rabikauskas. This book was essentially a photocopied and bound typescript (with some additions in pen!), in Latin, reproduced for his students and hard to obtain except from the bookstore of the Gregorianum.[33] Fernando De Lasala brought out, in Italian, a substantially revised and updated version of Rabikauskas.[34]

Comparison between Schmitz-Kallenberg and 'Rabikauskas & De Lasala' (henceforth 'De Lasala') is instructive.[35] There is a common approach. In both cases, the treatise on papal Diplomatics follows on from one on general Diplomatics (by a different author in Schmitz-Kallenberg's case). Both begin with a general preliminary section, including a short history of the discipline, with emphasis on registers of papal documents. Schmitz-Kallenberg gives the typical parts of a document here, notably the *arenga* (preamble) to which we must return, the *narratio* which gives the background, the *dispositio* which gives the papal decision, and the *sanctio* and *comminatio* which demand obedience and say what will happen if it is withheld.

The Diplomatics textbooks draw out attention to the crucial *narratio–dispositio* contrast, which goes back to Late Antiquity.[36] De Lasala had already laid out this structure in the general Diplomatics section, but the key distinction between *narratio* and *dispositio* is re-emphasised: the former is often in the words of the persons to whom the pope is replying and gives their version of the story, which the pope does not necessarily accept; the *dispositio* often includes a requirement that the story be verified by someone on the spot.[37]

---

[32] Schmitz-Kallenberg, *Papsturkunden*, 60–61.

[33] P. Rabikauskas, *Diplomatica pontificia. (Praelectionum lineamenta), Editio sexta emendata et aucta (ad usum auditorum)* (Rome, 1998). I purchased multiple copies of this for my UCL students, but, strangely, the Latin presentation did not cast the spell over them that I had expected.

[34] De Lasala, *Il Documento*.

[35] The respective tables of contents facilitate comparison: *Schmitz*-Kallenberg, *Papsturkunden*, pp. V–VI, and De Lasala, *Il Documento*, 344–346.

[36] Schmitz-Kallenberg, *Papsturkunden*, 78; Rabikauskas, *Diplomatica Pontificia*, 24; De Lasala, *Il Documento*, 165.

[37] De Lasala, *Il Documento*, 155.

It should be stressed, in parenthesis, that raising awareness of the difference between *narratio* and *dispositio* has been one of the key services of Diplomatics to historical interpretation. The transition point between the parts of a document can easily be missed. In an otherwise splendid article by Hans Eberhard Mayer, he misses the transition between *narratio* and *dispositio* in a letter of 28 August 1255 by Alexander IV. Mayer took this to be an annulment.[38] The letter does indeed retail the grounds for annulment as well as expounding the pope's duty to look after widows and orphans. (The lady in question, the interesting Plaisance of Cyprus, though very young, was already a widow.)[39] This is, however, a letter to judges delegate[40] and contains the key phrase 'if matters are as stated', which he commissioned them to investigate.[41] For the actual annulment Plaisance had to wait until 1258.[42] Another such case, where the whole history of the Bible in the Middle Ages has been misunderstood for want of awareness of technical diplomatics, is discussed below. These instances are a reminder that traditional Diplomatics remains indispensable.

Both Schmitz-Kallenberg and De Lasala go on to separate out successive periods of papal history. The periodisation is similar. Schmitz-Kallenberg takes the first period up to the second half of the eighth century, De Lasala up to 772, on the grounds that in the pontificate of

[38] H. E. Mayer, 'Ibelin versus Ibelin: The Struggle for the Regency of Jerusalem 1253–1258', *Proceedings of the American Philosophical Society* 122 (1978), 25–57, at 47; cf. D. L. d'Avray, *Dissolving Royal Marriages. A Documentary History, 860–1600* (Cambridge, 2014), 98–102.

[39] d'Avray, *Dissolving*, 101.

[40] On judges delegate, see above all P. Herde, *Audientia litterarum contradictarum: Untersuchungen über die päpstlichen Justizbriefe und die päpstliche Delegationsgerichtsbarkeit vom 13. bis zum Beginn des 16. Jahrhunderts*, 2 vols. (Bibliothek des Deutschen Historischen Instituts in Rom, 31, 32; Tübingen, 1970); idem, 'Papal Formularies for Letters of Justice (13th–16th Centuries): Their Development and Significance for Medieval Canon Law', in Bertram, *Stagnation oder Fortbildung?*, 221–247; Ute Pfeiffer, *Untersuchungen zu den Anfängen der päpstlichen Delegationsgerichtsbarkeit in 13 Jahrhundert. Edition und diplomatisch-kanonistische Auswertung zweier Vorläufersammlungen der Vulgataredaktion des Formularium Audientie Litterarum Contradictarum* (Vatican City, 2011); for England, R. Brentano, *York Metropolitan Jurisdiction and Papal Judges Delegate, 1279–1296* (Berkeley, CA, 1959) and J. E. Sayers, *Papal Judges Delegate in the Province of Canterbury, 1198–1254. A Study in Ecclesiastical Jurisdiction and Administration* (London, 1971); for Normandy, H. Müller, *Päpstliche Delegationsgerichtsbarkeit in der Normandie (12. und frühes 13. Jahrhundert)* 2 vols. (Bonn, 1997); idem, 'Generalisierung, dichte Beschreibung, kontrastierende Einzelstudien? Stand und Perspektiven der Erforschung delegierter Gerichtsbarkeit des Papstes im Hochmittelalter', in J. Johrendt and H. Müller, eds., *Rom und die Regionen. Studien zur Homogenisierung der lateinischen Kirche im Hochmittelalter* (Abhandlungen der Akademie der Wissenschaften zu Göttingen, n.s., 19; Berlin, 2012), 145–156.

[41] d'Avray, *Dissolving*, 102.   [42] *Ibid.*, 104–107.

Hadrian I (from 772), the papacy loses its institutional link with the Byzantine empire, and there is also a differentiation between kinds of documents (solemn privileges and other sorts).[43] Both historians bring the second period up to the pontificate of Leo IX (1049), the start of the 'papal turn', which was reflected in multiple ways by documentary practice.

Then they diverge, though the basic approach remains the same. De Lasala proposes a third period up to 1331 (to a reform of papal administration by John XXII), and a fourth to 1588, when the whole papal administration was being reorganised in the wake of the Council of Trent. A fifth period runs into the twenty-first century, but De Lasala does not devote much attention to generations after Trent. Schmitz-Kallenberg has a third period to the accession of Innocent III at the end of the twelfth century,[44] a fourth to the end of the great Schism of the West (1417),[45] and a fifth going up to near the end of the fifteenth century (1484).[46] The post-medieval period is dismissed in a couple of pages, though the appearance of an important new type of document, the brief, at the start of this final period, is given due emphasis.[47]

Topics covered in the treatises of Schmitz-Kallenberg and Rabikauskas & De Lasala

Within period sections the two treatises cover similar themes, especially for the first part of the medieval period. Thus for the second period, from the Carolingian period up to the Gregorian Reform, both start with different types of document, in particular the difference between letters and privileges, the latter more impressive because meant to be kept permanently. (It is Schmitz-Kallenberg who best conveys their huge size: up to three meters long and half a meter wide.)[48] Both books have sections on the Chancery, and both on the famous formulary book called the *Liber Diurnus*.

Thomas Frenz & Sergio Pagano

There is a thematic alternative to the period-based treatments of papal Diplomatics by Schmitz-Kallenberg and De Lasala: a short but

---

[43] De Lasala, *Il Documento*, 159–160.   [44] Schmitz-Kallenberg, *Papsturkunden*, 89–99.
[45] *Ibid.*, 99–109.   [46] *Ibid.*, 109–114.   [47] *Ibid.*, 114–116.
[48] *Ibid.*, 84. In *Pontificum Romanorum Diplomata Papyracea quae supersunt in tabulariis Hispaniae Italiae Germaniae* (Rome, 1928), itself a volume in an enormous format, the problem of length is solved by reproducing privileges over three consecutive sides.

invaluable synthesis by Thomas Frenz,[49] subsequently translated and updated in collaboration with Sergio Pagano.[50] (The thematic structure was also Bresslau's choice, incidentally.) Of course chronological developments are traced within the individual chapters and sections.

The first big theme is the variety of types of papal documents and their features. Notable topics (also on the agenda for discussion below) were the difference between the very formal and impressive-looking 'privileges', on the one hand, and letters on the other; within the 'letters' category we meet sub-distinctions between letters on silk thread (edging out privileges as the documents of a permanent right) and on string (documents intended for proximate action). From the mid-thirteenth century there are also 'solemn letters', which were meant to have a relatively long-term juridical effect or which were in other ways especially important. At the end of the medieval period a further major category, 'briefs', appears.

A chapter on 'style' brings together modes of address (e.g. different in letters to excommunicated persons), the prose rhythm (called the *cursus*) expected in the twelfth and much of the thirteenth centuries, practical hints on recurrent formulae, the *Liber Diurnus* with its history stretching back to Late Antiquity, and other formularies, including the so-called *Audientia* formulary of which much will be said below. Not much will be said, however, in the present volume about seals, the subject of Frenz & Pagano's chapter III.

Registration of papal documents is the next theme treated by Frenz & Pagano. It appears that this history too goes back to Late Antiquity, perhaps even to the fourth century,[51] though there are many uncertainties: we do not know how completely and continuously the registers were compiled or when the transition from papyrus to parchment and from roll to codex took place. We have a lot of letters of Gregory I, but they derive from copies made from the original 14 papyrus rolls, which have not survived. We have an eleventh-century copy of the register for six years (876–882) of the pontificate of John VIII, and the original register of Gregory VII. Other letters have come down to us indirectly, notably through canon law sources, though they present critical problems.

---

[49] T. Frenz, *Papsturkunden des Mittelalters und der Neuzeit* (Stuttgart, 1986).

[50] Frenz and Pagano, *I Documenti*. The overall structure is unchanged from the original German version by Thomas Frenz, but the Italian editions by Sergio Pagano have some new parts and an updated bibliography.

[51] Frenz and Pagano, *I Documenti*, 52–53; cf. R. Ronzani, 'Notes on the Diplomatic Aspects in the Documentation of the *Scrinium Romanae Ecclesiae*', in R. L. Testa and G. Marconi, eds., *The* Collectio Avellana *and its Revivals* (Cambridge, 2019), 260–279, at 273.

It should be noted that what evidence we have suggests that the registers recorded letters rather than privileges (a distinction to which we will return); the transmission of privileges derives from the beneficiaries. Only for the seventh century after Gregory I, and for the tenth and early eleventh centuries, is nothing known.[52] From Innocent III, 1198 on we have an almost continuous series, ramifying into an increasing number of different kinds of register.

Frenz & Pagano then devote two chapters to the key mechanisms of papal government, the Chancery and the path followed by documents from origin to execution (*Geschäftsgang, iter bureaucratico*). A final chapter deals with 'non-papal pontifical documents', issued by councils, cardinals, the Apostolic Penitentiary (which dealt with dispensations and absolutions from especially grave sins), and the papal financial organ, the *Camera*.

These general works reflect a state of scholarship which is impressive so far as the medieval period is concerned. From the time of Bresslau and Schmitz-Kallenberg onwards scholars have been equipped with reliable surveys of the ground, and these have been supplemented by high quality research on specific problems and periods, such as those of Leo Santifaller on the early medieval papal formulary (*Liber Diurnus*),[53] Hans-Henning Kortüm[54] and Judith Werner[55] on the major role of petitioners/recipients in the formulation of papal privileges, Peter Herde on thirteenth-century papal letters,[56] Patrick Zutshi on the -fourteenth-century papal Chancery (as well as on a series of other aspects of papal Diplomatics),[57] Othmar Hageneder[58] and Brigitte

---

[52] The foregoing closely follows R. Schieffer, 'Die päpstlichen Register vor 1198', in Herbers and Johrendt, *Das Papsttum und … Italien*, 261–273, at 263–266.

[53] L. Santifaller, *Liber diurnus. Studien und Forschungen*, ed. H. Zimmermann (Päpste und Papsttum, 10; Stuttgart, 1976).

[54] H.-H. Kortüm, *Zur päpstlichen Urkundensprache im frühen Mittelalter. Die päpstlichen Privilegien 896–1046* (Beiträge zur Geschichte und Quellenkunde des Mittelalters, 17; Sigmaringen, 1995).

[55] J. Werner, *Papsturkunden vom 9. bis ins 11. Jahrhundert. Untersuchungen zum Empfängereinfluss auf die äussere Urkundengestalt* (Berlin, 2017).

[56] P. Herde, *Beiträge zum päpstlichen Kanzlei-und Urkndenwesen im 13. Jahrhundert* (2nd edition, Kallmünz, 1967).

[57] See now his selected papers: P. Zutshi, *The Avignon Popes and their Chancery: Collected Essays* (Florence, 2021), fundamental contributions of the hightest quality. Note especially 'The Papal Chancery. Avignon and Beyond', in *ibid.*, 3–24.

[58] E.g. O. Hageneder, 'Die Rechtskraft spätmittelalterlicher Papst-und Herrscherurkunden "*ex certa scientia*", "*non obstantibus*" und "*propter importunitatem petentium*"', in P. Herde und H. Jakobs, eds., *Papsturkunde und europäisches Urkundenwesen: Studien zu ihrer formalen und rechtlichen Kohärenz vom 11. bis 15. Jahrhunderts* (Archiv für Diplomatik, Schriftgeschichte Siegel- und Wappenkunde, 7; Cologne, 1999), 401–429.

Meduna[59] on derogatory clauses, *clausulae*, in papal letters, Thomas Frenz on the Renaissance period,[60] or Barbara Bombi on the Diplomatics of diplomacy[61] – to name a random few of the plethora of excellent studies.[62]

It therefore comes as a shock to find how little early modern scholarship can show to compare with this. There is good work (discussed in the final chapter) on the workings of the Congregations set up after Trent (above all by Benedetta Albani on the Congregation of the Council and Francesco Beretta on the Inquisition); Thomas Frenz has pushed his researches forward beyond Trent,[63] though their centre of gravity remains the Renaissance; Olivier Poncet reconstructs the institutional setting of relations between the papacy and France;[64] but procedures of the central administration, the path of a document through the system – its *Geschäftsgang* – and that of the Apostolic Penitentiary after a major post-Tridentine reorganisation, have received far far less attention than their medieval counterparts. Guides to the Vatican Archives by K. A. Fink,[65] Leonard Boyle,[66] L. Pásztor,[67] and F. X. Blouin et al.[68] are

[59] B. Meduna, *Studien zum Formular der päpstlichen Justizbriefen von Alexander III. bis Innozenz III. (1159–1216): Die non obstantibus-Formel* (Vienna, 1989).

[60] T. Frenz, *Die Kanzlei der Päpste der Hochrenaissance (1471–1527)* (Tübingen 1986). This book is fundamental and invaluable, but a cryptic system of abbreviations of various sorts is a model of what scholars should avoid.

[61] B. Bombi, *Anglo-Papal Relations in the Early Fourteenth Century: A Study in Medieval Diplomacy* (Oxford, 2019).

[62] To get a sense of the sheer quantity and quality of publications on papal diplomatic and the papal Chancery in just one century, see A. Paravicini Bagliani, *Il Papato nel Secolo XIII. Cent'Anni di Bibliografia (1875–2009)* (Florence, 2010), 289–347, 362–374. For a survey of recent German scholarship, most of which it would be impossible to list here, and unnecessary after his admirable essay, see J. Johrendt, 'Papsturkunden und Papstbriefe bis zu Bonifaz VIII.', *Archiv für Diplomatik*, 66 (2020), 331–356 (Johrendt is himself one of the most important current contributors to the field). In addition to the printed works discussed and many others for which there is no space, there is an invaluable electronic resource, under the aegis of T. Frenz, at www.phil.uni-passau.de/histhw/forschung/lexikon-der-papstdiplomatik/ (consulted 9 May 2022).

[63] Frenz and Pagano, *I Documenti* includes 'l'età moderna' (i.e. the early modern period). Frenz, *Die Kanzlei* makes forays well beyond Trent.

[64] O. Poncet, *La France et le pouvoir pontifical (1595–1661). L'Ésprit des institutions* (Bibliothèque des Écoles françaises d'Athènes et de Rome, 347; Rome, 2011). Poncet is especially strong on major benefices (bishoprics and abbeys) and what one might call 'international relations'.

[65] K. A. Fink, *Das Vatikanische Archiv: Einführung in die Bestände und ihre Erforschung* (2nd edition, Rome, 1951).

[66] L. E. Boyle, *A Survey of the Vatican Archives and of its Medieval Holdings* (Toronto, 1972).

[67] L. Pásztor, *Guida delle fonti per la storia dell'America Latina negli archivi della Santa Sede e negli archivi ecclesiastici d'Italia* (Collectanea Archivi Vaticani, 2; Vatican City, 1970).

[68] F. X. Blouin et al., *Vatican Archives. An Inventory and Guide to Historical Documents of the Holy See* (New York, 1998). This was severely criticised by S. Pagano, the Vice-Prefect and then Prefect of the Archives: S. Pagano, 'Una Discutibile "Guida" degli Archivi

of course invaluable, but their primary function is to help the modern researcher navigate the collections, not to work out the processes that created the latter. In fact it might be impossible to do so without the help of early modern accounts of the workings of the system, which I have used in my own very provisional attempt to reconstruct it. This uncharted territory will be revisited at the end of this survey of papal Diplomatics.

Applied Diplomatics

There are new things to be said even about the territory so well mapped by Schmitz-Kallenberg, Rabikauskas, De Lasala, Frenz & Pagano, and others, if we look at it from the different vantage point of 'applied Diplomatics'. The surveys by Schmitz-Kallenberg, Bresslau, Frenz & Pagano, and De Lasala all belong to what the great Austrian scholar Heinrich Fichtenau called the 'strict observance' of Diplomatics – pure as opposed to applied Diplomatics, Diplomatics as a standalone discipline kept distinct from substantive historical analysis (see below). But there was and is another tradition, entirely compatible it should be said, and almost as venerable, for its origins go back to the eighteenth century.

Johann Christoph Gatterer

A tradition of applied Diplomatics can be traced back to Johann Christoph Gatterer, a professor at Göttingen in the second half of the eighteenth century. The approach has been described as 'an attempt to create a new paradigm'.[69] His integration of Diplomatics and manuscript studies generally into university historical training was certainly worlds away from anything one could find in eighteenth-century Oxford or

---

Vaticani', *Archivum Historiae Pontificiae*, 37 (1999), 191–201. For comments on that see F. X. Blouin, E. Yakel, and L. A. Coombs, '"Vatican Archives: An Inventory and Guide to Historical Documents of the Holy See" – A Ten-Year Retrospective', *American Archivist*, 71(2) (2008), 410–432, at 430–431: 'We encouraged review by the ASV, but … no one on the staff read the draft. The ASV section of the draft remained untouched in the prefect's office for five years prior to the publication of the guide.' For constructive criticisms see the review by P. Zutshi, *Journal of Ecclesiastical History* 53 (2002), 788–790. For all its faults, I have found the volume most useful for hands-on research, much fuller than the previous guides, and always take my own copy with me into the AAV, where no copy is available to readers. For a conspectus of series and the call marks for ordering documents see the *Indice dei Fondi e relativi mezzi di descrizione e di ricerca dell'Archivio Apostolico Vaticano* (Vatican City, 2021) (the website at www .archivioapostolicovaticano.va/content/aav/it/patrimonio.html is frequently updated and page numbers may change so I do not give them when citing this invaluable resource).
[69] Dorna, *Mabillon*, 235–248.

Cambridge and in fact stands up well to comparison with most graduate schools today.[70] Gatterer consciously broadened the scope of the discipline far beyond the discrimination between authentic and forged documents. Reviewing the exhaustive Maurist *Nouveau traité de diplomatique*, he commented that if the discipline had no other purpose than the one attributed to it by its authors Toustain and Tassin, he could hardly understand why a scholar would devote so much time to it as he, Gatterer, clearly also thought it deserved: for he saw it as a tool for historical interpretation.[71]

Heinrich Fichtenau

Since then, the two traditions of 'pure' and 'applied' Diplomatics have run side by side. Each needs the other: they are symbiotic.[72] So far as papal Diplomatics is concerned, Schmitz-Kallenberg, Rabikauskas, De Lasala, and Frenz & Pagano should on the whole be classified with the 'pure' school.

In the twentieth century, the difference between the two schools has never been better delineated than in a paper given by Heinrich Fichtenau at the École des Chartes on 10 November 1960.[73] Writing about Diplomatics as studied and taught in his native land of Austria (though by implication about the discipline in general), he compares it to a religious order, a small group of men prepared to make any sacrifice to devote themselves to the ideal of their master – in their case Theodor von Sickel, the founder of the Austrian school of Diplomatics. The tradition that held on to that austere ideal is the 'strict observance' mentioned above.[74] Alongside it grew up a laxer tradition which paid more attention to the things of the world; this was the school of Julius Ficker, who, like Gatterer before him, always wanted to be a historian as well as a Diplomatics expert and to use Diplomatics as a tool for the study of institutional history.[75]

Fichtenau himself clearly belonged to the 'applied' school – he brought out major interpretative books in addition to his contributions to Diplomatics, which were themselves integrated into interpretative

---

[70] *Ibid.*, 243–244 for his teaching collection of original documents and reproductions.
[71] *Ibid.*, 235–236.
[72] 'allgemeinhistorische und hilfswissenschaftliche Fragestellungen miteinander verknüpt sein sollen, um die Erkenntnispotenziale in beiden Bereichen auszuschöpfen' (Johrendt, 'Papsturkunden und Papstbriefe bis zu Bonifaz VIII.', 340.
[73] Published as 'La situation actuelle des études de diplomatique en Autriche', *Bibliothèque de l'École des chartes*, 119 (1961), 5–20.
[74] *Ibid.*, 8–9.   [75] *Ibid.*, 9.

history. Nonetheless he reaffirmed the value of both approaches. He also suggested that it was time that each tradition broadened out. The rubric he suggested is 'general diplomatic', by which he seems to mean Diplomatics which is not too focussed on very specific fields.[76]

He proposed that the 'pure Diplomatics' tradition, or 'strict observance', could broaden out, for instance by comparing charters with other survivals of the same period, tracing the evolution of certain forms over the centuries and beyond the medieval period, and comparing elements of the documents produced by more than one institution (he notes that Bresslau had already been doing this), the reciprocal relations between the diplomas of German kings and pontifical privileges, the influence of each on dukes and bishops, etc.[77] As for the applied Diplomatics tradition, it should now look at documents together with other media and with social and political conditions, and attempt to see documents as medieval people saw them.[78] In the pages which follow in Fichtenau's paper and among the questions he suggested,[79] one may perhaps perceive something like the 'history of mentalities', though the term was only beginning to become fashionable at the time of Fichtenau's talk, and may not have appealed to an intellectually conservative audience of *Chartistes*.[80]

Leonard Boyle

Very much in the spirit of Fichtenau's approach to Diplomatics are two key essays by Leonard Boyle. The first is his essay on the discipline in a general introduction to medieval studies.[81] Boyle saw Diplomatics as a method to be applied to any kind of source, not just to archival documents.[82] Furthermore, his Diplomatics questionnaire was calculated to

---

[76] In a personal communication, Werner Maleczek (from a younger generation of the same Vienna school) writes that 'Die Kritik Fichtenaus an der Diplomatik "strenger Observanz" ist zum Teil auch in den sehr start differierenden Temperamenten zwischen ihm und Leo Santifaller begründet. Nicht erst Fichtenau führte die Diplomatik aus der rein deskriptiven Richtung heraus [i.e. in the Vienna school – a Gatterer and a Ficker had anticipated this], schon Hans Hirsch war mit seinen Studien zur hohen Gerichtsbarkeit bahnbrechend ...'.

[77] Fichtenau, 'La situation', 14–16.   [78] *Ibid.*, 17   [79] *Ibid.*., 17–19.

[80] At that time the École des Chartes was almost the opposite pole of the Sixième Section of the École Pratique des hautes études (later EHESS), an institution at the heart of the *Annales* school, which was keen at the time on the history of *mentalités*. Yet one of the most distinguished *Annales* historians of mentalities is Jean-Claude Schmitt, Chartiste and Archiviste-paléographe – so things are never so simple.

[81] L. E. Boyle, 'Diplomatics', in J. M. Powell, ed., *Medieval Studies: An Introduction* (Syracuse, NY, 1992), 82–113.

[82] *Ibid.*, 88–89.

broaden interpretation of documents. Boyle proposed a set of questions taken from Aristotle and Cicero. Who? What? How? With what assistance? Why? Where? When? Some of these questions fit within a narrow conception of Diplomatics, but the 'How' question opens out into discussion of continuity from the ancient to the medieval world,[83] and the 'Why?' question takes one into the content of the document and its social role.[84]

More specifically relevant to papal Diplomatics is an essay by Boyle on the supposed condemnation of vernacular Bible reading by Innocent III; buried in a *Festschrift*, there is a danger of its great significance being overlooked.[85] The argument depended on technical Diplomatics, the difference between *narratio* and *dispositio*, but its implications for cultural and religious history were enormous. Before the essay (and after it for those who missed it), it was a standard view that Innocent III had banned the reading of the Bible in translation. This belief depended on the account in Margaret Deanesly's respected book on the Lollard Bible.[86] The key phrase that Deanesly took to be a condemnation of vernacular Bible reading is not Innocent's. It is part of the *narratio* which is a report of what the bishop of Metz had written to Innocent.[87] Since this letter appears to be the only medieval evidence of any papal condemnation of translations of the Bible, the diplomatic technicality is rather important.

Georg May

Boyle's paper illustrated how Diplomatics analysis of just one document can torpedo a big assumption about the medieval papacy – Boyle's natural genre was the essay rather than the big book. A big book is Georg May's vehicle for a *longue durée* essay in applied papal Diplomatics – the whole of papal history is its remit.[88] Though a particular formula – 'I [Name] bishop of the Catholic Church' – is the central theme, this study analyses technical papal diplomatics in granular detail to bring out the ideology embodied in papal documents. The contrast

[83] *Ibid.*, 97–99. [84] *Ibid.*, 101–102.
[85] L. E. Boyle, 'Innocent III and Vernacular Versions of Scripture', in K. Walsh and D. Wood, eds., *The Bible in the Medieval World. Essays in Memory of Beryl Smalley* (Oxford, 1985), 97–107.
[86] M. Deanesly, *The Lollard Bible and Other Medieval Biblical Versions* (Cambridge, 1920), 32–33.
[87] Boyle, 'Innocent III and Vernacular Versions of Scripture', 105.
[88] G. May, *Ego N.N. Catholicae Ecclesiae Episcopus. Entstehung, Entwicklung und Bedeutung einer Unterschriftsformel im Hinblick auf den Universalepiskopat des Papstes* (Kanonistische Studien und Texte, 43; Berlin, 1995). My thanks to Sergio Pagano for directing me to this, and for generously reading a draft of the present volume.

with Rabikauskas' approach could not be more striking: the technicalities are brought systematically into conjunction with historical scholarship on wider issues over an impressively wide time span, longer than attempted in the present volume.

Barbara Bombi and Benjamin Savill

Applied Diplomatics is fortunately now endemic as a skill among good historians of the papacy. An excellent recent example is Barbara Bombi's study of Anglo-Papal relations in the fourteenth century, which uses Diplomatics as a key to understanding diplomacy and shows the relevance of routine administration, the kind which is a central province of papal Diplomatics, to high-level interactions between states.[89] Moving back to the early end of the medieval period, Benjamin Savill's thesis and monograph apply Diplomatics systematically to elucidate the meaning of the papacy in Anglo-Saxon England.[90] One may note in passing that Anglophone contributions to the field of papal Diplomatics are sparse but of high quality,[91] as is work from France and Italy. Nonetheless it will become apparent to readers of this survey that German-language scholarship today dominates the field of applied papal Diplomatics (as it does papal history generally up until the Reformation period).

The scope of applied Diplomatics

An obvious implication of the foregoing is that papal Diplomatics can benefit from 'contamination' by wider interpretative historical scholarship. The common forms that Diplomatics uncovers are in fact recurrent structures of communication within social systems. Our attention to the genesis and setting in life of documents is an awareness that they are not just texts but key moments in social processes. Understanding those structures of communication and social processes adds a salutary extra dimension to Diplomatics as a discipline, while, conversely, the discipline of Diplomatics is almost indispensable for an accurate appreciation of the historical structures and processes. 'Pure' Diplomatics *à la*

---

[89] Bombi, *Anglo-Papal Relations*.

[90] B. Savill, 'Papal Privileges in Early Medieval England, c. 680-1073' (D.Phil. thesis, University of Oxford, 2017). A much revised 'book of the thesis' should appear at about the same time as the present volume, transforming our understanding of Anglo-Papal relations in the early Middle Ages: B. Savill, *England and the Papacy in the Early Middle Ages: Papal Privileges in European Perspective, c. 680–1073* (Oxford, 2023).

[91] Other Anglophone examples are Jane Sayers and Patrick Zutshi, currently one of the best specialists in the field anywhere. The list could be extended but would not be long.

Schmitz-Kallenberg and his modern successors remains the most succinct way of distilling and conveying the most crucial information, but it
can and should be complemented by the Gatterer–Fichtenau–Boyle
approach. Other areas where applied Diplomatics pays off are papal
privileges of protection and exemption, forgery, and mentalities.

Protection and exemption in Rabikauskas & De Lasala

In their sections on solemn privileges, Rabikauskas and De Lasala succinctly, perhaps too succinctly for the implications of these documents to
be evident, explain the difference between, on the one hand, grants of
protection, relating to the monasteries property, and, on the other, grants
of exemption from the authority of the bishop.[92] In the spirit of the strict
observance of Diplomatics, Frenz & Pagano do not analyse the distinction in their section on privileges.[93] When one reflects on the difference
between protection and exemption, however, large vistas of medieval
religious history open out.

Questions of a historical character present themselves; they are close to
the technicalities of Diplomatics but transcend them. As already noted,
early medieval papal privileges were enormous papyrus documents – up
to three metres long[94] – written in a script, the 'Roman Curiale', that
possibly few except the scribes themselves could read without great effort
or special training. Why so long physically and so hard to read?[95] Again,
what is their relation to royal charters for the same institutions (David
Knowles is still worth reading on this)?[96] Then, when one turns to
exemption, the whole question of the two elites – monks and bishops –
of medieval Christendom arises.

A remarkably high proportion of papal history consists of efforts to
manage the interactions of these quite different elites. The issues at stake
between monasteries and bishops changed over time, as the nature of
episcopal authority evolved, and in response to external factors like the

[92] Rabikauskas, *Diplomatica Pontificia*, 35–36, 49–51; De Lasala , *Il Documento*, 194–196.
[93] Frenz and Pagano, *I Documenti*, 20–23.
[94] Note however that Fatimid state documents could be twice as long and more: see M.
Rustow, 'Fatimid State Documents', *Jewish History*, 32 (2019), 221–277, at 241
and 249.
[95] For *some answers*, see Savill, 'Papal Privileges'. This is a path-breaking study both
conceptually and because it uses for the first time on English evidence the classic
Diplomatic technique of comparing purportedly papal privileges from different parts of
Europe to establish authenticity; furthermore, it is 'applied Diplomatics', exploring the
wider historical significance of his technical findings.
[96] D. Knowles, *The Monastic Order in England. A History of its Development from the Times of
St Dunstan to the Fourth Lateran Council 943–1216* (Cambridge, 1940), 575–591.

Gregorian Reform. This means that papal privileges have to be read closely and in the light of historical findings about exemption. Thus the scholarship on exemption is indirectly also part of the historiography of papal Diplomatics. The scholarly literature is substantial[97] and not easy to synthesise, though an attempt will be made below. Just as complex and much less well-explored is the history of exemption after the Council of Trent. One only skims the surface of documents relating to exemption if Diplomatics is not allowed to open out into the whole historical problem of the relation between the hierarchy and religious houses.

Forgery

Similarly, historical analysis of forgery should begin – rather than end – with establishing that a document is forged. The next stage is to ask questions from Boyle's, and classical rhetoric's, questionnaire. Who? What? How? With what assistance? Why? Forgery was a central theme from the start of Diplomatics as a discipline, and it remained important long after the period with respect to which it has attracted most attention. Its importance goes beyond establishing whether or not a document is

---

[97] G. Schreiber, *Kurie und Kloster im 12. Jahrhundert. Studien zur Privilegierung, Verfassung und besonders zum Eigenkirchenwesen der vorfranziskanishen Orden vornehmlich auf Grund der Papsturkunden von Paschalis II. bis auf Lucius III. (1099–1181)*, 2 vols. (Stuttgart, 1910) (still very interesting); cf. also F. Pfurtscheller *Die Privilegierung des Zisterzienserordens im Rahmen der allgemeinen Schutz- und Exemtionsgeschichte vom Anfang bis zur Bulle 'Parvus Fons' (1265). Ein Überblick unter besonderer Berücksichtigung von Schreibers Kurie und Kloster im 12. Jahrhundert* (Bern, 1972). Pfurtscheller emphasises the distinctiveness of the privileging of the Cistercian Order and the erosion of any episcopal authority in the course of the first half of the twelfth century; see especially 82–85, 145, 147. On the Cistercians, see now the exemplary dissertation by S. Morgan, 'The Religious Dimensions of English Cistercian Privileges' (PhD thesis, University College London, 2008); J.-F. Lemarignier, *Étude sur les privilèges d'exemption et de juridiction ecclésiastique des abbayes Normandes : depuis les origines jusqu'en 1140* (Paris, 1937); J.-L. Lemaître, 'Exemption', in P. Levillain, *The Papacy. An Encyclopaedia*, 3 vols. (London, 2002), i, 551–554; W. Szaivert, 'Die Entstehung und Entwicklung der Klösterexemtion bis zum Ausgang des XI. Jahrhunderts', *Mitteilung des Instituts für Österreichische Geschichtsforschung*, 59 (1951), 265–298; V. Pfaff, 'Die päpstlichen Klösterexemtionen in Italien bis zum Ende des zwölften Jahrhunderts. Versuch einer Bestandsaufnahme', *Zeitschrift der Savigny Stiftung für Rechtsgeschichte, kanonistische Abteilung*, 72 (1986), 76–114; L. Falkenstein, *La papauté et les abbayes françaises au XIe et XIIe siècles. Exemption et protection apostolique* (Paris, 1997); N. D'Acunto, ed., *Papato e monachesimo 'esente' nei secoli centrali del Medioevo* (Florence, 2003); L. Kéry, 'Klosterfreiheit und päpstliche Organisationsgewalt. Exemtion als Herrschaftsinstrument des Papsttums ?', in Johrendt and Müller, *Rom und die Regionen*, 83–144; K. R. Rennie, *Freedom and Protection. Monastic exemption in France, c. 590–c. 1100* (Manchester, 2018); L.-A. Dannenberg, *Das Recht der Religiosen in der Kanonistik des 12. und 13. Jahrhunderts* (Vita regularis, Abhandlungen, 39; Berlin, 2008), 118–120, with further references.

what it claims to be. When you have established that a document is forged, the next questions are: 'when?' and 'why?' Less obviously, also 'what?' What kind of text a forgery is may not be obvious. It is not necessarily a straightforward falsification for gain.

Writing about the Carolingian period (and about textual rather than documentary forgeries), Mayke de Jong has criticised 'a conflation between modern conceptions of forgery and early medieval notions of *inventio*/discovery';[98] 'borrowed authorial identities had nothing to do with what is now understood as forgery: they were a way of adding to one's own authority and honouring one's patristic models as well as one's audience, who were of course fully aware of this elegant ruse'.[99] Geoffrey Koziol takes a different view: ninth-century monks knew that forgery was wrong, but everyone did it and if one did not, one's monastery would be left behind.[100] (The analogy with performance enhancing drugs in certain sports suggests itself.) Koziol is writing about forged charters, de Jong about forged texts, but the difference goes deeper and each view has a historiography behind it.[101] There is still no consensus. The nature of medieval forgery may have to be classified under 'unsolved problems', but it is nowadays clear that its interest for historians has only begun when one has demonstrated inauthenticity.

Interest in forgery has primarily come from early medieval historians. For Christopher Brooke, 'down to the 1150s everyone engaged in it';[102] he dates the start of the great period of forgery to the mid-ninth century.[103] The ubiquity of forgery in this period is indeed a remarkable fact of social and cultural history. Not that it was rare in earlier periods. The famous Donation of Constantine probably dates from well before the start of Brooke's 'great period'[104] and forgery of conciliar proceedings at least goes back to Late Antiquity. Forgery also played a part in a disputed papal election circa 500; the same problems of how far fictions were

[98] M. de Jong, *Epitaph for an Era: Politics and Rhetoric in the Carolingian World* (Cambridge, 2019), 203.
[99] *Ibid.*, 204.
[100] G. Koziol, *The Politics of Memory and Identity in Carolingian Royal Diplomas: The West Frankish Kingdom (840–987)* (Turnhout, 2012).
[101] C. N. L. Brooke, 'Approaches to Medieval Forgery', *Journal of the Society of Archivists*, 3 (1968), 377–386, at 377, argues that 'In the period stretching from Pseudo-Isidore in the mid-ninth century to Geoffrey of Monmouth and the Westminster forgers in the mid-twelfth, forgery was an entirely respectable activity' – a position he goes on to qualify, but only in part; for the contrasting, 'forgery is forgery' view: E. A. R. Brown, '*Falsitas pia sive reprehensibilis*. Medieval Forgers and their Intentions', in *Fälschungen im Mittelalter*, 6 vols. (*MGH* Schriften, 33; Hanover, 1988–1990), i (1988), 109–119.
[102] Brooke, 'Approaches to Medieval Forgery', 384. [103] *Ibid.*, 377.
[104] The dating is a matter of dispute, and discussed below, but see F. Hartmann, *Hadrian I. (772–795)* (Päpste und Papsttum, 34; Stuttgart, 2006), 186.

outright deceptions apply here too.[105] For Brooke, however, after c. 1160 forgery 'rapidly declined into its normal place among human crimes'.[106]

Yet forgery as a cultural phenomenon remains worth studying into the late medieval period. In the late Middle Ages we find a whole series of forged indulgences – a new variety of documentary forgery. *1350 circa (BL Harley MS 273, fo. 7r) is a nice example. Forged indulgences can cast light on late medieval and post-medieval spirituality and were duly included in the multi-volume proceedings of the conference on medieval forgery held at the Monumenta Germaniae Historica institute in Munich.[107]

It is possible that inauthentic indulgences were transmitted by hearsay, mutating by a process of 'boy scouts' whispers'. According to the early fourteenth-century Dominican theologian Pierre de la Palud,[108] Nicolas Alberti, cardinal bishop of Ostia (1303–1321), had maintained in a public sermon that he had seen a bull granting an indulgence of a year and 40 days for a genuflexion when the name 'Jesus' was said – 'a highly suspicious indulgence!', comments Nikolaus Paulus in his history of the practice.[109] No doubt, but this gives an idea of how putative indulgences could circulate, mutating as they went. 'Fake news' could be spread without modern social media. Reflection on the genesis of the 'forgery' could lead us to the history of oral culture.

Mentalities

Though the *histoire des mentalités* was already in the air in French academic circles when Fichtenau gave his paper to the *Chartistes*, one of his own great contributions to the new subfield was almost certainly

[105] E. Wirbelauer, *Zwei Päpste in Rom. Der Konflikt zwischen Laurentius und Symmachus (498–514)* (Munich, 1993), 166: 'Es erscheint sinvoll, die Texte nicht als Fälschungen zu bezeichnen, sondern sie als *Documenta*, als Beispiele einer Produktion gegenwartsbezogener, "intentionaler Geschichte" (H.-J. Gehrke) zu verstehen.'
[106] Brooke, 'Approaches to Medieval Forgery', 378.
[107] H. Boockmann, 'Ablaßfälschungen im 15. Jahrhundert', in *Fälschungen im Mittelalter*, 5, *Briefe, Frömmigkeit und Fälschung, Realienfälschungen (MGH* Schriften, 35: 5; Hanover, 1988), 659–668. Cf B. Schimmelpfennig, 'Römische Ablaßfälschungen aus der Mitte des 14. Jahrhunderts', *Fälschungen im Mittelalter* v (*MGH* Schriften, 33, 5; Hanover, 1988), 637–658 (on indulgences for visits to Roman churches). Still valuable is N. Paulus, *Geschichte des Ablasses im Mittelalter, vom Ursprunge bis zur Mitte des 14. Jahrhunderts*, 2 vols. (Paderborn, 1922-23), ii (1923), chapter XXVI, 'Berühmte, doch unechte Ablässe', 292–338. 'These fantastic and fictitious indulgences are very common in books of hours (indulgenced prayers)' (Patrick Zutshi, personal communication).
[108] J. Dunbabin, *A Hound of God. Pierre de la Palud and the Fourteenth-Century Church* (Oxford, 1991).
[109] Paulus, *Geschichte*, ii, 234: 'Ein höchst verdächtiger Ablaß!'

independent of French influence, though it is a de facto contribution to *mentalités* history. This was his path-breaking 1957 book entitled *Arenga*.[110] The *arenga*, plural *arengae*, is the preamble of the document. Actually Fichtenau's book is about *prooemia* as well as *arengae*. He often pairs these (imperfectly distinct) concepts,[111] notably with relation to papal documents, without so far as I can see defining the difference between them. *Arenga* seems to be used to mean the introductory formulae of documents for the first time in the thirteenth century,[112] but Fichtenau is using it as a term of art and, in practice, bringing *prooemia* too within the frame of his study. In his chapter on 'Päpstliche Proömien und Arengen', which runs to the end of the twelfth century, he quotes another scholar's view that the letter of Pope Siricius to Himerius of Tarragona (commonly viewed as the first decretal) has no *arenga*, admits that this is right if one takes a formalist point of view ('wenn man sich auf einen formalistischen Standpunkt stellt'), responds that it has something approaching a *prooemium*, and proceeds to analyse it.[113] Probably the *arenga* is best classified as a subset of the wider category of *prooemia*, or a part of a *prooemium*, which stays on the level of the general, without referring to the specific occasion for the letter. Often it seems to consist of platitudinous generalities. Not all documents have *arengae*. English royal writs, notably, and even 'writ charters', skip the sententious section and go straight to the command. But other documents have long and elaborate *arengae*, the content of which seems only loosely related to what the document was actually doing.

Previously, the *arengae* had seemed unworthy of prolonged attention, and calendars of documentary series tended to skip over them. Fichtenau encouraged historians to look at *arengae* and *prooemia* in a new way. He realised that the platitudinous opening remarks of a period are a good source for the history of its mental attitudes. His book is in effect a study of *mentalités* on the basis of the preambles of documents.

His findings ran parallel not only to *mentalités* history but also to another trend in French historical scholarship of the immediate post-War period. (Again, it is unlikely that there was any actual mutual influence.) This was the investigation of long term – '*longue durée*' – patterns in history, continuities continuing over centuries if not millennia below the agitated surface of history . Fichtenau studied motifs, or *topoi*, which recur in documents over many centuries.

---

[110] H. Fichtenau, *Arenga. Spätantike und Mittelalter im Spiegel von Urkundenformeln* (Mitteilungen des Instituts für Österreichische Geschichtsforschung, Ergänzungsband, 18; Graz, 1957).
[111] *Ibid.*, 8, 14, 16, 21, 92, 97, 98, 99, 101.   [112] *Ibid.*, 20.   [113] *Ibid.*, 91–92.

He showed, for instance, how medieval documents used, individually or in combination, formulae about virtues that go back to the first Roman emperor, Augustus: *clementia/misericordia, iustitia, pietas*. He traced the roots in the ancient world of the comparison between the Holy Roman Emperor's relation to lesser rulers and the sun's relation to lesser heavenly bodies: the emperor wrote in 1245 to the duke of Austria that 'From the brightness of the imperial throne, like rays from the sun, the other offices come forth in such a way that the integrity of the original light suffers no detriment by losing light ...'.[114]

Fichtenau also illustrated how a theology of political authority could be embedded in the *arenga* of a document. Thus in 990 Pope John XV wrote to the monastery of Lobbes that:

Since it is well known that after the original sin of our first parent through the abuse of free will, the human race was subjected to the sentence both that man should be put over the heads of other men ... that is, to repress the illicit appetites[115] of the human will, and that we should be restrained by the rules not only of secular but of ecclesiastical law: the institution of authorities has progressed to such a point that places, holy ones that is, which have been founded by the devotion of the faithful, after being devoted to the service of God, have received gifts of income from various people, request not only royal and imperial commands to protect their immunity, but also desire privileges with our authority behind them to maintain their stability.[116]

It is possible to go a step further than Fichtenau but in the same direction by asking questions about different kinds of rationality in *arengae*.[117] A key distinction, going back to Max Weber, can be drawn between instrumental and value rationality in the process of thought or action that one is studying. To simplify drastically, value rationalities are coherent and tenaciously held sets of interlocking non-negotiable principles (e.g. liberty equality human rights democracy, or dharma karma samsara), while instrumental rationality is the calculation of logical or causal consequences – often, perhaps usually, within and shaped by a value framework, which colours the instrumental calculation to a greater or lesser degree.

We can put questions about the relation of the two rationalities in *arengae*. Now, one would expect to find value rational utterances all the

---

[114] *Ibid.*, no. 33, p. 37.

[115] 'ad compescendas ... appetitus': the case endings do not match, but this is typical of the faulty papal Latin of the tenth century, on which more below.

[116] Fichtenau, *Arenga*, no. 323, p. 149.

[117] I attempted this in an earlier study: D. L. d'Avray, chapter on 'Dispensations and their Diplomatic', in *Papacy, Monarchy and Marriage, 860–1600* (Cambridge, 2015), 218–237, at 221–226.

time, high-minded idealistic platitudes, but this is by no means necessarily the case. Papal *arengae* often emphasise case-by-case calculation, and also considerations that do not seem to have much to do with principle, such as the appropriateness of making special exceptions for members of great royal or noble families. This should make us pay attention. One thinks of the remark attributed to the mathematician G. H. Hardy: if the Archbishop of Canterbury says he believes in God, that's all in the way of business, but if he says he doesn't, one can take it he means what he says. Explaining how this can be so – why popes did not at least pretend to be applying some absolute unbending principle – can lead us to a deeper understanding of the forms of rationality underlying papal dispensations. The rules from which the dispensations granted exceptions were not in themselves absolute values, though they had a relation to values. Even in theory, dispensations belonged to the sphere of instrumental rationality, though of a kind coloured by principles.

The foregoing has been argued at length in an earlier study, with reference to the last three medieval centuries.[118] *Arengae* or (perhaps better) *prooemia* are also relevant to the early end of our period, from Late Antiquity on. Combined with the history of the reception of Late Antique papal decretals they help us explain how papal ideology took hold in the West.

Conclusion

Diplomatics began as a method for assessing the authenticity of charters, but broadened out into a method for elucidating the structures and settings in life of documents. Alongside the 'pure', standalone kind of Diplomatics there developed in the eighteenth century, with Johann Christoph Gatterer at Göttingen, an 'applied Diplomatics' which removed the barrier between the discipline and substantive historical investigation. In the twentieth century, applied Diplomatics found an articulate spokesman and successful practioner in Heinrich Fichtenau, though he did not specialise in papal documents. Papal documents have, however, been the object of numerous special monographs and, above all, articles and papers that show applied Diplomatics at its best. The textbooks on papal Diplomatics (which are in German, Italian and French), on the other hand, are austerely 'pure' and stay away from wider historical problems. This leaves a gap that the present volume attempts to fill.

---

[118] Cf. d'Avray, *Papacy, Monarchy and Marriage*, 208–217. There had to be a reason, as Patrick Zutshi reminds me, and if nothing more specific came to mind the phrase 'ex certis rationabilibus causis' could be used.

3   Papal Documents, c. 400–c. 1150

Insights from Diplomatics and the growth of papal authority

A theme running through modern scholarship in the field of papal Diplomatics and papal history generally is that the papal documents (within its remit as defined in the previous chapter) were predominantly responses. It was relatively exceptional for popes to initiate communications. This holds good too for the papal decretals from Late Antiquity.

In Late Antiquity, and to some extent in the early Middle Ages, popes had no way of enforcing their decisions. Even after the eleventh-century 'papal turn', the physical means of enforcement usually associated with what we call 'states' was lacking, but an excommunication system which could cause great inconvenience and no doubt with some people real terror was developed.[1] That presupposed, rather than caused, a general acceptance of papal authority. So how did papal authority come to be taken for granted?

Part of the answer lies outside the remit of Diplomatics and has been explored elsewhere: uncertainty and the complexities of partly incompatible religious sub-systems brought problems to the apostolic see.[2] Crucially, the apostolic see came up with replies, the period from the later ninth to the early eleventh century being an exception to a fairly general pattern. Diplomatics comes into its own when analysing these replies.

Popes often prefaced their responses with *prooemia* which legitimated their authority. These legitimations were not necessarily in the minds of the correspondents when they wrote to the apostolic see. Quite probably, they simply sought to have uncertainties resolved by an authority whose full claims they might have rejected if they thought about it. Perhaps the

---

[1] See now F. Hill, *Excommunication in Thirteenth-Century England: Communities, Politics and Publicity* (Oxford, 2022).

[2] d'Avray, *Papal Jurisprudence, 385–1234* develops this explanation.

individual correspondents did not pay too much attention to the *prooe-mia*. But these, together with the substantive responses, were transmitted in canon law collections that brought them to an increasingly wide clerical readership in the early medieval centuries, and this paved the way for the eleventh-century papal turn.

The foregoing puts two key insights from twentieth-century papal Diplomatics to work, moving them back to Late Antiquity and the early Middle Ages: firstly, Fichtenau's insight that the content of *arengae* and *prooemia* should matter to historians, and secondly, the generally accepted 'folk theorem' that the bulk of papal documents were replies. Taken together, these findings of Diplomatics point to an interpretation: the bishops who consulted popes may not have shared the Petrine ideology already established in Rome, but the preambles to the replies propagated that ideology.

As adumbrated above: in Late Antiquity, bishops consulted Rome as the senior see in the historical capital of the empire perhaps without any awareness of the Roman clergy's concept of their bishop as successor of St. Peter as head of the Church. That concept had been established in Rome from the mid-third century. We need to explain how it spread throughout the Latin West. *Prooemia* and the history of canon law collections help provide an explanation.

Prooemia from the first papal decretals

Early medieval canon law collections put the apostolic see before the minds of their users, who were numerous, to judge from the healthy surviving transmission of, especially, the *Dionysiana*. The popes not only responded with confident authority to the questionnaires that bishops sent them, but in some subsequently widely diffused decretals prefaced their responses with *prooemia* which invoked succession from St. Peter as the basis for their authority. The reception of Late Antique canon law magnified the impact of these arguments over the centuries, preparing minds for the eleventh-century revolution: the canon law collections were vehicles for the ideology which popes put in the *prooemia* of the responses which the collections transmitted. The *Dionysiana* had high status and great influence in the Carolingian period, and the *prooemia* that propagated the Petrine claims of the apostolic see were very widely copied in the post-Carolingian period as part of the Pseudo-Isidorian decretals.

The causal line is straightforward. The first large important decretal collections, the *Dionysiana* and *Quesnelliana* from around 500, transmit the Petrine ideology in the preambles of the first papal decretals. The transmission intensifies under Charlemagne, when an updated version of the *Dionysiana* was widely copied and evidently esteemed; then the ninth-century Pseudo-Isidorian decretals give the ideology more impetus still. The many exemplars copied put the *prooemia* before many pairs of eyes.

The chain of transmission is illustrated by the first of the documents at the end of the book, the *prooemium* of Innocent I's 404 letter to Victricius, bishop of Rouen.[3] The edition below, at ***404**, is designed to show the relation of the Late Antique version to the Pseudo-Isidorian version. As a base text I have used what is usually regarded as the best manuscript of the Late Antique version of the collection of Dionysius Exiguus (BAV Vat. Lat. 5845 [siglum *Db*]). I collate this against what may be the most important manuscript of the ninth-century Pseudo-Isidorian decretals, BAV Vat. Lat. 630, siglum *V630*, which was very close to the (mysterious) font and origin of the forgery, and which transmits genuine papal decretals like this letter alongside its forgeries. There is very little substantive deviation: the version in Pseudo-Isidore matches the early collections closely. There are quite a few minor variants, but none with a bearing on papal ideology. Moreover, most of the significant variants in *V630* are anticipated in the other manuscript of the Late Antique Dionysiana, MS Paris BNF 3837, siglum *Da*, and the other influential Late Antique decretal collection, the *Quesnelliana*, for which I have used MS Arras Bibliothèque Municipale 572 (644), siglum *Qa*.

Thus: the message to historians of the apparatus criticus is that the ninth-century Pseudo-Isidore collection acted as an effective transmitter of Petrine ideology in an early fifth-century *prooemium*. My introduction to the edition of the *prooemium* also notes other evidence of its influence. Clearly its contents did not go unnoticed.

The language of the *prooemium* would not have been out of place in the world of Innocent III.[4] Note that Victricius is asked to make the 'book of rules' known throughout surrounding dioceses.

Key passages are printed in bold:

Even if, brother, through the merit and honour – which you abundantly possess – of the priesthood, everything about living and teaching in accordance with the rules of the Church[5] is known, nor does there seem to be anything from the

---

[3] **J³.665** = Old Jaffé 286 (85).

[4] I translate for the most part from the *Db* version, the key manuscript for the *Dionysiana*; for variants see the text at ***404**.

[5] in accordance ... Church] I translate from the reading of *Qa* because it is grammatical, but the message is identical even with the ungrammatical reading of the base manuscript *Db*.

sacred scriptures which might seem to be less than fully grasped[6] by you, nevertheless, **since you have strongly requested the norm and authority of the Roman Church, I have adapted my behaviour somewhat to your desire and sent you attached to my letter the rules, in summary form, of discipline for life and approved behaviour[7] through which the peoples of the churches of your region may[8] perceive what conditions and rules should serve as a framework for the life of Christians in the walk of life of each individual, and what the discipline that should be observed in the churches of the city of Rome is.** It will be for your beloved self sedulously to make this book of rules known, as so to speak a primer and guide, throughout the neighbouring dioceses, and to our fellow bishops who preside over their own Churches in those regions, in order that they may able both to know our customs, and by their sedulous teaching shape the customs of those who are flocking to the faith in droves. For they will either recognise their own aims in our text, as it is in harmony with them, or, if they fall short of it, they will easily be able to make good what is lacking by following the model well. **Let us therefore begin, with the help of the holy apostle Peter, through whom both the apostolate and the episcopate had their beginning in Christ,** so that – since many cases often occur which in some respects are not cases but crimes – henceforth each bishop should devote to his Church the kind of care that the apostle Paul preaches, a Church such as can be presented to God as being without stain or wrinkle, and[9] our conscience be not contaminated and offended by the breath of any diseased sheep. Therefore on account of those who either out of ignorance or idleness fail to maintain ecclesiastical discipline, and take for granted many things which they should not take for granted, **you have rightly asked that the model to which the Roman Church holds should be followed in those parts:** not that we should want any new rules to be imposed, but that the ones that have been neglected though some people's negligence should be observed by all, rules which, in any case are established by apostolic and patristic[10] tradition. (*404)

There is also Petrine ideology in *prooemia* of at least two other key early decretals transmitted by Pseudo-Isidore. One of them, Innocent I's letter of 416 to Decentius of Gubbio,[11] was directed to an Italian diocese, so might speak only to patriarchal claims, but as transmitted in canon law collections it would have seemed like a message to Christendom in general. Its Petrine message seems to have attracted attention in the

---

[6] 'collectum esse': following the reading of *V630*, *Da*, and *Qa*.

[7] Adopting the reading of *V630*, Pseudo-Isidore, which also makes better sense. *Qa* adopts the reading after correction.

[8] Adopting the reading 'advertant', against *Db*.

[9] Or 'lest', if one adopts the reading 'ne' from *V630* (Pseudo-Isidore) against the base manuscript *Db*; *V630* represents an influential 'reception understanding' and possibly even the original text.

[10] 'Patrum'.

[11] **J[3].701** = Old Jaffé 311 (108) (Herbers et al., *Regesta Pontificum Romanorum*, i, pp. 128–129).

Carolingian period.[12] Another is Pope Siricius' 385 response to Himerius, bishop of Tarragona,[13] taken up by Nicholas I, probably via the 'Pseudo-Isidore' transmission.[14]

According to a common and probably correct view, the 385 letter of Siricius to Himerius is the earliest surviving papal document with intended legal force. The theory that Siricius' predecessor Damasus began the long series of papal decretals has been battered by recent scholarship, without being entirely knocked out; but if it was the first decretal its influence in the West was minimal.[15] Siricius' letter of 385, by contrast, not only had great influence in its own day but also for many centuries afterwards.[16] From this fourth-century source the decretal tradition would broaden out, eventually into a great river.

Roman synodal constitutions

Alongside papal decretals and on the edge of this book's remit are the acts of Roman synods – *constitutiones synodales*, which were signed by the pope among others and kept in the papal archive.[17] These have a definite form, which includes the time and place, the name of the presiding pope and members of the synod, and then a report of the business done and decisions made. At the end come the names of the participants and their acceptance of what had been decided.[18] The form strongly resembles that of Roman imperial senatorial decrees, but from the sixth century a Christian invocation of the divinity[19] habitually preceded the document.[20] Interestingly, Anglo-Saxon church councils were influenced by the Diplomatics of Roman synods.[21] Not much more will be said about

---

[12] Hadrian I: *MGH Epp.* 5: *Epistolae Karolini aevi (III)*, p. 3 at note 10; Nicholas I to Ado of Vienne, *MGH Epp* 6: *Epistolae Karolini aevi (IV)*, p. 637; Hincmar of Reims, *MGH Epp*, 8.1, pp. 124 and 135.

[13] J^3.605 = Old Jaffé 255 (65) (Herbers et al., *Regesta Pontificum Romanorum*, i, p. 113).

[14] Nicholas I 'Epistolae De Causis Rothadi et Wulfadi', *MGH Epp.* 6: *Epistolae Karolini aevi (IV)*, p. 415 at note 1.

[15] D. Jasper and H. Fuhrmann, *Papal Letters in the Early Middle Ages* (Washington, D.C., 2001), 28–32; D. L. d'Avray, 'Half a Century of Research on the First Papal Decretals (to c. 440)', *Bulletin of Medieval Canon Law* n.s. 35 (2018), 331–374, at 334.

[16] d'Avray, *Papal Jurisprudence, c. 400, passim*.

[17] On the acts of Roman synods, see the important paragraph in Bresslau, *Handbuch*, i, 74–75.

[18] Schmitz-Kallenberg, *Papsturkunden*, 75; cf. Frenz and Pagano, *I Documenti*, 17; Bresslau, *Handbuch*, i, 74–75.

[19] Cf. De Lasala, *Il Documento*, 51: he gives as examples of this 'Invocatio verbalis' the following: *In nomine Domini*; *In nomine sanctae et individuae Trinitatis, In nomine Domini nostri Iesu Christi Dei omnipotentis*.

[20] De Lasala, *Il Documento*, 167.

[21] C. Cubitt, *Anglo-Saxon Church Councils c. 650–c. 850* (London, 1995), 79, 82–84, 86–87.

line with the handbooks. They only get six lines in the
\[y\] Thomas Frenz[22] and the same number in the
a by Paulius Rabikauskas.[23]

Diplomatics of early papal decretals: the debt to imperial Diplomatics

In the same textbook on papal Diplomatics, Rabikauskas noted that early papal decretals followed the model of imperial edicts.[24] Studies that go beyond the remit of 'pure' Diplomatics unpack the meaning of his compressed comment. A model analysis is provided by Detlev Jasper. In his study of early papal letters Jasper writes that their internal structure 'is very similar to the charters and documents written in the form of letters by the Roman emperors and imperial officials: 'intitulatio', the body of the letter ('arenga', 'narratio', 'dispositio' and 'sanctio'), with a greeting and date at the end'.[25] The *intitulatio* is the sender's name with epithet, the *arenga* the preamble, the *narratio* the recapitulation of the situation, usually as told in a prior missive from the addressee, the *dispositio* the decision with legal force, and the *sanctio* is what it says, the sanction. As with the imperial rescript system, the papal decretal system was, as already noted, predominantly responsive, but the topics on which the responses were elicited were for the most part quite different from those which Roman emperors addressed.

Resolution of uncertainties in Late Antiquity

'The resolution of uncertainties' is the rubric which perhaps best covers the wide range of different questions put before the apostolic see in the late fourth and fifth centuries.[26] The uncertainties put before the popes around 400 C.E., Siricius and Innocent I, related to ritual, the relation between hierarchy of status and the hierarchy of command, the rules about celibacy in marriage for the higher stages of

---

[22] Frenz and Pagano, *I Documenti*, 17.   [23] Rabikauskas, *Diplomatica Pontificia*, 25
[24] '(litterae) decretales, ad formam edictorum imperialium conscriptae' (Rabikauskas, *Diplomatica Pontificia*, 23).
[25] D. Jasper in Jasper and Fuhrmann, *Papal Letters*, 13–14. For a good short analysis of the Diplomatics of the earliest papal decretals see D. Moreau, 'Non impar conciliorum extat auctoritas. L'origine de l'introduction des lettres pontificales dans le droit canonique', in J. Desmulliez, C. Hoët-van Cauwenberghe and J. -C. Jolivet, eds, *Étude des correspondances dans le monde Romain, de l'antiquité classique à l'antiquité tardive: permanences et mutations* (Lille, 2010), 487–506, at 492–493.
[26] d'Avray, *Papal Jurisprudence, c. 400*, 293.

clerical life, the ban on clerics remarrying or marrying a widow, the in
solubility of marriage, the difficulty of integrating the clerical syst
with the new and burgeoning monastic system, the rules about sacraments for repentant heretics, the penitential system, and the relation of
free-will to predestination. Except for the last topic, there is much less
of what would later be called 'theology' than one might expect, not
much in particular that reflects the fierce debates about the relation of
human and divine in Christ, and the same may be said of the most
important canon law collection to come out of Late Antiquity, that of
Dionysius Exiguus, who perhaps deliberately left out the papal letters
that dealt with Christology.[27] There are such papal letters about
Christology, however, from shortly after the pontificate of Innocent
I, and the other two main Late Antique canon law collections do
include them.[28]

One of these letters became famous as the 'Tome of Leo', because
Leo I's argument about the relation of humanity and divinity in the
person of Jesus Christ was well received two years later at the Council of
Chalcedon.[29] The Chalcedonian solution, that Jesus was one divine
person with two natures, one human and one divine, was a source of
controversy for the next two centuries because of fierce opposition in
the eastern half of the empire (now all that was left) and efforts by
emperors to broker theological compromises, in the vain hope of uniting
his subjects in belief. For this purpose emperors sought papal support, if
necessary by compulsion. From the reconquest of Africa and Italy by
Justinian to the eighth century, the eastern emperors were strong
enough in Italy to bring heavy pressure to bear. A great many papal
letters came out of these controversies, as well as other correspondence
with rulers that one could bring under the rubric of 'religious diplomacy', and miscellaneous business: but only a small subset of all this
had sufficient general legal force to be incorporated in early medieval
canon law collections.[30] They are on the margin of papal Diplomatics as
a field of study.

---

[27] The foregoing summarises some of the findings of d'Avray, *Papal Jurisprudence, c. 400*:
see 6–9 and *passim*.

[28] *Ibid.*, 191.

[29] J[3].934 = Old Jaffé 423 (201) (Herbers et al., *Regesta Pontificum Romanorum*, i, p. 167).

[30] F. Maassen, *Geschichte der Quellen und der Literatur des canonischen Rechts im Abendlande
bis zum Ausgange des Mittalalters, i* (Graz, 1870), 285–308 for the period from Anastasius
II (496–498) to Leo IV (d. 855). For the whole range of papal letters covering
approximately the same period, see Herbers et al., *Regesta Pontificum Romanorum*, i,
pp. 240–509; ii, ed. N. Herbers, W. Könighaus, T. Schlauwitz, et al. (2017), *passim*; iii,
ed. N. Herbers, J. Werner, and W. Könighaus, pp. 3–55.

Recent work on Late Antique papal Diplomatics

The diplomatic analysis of documents more central to the field is hampered by a lack of original documents, but Rocco Ronzani has recently made a brave attempt,[31] going beyond Detlev Jasper's analysis of structural parallels between papal decretals and imperial rescripts. Ronzani speculates that

The oldest documents very likely had a very simple external form, consisting of the *superscriptio*, that is the protocol, which regularly presented the bishop's name, followed by the word *episcopus* and, starting from the eighth century, by the *intitulatio* of Gregorian origin *seruus seruorum Dei*, by the *salutatio* which could greatly vary, and ultimately by an *in[s]criptio* which could be formed by the single name of the recipient, or enriched by various honorary attributes. Even a *subscriptio* ranged from the classic and neutral *bene vale* to more complex and explicit Christian greetings such as *Deus te incolumem custodiat*, but also there were more complex, refined expressions, appropriate to the circumstances and to the social class of the recipients.[32]

He points out that 'Towards the end of the fifth century, a Greek indiction was introduced'[33] (the indiction was a bizarrely complex way of dating a letter according to cycles of 15 years).[34] From c. 550 the phrase *imperante domino nostro N. piissimo Augusto anno n.* was introduced as another dating element, one which emphasised the continuing bond between papacy and Byzantine emperor.[35] That came to an end when the papacy switched its allegiance to the Carolingian north (see below), and began to date with the year of the pontificate and of Charlemagne's rule.[36] Ronzani even addresses the question of the appearance of Late Antique papal documents (no physical originals have survived) and makes a good case for a hierarchy of scripts distinguishing the formal elements from the body of the letter.[37] Ronzani also finds evidence that there were 'Chancery' annotations on letters.[38] The bishops of Rome may have had stenographers in their service in Late Antiquity. An interesting case has been made for their importance at the time of the controversial later fourth-century Pope Damasus, whose father may have been a stenographer.[39]

The papal writing office doubled up as an archive, according to Ronzani: it was not 'a complete collection of letters, but a miscellaneous

---

[31] Ronzani, 'Notes'.   [32] *Ibid.*, 265.   [33] *Ibid.*, 267.
[34] C. R. Cheney, *A Handbook of Dates for Students of English History* (Cambridge, 1995), 2–3.
[35] Ronzani, 'Notes', 267.   [36] *Ibid.*, 267,   [37] *Ibid.*, 270–273.   [38] *Ibid.*, 274–276.
[39] M. Raimondi, 'Damasus and the Papal *Scrinium*', in Testa and Marconi, *The* Collectio Avellana, 280–301, at 290.

collection of outgoing and incoming letters, applications, and other kinds
of documentation, such as minutes from the Synods, that besides being
deemed worthy of preservation also constituted useful precedents to
settling matters of [a] pastoral and administrative nature in the Roman
See'.[40]

Unsurprisingly, there are debates about the origins of the papal
archive,[41] but we do know that Jerome assumed that the authenticity of
a papal letter could be checked in the archive; the weight of probability
favours the view that there was an archive in Damasus' day if not
earlier.[42] Perhaps surprisingly, the three earliest substantial collections
of papal decretals (*Frisingensis Prima*, *Quesnelliana*, and *Dionysiana*) do
not appear to have been compiled from the papal archive.[43] It does seem
possible that the intriguing *Collectio Avellana*,[44] with its focus on documents not in other compilations,[45] used the papal archive for the documents from the pontificate of Pope Hormisdas.[46]

The *Codex Carolinus*

Very different from the canon law collections is the *Codex Carolinus*,
which reflects a world of high-level affairs distant from the Late
Antique setting of the *Dionysiana*, *Avellana*, et al. Most of the letters it
contains were for an audience of one. They are letters to Carolingian
rulers, brought together in one book. The readership of the letters
transmitted by the *Codex Carolinus*, and the readership of the compil-
ation, could not have been more targetted. The book was a brainchild of
Charlemagne. In 791 he had all the letters written by popes to him, his
father Pippin, and his grandfather Charles Martel collected, presumably
with an eye on his and his dynasty's image for posterity; the collection
survives in Österreichische Nationalbibliothek Cod. 449.[47]

The *Codex Carolinus* mirrors the papacy's turn away from the
Byzantine empire and towards the Frankish empire, which seemed more
likely to be able to offer protection of Rome and its territories from the
Lombards. In return, popes offered spiritual assistance. Charlemagne

[40] Ronzani, 'Notes', 273.   [41] Raimondi, 'Damasus', 284.   [42] *Ibid.*, 285–287.
[43] d'Avray, *Papal Jurisprudence, c. 400*, 24 at note 7.
[44] For up-to-date discussion and further bibliography see Testa and Marconi, *The Collectio Avellana*.
[45] Maassen, *Geschichte*, 791; L. Kéry, *Canonical Collections of the Early Middle Ages (ca. 400–1140). A Bibliographical Guide to the Manuscripts and Literature* (Washington, D.C., 1999), 37–38.
[46] Maassen, *Geschichte*, 792.
[47] F. Hartmann and T. B. Orth-Müller, eds., *Codex epistolaris Carolinus. Frühmittelalterliche Papstbriefe an die Karolingerherrscher* (Darmstadt, 2017), 11.

put papal political power in central Italy on a secure footing, and he received spiritual benefits: prayers for his soul, closeness to St. Peter, and the pope as godfather to his sons Ludwig and Carloman. All of this is reflected in letters included in the *Codex*.[48] The collection has been thoroughly studied.[49] Many, probably most, of the letters are only on the edge of the field of Diplomatics, or at most within the 'Diplomatics of common sense', but a couple of observations are in order.

A letter of Pope Zacharias to Charlemagne's father Pippin before the latter became king quotes liberally from the *Dionysiana* collection,[50] which brings it within the category of documents with legal force. It is also worth noting the *prooemia*. Some of these letters contain preambles which would have instilled in the Frankish leaders the Petrine legitimation of papal authority (even though the Latin grammar of at least some of the later letters is shockingly shaky).[51] In the powerful *prooemium* of a 756 letter appealing to King Pippin, Charles, and Carloman for help against the Lombards, Pope Stephen writes in the person of St. Peter:

I Peter the apostle, since I have been called by Christ, the son of the living God, by the judgment of his celestial mercy, [and] preordained by his power to be a source of light for the whole world, with the same Lord our God confirming it: 'Go, teach all nations, baptising them in the name of the Father and the Son and the Holy Spirit'; and again: 'Receive the Holy Spirit; whose sins you shall forgive, they will be forgiven' – and to me, his humble servant and one called to be an apostle, entrusting every one of his sheep, he said: 'Feed my sheep, feed my lambs'; and again: 'Thou are Peter, and upon this rock I will build my Church, and the gates of hell will not prevail against it, and I will give you the keys of the kingdom of heaven; whatever you bind on earth will be bound in the heavens, and whatever you loose on earth will be loosed in the heavens': because of this, those who listen to my preaching and obey it may assuredly believe that their sins are remitted in this world by God's command, and that they will go forward to that life purified and without stain; for indeed, since the light of the Holy Spirit shines forth in your resplendent hearts, and you have, through your reception of the word of Gospel preaching, become lovers of the holy and undivided Trinity, your

---

[48] *Ibid.*, 19.

[49] A. T. Hack, *Codex Carolinus. Päpstliche Epistolographie im 8. Jahrhundert*, 2 vols. (Päpste und Papsttum, 35; Stuttgart, 2006–2007).

[50] Hartmann and Orth-Müller, *Codex epistolaris Carolinus*, Nr. 5 (3), pp. 54–72, footnotes *passim*; J³.3917 (2277) (Herbers et al., *Regesta Pontificum Romanorum*, ii, p. 144).

[51] Hartmann and Orth-Müller, *Codex epistolaris Carolinus*, Nr. 37 (32) (date 761–766), p. 198: '... illa, quae ad nostris stipendiis [*sic!*] aguntur, ...'; Nr. 75 (75) (date 783) p. 320: I am quite unable to construe grammatically the long passage 'Quae dum tam firmam stabilemque annexa ... ab amore clavigeri regni celorum disiungi', though the message about the apostolic see and Peter comes through clearly enough.

hope of future reward is bound up with[52] this God's apostolic Roman Church which has been entrusted to us.[53]

This preamble is the cue for asking for Frankish help against the Lombards. The Lombards had been brought under Frankish rule by 782, when Hadrian I wrote to Charlemagne about a piece of territory to which he felt entitled:

> ... inasmuch as you love the head of the whole world, the same holy Roman Church, and its ruler and priest, by embracing or cherishing and glorifying them with honour, so too correspondingly does St. Peter the prince of the apostles ensure that you are an undisputedly triumphant military leader here and now, and, in the future, that you rule as a conqueror over all kings;[54] we are indeed absolutely confident that, just as your spiritual mother the Holy Catholic and Apostolic Roman Church is raised up in triumph through you, so too correspondingly does it grant you the power to strive for and inherit the heavenly kingdom in perpetuity through the intercession of the prince of the apostles.[55]

These *prooemia* are perhaps unusually full, but references to St. Peter and/or other legitimations of papal authority are frequent in the *prooemia* of the *Codex Carolinus*.[56] Similar Petrine themes were noted above in the *prooemia* of early papal decretals. There was a convergence of influence on Carolingian clerics and kings.

Letters and privileges

Before 772 papal letters generally have some common features. The dating clause includes the indiction as well as the date of the month, and there is a closing greeting in the pope's hand, in lieu of a signature in the modern sense.[57] From the later eighth century two different genres, letters and privileges, become differentiated by criteria that Diplomatics can identify, though scholars are hampered by the fact that no pre-ninth century original papal letters have survived entire, so that we do not know whether the support was parchment or papyrus (probably the latter but it is only an educated guess), whether they usually had a seal (again,

---

[52] 'adnexa'.

[53] Hartmann and Orth-Müller, *Codex epistolaris Carolinus*, Nr. 3 (10), pp. 38–40.

[54] This is another case of the somewhat dubious papal Latin of the period: 'tantum vos beatus Petrus apostolorum princeps inconcussos facit triumphos hic et in futuro victores super omnes regnare reges'.

[55] Hartmann and Orth-Müller, *Codex epistolaris Carolinus*, Nr. 78 (72), p. 332.

[56] *Ibid.*, pp. 82–84, 98, 106, 134, 172, 178, 182, 206, 212, 368.

[57] Bresslau, *Handbuch*, i, 74; De Lasala, *Il Documento*, 165–166.

more probably), and if so whether the seal closed up the letter (probably not).[58]

Despite all the uncertainties, letters such as those that the *Codex Carolinus* collected can be usefully distinguished in various ways from privileges. Under the rubric of letters, *litterae*, can be included exchanges between a pope and a personal friend, rescripts, invitations, commands and 'general communications to individual persons',[59] and they are less stereotyped in wording than privileges.[60] They end with formulae like 'Dextera Domini vos in omnibus inlesam conservare dignetur'.[61] As privileges emerge as a clear-cut genre in the late eighth century, in these such formulae come to be replaced by the shorter *Bene valete*.[62]

Privileges were documents designed to be kept, and this purpose is signalled in a number of ways.[63] A cross or crosses can be drawn by the pope's name at the beginning.[64] This introductory part, the protocol, ends with 'in perpetuum' or similar phrases.[65] Privileges are written in the archaic 'Roman Curiale' script,[66] and until the eleventh century they are written on papyrus. At the end they identify either the scribe or a senior Chancery official, or both.[67] They make use of the *Liber Diurnus*

---

[58] K. Herbers and V. Unger, eds., *Papstbriefe des 9. Jahrhunderts* (Darmstadt, 2019), 34–35.

[59] F. Engel, 'Päpstlicher als der Papst? Papstbriefe um das Jahr 1000', *Archiv für Diplomatik*, 66 (2020), 55–69, at 60.

[60] *Ibid.*, 62–68 discusses how far letters of individual popes show traces of individuality.

[61] De Lasala, *Il Documento*, 172 (and 171–174 with further details of the differences between letters and privileges); see also Schmitz-Kallenberg, *Papsturkunden*, 82–83.

[62] 'Während in den Briefen der Segenswunsch, der die Unterschrift des Papstes bildet, variabel bleibt und je nach der Stellung des Adressaten und den näheren oder entfernteren Beziehungen des Papstes zu ihm sich Umgestaltet, wird in den Privilegien gewöhnlich die kurze Formel *Bene valete* angewandt' (Bresslau, *Handbuch*, i, 77).

[63] '... lassen sich die meisten Privilegien, so man mehrere Kriterien zur Unterscheidung anwendet, recht eindeutig als solche identifizieren. Die "große" Datierung aus Datum- und Scriptumzeile in formaler Hinsicht, Liber Diurnus-Verwendung, eine deutliche Sanctio (negativ und positiv) in stilistischer Hinsicht, eine klar rechtlich bindende Verfügung wie etwa eine Schenkung oder Besitzbestätigung mit entsprechendem Güterverzeichnis in inhaltlicher Hinsicht sind solche Kriterien; nicht immer sind alle gleichzeitig zu finden, in der Regel aber sind wenigstens einige davon zweifelsfrei zu identifizieren.' V. Unger, *Päpstliche Schriftlichkeit im 9. Jahrhundert. Archiv, Register, Kanzlei* (Forschungen zur Kaiser-und Papstgeschichte des Mittelalters. Beihefte zu J. F. Böhmer, Regesta Imperii, 45; Vienna, 2018), 7–8 (with further references to Hack, *Codex Carolinus*).

[64] De Lasala, *Il Documento*, 76 (Tavola 1), 173.   [65] *Ibid.*, 173.   [66] *Ibid.*, 173.

[67] Bresslau, *Handbuch*, i, 76: 'Zuerst unter Hadrian I., soviel wir bis jetzt wissen, wird in zahlreichen Urkunden die Nennung der be der Ausfertigung beteiligten Kanzleibeamten im Eschatoll zur Regel. Die eine ... nennt den Schreiber der Urkunde ...; wir bezeichnen sie als die Screiberformel (Skriptumzeile). Die andere Formel, die wir nach den sie einleitenden Worten *Datum per manus* als große Datierung bezeichnen, nennt einen höheren Kanzleibeamten und gibt ausführlichere Zeitangaben, insbesondere die Regierungsjahre des Kaisers und, was gleichfalls unter Hadrian zuerst vorkommt, des

formulary. There is clear sanction to encourage obedience. Privileges had lasting value. All this goes with and expresses a definite legal function, such as a grant of 'protection' or 'exemption'.[68]

Privileges aimed to regulate the relation between monasteries and the world around them.[69] As usual, the initiative came from the localities, but the papacy developed documentary systems capable of satisfying demand. Privileges occupy a new space between 'religious diplomacy' and canon law which claimed to be valid generally. Particularly interesting are privileges bearing on the relation between monasteries and bishops.

Monasteries and bishops in papal privileges

Any reader of the letters of Gregory I will be struck by how often they give rulings about the liberties of religious communities,[70] including formulae from the *Liber Diurnus* that adumbrate later monastic exemption formulae.[71] This takes us to the Diplomatics of exemption. In a letter of 596 to Respecta, head of a religious house for women in Marseille – let us call her the abbess – we see something not so very different from a grant of exemption.[72] The house is a new foundation by lay patrons, a married couple. After stating this, Gregory I goes on to give the community the right to elect its abbess. Perhaps he also means to say that the bishop has the final say, but the scholarly editor of the *Monumenta Germaniae Historica* edition, Paul Ewald, did not take that view. The abbess is to have complete control of the governance of the house: 'Where the

---

Papstes.' For the eschatocol in the ninth century see Unger, *Päpstliche Schriftlichkeit*, 184–188.

[68] 'Schreiberformel und große Datierung treffen wir nur in den Urkunden an, die feierliche, auf die Dauer berechnete Verfügungen treffen; das Vorkommen beider Formeln oder einer von ihnen kann fortan als das Kennzeichen betrachtet werden, durch sich die Privilegien der Päpste von ihren Briefen unterscheiden' (Bresslau, *Handbuch*, i, 76–77).

[69] The pages that follow owe much to Benjamin Savill, who has repayed my teaching of early papal Diplomatics many times over.

[70] Cf. H. H. Anton, *Studien zu den Klosterprivilegien der Päpste im frühen Mittelalter. Unter besonderer Berücksichtigung der Privilegierung von St. Maurice d'Agaune* (Beiträge zur Geschichte und Quellenkunde des Mittelalters, 4; Berlin, 1975), 51–55.

[71] 'Für unsere Fragestellung ist nich unerhablich, daß unter den in so großer Zahl in den Briefen Gregors nachgewiesenen Formularen bzw. Formularteilen des LD gerade solche zu finden sind, die zumindest den grundstock für die formelbildung der späterenklostereximierungen bieten' (Anton, *Studien*, 52).

[72] J[3].2535 = Old Jaffé 1458 (1090) (Herbers et al., *Regesta Pontificum Romanorum*, i, p. 416). For a very definite statement of the view that Gregory I never granted exemption, see however Szaivert, 'Die Entstehung', 283: 'Die Streitfrage ... Schluß zuließe.'

monastery's business or its governance is concerned, however, we decree that neither the bishop nor any of the clergy[73] has any power.'[74] Then Gregory also rules that the bishop can only say mass in the monastery on the anniversaries of its foundation and dedication. He is not to keep an episcopal seat, a *cathedra*, in their church.[75] It is brought out on the very rare, specified occasions when he comes to say mass, then taken away again.[76] No need for an elaborate 'thick description' to see the significance of this! He does have oversight in case of serious wrongdoing, and a heavy responsibility is laid on the abbess's shoulders.

There are analogous provisions for male houses. In a letter of 597 Gregory reprimands the archbishop of Ravenna for letting his clergy oppress the monasteries in the area under him. Henceforth, the clergy are to have no access to monasteries except to pray and say mass if invited. If an abbot or monk becomes a cleric, they should no longer have any power in the monastery.[77]

We should pause to examine the assumptions underlying this last provision. It is assumed that 'monks' and 'clerics' are normally two separate categories. That had long since ceased to be the case, but the dichotomy is still in Gregory's mind. There was a practical reason. The fact not quite made explicit is that when monks or abbots become clerics, the archbishop used them as leverage to get control of monastic property. Defence of monastic property, even from bishops, would be a durable theme in later centuries, but not by this particular route – instrumentalising the transition of monks or the abbot to the clerical state. We are still in Late Antiquity so far as the relation between these two religious elites is concerned.

Clearly Gregory I has been asked by monastic communities to help them, and clearly his letters were meant to carry legal force. Furthermore, the 597 letter to the archbishop of Ravenna protects monastic property, and like the 596 letter to Respecta it firmly bars the bishop from interference in the running of the monastery. These documents point to the problem of monastic exemption and protection, a core

---

[73] 'ecclesiasticorum'.

[74] 'In rebus ... potestatem' (*MGH Epistolae (in Quart) (Epp.) Gregorii papae Registrum epistolarum Libri I–VII*, ed. P. Ewald and L. Hartmann, VII, 12, pp. 454–455).

[75] Benjamin Savill suggests to me in a personal communication that there is something 'especially "Provençal"' about the removal of the chair and that there may be a difference between Gregory's concerns about Provençal monasteries and about Italian monasteries.

[76] *MGH Epistolae (in Quart) (Epp.) Gregorii papae Registrum epistolarum Libri I–VII*, ed. P. Ewald and L. Hartmann, VII, 12, p. 455: 'Die siquidem natalis ... auferatur.'

[77] J³.2569 = Old Jaffé 1486 (1121) (Herbers et al., *Regesta Pontificum Romanorum*, i, p. 421); *MGH Epistolae (in Quart) (Epp.) Gregorii papae Registrum epistolarum Libri I–VII*, ed. P. Ewald, VII, 40, pp. 488–489.

topic in Diplomatics. On the other hand neither document is a formal privilege of the kind that would become so important, and which is a central issue in early medieval papal Diplomatics. The tradition of privileges is commonly traced back to Hadrian I (772–795).[78]

Three characteristics[79] of solemn privileges stand out: they were huge; they were written on papyrus; and they were written in a script, the 'Roman Curiale', that derived from the minuscule cursive of Late Antiquity.[80] The scale, the script, and the material were all unlike anything else anyone north of the Alps was likely to see. They were calculated to create awe. As Marina Rustow has put it (with regard to the even more enormous papyrus documents issued by Fatimid Caliphs), 'Documents communicate as much by how they look as by what they say.'[81] The combination of a mysterious script from another era, very hard to decipher, and the astonishing materiality of the documents – papyrus, great length – help us answer 'Hageneder's question' for the Carolingian and post-Carolingian period.

'Hageneder's question' needs to be posed for this period because (as hinted above) the papacy seems to have had difficulty in finding administrators who could write decent Latin! Some popes could: Nicholas I's Latin is complex but accomplished. Not so some other products of the papal administration, disgracefully ungrammatical. How did this not make the papacy look ridiculous in the eyes of any well-educated monk or cleric, especially north of the Alps, where the standard of Latin was high in some places at least?

Scholars do not make much of this but it was noted and documented in some detail by Harry Bresslau well over a century ago. He pointed out that the level of papal Latin in the first original documents that survive (from the pontificates of Hadrian I and Paschal I) is not at all good, and inferior to contemporary Frankish documents (from the reign of Louis the Pious).[82] Still working from the few surviving original documents, there seems to be an improvement in the pontificates of Benedict III, Nicholas I and John VIII, but there is a downturn after that: spelling

---

[78] Frenz and Pagano, *I Documenti*, 17.

[79] For the characteristics, see Schmitz-Kallenberg, *Papsturkunden*, 83–86; De Lasala, *Il Documento*, 172–174; Frenz and Pagano, *I Documenti*, 20–23. For facsimiles, see *Pontificum Romanorum Diplomata Papyracea*.

[80] P. Rabikauskas, *Die römische Kuriale in der päpstlichen Kanzlei* (Miscellanea Historiae Pontificiae, 20, Collectionis no. 59; Rome, 1958), 16.

[81] Rustow, 'Fatimid State Documents', 238. Cf. *ibid.*, 263: 'The impressive dimensions of the state decrees were meant for public performance, to inspire awe in subjects and to substitute for the person of the caliph.' The even longer documents she studies may have some as yet unelucidated relation to the great papyrus papal privileges.

[82] Bresslau, *Handbuch*, ii, erste Abteilung, 330 and note 1, and 344.

mistakes in a privilege of Stephan VI, then further decline towards what Bresslau kindly calls 'vulgar Latin'. Anticipating recent research,[83] he is well aware that the papal writing office worked from text presented by the beneficiary, but he rightly observes that they did not think it necessary to correct the Latin, and that it is also pretty bad in sentences that papal scribes had composed. Only under Benedict IX (actually regarded by historians as a 'bad pope') does papal Latin get back on track.[84]

We should pause to reflect on the implications of this for the educational and cultural level of the papal administration. Today, if documents emanating from an important international agency were written in the kind of English one might expect from menus in Mediterranean resorts, eyebrows would rise at the receiving end. Readers would wonder about the cultural niveau of the organisation that produced them.

Clerical education was entirely in Latin, and many of the relevant texts were in quite complex Latin: patristic writings, early papal decretals, etc. That kind of Latin is not a language that can be read with any precision by people who do not know their case endings. We should not be misled by the fact that historians can understand early medieval texts in poor Latin. The question is whether early medieval clerics with poor Latin could understand the Late Antique texts – their cultural heritage – in often complex and difficult Latin. North of the Alps there was no shortage of men who could do that without difficulty. What would they think of papal documents written by men who were so obviously inferior culturally?

Yet papal authority was much higher in this period of *non satis* Latin than one might expect, as a recent study by Sebastian Scholz has argued for Francia.[85] We should not be deceived by the fact that few of these privileges survive.[86] Papyrus is vulnerable, the more so the further north one gets, especially since they would have to have been folded up because of their great size: no original papyrus papal privileges have survived from Anglo-Saxon England though they certainly once existed and we have the texts of a significant number.[87] Given the slim survival rate, it is worth noting how many of those that are preserved were sent to bishops

---

[83] Kortüm, *Zur päpstlichen Urkundensprache.*

[84] Bresslau, *Handbuch*, ii, erste Abteilung, 344–346.

[85] S. Scholz, *Politik – Selbstverständnis – Selbstdarstellung. Die Päpste in karolingischer und ottonischer Zeit* (Stuttgart, 2006), 244–245.

[86] H. Omont, 'Bulles pontificales sur papyrus (IXe–XIe siècle)', *Bibliotèque de l'École des chartes*, 65 (1904), 575–582, at 575–576; catalogue 577–582.

[87] *Ibid.*, 576. Benjamin Savill's important forthcoming book, *England and the Papacy in the Early Middle Ages*, likely to appear around the same time as the present one, will put them on the scholarly map.

54 Papal Documents, c. 400–c. 1150

and monasteries in episcopal sees in Spain,[88] and testify to an astonishingly early connection between the papacy and what was then the periphery of Christendom.[89]

So we have a paradox: a papal government with a deplorable level of Latin, from which a poor general educational level would be an obvious inference, which nonetheless enjoyed an impressive European reputation. This is a problem that has not been posed with sufficient clarity and force.

Applied Diplomatics suggests answers. We can postulate that the script was too hard for the Latin to be checked and that the documents communicated papal prestige by how they looked, to paraphrase Marina Rustow's dictum. Furthermore, as will be discussed below with reference to some fine recent scholarship, the papal administrators did not need to do much original composition of Latin. For formulaic parts they could use the *Liber Diurnus* formulary (whose Latin could be terrible) and for the substantive parts they used material brought to them by the beneficiary. That material too might be in bad Latin, which the papal administrators seem not to have cared to correct. The prestige of the final product was protected by an otherwise obsolete script and a rather stunning physical appearance.

Protection of a monastery could be against all comers. Exemption, however, was about the relation between the monastery and the local bishop. The relation between monastic beneficiaries of the privileges and the bishop was recurrently problematic. On this topic there is a rich and discordant historiography.[90]

Exemption of monasteries in the early Middle Ages?

When the 'pure' Diplomatics treatise of De Lasala (and Rabikauskas) distinguishes between exemption from episcopal authority and papal 'protection' of monastic property, the reader could get the impression that true exemption from episcopal authority comes relatively late, in the late tenth and eleventh centuries.[91] There was also a trend from the

---

[88] Omont, 'Bulles pontificales', 575 at note 1.
[89] Werner Maleczek, in a personal communication, drew my attention to the 'gehäuften Überlieferung in nordspanischen Bischofssitzen und Klöstern, die auch heute noch irgenwo verloren in den Pyrenäen liegen, die auf die erstaunlich frühe Bindung von Kirchen an der Peripherie zum Hl. Petrus unterstreichen'.
[90] Good bibliography, not only on France, in Rennie, *Freedom and Protection*, 199–237.
[91] 'Molti antichi privilegi concedono soltanto la protezione; il primo privilegio d'esenzione completa che conosciamo è datato pochi anni prima dell' anno 1000, ed è stato concesso all'abbazia di Cluny' (De Lasala, *Il Documento*, 195–196).

1950s on to argue that what looked like exemption was really just protection.[92] For example, Mogens Rathsack argued robustly that the exemption formula from the *Liber Diurnus*,[93] *(LD V 32)* was not understood as an exemption formula until circa 1200.[94]

Yet the 'exemption-deniers' did not win general assent. In 1951 Willy Szaivert confidently asserted that the first exemption was granted by Honorius I to the monastery of Bobbio,[95] and that this was the basis for the *Liber Diurnus* formula 77 (= C 82 = A 77).[96] In the mid-1970s Hans Hubert Anton's thorough study of early medieval exemption took the view that the papacy had a clearly defined exemption practice in the seventh century.[97] Barbara Rosenwein has attacked the view that early privileges were only concerned with the protection of property.[98] Theo Kölzer strikes a salutary note of caution. True, papal privileges free monasteries from the 'iurisdictio' and 'ditio', which I would translate as 'control' in the formulae from the *Liber Diurnus*. It is not necessarily clear, however, exactly what 'iurisdictio' and 'ditio' meant: the key thing is that such phrases left the door wide open to interpretation.[99] Even contemporaries may have been vague about their meaning. Worth remembering from a different sector of early medieval history is F. W. Maitland's argument that in the language of early Anglo-Saxon charters the distinction between conveying

---

[92] On the 'Trendwende' see bibliography in T. Kölzer, 'Bonifatius und Fulda. Rechtliche, diplomatische und kulturelle Aspekte', *Archiv für mittelrheinische Kirchengeschichte* 57 (2005), 25–53, at 39–40 and note 78.

[93] H. Foerster, ed., *Liber Diurnus Romanorum Pontificum* (Bern, 1958), V 77 = C 82 = A 77, pp. 138–140.

[94] 'Erst Ende des 12. und Anfang des 13. Jh. wurde LD als Exemtionsformular aufgefasst' (M. Rathsack, *Die Fuldaer Fälschungen. Eine rechtshistorische analyse der päpstlichen privilegien des Klosters Fulda von 751 bis ca. 1158*, i (Stuttgart, 1989), 18.

[95] C. Cipolla, ed., *Codice Diplomatico des Monastero di S. Colombano di Bobbio fino all'Anno MCCVIII*, i (Rome, 1918), doc. X, pp. 100–103; J³.3239 = Old Jaffé 2017 (1563) (Herbers et al., *Regesta Pontificum Romanorum*, ii, pp. 17–18).

[96] Foerster, *Liber Diurnus*, 138–140: Szaivert, 'Die Entstehung', 285.

[97] 'Rom hat schon im 7. Jahrhundert eine bereits klarer konturierte Exemptionspraxis für sich in Anspruch genommen und auch ausgeübt, wie das dem Liber diurnus, dem päpstlichen Formularbuch, hervorgeht. Die Formulare 32, 77 und 86, von denen die ersten beiden sicher auf das 7. Jahrhundert zurückgehen, haben die Herausnahme des in Frage kommenden Klosters aus der Gewalt des zuständigen Bischofs und seine Unterstellung unter die Jurisdiction des heiligen Stuhles zum Inhalt' (Anton, *Studien*, 2).

[98] B. Rosenwein, *Negotiating Space: Power, Restraint and Privileges of Immunity in Early Medieval Europe* (Ithaca, NY, 1999), 107; Cf. Rennie, *Freedom and Protection*, 68–69.

[99] '... konstatierte schon Eugen Ewig bezüglich der analogen Urkunde für Bobbio: "Das Privileg ließ der Interpretation Tür und Tor offen". Das klingt banal, dürfte aber gleichwohl den Kern treffen.' Kölzer, 'Bonifatius und Fulda', 40.

property and alienating public authority over land could not be or was not articulated.[100]

This has implications for the answer to the early medieval version of 'Hageneder's question'. It seems unlikely that the papacy had a well-thought-out plan to strengthen monasteries at the expense of episcopal authority – a sort of divide and rule programme. There is no evidence for anything so coherent. On the other hand, the papacy was confident enough to employ formulae that 'left the door and gate open to interpretation', to borrow Eugen Ewig's phrase. The meaning of these formulae could expand over time, provided that the monks could decipher the documents. But if the beneficiary houses had done the drafting of the documents subsequently issued by popes – we will see that this was regularly the case – they would probably have known the contents anyway. Thus there would be an institutional awareness of the monastery's special position vis-à-vis the local bishop, and as the latter's power became more intrusive, as we shall see that it did, the special position would become increasingly imporant.

How privileges were interpreted was surely affected by the evolution of monasticism, on the one hand, and episcopal authority on the other: neither were static. Two developments deserve special attention. On the one hand, monasteries were becoming clericalised. On the other hand, many bishops were tightening control of their dioceses – a *longue durée* process that in England at least would eventually go very far.[101]

In the ninth and tenth centuries, that meant public penance increasingly controlled by bishops.[102] An influential handbook to help bishops administer public penance was provided by Regino of Prüm (d. c. 915).[103] This includes sins by monks: three months fasting on bread and water as a penance for drunkeness,[104] for instance, or alternatively 30 days penance of vomiting because of drunkenness.[105] A priest

---

[100] F. W. Maitland, *Domesday Book and Beyond. Three Essays in the Early History of England* (Cambridge, 1897, London, 1960), 287.

[101] This train of thought was first suggested to me by Benjamin Savill. I. Forrest, *Trustworthy Men: How Inequality and Faith Made the Medieval Church* (Princeton, NJ, 2018) (really about late medieval England, after a *Begriffsgeschichtliche* survey of the notion of 'fides' shows bishops and local peasant elites working together to exercise a high degree of local control over priests).

[102] R. Meens, 'Remedies for Sins', in T. F. X. Noble, and J. M. H. Smith, eds., *The Cambridge History of Christianity*, iii. *Early Medieval Christianities, c. 600–c. 1100* (Cambridge, 2008), 399–415, at 412–413.

[103] *Ibid.*, 412. Edition and German translation by W. Hartmann, *Das Sendhandbuch des Regino von Prüm* (Darmstadt, 2004) (below I quote the *PL* edition for convenience).

[104] Regino of Prüm, *Libellus de Ecclesiasticis Disciplinis et Religione Christiana*, in *PL* 132, Lib. I, CXXXV, col. 218.

[105] Regino, *Libellus*, *PL* 132, CXLV, col. 220.

who celebrates mass on his own is suspended, and Regino thinks this is especially a problem in monasteries.[106]

It would seem to follow that bishops regarded monks as within their remit. If energetic bishops were imposing public penances on members of monastic communities, the latter were unlikely to be enthusiastic. Consequently, a papal privilege giving the community immunity from the control (*ditio*) and 'jurisdiction' of the bishop – whatever those words originally meant – would become an increasingly valuable asset.

Furthermore, in the period around 800 synods were common at the provincial level[107] and probably even more so at the diocesan level.[108] Abbots could and perhaps had to attend.[109] There are indications that the abbots would be second-class citizens. If so, perhaps better not to be there at all! One ritual, the 'Ordo' for councils in Pseudo-Isidore, describes a hierarchy made visible: priests behind bishops, deacons standing – but there is nothing at all about abbots.[110]

At the Council of Ravenna of 955 it looks as though abbots had to stand with the priests and deacons, while the bishops were seated.[111] An account of a synod in 1027 in Frankfurt does suggest that abbots could be seated, like bishops, whereas lower clergy had to stand, but a description of the decision-making mentions only the bishops.[112] That only bishops were voting members of councils and synods probably holds good more generally.[113] If so, the obligation of abbots to be present at a council emphasised their inferior status: they had obeyed a summons and were on the margins once they were there.

---

[106] 'periculosa superstitio maxime a monasteriis exterminanda est.' Regino, *Libellus*, PL 132, CXCI, col 225.

[107] A. Hauck, *Kirchengeschichte Deutschlands, ii* (9th edition, Berlin, 1958), 732–735.

[108] *Ibid.*, 735–736.

[109] 'cum cetu abbatum, canonicorum, nec non et monachorum' (Council of Ingelheim, 7 June 948, MGH Concilia (Conc.), 6. 1, *Die Konzilien Deutschlands und Reichsitaliens 916–1001, Teil 1 916–961*, ed. E.-D. Hehl et al. (Hanover, 1987), 158–159. It would be quite easy to map the growing presence of abbots at councils and synods by working through the subscriptions to them available in critical editions in the MGH Concilia volumes. For the period 916–1056 see H. Wolter, *Die Synoden im Reichsgebiet und in Reichsitalien von 916–1056* (Paderborn, 1988), Sachregister p. 520, *s.v.* 'Äbte ... als Synodalteilnehmer'. At the Council of Seligenstadt in 1023 there were ten abbots according to the record of the synod, those from the Gorze reform movement, probably as back up for the archbishop of Mainz who summoned the synod and had a reform agenda too: see *ibid.*, 298–299.

[110] Wolter, *Die Synoden*, 467.

[111] 'cum eo ibique residentes reverentissimi episcopi atque astantibus religiosissimis abbatibus atque presbiteri [sic] et diaconibus [etc.]'. MGH Concilia (Conc.), 6. 1, *Die Konzilien Deutschlands und Reichsitaliens 916–1001, Teil 1 916–961*, ed. E.-D. Hehl et al. (Hanover, 1987), p. 198.

[112] Wolter, *Die Synoden*, 467–468.   [113] *Ibid.*, 468–469.

All this amounted to motive for absence if one could legitimate it. To judge by later medieval monastic attitudes, abbots might have preferred not to demonstrate inferior status in this way. Papal privileges like the letter of a Pope Gregory, probably Gregory II, to Vitalian[114] (715–724), or those in the *Liber Diurnus*,[115] dating from around 629 and available into the eleventh century, would legitimate a refusal to attend.

Monasteries were also changing in a way that must have pushed in the same direction – encouraged an aversion to dependence, a wish for some sort of exemption from episcopal power. The process of clericalisation was making monks more reliant on their local bishop, with potentially undesirable consequences (from a monastery's point of view) that may not have been fully understood in the scholarly literature. Clericalisation was in full swing in Carolingian monasticism, to judge by a study of Saint-Germain-des-Près, where the proportion of laymen monks to priest-monks was turned upside down between the eighth and ninth centuries.[116] By the ninth century, Benedictine monasticism had travelled a long way from the 'lay' monasticism of the order's first couple of centuries.

One implication of this, in particular, may not – *nisi fallor* – have sufficiently sunk into the consciousness of historians. There were many stages on the road to the priesthood, a whole series of ordinations.[117] The more a monastery was clericalised, the more dependent on the bishop it became. It was not just a matter of priestly ordination. There were many ordinations before one got to that final stage. The number of clerical 'orders' was not fixed for a long time – the *Sentences* of Peter Lombard made a total of seven popular, but there could be even more stages.[118] In a well-populated monastery – think of Cluny! – where it was normal for monks to work their way up through the hierarchy to the priesthood, that meant a great many ordinations. If the monastery depended entirely on the local bishop, he had a hold over them that he could use in other areas

---

[114] J[3].3719 = Old Jaffé 1926 (not in first edition) (Herbers et al., *Regesta Pontificum Romanorum*, ii, p. 104); *MGH Epistolae (in Quart) (Epp.)*, 2, *Gregorii I papae Regisrum epistolarum Libri VIII–XIV*, ed. L. M. Hartmann, 'Appendix IV', pp. 468–469.

[115] Foerster, *Liber Diurnus*, V32 = C 29 = A 24, pp. 93–94; V 77 = C 82 = A 77, pp. 138–140; and A 77 = V 77 = C 82, pp. 395–398.

[116] J.-L. Lemaître, review of O.-G. Oexle, *Forschungen zu monastischen und geistlichen Gemeinschaften in Westfränkischen Bereich*, 1978 'Münsters. Mittelalt.-Schr., 31'), in *Cahiers de Civilisation Médiévale* 23 (1980), 270–273, at 271.

[117] A. Faivre, *Naissance d'une hiérarchie. Les premières étapes du cursus clérical* (Théologie historique, 40; Paris, 1977).

[118] R. E. Reynolds, *Clerics in the Early Middle Ages. Hierarchy and Image* (Aldershot, 1999), ch. III, '"At Sixes and Sevens" – and Eights and Nines: The Sacred Mathematics of Sacred Orders in the Early Middle Ages', 669–684, at 669 and 679.

of life, including the economic. The monastery would be very dependent on the bishop's good will and even his timetable. Thus freedom from control of that one bishop mattered much more in the ninth century than before. Consequently, the force of a papal exemption from 'iurisdictio' and 'ditio' would increase over time without any further action by popes.

Chronology: Carolingians and protection

Papal privileges removing monasteries from episcopal 'iurisdictio' and control ('dicio') seem not to have met Charlemagne's approval: according to Jean-Loup Lemaître, he 'proclaimed that all monasteries would submit to episcopal jurisdiction, granting them only the freedom to elect their abbot and administer their daily affairs'; later, 'With the weakening of royal power in the second half of the ninth century, the monasteries ... again sought the protection of the pope.'[119]

A rough and ready chronology goes like this: initially, before the Carolingians came to power, there were a few special papal privileges, the precise import of whose powerful sounding formulae is obscure, and may have been unclear even at the time; next came a period when protection from the great new Carolingian dynasty sidelined papal privileges; then in the second half of the ninth century a new age of papal privileges began, with the focus on the protection of property rather than exemption from the bishop's spiritual power, which remained more-or-less out of the picture until c. 1000.[120] *Protectio* was about safeguarding lands rather than getting out from under the bishop's legal power. There was no necessary contradiction between papal and royal power when it came to monastic privileges in this period.

Decline of royal power and rise of exemption

Royal power west of Germany lost its grip in the post-Carolingian world. This had implications for monasteries, as Cinzio Violante perceived long ago.[121] Strong kings were natural protectors of monasteries, from lay lords but also from bishops, who would be tempted to cast covetous eyes on their properties. That encouraged appeals to the apostolic see for

[119] Lemaître, 'Exemption', 552.
[120] J. Dubois, 'Esenzione Monastica', in G. Pelliccia and G. Rocca, eds., *Dizionario degli Istituti di Perfezione, iii* (Rome, 1976), cols. 1295–1306, at 1299–1300. Still well worth reading on this is Knowles, *The Monastic Order in England*, 577–578.
[121] C. Violante, 'Il Monachesimo Cluniacense di Fronte al Mondo Politico ed Ecclesiastico. Secoli X e XI', in *idem, Studi Sulla Cristianità Medioevale. Società, Istituzioni, Spiritualità*, ed. P. Zerbi (Milan, 1975), 3–67.

privileges of protection, which must have counted for something, at least as a deterrent to bishops. Since as we have seen bishops had the potential to put pressure on monasteries because the latter were dependent on them for ordinations of monks as they progressed up the clerical hierarchy, it made sense to ask for exemption from the bishop's spiritual power as well; conversely, it is unsurprising that the bishop of Mâcon argued on the authority of conciliar decisions against Cluny's privilege of going to any bishop for the ordination of its monks; John XIX reacted against this with Petrine arguments at the Lateran synod of 1027.[122] The intellectual arguments for exemption were ready. In the eleventh and twelfth centuries would come a crescendo of actual and genuine papal exemptions. It is safe to assume that the initiative always came from the monasteries.

Responsive government

That had always been the default setting. An earlier Anglo-Saxon king, Offa (d. 796) had asked for an – at first sight – more puzzling privilege from the apostolic see.[123] It is a surprise to meet the name of an Anglo-Saxon queen, Offa's wife, in the standard formulary of the early medieval papacy – the *Liber Diurnus*. Clearly this papal document was a response to a special request by the king. What seems to have been happening is this: Offa is endowing a monastery from land he controlled thanks to his 'kingly superiority', as Maitland put it,[124] or 'publicly owned land', as one might anachronistically call it. The monastery is to be controlled by his wife and their 'genealogy' – i.e. their descendants?[125] The fact that it is a monastery will help keep it safe from land-grabbers (a category which might include bishops). Offa's plan fits a pattern that one also finds in Byzantium and with Islamic *wakfs*: keeping land in the family by making it a religious endowment controlled by the family.[126] In this case, the land was not strictly speaking his family's in the first place, since royal power in Anglo-Saxon England did not follow strict family inheritance

---

[122] *Ibid.*, 13.

[123] Foerster, *Liber Diurnus V 93 = C 78 = A 73*, pp. 172–173; **J³.4612** (Herbers et al., *Regesta*, ii, p. 244); they date it to 772–795; the previous versions of Jaffé do not have an entry for it.

[124] Maitland, *Domesday Book*, 287.

[125] In a personal communication, Benjamin Savill points out that 'genealogia' is 'a very unusual term in early medieval charter Diplomatic' and 'openly doing something peculiar'.

[126] M. Weber, *Wirtschaft und Gesellschaft*, 5th edn., 3 vols. (Tübingen, 1976), ii, 643–644; M. Borgolte, *World History as the History of Foundations, 3000 BCE to 1500 CE* (Leiden, 2020), p. 271.

rules, as it would in a later period. Presumably the pope who issued the privilege had very little idea of any of this, but was happy to oblige when asked by a distant and powerful king in the North.

The meaning of papal privileges at the receiving end

The beneficiary's reasons for obtaining a privilege and the valency of the privilege once they had got it differed regionally. In England or Germany, papal privileges were a reinforcement of royal privileges. Not so in southern France. There the papal privilege had independent legal force, created a closer relationship between the religious house and the pope, and might even be directed against the king.[127]

A formula for responses to solve conflicts

Even with papal documents that rebuke the recipient, the *a priori* likelihood is that they are responses. To be sure, these would not be responses to the recipient. The likely context is a complaint by a third party to the pope about the recipient.[128]

A model *arenga* in same formulary, the *Liber Diurnus C 79 = V 94 = A 74*,[129] shows that the pope could be asked to resolve conflicts. The words 'to put a stop to the turning and twisting of disputants, we devote the more vigilant care to make sure that if any dispute arises between parties it may be investigated directly with a transparent investigation and cleared up in an appropriate way' looks like the preamble to a judge or judges delegate, most probably away from Rome (otherwise a document would not be necessary). Documents commissioning judgment of a dispute, and the privileges discussed in the previous section, anticipate two main categories of papal Diplomatics at the apogée of the papacy's medieval power: commissions to judges delegate and favours granted by letters of grace.

When we come to examine that thirteenth- and earlier-fourteenth-century high point of governance we will see how large a part could be played by the beneficiary – the recipient of the document. This did not actually preclude the application of thought by popes or curial officials, but it did mean that not much thought needed to be applied to the whole of the widening flood of business. (A similar pattern may be observed in

---

[127] J. Johrendt, *Papsttum und Landeskirchen im Spiegel der päpstlichen Urkunden (896–1046)* (*MGH* Studien und Texte, 33; Hanover, 2004), 272–273 (contrasting meanings of papal privileges in southern France and Germany, at the reception end).
[128] Werner, *Papsturkunden*, 29.   [129] Foerster, *Liber Diurnus*, 352.

high medieval England, with its system of stereotyped writs.) It will be argued that this explains how the massive turnover of the system was possible: thought in devising systems made it unnecessary to devote thought to the complexities of each individual case. In the early Middle Ages the turnover was tiny in comparison, but the beneficiary seems to have played an even larger role. In fact the role of the central 'administration' (if one may call it that) of the post-Carolingian papacy seems to have been largely confined to assembling pre-prepared parts.

The contribution of beneficiaries to papal privileges, 896–1046

The substantive parts of papal privileges between the Carolingian era and the Gregorian Reform tended to owe a great deal to the work of the beneficiaries of those same privileges. This is a key finding of a remarkable investigation by Hans-Henning Kortüm.[130] His methodology is simple in conception though it required considerable sensitivity to medieval Latin. He showed that in these substantive sections the Latinity corresponded to stylistic and linguistic traits characteristic of the regions in which the beneficiary monastery was set – an elegant argument which brings philological and Diplomatics expertise into play together.

The externals of papal documents

The same line of interpretation has been developed still further by Judith Werner, with reference to the external appearance of the privileges.[131] She argues that 'from the ninth to the eleventh century, remarkably frequently, the external appearance [*Gestalt*] of papal documents was influenced, with varying degrees of obviousness, by the institution which was the beneficiary'.[132] This holds good for both papyrus and parchment documents. She notes an extravagance in the use of writing material in Lorraine and in general features designed to make a powerful impression – she uses the neologism *Wirkmächtigkeit* – and to stress papal authority in documents addressed to institutions there. She finds a striking correlation between this geographical area of 'wirkmächtig'

---

[130] Kortüm, *Zur päpstlichen Urkundensprache.*   [131] Werner, *Papsturkunden.*
[132] '... wurde im 9. bis 11. Jahrhundert bemerkenswert oft die äußere Gestalt der Papsturkunden in unterschiedlicher Deutlichkeit von der empfangenden Institution beeinflusst.' Werner, *Papsturkunden*, 468.

documents and monastic reform[133] and argues that the high regard for the successor of St. Peter was reflected in the impressiveness of the documents made.[134]

Pre-fabricated parts: the *Liber Diurnus*

The influence of the beneficiary has been detected by Jochen Johrendt[135] even in the formulaic beginnings and endings of privileges, the *arenga* and the *sanctio*. These seem often to be taken from the often-mentioned *Liber Diurnus*, the earliest surviving formulary used by writers of papal documents. The *Liber Diurnus* made it easy to write the opening and closing passages of privileges, but it seems that the beneficiaries gave the Chancery a hand even in the choice of formulae.

Only German and Italian beneficiaries can be shown to have used the *arenga* formula from the *Liber Diurnus* known as *LD 32* (discussed above in connection with exemption): it is not used in France or Catalonia.[136] At the other end of documents, a phrase used in the sanction of *Liber Diurnus* formula *LD A89* is used in 20 per cent of relevant letters for Catalonia, but only 2 per cent of letters for beneficiaries in German lands. Johrendt's explanation, which is surely correct, is that beneficiaries could give a steer towards one formula or another.[137]

Johrendt built on the earlier path-breaking work of Hans-Henning Kortüm,[138] who in turn could rely on the critical edition of papal documents from 896–1046 by Harald Zimmermann.[139] Thanks to these scholars we now have a good idea of how the *Liber Diurnus* was used. Frequent close matches between genuine documents and the formulae in the *Liber Diurnus* show that the latter was not just a 'school-book' for the training of notaries, as was once thought,[140] or a 'canon law collection' unconnected with the practical needs of the papal

---

[133] *Ibid.*, 469–470.　　[134] *Ibid.*, 470: 'Hierin ist möglicherweise … Urkunden wider.'

[135] J. Johrendt, 'Der Empfängereinfluß auf die Gestaltung der Arenga und Sanctio in den päpstlichen Privilegien (896–1046)', *Archiv für Diplomatik* 50 (2004), 1–11.

[136] *Ibid.*, 5.　　[137] *Ibid.*, 10–11 and *passim*.

[138] Kortüm, *Zur päpstlichen Urkundensprache*, especially 312–387. For older scholarship, see especially Frenz and Pagano, *I Documenti*, 45–46; De Lasala, *Il Documento*, 178–187; Santifaller, *Liber diurnus*, ed. Zimmermann.

[139] H. Zimmermann, *Papsturkunden 896–1046*, 3 vols. (Österreichische Akademie der Wissenschaften, phil.-hist. Klasse, Denkschriften, 174, 177, 198; Vienna, 1984–1989).

[140] Kortüm, *Zur päpstlichen Urkundensprache*, 385–386: 'Die von Santifaller zeitweise vertretene These, bei dem LD. handle es sich um ein "Schulbuch" zur Ausbildung der Notare, bestätigt die urkundliche Praxis nicht.'

documentary production.[141] The surviving manuscripts were not written by papal scribes,[142] but they do go back to a manuscript exemplar or
exemplars used by papal scribes. The formulary behind the manuscripts
that have survived was indeed used by the scribes, above all for the
arengae and for the concluding formulae of the substantive parts and for
the 'sanctions' at the end.[143]

How they did so, we do not know. Perhaps the representative of the
institution in question dealt directly with a papal scribe. Perhaps the
prospective beneficiaries looked to earlier documents in their archives
for models for drafts. Their advisers in Rome may have worked from
private copies of the *Liber Diurnus*; indeed, such copies may well have
been available away from Rome. As already noted, it is now accepted that
all three manuscripts of the *Liber Diurnus* are from outside the papal
'Chancery' even though they derive from an in-house formulary. It is
possible that a pattern we will meet in a later period was already anticipated, namely, that those who wanted a papal document prepared even
the formulaic parts with the help of a copy of the formulary. This meant
that the draft form of the finished document could be provided, saving
trouble for all concerned at Rome.

The production of papal documents

If the formulaic parts of papal documents tended to be lifted from the *Liber
Diurnus*, possibly by the beneficiary in the draft put before the papacy, and
if the substantive parts too were drafted by the beneficiary, all that
remained was to assemble prefabricated sections and copy them out.
That was the task of the Roman city scribes whom the pope used, his
'Chancery': while 'Chancery' is a misleadingly grandiose title for the
modest reality,[144] it is convenient to keep the word, as Veronika Unger
has argued.[145] Unger, in her important study of the papacy and writing in

---

[141] Kortüm, *Zur päpstlichen Urkundensprache*, 316.

[142] The decisive argument is that the copyists were clearly unable to read the abbreviations
of the weird 'Roman *Curiale*' script used in the papal Chancery: Kortüm, *Zur päpstlichen
Urkundensprache*, 316.

[143] Kortüm, *Zur päpstlichen Urkundensprache*, 347, 385.

[144] Klaus Herbers comments thus on the tenth century (and by implication on the
preceding two): 'Noch mehr als für die Karolingerzeit – die noch beachtenswerte
Ausprägungen päpstlicher Schriftlichkeit zeigt – wird man sich von der Vorstellung
einer Kanzlei als fester Behörde verabschieden müssen. Vielmehr schrieben römische
Stadtschreiber (Scriniare, Notare oder Tabellionen) wohl häufig in Auftragsarbeit auch
die päpstlichen Dokumente.' K. Herbers, *Geschichte des Papsttums im Mittelalter*
(Darmstadt, 2012), 110.

[145] Unger, *Päpstliche Schriftlichkeit*, 291–292: 'Auch wenn in den letzten Jahrzehnten öfter
der geringe Organisationsgrad und die mangelnde Institutionalisierung hervorgehoben

the ninth century, does warn us against imagining anything like a cut-and-dried division of labour such as one might find in a real bureaucracy.

She characterises this 'Chancery' succinctly and convincingly. Papyrus was used for privileges and probably also for letters, parchment for 'the records of synods, thematic collections, and translations'; the same men could write both the strange 'Roman Curiale' and minuscule; privileges were issued as rolls, as were – possibly – letters; texts that were to be kept in the archive were probably in quire or codex form.[146] We cannot be sure that titles like *scriniarii* and *notarii* represented distinct offices.[147] Her caution on the basis of thorough work on one century is a warning against overconfidence about the infrastructure producing papal documents in the preceding and following periods.

The 'Chancery' in Late Antiquity and the early Middle Ages

It is possible that the papal administration became less rather than more developed as what we call 'Late Antiquity' faded into 'the early Middle Ages': in Late Antiquity the papal 'Chancery' may have been significantly more structured than in Carolingian times. In the records of Roman synods references to *notarii* are not uncommon. Andreas Weckwerth takes it for granted that these were members of the papal Chancery and that it was organised along the lines of the Roman imperial Chancery;[148] other episcopal administrations were similar in structure[149] if not perhaps in scale. The men who staffed the papal administration were not just low-level clerks; they also collected the 'deeds' of the martyrs and went on diplomatic missions.[150] The developing sophistication of the papal

wurden, möchte ich am Begriff der päpstlichen Kanzlei festhalten. Er soll … als "Verabredungswort" gebraucht werden, nicht im Sinne einer fest umrissenen Behörde, sondern als Bezeichnng des (möglicherweise nicht ganzlich festgelegten) Personenkreises, der für die Abfassung von unterschiedlichen Schriften verantwortlich war.'

[146] Unger, *Päpstliche Schriftlichkeit*, 292: 'In dieser Kanzlei … abgefasst worden sein.'

[147] Unger, *Päpstliche Schriftlichkeit*, 258–259.

[148] A. Weckwerth, *Ablauf, Organisation und Selbstverständnis westlicher antiker Synoden im Spiegel ihrer Akten* (Jahrbuch für Antike und Christentum, Eränzungsband Kleine Reihe 5; Münster, 2010), D. 3. 4. 3, p. 190. The papal administration would also presumably have resembled those of other bishoprics.

[149] E. Pásztor, 'La Curia Romana', in *Le istituzioni ecclesiastiche della 'Societas Christiana' dei secoli XI–XII. Papato, cardinalato ed episcopato* (Milan, 1974), 490–504, at 492: 'segue il modello degli altri vescovati'.

[150] 'Del primo nucleo di organizzazione attorno al papato, detto nelle fonti "episcopium Lateranense" (dalla "Domus Faustae" in Laterano), fanno parte notai e, a partire dal quarto secolo, "defensores". Ai primi è affidata la preparazione delle lettere e dei

scrinium (that is, the writing office and archive) in and after the period of imperial collapse in the West has been outlined by Sophia Boesch Gajano:

one can trace the *scrinium* back to the times of the emperors Gratian and Valentinian, who had granted to the bishops of Rome the same privileges that the emperor exercised in civil matters. Thus began, from the time of Pope Siricius (384–399) a process of imitation of the imperial Chancery, and the *scrinium* looks like a well-developed structure by the end of the fifth century, responsible for the production and archiving of documents, and with its own staff consisting of notaries ....[151]

This trajectory appears to have reached a high point under Gregory I:

The Chancery's function, as a writing office responsible for papal documents – structured by forms which were by then well established by practice – and indeed for the preservation of papal privileges, conciliar decrees, and administrative documents, was consolidated, ... The institutionalisation of the *scrinium* is made evident also by the presence of its own special staff, the ... *notarii*, who constituted a *schola notariorum*, with seven *notarii regionarii*, directed by a *primicerius* and by a *secundicerius*. The prestige of this institution is confirmed by the fact that positions of trust and responsibility were also given to its members, for instance the positions of rectors of the patrimonies of the Church ... Though the custom of preserving papal letters was already ancient, and though the *scrinium* was already a well-established institution, what does appear to be new is the form of the preservation of the letters in what can properly be called a collection, the structure of which Gregory himself would establish and to which he would give the title of *Registrum* [according to one source].[152]

The evidence for letter production by the writing office under Gregory I is exceptionally rich and thoroughly studied.[153] For the subsequent early medieval history of the production of papal documents the old survey by Edith Pásztor remains useful,[154] as is Harry Bresslau's older but classic

documenti; raccolgono, inoltre, I "gesta" dei martiri e compiono missioni diplomatiche.' Pásztor, 'La Curia Romana', 492.

[151] S. Boesch Gajano, *Gregorio Magno. Alle origini del Medioevo* (Rome, 2004), 59, passage beginning 'l'esistenza dello *scrinium* ...' and ending '... costituito da notari' (my translation).

[152] Boesch Gajano, *Gregorio Magno*, 59–60: passage beginning 'Si conferma la funzione ...' and ending '... titolo di *Registrum*'.

[153] E. Pitz, *Papstreskripte im frühen Mittelalter. Diplomatische und rechtsgeschichtliche Studien zum Brief-Corpus Gregors des Großen* (Beiträge zur Geschichte und Quellenkunde des Mittelalters, 14; Sigmaringen, 1990), and criticism (combined with polite appreciation) by B. Pferschy-Maleczek, 'Rechtsbildung durch Reskripte unter Gregor dem Großen? Zu einem neuen Buch', *Mitteilungen des Instituts für österreichische Geschichtsforschung*, 99 (1991), 505–512. See too the excellent clear summary in the broadly positive review of the book by T. F. X. Noble, *Speculum* 68 (1993), 1195–1197.

[154] E. Pásztor, 'La Curia Romana'.

analysis, still invaluable for papal administration between the end of the Roman empire and the 'papal turn' of the eleventh century, notably on registration of papal documents,[155] their archival preservation,[156] and the personnel of the writing office.[157]

On the latter: from the seventh century there was a college of seven *iudices cleri* – here the word 'judge' just means 'official'.[158] As we have seen, two of these, a *primicerius notariorum* and a *secundicerius notariorum*, presided over the notaries.[159] With time, not only these two but also the other *iudices de clero* came to be involved in the preparation of papal privileges.[160] The writing of papal documents was still in the hands of the *notarii*, also called *scriniarii*.[161]

The writing of documents in the ninth and tenth centuries

This takes us again to the ninth century and its unstructured writing arrangements. Structure may have been slowly emerging. One significant ninth-century development in that direction was the involvement of the papal *bibliothecarius* (which one could probably translate as 'librarian and archivist') in papal correspondence, from the pontificate of Paschal I (817–824). The *Hofkapelle* (court chapel) of the German emperors may have been a model.[162] From 983, according to De Lasala, the *bibliothecarius* appears to have had sole responsibility for the dating clause on privileges.[163] Previously the *iudices de clero*, recruited from local Roman families,[164] could do that. The new arrangement may be the first stage, or perhaps rather an adumbration, of the process of detachment of papal administration from the local nobility.[165] The office of *bibliothecarius* was not always filled. That may reflect the dominance of the Roman nobility in the ninth and tenth centuries. When there was a *bibliothecarius*

---

[155] Bresslau, *Handbuch*, i, 104–108.   [156] *Ibid.*, i, 152–155.   [157] *Ibid.*, i, 193–229.
[158] *Ibid.*, i, 200–208.
[159] Pásztor, 'La Curia Romana', 492–493; Bresslau, *Handbuch*, i, 193–195 and 200–201. He is clearer than Edith Pásztor, who does not make the relation between *notarii* and *iudices* as clear as she might.
[160] Bresslau, *Handbuch*, i, 208.   [161] Good pages in Bresslau, *Handbuch*, i, 196–200.
[162] Pásztor, 'La Curia Romana', 496–499.   [163] De Lasala, *Il Documento*, 175.
[164] Pásztor, 'La Curia Romana', 493.
[165] The process is one of the main themes of C. Wickham, *Medieval Rome. Stability and Crisis of a City, 900–1150* (Oxford, 2015), which refreshingly presents it from the point of view of political harmony and its breakdown. On the palatine judges / *iudices de clero* see Bresslau, *Handbuch*, i, 200–211; 212 for their recruitment from the Roman elite. Thanks to the office of *bibliothecarius*, according to Bresslau, the *iudices de clero* were 'völlig aus dem Dienst in der Kanzlei, sowie aus dem Genuß der Einkünfte und des Einflusses, die damit wahrscheinlich schon damals verbunden waren, verdrängt worden' in the second half of the tenth century (211; cf. 213).

he was also involved in the composition of letters.[166] These were high status men, bishops apart from the famous Anastasius Bibliothecarius.[167] In 1023 the archbishop of Cologne was made *bibliothecarius*; he appointed a deputy to do the work in Rome.[168] After that the office regularly went to one of the bishops in proximity to Rome.[169]

The papal Chancery under the reformed papacy

The process of detaching the papal Chancery from the grip of the Roman notaries and the Roman nobility speeded up under the 'Reform papacy', from the mid-eleventh century, with Clement II and Leo IX. They were protegés of the German empire and began to recruit imperial scribes.[170] This marked the beginning of a transformation of the papal Chancery.

The Chancery was becoming international. It was no longer such a good source of jobs for Roman nobles. Not accidentally, we see here the beginning of a long period of tension between papal government and the Roman elite, of which the Avignon papacy was in part a result. From the point of view of papal history this can be characterised as evolution towards greater efficiency. From the point of view of Roman history, it was the end of an era of happy cooperation between bishop and city. Chris Wickham's *Medieval Rome. Stability and Crisis of a City* (2015), written from the city's point of view, is a fascinating photo-negative of the usual picture. Arguably, this period of tension ended only in the fifteenth century, with the system of sale of offices which gave Roman and neighbouring aristocratic elites a stake in papal administration reminiscent of the good old days of the ninth and tenth centuries – so that the sale of offices functioned, though it was hardly intended, as a force for stability. This digression should be called to mind when we reach the Renaissance Chancery.

---

[166] 'Il bibliotecario della Sede apostolica partecipa a missioni diplomatiche e alla preparazione delle lettere: non solo apponendo la data sui privilegi, ma stendendone egli stesso [according to his and the pope's capacities] ... il testo medesimo ...'; Pásztor, 'La Curia Romana', 494.

[167] 'già sotto Pasquale I, partecipa alle funzioni cancelleresche, apponendo la data sui privilegi; entra a far parte dell'amministrazione pontificia, a partire dall'829, un vescovo: la sola eccezione è rappresentata da Anastasio, bibliotecario di Adriano II e di Giovanni VIII; ... sarà appunto la carica di bibliotecario che permetterà future cardinali vesovi di inserirsi nell'amministrazione della Chiesa Romana'; Pásztor, 'La Curia Romana', 493.

[168] Bresslau, *Handbuch*, i, 220. De Lasala, *Il Documento*, 175 infers from the conferral of the title on the archbishop of Cologne that the office had become honorific.

[169] Bresslau, *Handbuch*, i, 222–223.

[170] Pásztor, 'La Curia Romana', 500; Bresslau, *Handbuch*, i, 228–231.

The real initiator of the 'papal turn', Leo IX, was constantly in motion not just in Italy but also in France and Germany, and the scribes he used when on the road were a new breed.[171] A few Roman scribes (*scriniarii*) continued in Rome to work in the traditional style, but it was on the way out. The change was reflected in the appearance of the documents.[172]

Papal privileges: a new look

The change in the appearance of papal privileges in fact started before the mid-century movement. The huge papyrus documents of the early Middle Ages were being replaced by parchment privileges, the transition period being from 1005 to 1057.[173] That affected format: the size of sheepskins limited the format of parchment documents, since it was not the practice of papal scribes to sew them together, whereas it was acceptable to fasten papyrus sheets together.[174]

The pace of change speeded up with the short pontificate of Clement II and with Leo IX.[175] The 'Roman Curiale' used in the traditional papal administration took some time to die out in documents written in Rome by scribes of the old sort,[176] but was never adopted by the new scribes. The Germans among them[177] probably had no reason or inclination to learn how to write a script that nobody except Roman scribes could even easily read.[178]

---

[171] Bresslau, *Handbuch*, i, 230. Where the Diplomatics of the 'reform' period is concerned my debt to Benjamin Savill is especially great.

[172] For a broad and original interpretative perspective see I. Fees, 'Diplomatik und Paläographie als Schlüssel zur Kulturgeschichte: Papsgeschichtliche Wende und Urkundengestaltung', in K. Herbers and V. Trenkle, eds., *Papstgeschichte im digitalen Zeitalter. Neue Zugangsweisen zu einer Kulturgeschichte Europas* (Cologne, 2018), 95–107, especially 96.

[173] Werner, *Papsturkunden*, 32; cf. Bresslau, *Handbuch*, ii, zweite Abteilung, 491–493.

[174] Werner, *Papsturkunden*, 39.

[175] Cf. H. Engl, 'Rupture radicale ou mise en oeuvre d'une conception ancienne? Le concept de "réforme grégorienne" à travers les recherches récentes sur la diplomatique pontificale en Allemagne', in T. Martine and J. Winandy, eds., *La Réforme grégorienne, une 'révolution totale'?* (Paris, 2021), 176–189, especially 189, on use of signs and images in Chancery documents which reflected and propagated the idea of papal primacy, and on 'une certaine disposition à collaborer ou plus précisément à interagir' on the part of the governed.

[176] De Lasala, *Il Documento*, 190.   [177] Bresslau, *Handbuch*, i, 233.

[178] I respectfully dissent from Irmgard Fees's inference from the length of the privileges that these privileges were for to be read rather than viewed: '... diese Stücke gar nicht für einen Betrachter, sondern für einen Leser bestimmt waren' ('Diplomatik und Paläographie als Schlüssel zur Kulturgeschichte', 99). It was precisely their extraordinary size that would impress the viewer, while few beneficiaries would have been able to read the script without a great effort aggravated by the unwieldy format.

The old script did have the advantage of mystery. It looked like something from an earlier civilisation, as in fact it was, since it went back to a Roman cursive minuscule script.[179] Other ways to give a solemn privilege a special aura had to be found, and under Leo IX they were.

Graphic symbols replaced script as the method of marking out papal documents as special[180] Leo IX himself must have played a decisive role in the introduction of the new signs.[181] It has been said that 'The changes brought about by Leo IX were so striking and radical that it is clear that his pontificate represented a veritable upheaval so far as papal diplomatic is concerned.'[182] The most important and long-lasting innovations were the monogram of the words *Bene valete* and the Rota[183] (the 'comma' was a secondary and more temporary innovation which requires less attention).[184] The *Bene valete* and the Rota both remained features of solemn privileges until the genre died out in the fourteenth century.[185] The Rota consisted of a sign of the cross surrounded by two concentric circles. Leo put the letters of his name plus P for pope in the compartments marked by the cross:

---

[179] 'Es besteht kein Zweifel, dass die Schrift als Ganzes und in ihren vielen Einzelformen direkt auf die römische Minuskelkursive zurückgeht.' Rabikauskas, *Die römische Kuriale*, 16.

[180] Leo IX 'hatte in Anlehnung an die Herrsherurkunde den Wandel von einem ausschließlich durch Schrift gekennzeichneten Urkunde zu einem durch graphische Symbole wirkenden Schriftstück vollzogen'; I. Fees, 'Rota und Siegel der Päpste in der zweiten Hälfte des 11. Jahrhunderts', in C. Alraum, A. Holndonner, H.-C. Lehner, C. Scherer, T. Schlauwitz und V. Unger, eds., *Zwischen Rom und Santiago. Festschrift für Klaus Herbers zum 65. Geburtstag* (Bochum, 2016), 285–298, at 292.

[181] J. Dahlhaus, 'Rota oder Unterschrift. Zur Unterfertigung päpstlicher Urkunden durch ihre Aussteller in der zweiten Hälfte des 11. Jahrhunderts', in I. Fees, A. Hedwig and F. Roberg, eds., *Papsturkunden des frühen und hohen Mittelalters. Äußere Merkmale – Konservierung – Restaurierung* (Leipzig, 2011), 249–290 (with 'Anhang: Die Originalurkunden der Päpste von 1055–1099', 291–303), at 251: 'Die neuen Zeichen, an deren Konzeption Leo entscheidenden Anteil gehabt haben muss, ...'.

[182] Engl, 'Rupture radicale ou mise en oeuvre d'une conception ancienne?', 180: 'Les changements ... diplomatique papale.'

[183] Werner, *Papsturkunden*, 335–337; Fees, 'Rota und Siegel'; Dahlhaus, 'Rota oder Unterschrift'. See also older studies: Schmitz-Kallenberg, *Papsturkunden*, 91 (full and lucid) Poole, *Lectures*, 101–105; De Lasala, *Il Documento*, 191; Frenz and Pagano, *I Documenti*, 21; and J. Dahlhaus, 'Aufkommen und Bedeutung der Rota in den Urkunden des Papstes Leo IX.', *Archivum Historiae Pontificiae*, 27 (1989), 7–84, which offers a thick description of the meaning of the sign for Leo and gives a full account of the scholarship up to the time of the article's writing. For examples, see I. Battelli, *Acta Pontificum* (Exempla Scripturarum, 3; Vatican City, 1965), facsimiles nos. 5 and 6, 8, 10; also I. Fees and F. Roberg, *Papsturkunden der zweiten Hälfte des 11. Jahrhunderts (1057–1098)* (Digitale Urkundenbilder aus dem Marburger Lichtbildarchiv älterer Originalurkunden; Leipzig, 2007): many examples of both Rota and *Bene valete* monogram among the documents beautifully reproduced. Werner, *Papsturkunden*, gives pictures of Rota signs on 352, 369, 379.

[184] Frenz and Pagano, *Documenti*, 22.   [185] Dahlhaus, 'Rota oder Unterschrift', 251.

L	E
O	P

with a motto written in his own hand around the concentric circles: starting from 9 o'clock:

of the mercy [misericordia] | of the Lord [Domini]| is full [plena] | the earth [terra].

– the earth is full of the mercy of the Lord.

Both the form and the words express Leo's idea of his office.[186]

Subsequent popes had different mottos. After Leo the compartments of the inner circle were not filled with the pope's name but with edifying texts.[187] There is some variation in the form taken by the Rota until Paschal II (1099–1118).[188] Judith Werner calls the Rota, together with the *Bene valete* monogram, the 'logo' of the papal curia in the reform age.[189]

A whole book could be – and in fact has been! – written about the *Bene valete* monogram.[190] The monogram developed from those words, meaning 'be well', written out in full often by the pope himself.[191] When the words turned into a mysterious looking monogram the pope himself no longer wrote it.[192] A symptom of the symbolic power of the monogram is that it is often imitated in copies of papal privileges.[193]

From around 1100 the pope inserted his signature in the form 'I Paschal [for example] bishop of the Catholic Church have subscribed'.[194] After 1145 the pope only wrote 'Ego', or just 'E' (but always a small cross at the top of the Rota).[195] The signatures of cardinals or

---

[186] Schmitz-Kallenberg, *Papsturkunden*, 91; cf. Werner, *Papsturkunden*, 335–336.
[187] Poole, *Lectures*, 101–104 (old but as usual very clear), and Frenz and Pagano, *I Documenti*, 21, give lists.
[188] De Lasala, *Il Documento*, 191. Note the distintive features of Gregory VII's privileges: *ibid.*, 192. Joachim Dahlhaus has shown that at least in the period before 1099 privileges either had a papal signature or the Rota but not both, though the Rota could be combined with a signature of an official other than the pope ('Rota oder Unterschrift', 288).
[189] Werner, *Papsturkunden*, 336.
[190] O. Krafft, *Bene Valete. Entwicklung und Typologie des Monogramms in Urkunden der Päpste und anderer Austeller seit 1049* (Leipzig, 2010) and *idem*, 'Der monogrammatische Schlußgruß (*Bene Valete*). Über methodische Probleme, historisch-diplomatische Erkenntnis zu gewinnen', in I. Fees, A. Hedwig, and F. Roberg, eds., *Papsturkunden des frühen und hohen Mittelalters. Äußere Merkmale – Konservierung – Restaurierung* (Leipzig, 2011), 209–247 (good summary of evolution at 240–243).
[191] Werner, *Papsturkunden*, 391–435; also Bresslau, *Handbuch*, i, 78–79.
[192] De Lasala, *Il Documento*, 191–192.   [193] Werner, *Papsturkunden*, 392.
[194] Rabikauskas, *Diplomatica Pontificia*, 46.   [195] *Ibid.*

others were often added at the foot of privileges from 1100, and from 1130 this was a regular practice, and only cardinals subscribed.[196]

The outcome of these innovations was a visually imposing genre of documents, as anyone who browses through the photographs published by Irmgard Fees and Francesco Roberg can see.[197] The innovations may have made up for anything lost by the abandonment of the mysterious 'Roman Curiale' script.[198] As its historian said, when the papacy was the apex of the West a script that everyone could read was needed.[199]

A new age of exemption

Legibility of papal privileges had begun to matter a great deal, and there were many more of them, because monasteries had more reason to want independence of episcopal power. We saw that bishops had more potential power over monasteries from the ninth century onwards than had earlier been the case, because far more ordinations were required, and for these the monastery was dependent on a bishop; and perhaps also because bishops could exercise penitential jurisdiction over monks. That may have breathed new meaning into the strong-sounding but imprecise formulae that we meet in the *Liber Diurnus*. Perhaps because old formulae were deemed unspecific, however, some monasteries began around 1000 to ask for more clearly defined privileges. Thus in 998 monks of the flagship reform monastery of Cluny obtained from Gregory V the privilege of receiving the various degrees of ordination in any place that the abbot wanted, and in 1024 John XIX forbade bishops to put the abbey under interdict or excommunicate any of its monks. Other monasteries succeeded in following this example.[200]

The more specific the privileges, the more it mattered whether one could read them. Thus it was lucky that the 'Roman Curiale' script began to be phased out from the mid-eleventh century. The change coincided with the start of the 'papal turn', which lead into the Investiture Contest between popes and secular rulers. That was a context that favoured an increase in grants to monasteries of privileges. Monasteries tended to be allies of the reformers, while secular rulers and the bishops they had appointed were often the opponents. Grants of protection or liberty were a natural move in these circumstances.

---

[196] *Ibid.*, 46–47.   [197] Fees and Roberg, *Papsturkunden, passim.*
[198] See Rabikauskas, *Die römische Kuriale.*
[199] *Ibid.*, 100: '… an der Spitze des Abendlandes stehend, bedurfte es einer allgemein verständlichen Schrift'.
[200] L. Falkenstein, *La papauté,* 6–7.

Protection or liberty – which? It is not so easy for historians to tell with privileges before the second half of the twelfth century, and contemporaries may not have been too sure either – clarity would come later.[201] Until the pontificate of Alexander III (1159–1181) 'one must always put together several elements in a privilege to be sure that the church concerned is an exempt church'.[202] Indications are: mention of a 'special' relation with the papacy in the *arenga*; attachment with no intermediary (*nullo mediante*) to the pope; denial to the bishop of the right to hold public masses in the monastery or community in question; right to have direct recourse to the apostolic see; the right to excommunicate; rights regarding holy oil and chrism (so that the church was not dependent on the local bishop); the clause 'saving the authority of the apostolic see'.[203] However hard it may be for modern historians to decide whether, or how far, a monastery was exempt from its bishop, or if the relation with the papacy was merely one of protection, the precise terms really were important to the monastery (and bishop). The phasing out of the old script removed one obstacle to working out what the relation was.

Thus the 'papal turn' of the mid-eleventh century transformed diplomatic practice. We find instead a script that was and is easy to read; the abandonment of the 'Roman Curiale' and new ways – especially the Rota and the monogram – to communicate the awe earlier instilled by massive papyrus documents in a strange unreadable script; a Chancery recruiting internationally, and above all no longer controlled by the Roman nobility; and, as we have seen, also more specificity with regard to the relation between bishops and religious houses.

Development of the papal letter before 1150

The attention of papal Diplomatics has traditionally been focussed on the solemn privilege so far as the period before 1150 is concerned. Recently other kinds of papal document have received attention: the simple privilege and papal letters. We will see that two predominant categories of papal letters would emerge by the period c. 1150–1200: letters of grace and letters of justice. Before that there was a period of flux which – solemn privileges aside – has only recently received attention, notably

---

[201] Cf. Schreiber, *Kurie und Kloster*, i, 8, writes of 'der grossen, dem 12. Jahrhundert gestellten und auch von ihm gelösten Aufgabe: der Scheidung, und zwar einer klaren und deutlichen Scheidung der Klöster des Schutzinstitutes in exemte und nicht exemte'.

[202] '... il faut toujours réunir plusieurs élements dans un privilège pour être sûr que l'église concernée est une église exempte'. Falkenstein, *La papauté*, 156.

[203] Closely following Falkenstein, *La papauté*, 155–156.

in a published dissertation by Benedikt Hotz.[204] The principal conclusions of his study would seem to be as follows. On the one hand, the rapid development of a papal judge delegate system led to an evolution in the direction of simplicity, culminating in the genre of 'letters of justice' (to which the seal was as a rule attached by hemp string).[205] This will be studied in the following chapter. On the other hand, Hotz traces an evolution which would eventually lead to the diminution in importance of the solemn privilege. He plays down, without trying to eliminate, the distinction between solemn and simple privileges, arguing instead for a series of gradations of degrees of formality,[206] with room for manoeuvre and experimentation.[207] Simple privileges are the 'mother genre' for letters which one would want to keep, sealed on silk thread.[208] Letters sealed with silk thread are heavily influenced by the privilege tradition, taking over the *arenga* (frequently) and a *prohibitio* and *sanctio*, saying that the decision must be obeyed and that terrible if vague consequences will follow if it is not.[209]

Thirteenth-century rules for letters of grace cannot be read back into the twelfth century.[210] However, simple privileges, as we find them around 1100, would evolve into the 'letters of grace', whose seal was attached by coloured silk thread. As later, coloured silk thread might also be employed for the forerunners of letters of justice when the letter's recipient was not the addressee but a de facto beneficiary on a lasting basis of the decision contained in the letter.[211] If a monastery asked for a protection against a bishop, the letter to the bishop would normally be given to the monastery, to be produced to silence the bishop when it was needed.

Mid-twelfth-century changes

Another dissertation, by Stefan Hirschmann,[212] focusses on the decades in the middle of the twelfth century. It connects a growth in importance of solemn privileges with the development of the college of cardinals – the connection being the signing of privileges by cardinals. Hirschmann

[204] B. Hotz, *Litterae apostolicae. Untersuchungen zu päpstlichen Briefen und einfachen Privilegien im 11. und 12. Jahrhundert* (Münchener Beiträge zur Geschichtswissenschaft, 9; Munich, 2018).
[205] *Ibid.*, 175–176, 219; cf. Rabikauskas, *Diplomatica Pontificia*, 58; De Lasala, *Il Documento*, 201, 204; Frenz and Pagano, *I Documenti*, 25.
[206] Hotz, *Litterae*, 58–60, 177.   [207] *Ibid.*, 59, 219.   [208] *Ibid.*, 177–178.
[209] *Ibid.*, 65.   [210] *Ibid.*, 63.   [211] *Ibid.*, 67–68.
[212] S. Hirschmann, *Die päpstliche Kanzlei und ihre Urkundenproduktion (1141–1159)* (Frankfurt am Main, 2001).

stresses the energy of mid-century chancellors in reorganising the Chancery, and sees a tendency towards standardisation,[213] but he also emphasises graduality and continuity, especially in *arengae*.[214] In his view the middle years of the twelfth century were a bridge between the world of the *Liber Diurnus* and the bureaucratic papacy of the later Middle Ages.[215] One can argue about (or rather against) the term 'bureaucratic', but the subsequent period certainly saw far-going administrative rationalisation to cope with massive quantitative expansion of demand for and supply of documents, to which the next chapter turns, concentrating on the question of how papal government coped with the pressure.[216]

Conclusion

The Diplomatics of Late Antique papal documents mirrors Roman imperial Diplomatics, though the content is naturally different. Like Roman imperial documents, Late Antique papal decretals were for the most part responses, rather than communications initiated by the papacy. Especially important from a long-term perspective are some *arengae* or preambles, because they legitimated papal authority in terms of succession from St. Peter. These *arengae* reached a widening audience through canon law collections, especially through the ninth century 'Pseudo-Isidorian' decretals, which included genuine decretals and reproduced the Late Antique papal *prooemia*. The *Codex Carolinus* shows us that

---

[213] *Ibid.*, 221; for standardisation also 374.   [214] *Ibid.*, 371, 374–375.   [215] *Ibid.*, 370.
[216] Existing scholarship provides a secure framework. To name some recent outstanding contributions: A. Meyer, 'The Curia: The Apostolic Chancery', in K. Sisson and A. A. Larson, eds., *A Companion to the Medieval Papacy. Growth of an Ideology and Institution* (Brill Companions to the Christian Tradition, 70; Leiden, 2016), 239–258, noting especially his comment, at 256, that 'in this mass of transmitted letters, the pope is … not the hunter but the hunted' (he notes at 239 note 1, that this chapter is a distillation of his 'Die päpstliche Kanzlei im Mittelalter – ein Versuch', *Archiv für Diplomatik, Schriftgeschichte, Siegel-und Wappenkunde* 61 (2015), 291–342); idem, 'Regieren mit Urkunden im Spätmittelalter. Päpstliche Kanzlei und weltliche Kanzleien im Vergleich', in W. Maleczek (ed.), *Urkunden und ihre Erforschung. Zum Gedenken an Heinrich Appelt* (Veröffentlichungen des Instituts für Österreichische Geschichtsforschung, 62; Vienna, 2014), 71–91; B. Schwarz, 'The Roman Curia (until about 1300)', in W. Hartmann and K. Pennington, eds., *The History of Courts and Procedure in Medieval Canon Law* (Washington, D.C., 2016), 160–228 (195–196, 209–213 for the Chancery); from a historiographical perspective, *eadem*, 'Die Erforschung der mittelalterlichen römischen Kurie von Ludwig Quidde bis heute' (with an 'organogram' of papal governance, 420–421, and key historiographical but also interpretative pages especially on 424–436); P. Zutshi, 'The Papal Chancery: Avignon and Beyond', in *idem*, *The Avignon Popes and their Chancery*, 3–24. When the profound insights of Schwarz and Meyer have penetrated into the general historical consciousness, papal history will look quite different.

arengae legitimating papal authority could also be directly before the eyes of Carolingian rulers. In the early Middle Ages popes were increasingly called upon to regulate relations between monasteries and bishops. One outcome was the strange genre of papyrus papal privileges two or three metres long, written in a late Roman script, hard for contemporaries to decipher. (The illegibility may have helped cover up shaky Latin.) Only in the eleventh century, as monastic exemption from bishops became common in varying degrees, did it become important to understand in detail the content of such privileges, though it was only under Alexander III, after the period covered by this chapter, that the terminology began to catch up with the need for clarity, to make it more evident whether a privilege was conveying exemption from the bishop, or merely protection of its property from all comers. The Diplomatics of privileges changed. The mysteriously antique Roman Curiale script was abandoned, and privileges became legible – and physically shorter since they were now on parchment and had to fit on a sheepskin. New ways to make them impressive were created, notable the striking Rota and *Bene valete*. In the course of the twelfth century various shades of 'simple privileges' can be seen, from which 'letters of grace' (to be discussed in the next chapter) emerge alongside the solemn privileges, whose heyday was almost over.

4 The Religious Governance of the Latin World, 1150–1378

As the twelfth century progressed, Latin Christendom was becoming a more complicated society, especially in its legal aspects. Random examples: there were new international orders, special legal rules for crusaders, indulgences, excommunication as a routine enforcement mechanism – the list could go on. The growth of papal government was driven in part by the demand for rational management of the increased complexity. Another driving force was legislation by councils, in 1123, 1139 and 1179. Like most legislation, it was too simplistic for the world it sought to improve, and the new canons created new problems for which the papacy, more flexible than a general council, was called upon to find solutions. Gradually, the solutions would be routinised. All this would lead to a quantum leap in the amount of business handled by the curia with the help of routine procedures which will be examined below from the point of view of Diplomatics.

The papacy was also now a major player in top level ecclesiastical politics and diplomacy, dealing on an equal level with the rulers of Europe, ecclesiastical and secular. The kind of documents in which such communications were conducted have their own Diplomatics. As administration intensifies, a gap widens between routine business and business to which the ruler gives personal attention. Each kind of business has its own Diplomatics.

High-level business

From the twelfth century on, a capacity to cope with the heavy burden of high-level business was an essential qualification for a pope, and for all the other faults and weaknesses they may have had, most of them could take the pressure, the exception proving the rule being Celestine V, briefly pope in 1294; he was as incompetent as he was holy. His case shows that admininistrative ability was a *sine qua non*. It is true, obviously, that popes did not manage on their own. No ruler governs without help,

and a possible management style is to avoid micro-management, relying
on a competent staff (how far this or that ruler directed policy personally
is a favourite question for historians). At the top level, however, in almost
any organisation, even the tendency to follow advice is a decision by the
leader. With later medieval popes, as with modern premiers, we may be
sure they were involved in some way in decisions about legal precedents,
theological questions, relations with secular rulers, etc.[1] Around the mid-
thirteenth century, letters about such matters came to be called *litterae de
curia* or *litterae curiales*.[2]

The special status of such documents could be reflected in the
Diplomatics of the registration of documents. Distinct volumes or fascicules came to be reserved for *litterae de curia*, which were thus segregated
from the *litterae communes*. From the pontificate of John XXII (d. 1334),
a series of *registra secreta* begins (or at least, only from his pontificate do
such registers survive).[3] The texts of the letters were composed by aids
known as *secretarii*[4] from the pontificate of Benedict XII (d. 1342) on,[5]
with the pope closely involved.[6] Under Gregory XI (d. 1378) we meet the
phrase: letters 'that went via the secretaries' ('que transiverunt per ...
secretarios').[7]

The account by Patrick Zutshi is worth quoting:

Following a breach of confidence in the chancery, Benedict XII removed curial
letters from the notaries' control and entrusted them to secretaries. The
secretaries [qua secretaries] were not chancery officials; rather they were
members of the pope's entourage who enjoyed his special confidence, although

---

[1] For relations with the kings of England in the fourteenth century we now have a model
study by Bombi, *Anglo-Papal Relations*. See also her *Il Registro di Andrea Sapiti, procuratore
alla Curia Avignonese* (Rome, 2007). Sapiti was the English king's proctor at the
papal court.

[2] De Lasala, *Il Documento*, 203; Bresslau, *Handbuch*, i, 114. This and the following
paragraph are heavily indebted to Werner Maleczek. For the fourteenth century there is
a magisterial discussion by P. Zutshi, 'The Political and Administratve Correspondence
of the Avignon Popes, 1305–1378: A Contribution to Papal Diplomatic', in *Aux origines
de l'état moderne. La fonctionnement administratif de la papauté d'Avignon* (Collection de
l'École Française de Rome, 138; Rome, 1990), 371–384.

[3] See P. Zutshi, 'Changes in the Registration of Papal Letters under the Avignon Popes
(1305–1378)', in *idem, The Avignon Popes and their Chancery*, 107–138, at 127–130.
According to Frenz and Pagano, *I Documenti*, 55, the registers 'contengono gli scritti *de
curia*, redatti nella *camera secreta* del papa ... da quelli che in seguito saranno chiamati
segretari'. Read closely, this is an assertion that the 'scritti' (rather than the registers) were
written by the secretaries.

[4] P. Gasnault, 'L'élaboration des lettres secrètes des papes d'Avignon: Chambre et
Chancellerie', in *Aux origines de l'état moderne*, 209–222.

[5] 'The texts ... on': I owe the formulation to Patrick Zutshi.

[6] Gasnault, 'L'élaboration', 213.

[7] *Ibid.*, 221; Zutshi, 'Changes in the Registration', 131.

they often combined a chancery office with that of secretary.[8] The change ... meant the end of the chancery's responsibility for curial letters, although the scribes of the chancery continued to engross [= make fair copies of] them. This in turn meant the end of the monopoly that the chancery had hitherto enjoyed in the production of papal letters.[9]

From the time of Gregory XI each secretary would keep his own register.[10] From Benedict XII's time the drafts for the *registra secreta* were written directly onto parchment.[11] In the modern Vatican Archives they are classified with the *Reg. Vat.* series.[12]

In this connection, and in parenthesis, a controversy among specialists must be mentioned. Some letters are described as *de Camera*. There are references to 'letters that passed through the *Camera*' ('littere que transiverunt per Cameram'). About the word *Camera* in this context there are two theories, neither of which appear to have been definitively demonstrated. According to Martino Giusti (following Emil Göller) and others, it refers to the *Camera apostolica* (the pope's 'finance ministry'). There are some non-neglible arguments in favour of this view. Some of the letters in question in the registers are described there as 'tangentes Cameram apostolicam' and in three of the *Registra Vaticana* (235–237) we find on the first folio the words 'Littere ... et commissiones ... pro Camera Apostolica'.[13] Against that, Thomas Frenz[14] and Pierre Gasnault[15] argue for the pre-Göller view that the Chamber in question was the pope's private apartment.[16] Gasnault argues that the apparent replacement of the formula *que transiverunt per Cameram* by references to the role of the secretaries suggests that the latter and the former systems were the same, so that one can infer that the setting was the private *Camera secreta* rather than the *Camera apostolica*.[17] I do not think that this non-trivial disagreement can be regarded as settled either way.

Frenz notes that from the mid-fourteenth century the *Camera apostolica* kept its own register.[18] The *Camera*'s special registers were on paper (but they are nonetheless classified with the *Registra Vaticana*). Some of the letters in question are registered in the *litterae secretae* registers too.

---

[8] Cf. Gasnault, 'L'élaboration', 218 (following Brigide Schwarz): he comments that with rare exceptions ('sauf exception') the secretaries would also have posts in the Chancery.

[9] P. Zutshi, 'The Papal Chancery: Avignon and Beyond', 10.

[10] Frenz and Pagano, *I Documenti*, 55.   [11] Zutshi, 'Changes in the Registration', 128.

[12] Frenz and Pagano, *I Documenti*, 55.

[13] M. Giusti, *Studi sui Registri di Bolle Papali* (Collectanea Archivi Vaticani, 1; Vatican City, 1979), 28.

[14] Frenz and Pagano, *I Documenti*, 55 ('redatti nella *camera secreta*').

[15] Gasnault, 'L'élaboration', 221

[16] On the historiography of the disagreement, see *ibid.*, 221   [17] *Ibid.*, 221.

[18] Frenz and Pagano, *I Documenti*, 55.

Thus, as Frenz says, that the boundary with the 'secret' registers was fluid or sometimes non-existent.[19]

Possibly the answer to Göller's weighty arguments about *de Camera* registers is to be found there: the duplication. Given the dissent between excellent specialists, the problem deserves further attention. There seems, however, to be a consensus that, whichever 'Camera' is in question, the papal secretaries played a key role in the production of the letters.[20]

The register from which ***1363, May 30**[21] is printed is structured by months and divided into 'secret' letters and *De Camera* or *De Curia* letters.[22] This letter is the last in the section of the 'secret' letters for May of that year.[23] According to Martino Giusti his hybrid register is on parchment (*'Membran.'*).[24] In the light of the foregoing it would seem to be a product of the *Camera secreta* rather than the *Camera apostolica*, or possibly of both.[25]

The designation *litterae de curia/litterae curiales* can be found in the thirteenth century too, from the second quarter of the thirteenth century; names aside, from at least a century before that there was a de facto distinction between routine letters (whether of justice or of grace) and letters requiring thought at the top level: judicial and theological writings, and political letters (taking the term to include ecclesiastical politics). Qualitatively if not quantitatively, such letters were an essential

---

[19] 'Dalla metà del XIV sec. la Camera apostolica tiene un registro a parte dove vengono riuniti quei documenti che la riguardano particolarmente; anche tali documenti però sono spediti dai segretari, cosicché il confine con i regisri segreti diviene labile o può sfumare addirittura. Ricorrono anche doppie registrazioni in entrambi le serie' (Frenz and Pagano, *I Documenti*, 55–56). Cf. Giusti, *Studi sui Registri*, 27.

[20] Giusti, *Studi sui Registri*, 28; Zutshi, 'Changes in the Registration', 130; Gasnault, 'L'élaboration', 221: 'secrétaires, assistés de *scriptores*'.

[21] AAV Reg. Vat. 245, fo. 174v–175r.

[22] Giusti, *Inventario dei Registri Vaticani* (Collectanea Archivi Vaticani, 8; Vatican City, 1981), 66, on AAV Reg. Vat. 245; cf. *idem*, *Studi sui Registri*, 27.

[23] 'Littere secrete de mense maii anno primo' (AAV Reg. Vat. 245, fo. 146v). The section ends – with ***1363, May 30** – on fo. 175v.

[24] Giusti, *Inventario*, 66 – though on the digitised version I have used it looks as if it could be paper!

[25] The foregoing discussion of fourteenth-century registration is virtually a translation of Frenz and Pagano, *I Documenti*, 54–56. See also the discussion, *ibid.*, 56, of the vexed question of what copied from the minute of a papal letter and what was copied from the letter. One hypothesis is that cameral and secret registers were copied from the minute, *litterae communes* from the original, but with the latter it has been argued that the *registrator* worked from the minute but then checked it against the original. Against that, the best specialist, Zutshi, 'Changes in the Registration', 116, concludes that 'There is no reason to assume that there was a single method of registration ... But it is much more likely that the normal method of registration [for the Avignon Registers] was to use originals alone.'

component of papal government, and it seems likely that popes personally were involved in their composition.[26] (Indeed, the kind of letters
collected by Charlemagne in the *Codex Carolinus* could be regarded as
distant ancestors of *litterae curiales*.) There was an economic aspect to the
distinction between such special letters, separately registered, on the one
hand, and *litterae communes* on the other. While most letters in the
thirteenth century (and *a fortiori* earlier) were only registered if the recipient paid extra, top level letters were registered at the curia's expense;[27]
'since they were issued on the initiative of the curia, ... there was no
beneficiary who could be expected to pay for them'.[28]

It may be added that special *ad hoc* registers were sometimes compiled
for high-level letters relating to a particular problem: under Innocent III
for the business of the succession to the Empire after the death of Henry
VI of Germany, and (two separate surviving instances) for Sicilian
affairs.[29]

Unfortunately we seldom – by comparison with the post-Trent period –
have documentation revealing the curial debates behind the letters that
eventually emerged. An exception is the pontificate of John XXII, which
has left a lot of evidence about the decision-making process, notably on
theological discussions which he hoped would lead to a binding document (a page is reproduced below as Plate 4).[30] His strong interest in

---

[26] 'Wohl schon unter Alexander III. sind die Papstbriefe in zwei große Kategorien zu
scheiden, Routineangelegenheiten (wie zum Beispiel einfache Gratialbriefe oder
Justizbriefe, die von den Suppliken abhingen) und Briefe, die einen differenzierten
Prozeß der Entstehung zeigen (Urteile des päpstlichen Gerichtes, Rechtsauskünfte,
theologische Schreiben, politische Schreiben). Bei der zweiten Kategorie ist die Frage
zu stellen, wer sie redigiert hat. Der Papst wird einen Teil selbst formuliert haben. Ab
etwa Gregor IX. heißt ein Teil diese Briefe litterae curiales; dafür gibt es sogar
Spezialregister, z. B. das Thronstreitregister Innocenz' III.' (Werner Maleczek,
personal communication). Cf. P. Herde, 'Die Urkundenarten im dreizehnten
Jahrhundert', in idem, *Beiträge*, 57–71, at 68: '... Briefe, die im Interesse der Kurie
selbst entstanden sint, vornehmlich politische Korrespondenz der Päpste'; Herde, 'Der
Geschäftsgang in der päpstlichen Kanzlei des dreizehnten Jahrhunderts', in idem,
Beiträge, 149–242 (+ 'Exkurs. Wesen und Merkmale von Kanzleikorekturen an
Papsturkunden', 243–246), at 179.

[27] As pointed out to me by Werner Maleczek.

[28] Patrick Zutshi, personal communication.

[29] Frenz and Pagano, *I Documenti*, 55. Cf. R. Fawtier, 'Documents négligés sur l'activité de
la Chancellerie apostolique à la fin du XIIIe siècle. Le registre 46A et les comptes de la
Chambre sous Boniface VIII', *Mélanges d'archéologie et d'histoire* 52 (1935), 244–272,
studies the second case: a register containing letters of Nicholas IV, Celestine V, and
Boniface VIII. (Incidentally this article anticipates Michael Clanchy's use of records of
purchase of lead for sealing as an index of the number of documents produced.)
Probably other such *ad hoc* registers have been lost.

[30] *1333, September 6 and 7, and, more generally, P. Nold, *John XXII and his Franciscan
Cardinal: Bertrand de la Tour and the Apostolic Poverty Controversy* (Oxford, 2003) and
idem, *Marriage Advice for a Pope: John XXII and the Power to Dissolve* (Leiden, 2009);

theology and his idea that the papacy would actively shape the development of doctrine were exceptional in medieval papal history.

The Diplomatics of high-level decision-making would normally
include the typical *de haut en bas* language of authority, often with an
arenga redolent of authority or a sanction clause threatening the dis-
obedient with the wrath of the apostles Peter and Paul, but another kind
of discourse was possible, when the pope was not exercising spiritual
power, or trying to. Urban V was not doing so in the document printed at
*1363, May 30,[31] addressed to King John the Good of France. The pope
is interceding on behalf of the 'consuls and community', the community,
a *universitas*, near Uzès and Avignon. Presumably it had commercial
relations with the papal court. The community in question had obtained
permission from the French king to hold a market once a week and a fair
twice a year, but another community together with the Comte de
Beaufort challenged this. The case was to come before the French
Parlement, and the pope begs the king to make that costly process go
away and let the first town keep its privilege. The town was across the
border from the papal city state of Avignon and in the kingdom of
France, and the issue was purely commercial. Consequently, the pope
did not 'pontificate', but instead wrote like someone asking a favour, as
indeed he was, since he had no authority over the matter. This is worth
noting. It should be a corrective to the many who misunderstand the
concept of *plenitudo potestatis*.[32] Since the letter was a rather specific
request to a king rather than, say, a routine response to a request for a
minor indulgence, it was registered with the 'secret' rather than
'common' letters, at the end of the section for 'secret' letters for
May 1363.

The thirteenth-century developments outlined above – *litterae de curia*,
the appearance of 'secretaries' alongside and distinct from Chancery
staff, etc. – would be followed by others in the later Middle Ages and
afterwards: most notably, the creation of a Secretariate of State (*Segreteria
di Stato*) in the sixteenth century. Without passing over these important
topics altogether (we will return to them in the next chapter), the main
emphasis of the present study is on the Diplomatics of routine business.

L. Duval-Arnould, 'Élaboration d'un document pontifical: les travaux préparatoires à la
constitution apostolique *Cum inter nonnullos* (12 novembre 1323)', in *Aux origines de l'état
moderne*, 385–409.

[31] AAV Reg. Vat. 245, fo. 174v–175r.

[32] For an analogous case, where Gregory X intercedes for Italian merchants who have tried
to break royal trade sanctions, see TNA SC 7/47/1; for context see J. Prestwich, *Edward I*
(London, 1988), 98–99, and F. M. Powicke, *The Thirteenth Century, 1216–1307* (Oxford,
1953), 621–622.

The divergence between the high-level systems and the routine systems becomes evident from the pontificate of Alexander III.

The increasing burden of routine business

Understanding the Diplomatics of routine business is the best way to solve the major historical problem of how the papacy coped with the colossal demand for its services in the later medieval and early modern centuries, in the absence of the political and financial infrastructure of a secular state other than the puny one in central Italy. The burden of routine business expanded dramatically from the mid- twelfth century.

It seemed as if everyone wanted something from the papacy! Almost random examples from an enormous mass of material are in the Transcriptions section below. Thus in *1195[33] Celestine grants an indulgence of 100 days to anyone who visits the Church of St. Mary of 'Wika' and gives some 'beneficia' to the nuns; he asks archbishops, bishops, abbots, priors and other prelates to encourage the faithful to do so. The letter is sealed on silk thread, showing that it was a document to be kept, recording a papal favour. Though addressed to prelates, the letter must have been given to a representative of the nuns, who would be responsible for bringing it to the attention of the ostensible addressees. Behind the document lies a request of a community of women to the pope for a favour, a document which will help their precarious finances.

*1200, March 8 (TNA SC 7/19/16) is a somewhat different case, a document for a powerful military order rather than an impoverished community of nuns. Like the earlier document, however, it is sealed on silk thread, a sign that it is a privilege to be kept, and it too would have been entrusted not to the addressees but to those who stood to benefit, the Knights Templar. Powerful though they were, the Templars felt themselves to be victims of malefactors and, furthermore, insufficiently protected by prelates. Innocent III tells the prelates to give them full justice, so that they don't have to take matters up to the pope.

As demand grew, papal administration became increasingly complex. The Diplomatics of papal documents becomes correspondingly difficult to explicate in an accessible manner. Rather than try to capture all its labyrinthine details, well explained by Bresslau, Schmitz-Kallenberg, Herde, Rabikauskas, Frenz & Pagano, and others, I will focus on those aspects which help most to understand how the papacy was able to function – with only a fourth-class army and with less money than most

---

[33] TNA SC 7/9/35.

assume – as a government controlling aspects of life all over Latin Europe.

So we return to Othmar Hageneder's question: 'how was it possible to rule the Church and Christendom without an administrative apparatus equal to the task, one which would be able to check and oversee that the documents that the Chancery produced were based on correct assumptions and implemented in the localities?'[34] This chapter and the next attempt to provide answers.[35]

Demand-driven, self-funded and resented government

There would be no problem to solve had there not been heavy demand for papal government. The whole system was demand-driven. People came to the curia to ask for things and to get disputes settled – and the two great diplomatic categories of 'letters of grace' and 'letters of justice' correspond to these two powerful pistons of the engine of papal government. The first part of the answer to 'Hageneder's question' is that payment for each piece of work done by the curia funded the administration, by contrast with the 'taxation and salary' system. In addition, there might be 'presents',[36] de facto expected (like a tip in a restaurant today) even if not formally demanded, and the cost of a lawyer, the 'proctor'. Consequently, from the twelfth century on, burgeoning demand for the curia's services was accompanied by a tenacious sense of grievance about the cost of dealing with it. Satires and moralising

---

[34] Hageneder, 'Päpstliche Reskripttechnik', 194: '... wie waren Kirche ... zu regieren?'; D. L. d'Avray, *Medieval Religious Rationalities. A Weberian Analysis* (Cambridge, 2010), 142 at note 79. Much of the current chapter is based on my earlier book. The excuse for the (limited) recycling is that students of papal Diplomatics are highly unlikely, given the specialisation of modern research, to crack open a book with a title of this kind.

[35] In a highly compressed form 'Hageneder's question' is answered, with deep insight into the whole nature of later medieval papal government, by Meyer, 'Regieren'. Cf. also A. Meyer, 'Spätmittelalterliche päpstliche Kanzleiregeln', in G. Drossbach, ed., *Von der Ordnung zur Norm: Statuten in Mittelalter und Früher Neuzeit* (Paderborn, 2010), 95–108, which brings out the importance of *regulae cancellariae* as law. On this cf. yet another gem of a synthesis by A. Meyer, 'Das spätmittelalterliche Kirchenrecht', in C. R. Lange, W. P. Müller and C. K. Neumann, eds., *Islamische und westliche Jurisprudenz des Mittelalters im Vergleich* (Tübingen, 2018), 169–181, at 173–176, on the various versions of the *Liber Cancellariae* and the *regulae cancellariae*, and 179–181 on the same but above all for profound paragraphs about medieval papal law in general. My thanks to Werner Maleczek for drawing my attention to these important papers.

[36] M. Tangl, 'Das Taxwesen der päpstlichen Kanzlei vom 13. bis zur Mitte des 15. Jahrhunderts', reprinted in *idem, Das Mittelalter in Quellenkunde und Diplomatik. Ausgewählte Schriften*, ii (Graz, 1966), 734–838, at 784 (writing about the Avignon period): 'neben Sporteln und Trinkgelder werden nach dem Zeugnis des Alvarus Pelagius wohl ... an einzelne Beamte ... geflossen sein'.

complaint gave expression to this resentment: it was a literary topos with a life of its own.[37] To get a balanced objective picture on the basis of actual case costs in real terms would be a daunting task which has not to my knowledge been attempted and may not be possible.[38] The problem is complicated by the multiplicity of currencies in circulation[39] and the difficulty of establishing what a given fee meant in real terms – though I have made an attempt to do this below for fees of *abbreviatores*.[40] In estimating real costs over time one should also take inflation into account, though – another conspicuous omission – nobody to my knowledge has tried to calculate the impact of that. Even harder would be a comparison with the cost of comparable services from a modern government, which would have to be a calculation of taxation-funded costs and costs of civil litigation (notoriously expensive in modern England or the USA, for instance). So far as comparisons within the medieval period are concerned, Harald Müller suggests that litigation in the localities was not necessarily regarded as a cheaper option than papal justice.[41] He also analyses the measures taken by the curia in the later Middle Ages to limit the costs of litigation, or at least to streamline the procedures.[42]

Production of documents

To understand how the papacy met the increased demand for documents, we need to realise that it did not have a bureaucracy as conventionally understood. Half a century ago Brigide Schwarz demolished the idea that papal administration in its heyday fits the ideal-type of a bureaucracy as defined by Max Weber.[43] (Weber *aficionados* will realise that, far from being a critique of Weber, this is a consummate application of his methodology.) She pointed out that 'with the enormous

[37] T. Wetzstein, '*Roma carpit marcas, bursas exhaurit et arcas.* Die Gier des Papstes und der Groll der Christenheit', in Maleczek, *Die römische Kurie und das Geld*, 337–372, at 371 (Maleczek's volume is fundamental for many aspects of papal finance in the twelfth and thirteenth centuries); M. Tangl, 'Das Taxwesen', at 767–768, and 768 note 134 quoting Alvarus Pelagius: a moralising judgment by both Tangl and his source. In addition to its sermonising ('nie entschuldigt, nie gerechtfertigt', p. 767) Tangl's article gives rich detail on fees at the papal court.
[38] Cf. H. Müller, 'Päpste und Prozeßkosten im späten Mittelalter', in Bertram, *Stagnation oder Fortbildung?*, 249–270, at 250–251.
[39] Tangl, 'Das Taxwesen', 744–748.   [40] See below, 123–124.
[41] '... die Verfolgung eines Rechsstreits *in partibus* nicht zwingend als die kostengünstigere Variante angesehen wurde' (Müller, 'Päpste und Prozeßkosten', 270).
[42] Müller, 'Päpste und Prozeßkosten', 251–269: 'den Geschäftsgang zu optimieren und die Verfahren zu straffen'.
[43] B. Schwarz, *Die Organisation kurialer Schreiberkollegien von ihrer Entstehung bis zur Mitte des 15. Jahrhunderts* (Tübingen, 1972).

intensification in the pressure of business on the curia from the middle of the twelfth century, the officials of the Chancery outsourced [*abwälzten*] part of their duties by getting private assistants from outside the curia to make the fair copies of documents'.[44] 'People who were equipped to make fair copies of papal letters were available in large numbers in the environs of the curia: namely, above all public notaries.'[45] Such men were the main recruitment pool. They were mostly clerics and non-Romans, and should probably not be identified with the *scriniarii* who had been more-or-less sidelined in the course of the eleventh-century 'papal turn' by the *notarii palatini* who wrote papal minuscule and who could travel with an itinerant curia.[46] The informal use of these assistants helped handle the business but needed quality control. Innocent III saw the problem (it is possible that discovery of forgeries triggered his plan to regulate the relation between notaries' assistants and the curia).[47] His solution was precisely *not* to turn them into a bureaucracy.

To be precise and qualify this generalisation: the thirteenth-century papal curia as shaped by Innocent III did have one feature of Weber's famous ideal-type of bureaucracy, namely, clear rules of procedure. Rudolf von Heckel argued convincingly that there was a 'statute book of the Lateran Palace', including among other things the elements of a Diplomatics, *avant le mot*, of forgery.[48] (Much more will be said about administration through rules below.) What the curia lacked was the system hierarchy of salaried officials, working in an office, that Weber's ideal-type foregrounds.

To turn the administrative labour force attached to the curia into a bureaucracy would have required a salary system funded by the curia. The papacy did not have the financial resources for that. Instead, Innocent III turned the men who made fair copies of papal documents, the *scriptores*, into a kind of self-regulating and financially self-supporting guild under the aegis of the Chancellor (or, from 1216, the College of the Vice Chancellor and Notaries). They did not have an office but worked from home. Rather than receiving salaries in cash or kind, papal *scriptores* would be paid for each piece of work they did. To achieve parity of

[44] 'daß mit dem ungeheuren Anwachsen ... heranzogen' (Schwarz, *Die Organisation*, 14).
[45] 'Leute ... Notare' (Schwarz, *Die Organisation*, 15).
[46] Schwarz, *Die Organisation*, 83, and note 328. See Rabikauskas, *Diplomatica Pontificia*, 38, and Frenz and Pagano, *I Documenti*, 63, on the *scriniarii*. Cf. Schmitz-Kallenberg, *Papsturkunden*, 99, on their decline.
[47] Schwarz, *Die Organisation*, 16.
[48] R. von Heckel, 'Studien über die Kanzleiordnung Innozenz' III', *Historisches Jahrbuch* 57 (1937), 258–289, at 265–266. My thanks for Patrick Zutshi for pointing out the relevance.

remuneration, one of their number would have the task – not a permanent post but a rotating duty – of allocating work evenly to the others. The name of the scribe of the document would be written on the fold, so that it was possible to check who was responsible. *Scriptores* were examined before being appointed by the pope, to whom they had to give a present.[49] Thus was formed the college of papal *scriptores*, who would monopolise production of papal letters (until the pontificat of Benedict XII [1334–1342], who took the pope's top level correspondence ['curial letters'] away from them and handed it over to a new class of 'secretaries').[50]

The *cursus*

From the later twelfth century, the documents these men copied were in a special prose rhythm, based on a stress accent, called the *cursus*.[51] Its absence in a papal document in the period between the mid-twelfth and the end of the thirteenth centuries calls into question the authenticity of the document. The use of the *cursus* is a symptom of the mastery of complex Latin characteristic of papal letters in this age – a contrast with the late- and post-Carolingian period. The drafting of the letters, insofar as the words were not lifted directly from a formulary, was the work of more elevated officials, senior to the *scriptores*, and evidently able to handle the *cursus*.

New administrative roles

The officials above the *scriptores* were seven or six notaries (six after the vice-chancellor[52] joined the college), who might be called unofficially 'protonotaries' – an elite group who were in charge of drafting documents (not to be confused with the city notaries from whom the *scriptores* were recruited).[53] To the notaries were added *abbreviatores*: the volume of letters to be drafted became too large for the six or seven notaries to cope with, so they employed *abbreviatores* to pick up some of the burden. The *abbreviatores* are discussed in more detail below.

---

[49] For the foregoing, Schwarz, *Die Organisation*, 16–17; 32–34 for distribution of work.
[50] Zutshi, 'The Papal Chancery: Avignon and Beyond', 10.
[51] There are many accounts of this but the clearest I have found is in Poole, *Lectures*, 78–97. The rhythms were for the ends of sentences, but nobody to my knowledge has looked at the punctuation of original papal documents from the point of view of use of the *cursus*.
[52] For the office of vice-chancellor see B. Schwarz, 'Rolle und Rang des (Vize-)Kanzlers an der Kurie', in Herbers and Trenkle, *Papstgeschichte im digitalen Zeitalter*, 171–190.
[53] Frenz and Pagano, *I Documenti*, 63–64.

The post of *auditor litterarum contradictarum* was one of Innocent III's key innovations and will also be discussed below. Another was the *corrector litterarum apostolicarum*, probably also introduced by Innocent III and certainly first attested for his pontificate.[54] This official checked the fair copies of letters and also came to play a part in one of the quick ways of expediting documents, *expeditio per correctorem* (also discussed below). Yet another new role was that of *referendarii*. *Referendarii* appear around the turn of the thirteenth and fourteenth centuries, senior men who took over the task of making the first judgment call on supplications and, more generally, who relieved the senior notaries of a lot of their administrative labour.[55]

Differentiation of documentary types

Another way in which the papacy coped with the increased complexity, as well as with the pressure, of business was by differentiation of documentary terminology, functions, and types. By comparison with the early medieval period, the spectrum of papal business had become much more diversified, and the capacity of the system of papal documents to absorb the complexity of the demands made on it needed to be enhanced by a corresponding expansion of the range of papal documents. In the early Middle Ages, there had been decretals, privileges, and letters. In the period that concerns us here, the typology of documents becomes far richer and subtler.

In addition to the older contrast between privileges and letters, the broad category of 'papal letters' became differentiated in multiple ways. A range of types is listed in the standard works on papal Diplomatics. Letters linked to their seals by silk thread had a series of visual characteristics (described below) and a commonality of function, in that they conferred favours and were not 'for one use only'. These will be referred to henceforth as 'letters of grace' or silk-thread letters. Then there are hemp-thread letters, whose seal was attached by ordinary string, hemp. The principal functions were executive instructions (*litterae executoriae*), including instructions to see that letters of grace took effect, or commissions to judges delegate to take a case between parties who might be far

---

[54] B. Schwarz, 'Der Corrector litterarum apostolicarum. Entwicklung des Korrektorenamtes in der päpstlichen Kanzlei von Innozenz III. bis Martin V.', *Quellen und Forschungen aus Italienischen Archiven und Bibliotheken*, 54 (1974), 122–191, at 124. Schwarz traces the history of the office – another of her fundamental contributions.

[55] B. Katterbach, *Referendarii utriusque Signaturae a Martino V ad Clementem IX et Praelati Signaturae Supplicationum a Martino V ad Leonem XIII*, Sussidi per la Consultazione dell'Archivio Vaticano ii (Studi e Testi, 55; Vatican City, 1931), XII.

distant from the curia (*litterae de iustitia*).[56] For practical purposes, 'letters of justice' and 'letters sealed with string/hemp' will be used cavalierly as more-or-less interchangeable concepts. Also within the category of 'hemp thread letters' are letters sealed in such a way that the contents could not be read, *litterae clausae*, letters close; *litterae secretae*, for special business, controlled as we saw by secretaries after an incident under Benedict XII, and for which the Chancery was not necessarily used;[57] and *litterae de curia* (or *curiales*), sent on the initiative and at the expense of the Roman curia. From the pontificate of Innocent IV we also have *litterae solemnes*.[58] (For purists, the phrase 'papal bull' should be reserved for these, though in practice it is often used loosely for papal letters generally.) These letters published politically important excommunications but also decrees and decisions with general applicability,[59] such as John XXII's constitutions for the Chancery, to be discussed below. Original *litterae solemnes* may be recognised by the opening: 'Ad perpetuam rei memoriam', or closely related formulae. The top line has elongated and decorated letters, while the document ends like other papal letters.

Important as these last types are for 'religious politics' and other high-level business, our focus here is on the more routine capillary connections that constituted the greater part of papal business. Religious politics and canon law aside, the bulk of papal business in the early Middle Ages had been the grant of privileges to monasteries, so it is logical to start with these before moving on to the newer types of document. The precise legal import of papal privileges became clearer in the second half of the twelfth century as linguistic indices of the difference between protection and exemption became more explicit. This mattered because relations between monasteries and bishops remained important, and indeed became more so, in the course of the Investiture Contest.

Exemption and protection

A differentiation of terminology in the later twelfth century dispelled the potential confusion between the protection and the exemption of a

---

[56] Herde, 'Die Urkundenarten', 59.

[57] De Lasala, *Il Documento*, 203. If on paper rather than parchment they were sealed with wax, as briefs would be after they had taken their place in the repertory of documents (personal communication from Patrick Zutshi). For further classification and terminology: *litterae legendae*, *litterae dandae*, *litterae communes*, *litterae speciales*, *litterae simplices*, *litterae rescribendae*, and *litterae revocatoriae*, see De Lasala, *Il Documento*, 203–205, and Herde, 'Die Urkundenarten'.

[58] Rabikauskas, *Diplomatica Pontificia*, 54–55.   [59] Bresslau, *Handbuch*, i, 82–83.

monastery. The elements of full exemption were listed long ago by David Knowles, with his customary lucidity:

(1) The abbot on election would normally be blessed by the diocesan in his cathedral and make profession to him of canonical obedience. Papal privileges freed him from this in varying degrees:
 (a) In all cases he was exempt from the oath of obedience.
 (b) He might be permitted to be blessed in the abbey church.
 (c) He might be given free choice of the officiating prelate.
 (d) He might be allowed to apply for consecration directly to the pope.
(2) The monastery became free from the bishop's excommunication and from general interdicts.
(3) The abbot might invite any bishop to perform ordinations and consecrations which required the episcopal character in the officiant.
(4) The bishop could not claim hospitality for himself and his retinue when on his official visitation of his diocese (*procuratio canonica*), nor the right of celebrating a solemn Mass and holding ordinations in the church ...
(5) The abbot was freed from attendance at the diocesan synod, from observing its decrees, and from paying its tax.
(6) The abbot had the right of wearing some, or all, of the seven garments or articles comprehended under the term *insignia pontificalia*.[60]

It will be clear from Knowles's checklist that there was much more for a monastery to be exempt *from*, c. 1200, than in the early Middle Ages.[61] The issues tackled and resolved by Innocent III in the document printed and translated below at *1212[62] shows how complicated the question of exemption had become by the thirteenth century. *1244, **March** 7 (BL Add Ch 17857) deals with a further complication to the privilege of exemption from excommunication. It appears that prelates had found a circumvention of the ban on excommunicating Cistercians. Instead they could excommunicate the staff of the monasteries: servants, those who used their mills or cooked in their furnaces, people involved in buying from and selling to an abbey, and benefactors of abbeys. The knock-on effect would be to make the life of the monks themselves impossible, if they wanted to avoid excommunication by contagion. Innocent IV bans this ingenious way around the system. The sheer complexity of the apparently simple concept of exemption needs to be kept before the mind.

At least a much clearer terminology to indicate true exemption as opposed to protection emerges from the time of Alexander III

---

[60] Knowles, *The Monastic Order in England*, 585–586.
[61] For essays on exemption that cross the 1200 line see D'Acunto, *Papato e monachesimo 'esente'*.
[62] BL Add Ch 1542.

(1159–1181):[63] *nullo mediante; specialiter beati Petri iuris* and *ad indicium perceptae libertatis* (exemption), as opposed to *ad indicium perceptae protectionis* (protection); and *salva sedis apostolicae auctoritate* (exemption), without further qualification, as opposed to *salva sedis apostolicae auctoritate et diocesani episcopi canonica iustitia* (protection).[64] (Payment of a census to the pope does not in itself tell one much about a monastery's relation to bishop and pope.)[65] These were important strides towards legal clarity, but even after Alexander III the goal had not been reached:[66] to be sure whether a monastery was exempt one must take account of all the privileges and papal communications addressed to it.[67] Furthermore the problem of exemption would continue to re-surface in different forms – for instance, with regard to parish churches which had been given by lay patrons to exempt monasteries.

The complexities that continued to be tangled up with exemption are illustrated by *1212[68] (already mentioned) and *1277.[69] In *1212 Pope Innocent III resolves a long-running dispute between the Cluniac house of Montierneuf and the local bishop. Rights of criminal justice were one area of dispute. Limited powers of justice over 'malefactors' in the territory of the monastery are conceded to the bishop. The bishop's ritual powers over the monastery – ordaining clerics etc – have a crucial limitation: if the bishop does not behave responsibly the monastery can go to another bishop, as laid down in the monastery's existing documents, which Innocent had seen. Interdicts were a contentious issue where exempt houses were concerned. The ruling is that during interdicts the monastery will not celebrate services in a public way. The abbot will attend the bishop's synod by reason of the chapels and churches that the monastery controls (i.e. not because the bishop has authority over the monastery itself), and if the chaplains ignore the decisions of the synod the bishop can take measures against them, but

---

[63] Rabikauskas, *Diplomatica Pontificia*, 49; De Lasala, *Il Documento*, 196.

[64] De Lasala, *Il Documento*, 196; Kéry, 'Klosterfreiheit', 99, 103, 111.

[65] Kéry, 'Klosterfreiheit', 87; for the way monastic census worked, see B. Wiedemann, 'The Papal Camera and the Monastic Census. Evidence from Portugal, c. 1150–1190', *Zeitschrift für Kirchengeschichte*, 126 (2015), 181–196.

[66] Kéry, 'Klosterfreiheit', 95.

[67] *Ibid.*, 96. Cf. 93: 'Generell war und ist auch aus heutiger Sicht die Exemtion nur schwer von anderen Formen des apostolischen Schutzes zu unterscheiden'. Kéry argues convincingly (e.g. 111, 143) that twelfth-century popes had no 'master plan' to extend monastic exemption. In the eleventh century, in the context of the Gregorian Reform, Gregory VII and Urban II tended to limit the bishops' power to consecrate and ordain ('*Weihegewalt*') in order to combat simony (*ibid.*, 107, 143), and Urban II, by contrast with twelfth-century popes, favoured exemption generally as a way of intensifying links between papacy and locality (*ibid.*, 107).

[68] BL Add Ch 1542.   [69] BL Add Ch 1548.

not against the abbot or monastery. The many churches and chapels controlled by exempt monasteries were, as this suggests, a major structural problem. They were outside the monastery so they were not covered by the exemption, but the bishop could use his powers over them against the monastery.

Exactly that is what *1279 (BL Add Ch 1551) suggests, though it requires a close reading. The abbot and community of Cluny have complained that the bishops and other prelates of the secular clergy 'by the tallages, exactions, and procurations that they require to be given to them outside the houses, presume mercilessly to oppress also the houses themselves, exceeding contrary to the Lateran Council the number of horsemen in attendance and of individuals'. This must be a reference to canon 4 of the Third Lateran Council (1179), which limited the entourage of bishops conducting visitations.[70] But an exempt house should not have been liable to visitation, so what is going on? Probably the prelates were conducting visitations of the churches and chapels belonging to Cluniac houses, bringing larger entourages than Lateran III allowed, and expecting the Cluniac houses to pay for them. (It is true that papal confirmations of various Cluniac daughter priories have the formula *salvo iure episcoporum* which would seem to imply that they were not exempt[71] and that the bishop could conduct a visitation of the community as well as the churches attached to it; perhaps the status of daughter houses was not uniform with regard to exemption.) The other complaint of the Cluniacs is that churches belonging to them are being put under interdict without reasonable causes, and 'the priests' suspended. The priests in question must be the priests serving the churches controlled by Cluniac houses. The pope rules that there must be reasonable cause and due process.

The general thrust of this letter is to protect the Cluniacs who must have asked for it, but it is not a privilege; rather it is an instruction to investigate abuses. It is a 'letter of justice' rather than a 'letter of grace' – an antithesis that requires a closer look.

Letters of grace and letters of justice

Solemn privileges became rare during the thirteenth century, though the genre had not entirely died out even far into the fourteenth.[72]

---

[70] Cf. D. Summerlin, *The Canons of the Third Lateran Council of 1179. Their Origins and Reception* (Cambridge, 2019), 79–80.
[71] Dannenberg, *Das Recht der Religiosen*, 120.
[72] Frenz and Pagano, *I Documenti*, 20; cf. M. Tangl, ed., Die päpstlichen Kanzleiordnungen von 1200–1500 (Innsbruck, 1894), CIII, 304–305.

Increasingly, they were replaced by the more-or-less functionally equivalent letters of grace, attached to their seals with coloured silk thread. The development c. 1100–c. 1150 of the latter genre of letters by incorporating key features of 'simple' privileges was discussed in the previous chapter.

The scope of letters of grace was, however, far broader than privileges for religious houses. This expanded range reflects the wider band of social systems with which the papacy interacted (usually responding to demand). The common factor is that letters of grace, as their name suggests, confer a right or a favour.

As will be clear by now, letters of grace are only one of a range of categories (overlapping in some cases) of papal letters,[73] but the other most important category in the period up to the mid-thirteenth century, one with which letters of grace are frequently paired, is the one already mentioned, namely the various sorts of letters whose seal was attached not by silk thread but by string, hemp: the 'letters of justice', starting litigation of a relatively routine kind, and other executive orders of one sort or another. A subset of such 'hemp letters' is the category of letters close, *litterae clausae*, sent folded in such a way that the message could not be read.[74] In the thirteenth century at least the papacy relatively rarely sent letters closed, at least by comparison with the English monarchy in the same period.

The pairing of letters of justice and letters of grace is convenient so far as external features are concerned because these are most easily described by contrasts between the two categories.[75] The differences may be set out schematically as follows:

---

[73] De Lasala, *Il Documento*, 198–205. We have already repeatedly made reference to the classic collection of studies by Herde, *Beiträge*, especially 'Die Urkundenarten'.

[74] Magisterial study by W. Maleczek, '*Litterae clausae* der Päpste vom 12. bis zum frühen 14. Jahrhundert' in T. Broser, A. Fischer and M. Thumser, eds., *Kuriale Briefkultur im späteren Mittelalter* (Forschungen zur Kaiser-und Papstgeschichte des Mittelalters. Beihefte zu J. F. Böhmer, Regesta Imperii, 37; Cologne, 2015), 55–128 (followed by some beautiful facsimile reproductions). See also Herde, '*Litterae clausae*', in *idem*, *Beiträge*, 72–78; S. Pagano, 'Documenti Pontifici', in B. Ardura, ed., *Lessico di Storia della Chiesa* (Rome, 2020), 261–265, at 262; De Lasala, *Il Documento*, 202–203.

[75] For convenient analyses, see Rabikauskas, *Diplomatica Pontificia*, 56; De Lasala, *Il Documento*, 201–202. For facsimiles of letters of grace, see Battelli, *Acta Pontificum*, facsimile 19 and De Lasala, *Il Documento*, *Appendici* (published as a separate folder), Tavola 18; a letter of justice proper is reproduced at the end of the present volume: TNA SC 7/64/40 (*1281, August 23; Plate 3). For facsimiles of *litterae executoriae*: Battelli, *Acta Pontificum*, facsimile 20, and De Lasala, *Il Documento*, *Appendici*, Tavola 17. In external appearance *litterae executoriae* and *litterae de iustitia* are virtually the same. Nowadays it is relatively easy to find good facsimiles on the internet, even if one cannot rely on the stability of any given site. At the time of writing, monasterium.net is a wonderful source of documents; see also the 'Theleme' strand within the website of the

Letters of grace

- The whole of the pope's name is in capitals
- The ascenders of the first line are extra high, and elaborate
- The 'tittle' sign – it looks like a little loop, or an alpha turned clockwise 45 per cent, or an ampersand in reverse – is used as an abbreviation
- There are long ligatures in *ct* and *st*: thus c⁻t, s⁻t
- The prohibition clause *Nulli ergo* and the sanction clause *Si quis autem* are usually included, and their first letters are in heavy capitals: in fact such capitals show the whole structure of the document
- They are sealed using silk thread

Letters of justice or mandates

- Only the first letter of the pope's name is in capitals.
- The ascenders of the first line are less egregious than with letters of grace
- Instead of the loop-like tittle, the normal simple horizontal line indicates abbreviation
- There are no exaggerated ligatures joining *c* to *t* and *s* to *t*
- The '**N**ulli ergo' and '**S**i quis autem' clauses are rarer
- They are sealed with hemp (string).

It is worth repeating that strictly speaking 'letters of justice' are only a subset of the larger set of papal commands or mandates; not all mandates appointed judges delegate. The large class of mandates included, as noted above, the *litterae executoriae*,[76] which appoint men to ensure that letters of grace were translated into fact, and all sorts of other instructions. A document like *1277 (BL Add Ch 1548, discussed above), for instance, seems to be a kind of roving commission to the abbot of Saint Corneille de Compiègne to investigate improper alienations of property by the Cluniac order. Presumably the abbot of Cluny initiated this in the hope of recovering some of it. The letter has none of the distinctive external features of a letter of grace. It may be contrasted with *1279, **January 23** (BL Add Ch 1551), also to help (and no doubt requested by) Cluniacs. This is an unprepossessing document which might at a superficial glance look like a routine letter of justice or instruction. It does not have the crazy ascenders on the top line that catch the eye with more

---

École nationale des chartes: dossier 45 for a letter of justice (1245), dossier 49 for a letter of grace (1344).

[76] See now the important article by T. W. Smith, 'Papal Executors and the Veracity of Petitions from Thirteenth-Century England', *Revue d'Histoire Ecclésiastique* 110 (2015), 662–683.

elaborate letters of grace. Nonetheless, perusal of the content (protection of the Cluniac order, not time-limited) shows that it was a document to keep, and externally it has the key features of a letter of grace: whole of the pope's name in capitals, tittles instead of the usual straight line superscript abbreviation mark, the 'Nulli ergo' and 'Si quis autem' clauses with the initials **N** and **S** in bold, and long ligatures between 'c' and 't' and 's' and 't'. To the student of Diplomatics, there is no doubt that it is a letter of grace, and it illustrates the need both to study Diplomatics and to understand content and setting in life if one is to interpret a papal document properly. The contrast drawn below between ANF J.709.297.5 and ANF J.709.298.10 reinforces this informal rule of Diplomatics. In both the transcriptions of documents and the plates at the end of this book – BL Add Ch 17857, *1244, March 7 (letter of grace protecting Foucarmont abbey *and* its servants from exommunication), on the one hand, and TNA SC 7/64/40, *1281, August 23 (letter of justice, appointing a judge delegate), on the other – serve as illustrations of the difference between the two great categories of letters of grace and letters of justice.

Letters of justice are a particularly crucial subset of the set of 'mandate' documents, because they appoint judges and enabled the papacy to deal with the enormous volume of litigation that flowed towards it from all over Christendom.

There are exceptions to the rule that letters of justice are sealed with hemp, but the exceptions uncover the underlying logic of the rule. The pope might address to bishops an executive instruction not to obstruct a monastery or religious order, but he would probably give the document or documents not to the bishop in question but to the monastery or the order's representatives to use when they needed it, which is why such letters can turn up not in the archive of the addressee but of the party that stood to benefit from the instruction.[77] In such cases it was functionally equivalent to a letter of grace and might have silk thread rather than string.[78]

Incidentally, a corollary of the 'responsive' character of papal government is that the curia did not normally have to worry about 'the post'. The person or institution that had requested a papal letter would be responsible for getting the letter to the addressee and had the motivation to do so. This holds good for both letters of grace and letters of justice.

[77] My thanks to Christoph Egger for making this clear to me.
[78] Herde, 'Die Urkundenarten', 59–61. See also below, discussion of British Library Add Ch 1542, edited at *1212.

When the external features of these two great categories are contrasted, as above, the distinction seems sharp and straightforward, but in practice it would often be hard for anyone unfamiliar with this corner of papal Diplomatics to perceive the difference; and even after one has seen it, it is not always easy to explain the relation of appearance to content. To do that one must pay close attention to both.

By way of illustration, we may compare two Archives Nationales de France documents: ANF J.709.297.5[79] with ANF J.709.298.10.[80] Impressionistically, they look rather alike and the message seems very similar: the pope is allowing the king of France and his agents to come down hard on clerics who are living like laymen. (It should be explained that there were enormous numbers of clerics in minor orders who could be married quite legally in canon law, though not a second time or to a widow, and who lived secular lives, while availing themselves of immunity from secular justice and taxation.) Both documents are quite elegantly written in the same script, with plenty of space between the lines, and in both the ascenders in the first line are tall. On closer inspection and with the checklist above in mind, the differences begin to seem obvious. In the letter of grace, ANF J.709.297.5, the whole of the name 'Johannes' is in very large letters, which are decorated with fringes and flourishes. There are similar adornments on the 'C' of 'Carissimo', and the ascenders of the first line have 'streamers'. The tittle is used as the superscript abbreviation, and there are extensive s‾t ligatures. The first letters of 'Nulli' and 'Si quis' are heavily black and decorated. In ANF J.709.298.10 only the first letter of 'Iohannes' is tall and heavily inked, but it is not decorated. It is true that the E of 'Ex parte' is tall and heavily inked but there are no other such cases. There are no tittle abbreviations or long ligatures.

How far do contrasts in content account for the difference in appearance? It is not a straightforward case because ANF J.709.298.10 is also giving the king a document he will want to keep. Essentially, he is saying that clerics in minor orders who do not live like clerics can be treated like lay people, despite any attempt to invoke clerical immunity. But John XXII, like the predecessor whom he quotes (whose document is transcribed and translated at *1278)[81] does not want to actually make this a *privilege* of the French king. A formal legal removal of their immunity would be a blow to the clergy as a status group to which the pope was in

<hr>

[79] Barbiche, *Les actes pontificaux originaux*, iii, no. 2548, pp. 129–130.
[80] *Ibid.*, no. 2547, p. 129, transcribed in D. L. d'Avray, *Medieval Marriage. Symbolism and Society* (Oxford, 2005), p. 255.
[81] ANF J.709.296.5.

the last analysis loyal, and also raise ticklish legal questions about how far a cleric in minor orders could actually go. Much better simply to indicate to the king that the pope would 'tolerate it with equanimity' if they were treated like laymen. The pope does not want to erode the principle of clerical immunity, but in practice, with a nudge and a wink, he makes it clear that the king and his enforcers have a free hand.

The pope's anxiety not to seem an enemy of his own clerical caste is apparent in the other letter, the letter of grace J.709.297.5, towards the end of which the pope stresses that he is not giving the king or his men a licence to capture clerics in this way nor even approving of this capture or detention. What then is he giving? This document, like the other, is a de facto green light to ignore the protests of clerics in minor orders, but it also had a precisely delimited legal force. It is a block on excommunication of royal officers who arrest clerics who have committed, or are credibly accused of, serious crimes – murder, grievous bodily harm, etc. In doing so they must show 'such restraint as can be maintained with such men' – but how much restraint would that be, with men of violence? The sub-text is that the arresting officers might, if driven to it, have to use reasonable violence in return, the kind that might otherwise get them excommunicated. From the foregoing it should be clear that to understand the relation between the appearance and the content or function of a letter one has to drill down quite deep, much further than 'pure' Diplomatics can take one.

According to the decree *Si quis suadente* of the Second Lateran Council (in 1139), firmly embedded in canon law, violence against a cleric could only be absolved by the pope (unless in danger of death).[82] Clearly these French kings were worried about this, and successfully asked popes for a legal shield for their agents. That was, accordingly, more than a nod or hint about what could be done without the pope taking action – which is the likely reading of J.709.298.10 – but, rather, a formal privilege: yet it was only with regard to excommunication, not a permit to manhandle clerics.

Dispensations for marriage within the forbidden degrees

An increasingly common genre of privilege, at all levels but especially generous towards French kings, was a dispensation to marry within the forbidden degrees of consanguinity and affinity; with monarchs and their family members the degrees permitted by way of exception would be

---

[82] Gratian, *Decretum*, PARS II, C. 17 q. 4 c. 29; i, col. 822.

closer, in that advantages such as cementing peace were taken into account.[83] (Dispensations and spiritual favours to the French monarchy were so common that one can classify them as 'routine business'.) One example out of many is ANF J.435.8, a dispensation from Celestine V to Philip IV of France for children and siblings of the king to marry within specified forbidden degrees.[84] It obeys all the rules of a letter of grace, as set out above, though the decoration of the pope's name is much less exuberant than usual, which perhaps reflects this pope's modesty (a hermit, he had bizarrely been elected pope, for which administratively demanding office he was unsuited). One may contrast this with, say, ANF J.435.10, from Pope Boniface VIII to Philip IV of France,[85] which from its appearance would probably be classified as a letter of justice. Only the initial B of the pope's name is large, it and the ascenders of the top line are not decorated, there are no long ligatures or tittles. In fact, however, it does not actually command the king to do anything, but merely asks for help in arranging an important marriage, so it is not even a *mandatum* or *litterae executoriae*. This is a reminder that letters of justice proper looked just like letters without legal force.

Of the eleventh and twelfth centuries Benedikt Hotz wrote that 'the content and internal features must underpin diplomatic investigations also',[86] and this holds good for later periods as well. While the crude contrast between between features of letters sealed with silk thread and of letters sealed with hemp/string is easy enough to present, in many cases one must understand the precise content and function of the letter to elucidate its formal and physical features. The following cases further illustrate this point.

Hybrids

Life being more complicated than bureaucratic systems set up to manage it, not every document fits the rules neatly. Compare, for instance, the letter of grace from Celestine V just discussed, ANF J.435.8, which ticks all the diplomatic boxes, with ANF J.435.8bis,[87] also by Celestine and bearing the same date, 12 November 1294. ANF J.435.8bis is more ambiguous from a Diplomatics point of view. It says that King Sancho of Castile and his children are excluded from the previous permission.

---

[83] This is a principle theme of d'Avray, *Papacy, Monarchy and Marriage*.
[84] Transcribed and translated in *ibid.*, 262–265.   [85] *Ibid.*, 266–268.
[86] '... der Inhalt und die inneren Merkmale die Basis auch Diplomatischer Untersuchungen bilden müssen'; Hotz, *Litterae*, 24.
[87] d'Avray, *Papacy, Monarchy and Marriage*, 265–266.

(Sancho was married without dispensation to his grandfather's niece.)[88] Now, this second letter starts off looking like a letter of justice. Only the first letter of Celestine's name is in capitals, the ascenders of the first line, though tall, do not have little streamers like those in ANF J.435.8, and the superscript abbreviations are straight lines – until line 6, when we meet the 'Christo' abbreviation with a tittle, and there are s‾t ligatures not much less long than in ANF J.435.8.

What is going on here? The document is a sort of negative dispensation of a kind that would seldom occur. In a way it was an executive command, but it was also presumably to be kept with the dispensation, as a qualification of it, limiting its applicability. Celestine is not famous for his mastery of business. Could he not have put the exclusion clause in ANF J.435.8? Perhaps he didn't think of it and ANF J.435.8bis was an afterthought. He and his drafters perhaps wavered about which form to adopt.

Another hybrid is British Library Add Ch 1542, edited and translated at *1212. The reasons for the mixture of features are different. The document looks superficially a letter of grace, but some of the elements are missing (notably ligatures). It is not a forgery, however. It looks like a sort of facsimile of the letter of grace held by Montierneuf. Montierneuf made the copy sent to Cluny look like their original, and Add Ch 1542 is that copy. It was functionally a letter of grace despite the fact that it was the settlement of a legal case, because the outcome of the case was a clarification of the abbey's rights. Without seeing the Montierneuf original I cannot be sure whether the copy sent to Cluny chose not to include all the 'letter of grace' features of its exemplar, or if the exemplar itself was a hybrid.

Also printed below is yet another hybrid from the pontificate of Innocent III: *1200, March 8.[89] It is a mandate to prelates to do justice to the Knights Templar when they are oppressed by evildoers. In content it is not a letter of grace and does not have key features of the genre: long ligatures, tittles instead of normal linear superscript abbreviations, and very high ascenders on the top line. On the other hand, the whole of Innocent's name is in capitals, a feature of a letter of grace. The explanation for the mixture could be that it was formally speaking a mandate, but its function would be to confer a privilege, so it has some of the signs of a letter of grace to make that evident. The above also applies to *1195, January 21 (TNA SC 7/9/35), Celestine III's instruction to prelates to encourage the faithful (by word and example) to take advantage of the

---

[88] *Ibid.*, 78 and 96–97.   [89] TNA SC 7/19/16.

indulgence he is granting to those who visit and help out a poor community of nuns.[90]

The foregoing analyses show again that to assess the import and character of a papal document of this period one needs to look at the external features in conjunction with the contents. The documents relating to excommunication[91] and dispensations[92] are a reminder, furthermore, that the scope of papal action, the range of matters which a papal letter might address (usually on request rather than as a papal initiative), was far wider from the twelfth century than in the early medieval period or even in the period of the 'papal turn'. This expansion of range may not be manifested by too 'pure' a presentation of the Diplomatics of the period: one needs to attend to substance as well as form to understand the true typology, and to be alert to the social life that the document was meant to manage.

Enlarged scope of papal action

From the foregoing two examples, this increase in the range of papal action will be clear. Popes could shield whole categories of people, or a particular monarch, from excommunications that might be incurred automatically or laid on them by some lesser prelate (cf. ***1244**[93] and ***1281 October 7**[94]) – apparently such privileges only lasted for the lifetime of the king in question[95] – and popes could grant dispensations for things otherwise forbidden (such as marriage within the 'forbidden degrees'), provided that natural or divine law was not infringed.[96] Hence a special subfield of papal Diplomatics deals with marriage dispensations, especially to royalty.[97]

---

[90] In these two cases it may also be that the differences between letters of grace and letters of justice/mandates had not yet fully crystallised.

[91] On excommunication see now Hill, *Excommunication in Thirteenth-Century England*.

[92] Arnaud Fossier is leading an international collective investigation of dispensation, in a comparative framework. There is already much about dispensations in his *Le Bureau des âmes. Écritures et pratiques administratives de la Pénitencerie apostolique (XIIIe–XIVe siècle)* (Bibliothèque des Écoles françaises d'Athènes et de Rome, 378; Rome, 2018), since granting them was one of the primary functions of the Apostolic Penitentiary (on which more below).

[93] BL Add Ch 17857.   [94] ANF J.683.4.

[95] 'Until 1351, the privileges of the French kings had to be renewed at each change of king. On April 20, 1351, Clement VI granted them to the reigning king and queen (Jean II and Jeanne de Boulogne) and their successors. I suppose it was the same for the kings of other countries. But I did not search for confirmation of these dispositions in the general treatises' (so Bernard Barbiche, a leader in the field of papal documents, in a personal communication).

[96] Cf. d'Avray, *Papacy, Monarchy and Marriage*, 210–216.

[97] *Ibid.*, 218–237: chapter on 'Dispensations and their Diplomatic', and see above, 97–98.

A spectrum of papal documents

A class of document which could go to anyone from kings downwards was the indulgence, another example of the expansion of the range of documentary categories.[98] The Capetian kings of France from Louis IX on were particularly associated with the indulgence system and its development, and they served as a model for other rulers.[99] This is the example of the trend towards the sacralisation of late medieval monarchy which historians have come to emphasise[100] as compatible with the more traditional theme of 'secularisation'.

An example of an indulgence for less elevated recipients is printed below at *1195, January 21 (TNA SC 7/9/35). Indulgences remitted penance on earth, just as penance on earth replaced suffering in purgatory: so it was by a knock-on effect that indulgences replaced suffering in purgatory. In this case the pope granted an 'indulgence of 100 days to all those who, given that they are truly penitent and have confessed their sins, visit the aforesaid place, and dispense some benefits to the nuns serving God there'. That meant that a visit and contribution to the nuns' church would take the place of 100 days of penance on earth, with the same implications for suffering in purgatory, whatever those might be. What kind of time there was in purgatory was left undefined.

There are many other sorts of papal responses. Further examples: Grants of protection remained important, but now they could extend to unified international orders like the Knights Templar: see *1200, March 8 (TNA SC 7/19/16). In the early Middle Ages there were no international orders in the sense of orders with an international organisation. The Benedictines had no organisation above the level of the individual monastery. They

---

[98] An important recent set of studies is E. Doublier and J. Johrendt, eds., *Economia della Salvezza e Indulgenza nel Medioevo* (Milan, 2017). For a list of some of the recent studies see L. Wolfinger, 'König Ludwig der Heilige und die Genese fürstlicher Ablasspolitik. Beobachtungen zur Heilsökonomie weltlicher Herrschaft im Spätmittelalter', in *ibid.*, 149–181. See too E. Doublier, *Ablass, Papsttum und Bettelorden im 13. Jahrhundert* (Cologne, 2017) and E. Dehoux, C. Galland, and C. Vincent, eds., *Des usages de la grâce. Pratiques des indulgences du Moyen Âge à l'époque contemporaine* (Villeneuve d'Ascq, 2021), 45–104, with contributions by Charles Mériaux, Matthieu Rajohnson, Amandine Le Roux, and Benoît Schmitz, dealing with 'La papauté'.

[99] Wolfinger, 'König Ludwig der Heilige', esp. 161–181.

[100] J. Dale, *Inauguration and Liturgical Kingship in the Long Twelfth Century: Male and Female Accession Rituals in England, France and the Empire* (York, 2019); J. Théry, 'Allo Scoppio del Conflitto tra Filippo il Bello di Francia e Bonifacio VIII. L'affare Saisset (1301). Primi Spunti per una rilettura', in G. Minucci (ed.), *I Poteri Universali e la Fondazione dello Studium Orbis. Il pontifice Bonifacio VIII dalla Unam sanctam allo schiaffo di Anagni* (Archivio per la storia del diritto medioevale e moderno, Miscellanee, 1; Bologna, 2008), 21–68.

were an 'order' only in the sense that they followed the same or a similar rule. But, with the Cluniacs, international organisation is under way, though in a rather crude form: the abbot of Cluny was abbot of all Cluniac houses, which had priors instead of an abbot. In the twelfth century, however, the Cistercians and Templars, among others, would have well-thought-out constitutions underpinning their corporate exist-ence, while the constitutions of the friars, the Dominicans particularly, were impressive intellectual and practical constructs. Papal documents adjusted to the phenomenon of international orders.

Again, a pope might be called upon to authorise the 'appropriation' of a parish church to a religious community, which, probably replacing a lay patron, accessed a proportion of the church's income and appointed someone to serve the parish. British Library Add Ch 6306 is a case in point (see *1268). It is unclear why the pope was brought in to endorse this decision. An authoritative survey of the system gives no hint that the papacy had to be involved in appropriation.[101] But the genesis of the document must have been in the locality: somebody wanted a papal letter.

Formulary evidence for the expanding spectrum of business

One can get an idea of the expansion of papal government from formu-laries. Formularies of the Apostolic Penitentiary, for instance, reveal a whole range of letter types.[102] The Penitentiary was an organ of papal government that crystallised in the thirteenth century. It dealt with absolution of confessional cases reserved to the pope, but we do not have records of this because of the secrecy of the confessional, and the Penitentiary formularies do not deal with secret sins. The Penitentiary did much other business, however: a range of dispensations and of

---

[101] C. H. Lawrence, 'The English Church and Its Clergy in the Thirteenth Century', in *The Medieval World*, Routledge, accessed 9 June 2022), 746–769, at 748–751.

[102] Fossier, *Le Bureau*, especially 152–189; formulary for minor penitentiaries: P. D. Clarke, 'Between Avignon and Rome: Minor Penitentiaries at the Papal Curia in the Thirteenth and Fourteenth Centuries', *Rivista di Storia della Chiesa in Italia*, 63 (2009), 455–510. From the fifteenth century the evidence of formularies is supplemented, or perhaps one should say sidelined, by the survival of registers, but of course these cast light on how things worked earlier. The study of the Apostolic Penitentiary is especially indebted to Kirsi Salonen and Ludwig Schmugge: see e.g. K. Salonen, *The Penitentiary as a Well of Grace in the Later Middle Ages: The Example of the Province of Uppsala, 1448–1527* (Helsinki, 2001); K. Salonen and L. Schmugge, *A Sip from the 'Well of Grace'. Medieval Texts from the Papal Penitentiary* (Washington, D.C., 2009).

absolutions from excommunication (as well as miscellaneous matters
such as authentication of marital status that might not get into a formulary). Conscience or concern for reputation appear to be the main driving
forces behind this last side of papal business. The routinisation, reflected
in formularies, of cases involving conscience was a development in this
period, parallel to the proliferation of form letters of grace and of justice,
as revealed by the formularies of the *Audientia litterarum contradictarum*.

The formularies of the *Audientia litterarum contradictarum* have been
well studied by Peter Herde,[103] and more recently by Ute Pfeiffer.[104]
The table of contents of Pfeiffer's edition and study reflects the broad
spectrum of business:[105] property offences, usury and pawn matters,
false sales (concealing usury), violence against clerics, execution of wills,
testamentary matters, sacrilege, illegal dispossession, patronage of
churches, benefice cases, clerics acting as guarantors, breaches of the
seal of confession, building on Church land, cases involving burial rights,
neglect of pastoral duties in a parish, just price, excommunication and
suspension, academic study while drawing income from a benefice,
procuration (compulsory payments, during a visitation etc., to the
visiting party), tithes (investigation of rights to), marriage matters, payments from ecclesiastic property and income, procurators, cases involving deputies (vicars) paid by benefice holders, return of alienated church
property, dispensation to receive orders despite illegitimacy, cases (many
different kinds of them) involving monastic status, ordination without a
benefice, appointing additional judges delegate to cases, damage done to
pilgrims, protection of crusaders, confirmation of rights, punishment of
monks, offences against papal privileges etc., appeals, arbitration, and
miscellaneous. Letters of grace which would have been sealed with silk
thread are included, notably confirmation of papal protection of monasteries, etc. Herde makes it clear that routine letters of grace too passed
through the *Audientia litterarum contradictarum*.[106] Whether *litterae executoriae* were read at the *Audientia litterarum contradictarum* seems to be
uncertain.[107]

The formulary tells us a lot about what papal government was really
about, and what studies of papal ideology like Walter Ullmann's *Growth*

---

[103] Herde, *Audientia*.
[104] Pfeiffer, *Untersuchungen*: edition of and commentary on two forerunner formularies.
[105] My précis/translation is based on the table of contents to Pfeiffer, *Untersuchungen*, III–
IV.
[106] P. Herde, 'Zur Audientia litterarum contradictarum und zur "Reskripttechnik"',
Archivalische Zeitschrift, 69 (1973), 54–90, at 73–74.
[107] Peter Herde thought that they did so (personal communication).

of Papal Government in the Middle Ages (London, 1955) leave out. To understand government, one must examine content as well as theory.

Papal provisions

Papal provisions, conferral of benefices all over Europe, were a prominent and controversial new class of business: popes did not do this in the early medieval period, while in the later medieval period the sheer volume is staggering![108] There is a deeply rooted tendency to treat this as a symptom of the corruption of the medieval church and an example of the papacy's will to power.[109] This historiographical tendency is an instance of the danger of taking at face value the reform indignation of medieval sources. For one thing, for this period and indeed for most periods, it is a fallacy to assume that morally self-righteous men actually understand the society in which they live. For another, reform indignation can conceal self-interest. To put it crudely, papal provisions whisked away from noble and or wealthy and powerful families in the localities an invaluable way of providing for younger sons. By the end of the Middle Ages they had got a lot of it back.[110] The few historians with a better

---

[108] On papal provisions see (notably but far from exhaustively) Hermann Baier, *Päpstliche Provisionen für niedere Pfründen bis zum Jahre 1304* (Vorreformationsgeschichtliche Forschungen, 7; Munster i. W., 1911); G. Barraclough, *Papal Provisions. Aspects of Church History, Constitutional, Legal and Administrative, in the Later Middle Ages* (Oxford, 1935); A. Meyer, *Arme Kleriker auf Pfründensuche. Eine Studie über das* in forma pauperum-*Register Gregors XII. von 1407 und über päpstliche Anwartschaften im Spätmittelalter* (Forschungen zur kirchlichen Rechtsgeschichte und zum Kirchenrecht; Cologne, 1990); A. Meyer, *Zürich und Rom. Ordentliche Kollatur und päpstliche Provisionen am Frau-und Grossmünster 1316–1523* (Bibliothek des deutschen historischen Instituts in Rom, 64; Tübingen, 1986); B. Schwarz, 'Römische Kurie und Pfründenmarkt im Spätmittelalter', *Zeitschrift für historische Forschung*, 20 (1993), 129–152; P. Zutshi, 'Petitioners, Popes, Proctors: The Development of Curial Institutions, c. 1150–1250', in G. Andenna (ed.), *Pensiero e sperimentazioni istituzionali nella 'Societas Christiana' (1046–1250)* (Milan, 2007), 265–293, at 291; T. W. Smith, 'The Development of Papal Provisions in Medieval Europe' *History Compass* 13 (2015), 110–121 (online resource, https://onlinelibrary.wiley.com/doi/full/10.1111/hic3.12223, accessed 21 September 2021)(excellent account of the state of research up to the time Smith was writing); T. W. Smith, 'The Papacy, Petitioners and Benefices in Thirteenth-Century England', in T. W. Smith and H. Killick, eds., *Petitions and Strategies of Persuasion in the Middle Ages: The English Crown and the Church, 1200–1550* (Woodbridge, 2018), 164–184; T. W. Smith, 'The Italian Connection Reconsidered: Papal Provisions in Thirteenth-Century England', in A. Spencer and C. Watkins, eds., *Thirteenth Century England XVII. Proceedings of the Cambridge Conference, 2017* (Woodbridge, 2021), 147–162: shows that the complaints of Matthew Paris were a caricature.

[109] As noted by Meyer, 'Regieren', 72–73.

[110] Meyer, *Arme Kleriker auf Pfründensuche*, e.g. 64; *idem, Zürich und Rom; idem,* 'Das Wiener Konkordat von 1448 – eine erfolgreiche Reform des Spätmittelalters', *Quellen*

understanding of the system[111] did not have much effect on the main-stream view. Probably the powerful recent contributions by Andreas Meyer[112] and Brigide Schwarz[113] will meet the same fate. Meyer and Schwarz point out the papacy was the prey rather than the hunter: the system was demand-driven.[114]

Consequently, benefices were the subject of an increasing number of letters of grace of various sorts and of letters to those who had to execute the letters of grace in the locality (or not to execute them, if the situation on the ground differed from what the pope or his officials had been led to believe). 'Letters sealed with hemp were also involved in that a papal grant of a benefice would be accompanied by *littere executorie* addressed to men charged with the task of executing the grant.'[115] Recent work by Kerstin Hitzbleck calls into question the old thesis of Geoffrey Barraclough that the system of executors was 'clear and structured'.[116] Executors were not bound to any clear procedure for testing 'on the ground' the validity of the claim to the benefice. They could look into that if they wanted to, but they did not have to.

Hitzbleck's sharp reaction against Barraclough should not obscure what she also says about the functional aspects of the system. The executor could react to objections if these arose but could also proceed rapidly and without complications to install the recipient of the provision as a canon or as a holder of a benefice. If there was no rival claimant, they could proceed directly to installation. Executors were a remarkably flex-ible instrument for carrying out papal rescripts. The form of the letter obliged them to take account of the interests of the regular 'collator' (person normally responsible for allocating the benefice) or of someone who was already occupying it.[117] Read closely, Hitzbleck is perhaps criticising her scholarly predecessor more than the functionality of the

---

und Forschungen aus italienischen Bibliotheken und Archiven, 66 (1986), 108–152; *idem,* 'Der deutsche Pfründenmarkt im Spätmittelalter', *Quellen und Forschungen aus italienischen Bibliotheken und Archiven,* 71 (1991), 266–279.

[111] Meyer, 'Regieren', 73 at note 8, for some of them.   [112] *Ibid.*

[113] Schwarz, 'Die Erforschung der mittelalterlichen römischen Kurie'.

[114] Meyer, 'Regieren', 73; Schwarz, 'Die Erforschung der mittelalterlichen römischen Kurie', 433 (she gives due acknowledgment to Pitz, flaws in whose work seem to have aroused much probably justified annoyance, but whose core insight was on the mark).

[115] Patrick Zutshi, personal communication.

[116] 'klar und strukturiert': K. Hitzbleck, *Exekutoren: Die ausserordentliche Kollatur von Benefizien im Pontifikat Johannes' XXII.* (Tübingen, 2009), 131; cf. 553: 'Das päpstliche Benefizialsystem, das Barraclough schon auf dem Exekutoreninstitut des 13. Jahrhunderts had aufbauen wollen, hat es in der Form auch zu dieser Zeit [pontificate of John XXII] noch nicht gegeben.'

[117] Hitzbleck, *Exekutoren,* 132, especially from 'Und also solcher kann er auf Einwände reagieren ...' to '... gegen eine Kollation klagte'.

executor system. She does, however, find that the choice of executors was unregulated to a striking degree: a functional weakness of the system at least in the period she studies.[118]

The consensus of scholars seems to be that all letters of grace involving benefices were read aloud to the pope.[119] If so – and to me it is counter-intuitive – this may have been a pure formality with the simplest kind of letters: there is reason to think that the drafting and approval of highly formulaic letters of all kinds, including letters of grace, was left to *abbreviatores*, with higher authority, the vice-chancellor or a notary, being called in only when substantial changes to the stereotyped formula were needed.[120] More on that below.

Contradictory provisions as a record-keeping problem

The men in the localities who received *litterae executoriae* telling them to turn the provision into a reality on the ground might face a tricky task, because there might be more than one letter of grace providing hopeful candidates to the same benefice. It could easily happen because the thirteenth-century curia did not keep a record of all the grants it had made. Officials could not consult the papal registers to see whether the benefice had already been granted.

The limitations of papal record keeping

It is easy to exaggerate the scale and rationality of papal record keeping in the thirteenth century; it looks less impressive when comparisons are drawn with England or Italian cities. It is true that there is some progressive rationalisation of registration, in the form of differentiation of letter types, even in the thirteenth century. In the middle years of the century *litterae curiales/de curia*, registered on the initiative of the curia without a fee being charged, were kept in separate volumes or fascicules.[121] In the later thirteenth century, then in the fourteenth systematically under John XXII, secret letters are registered separately.[122]

---

[118] *Ibid.*, 552.
[119] Herde, *Audientia*, i, 419. On the same page he implies that in both the thirteenth and fourteenth centuries all letters regarding provisions and indeed all letters of grace were 'der *audientia* vorenthalten', not the business of the *audientia*, apart from confirmations of legally conferred benefices. I am not so sure, given that (as Herde was well aware) we find *de gratia* specimen letters in *audientia* formularies (Pfeiffer, *Untersuchungen*, 70 p. 194, 73 pp. 196–197, and 74 p. 197; BL Lansdowne MS 397, fo. 162r–v.
[120] Tangl, *Die päpstlichen Kanzleiordnungen*, 92–101, items 3 and 5, at 92–93.
[121] Frenz and Pagano, *I Documenti*, 54; Bresslau, *Handbuch*, i, 114.
[122] Bresslau, *Handbuch*, i, 114–115.

Even given these small steps towards rational registration, papal recording of documents, for all its much longer history, looks positively retarded by comparison with the record keeping of the English monarchy from circa 1200. The volume of documents recorded by the thirteenth-century papacy was tiny by comparison with the records of that government in the same period,[123] and English royal government not only kept a huge volume of records, but also increasingly diversified its range of record categories.

Papal government followed at some distance so far as registration was concerned.[124] It is not generally realised how undeveloped papal record keeping looks in comparison with England's from the thirteenth century on. It would also be a mistake to assume that the direction of influence was from Rome to Westminster so far as documentary techniques in general are concerned. The two administrations and their Diplomatics are seldom compared (for the usual reason – overspecialisation).[125]

---

[123] Meyer, 'Regieren', 83–90 gives a compressed comparison of the papal with other chanceries, but there is more to be done. At a memorable seminar at the Institute of Historical Research in London, the famous 'England versus Italy' match between Prof. David Carpenter and Prof. Trevor Dean, it became clear that while documentary survival from thirteenth-century England is colossal, the volume surviving from Italian cities is colossal cubed. The thirteenth-century papal registers are small in quantity in comparison with either.

[124] Good summary surveys of the history of papal registration generally in Frenz and Pagano, *I Documenti*, 52–60, and S. Pagano, 'Registri pontifici', in Ardura, *Lessico di Storia della Chiesa*, 515–517.

[125] The excellent survey by W. Maleczek, 'Les registres pontificaux du XIIIᵉ siècle', in O. Guyotjeannin, ed., *L'art médiéval du registre. Chancelleries royales et princières* (Études et rencontres de l'École des Chartes, 51; Paris, 2018), 37–54, ends by stating as common knowledge that the papal registres were richer and more precise than those of secular rulers: 'Il ne fait aucun doute que les registres pontificaux du XIIIᵉ siècle dépassent ceux des puissances séculières en richesse, en précision, et en envergure' (p. 53). In fact, however, the thirteenth-century papal registers can only be described as primitive record keeping by comparison with that of the English monarchy in the same period: see R. Bartlett, *England under the Norman and Angevin Kings, 1075–1225* (Oxford, 2000), 697–699, and D. A. Carpenter, 'The English Royal Chancery in the Thirteenth Century', in A. Jobson, ed., *English Government in the Thirteenth Century* (Boydell, 2004), 49–69. A joint seminar on English royal and papal government in the thirteenth century taught by Professor David Carpenter and myself tended to suggest not only that English royal administration kept far more records – the gap is huge – but also that its documentary practice was in general more sophisticated – to the surprise of us both. Specialists with a grasp of both have been thin on the ground, and the classic general textbooks of Diplomatics do not include England. On comparison from the point of view of the influence of papal forms, see G. Barraclough, 'The English Royal Chancery and the Papal Chancery in the Reign of Henry III', *Mitteilungen des Instituts für Österreichische Geschichtsforschung*, 62 (1954), 365-378; see J. E. Sayers, 'The Influence of Papal Documents on English Documents before 1305', in P. Herde and H. Jacobs, eds., *Papsturkunden und europäisches Urkundenwesen* (Archiv für Diplomatik, Beiheft 7; Cologne, 1999), 161–199, at 170–172 for 'possible influence on royal documents', and

In sharp contrast with English royal government, only a modest proportion of papal letters were registered (predominantly outgoing letters).[126] Before John XXII in the fourteenth century, at least, there was no attempt systematically to register outgoing (let alone incoming) correspondence. A small minority of letters were registered by the curia because they were especially important (for 'religious politics', notably). Apart from that, a letter would be registered if someone – the beneficiary or the litigant – wanted to pay for it. Often the expense would be worth it. *1243[127] records a letter from Innocent IV to the bishop of Agen which grants a valuable privilege. Agen was in the territory of the count of Toulouse, which was liable to fall under interdict because of misdeeds of the count or his officials. Innocent IV gives the city the privilege of exemption from interdict unless the bishop or cathedral chapter assent to it or the pope himself directly commands it. The cost of registering documents was worth it often enough to produce a series of registers that looks impressive – until one starts to draw the comparisons touched on above.

The limitations of papal record keeping led to a problem. If the person or institution that had obtained the letter had baulked at the expense of having it registered, a pope might be quite uncertain whether a letter had been dispatched or not. That was financially rational. It meant that the administration of registration paid for itself: a recurrent papal pattern. But if one prescinds from the financial aspect, the pattern hardly suggests administrative rationality.

The fact is that the popes of this period (of most medieval periods, come to that) hated to say 'no' but could not always, or perhaps even often, guess the implications of their all-to-ready assents. As noted above, this was potentially a major problem when it came to provisions, because a bishop was liable to be confronted with a number of men claiming a benefice, all with a papal letter of grace in hand.

An ingenious solution to the deficiencies of record keeping

The to me entirely convincing argument of Brigide Schwarz that medieval papal administration meets few of the criteria of a bureaucracy,[128]

at 172–173 for 'parallel developements'; parallel development is also stressed in *ibid.*, by P. Zutshi, 'The Papal Chancery and English Documents in the Fourteenth and Early Fifteenth Centuries', 201–217, at 215–216; on 210 Zutshi argues that 'There seems little reason to suppose that English royal documents were substantially modelled on documents emanating from the papal curia.'
[126] Maleczek, 'Les registres', 47.   [127] AAV Reg. Vat. 21i, fo. 4r.
[128] Schwarz, *Die Organisation*, especially 210–212.

unless the word is used very loosely to mean any sort of administration, has already been mentioned. One of the criteria it does meet, however, is: the use of formal rules to manage complexity. Without any systematic method of checking what had already been granted, the papacy developed over the course of the thirteenth century a way of ranking documents, like cards in a standard pack, so that anyone familiar with the rules would know which letter of grace out-trumped the others. At the risk of oversimplification, we find the following ranking, in ascending order of priority (from Ten of Clubs to Ace of Spades as it were):

1. *Litterae communes* without *non obstantibus* clauses.
2. Letters with *non obstantibus* or *ex certa scientia* clauses. These ranked equal and in the event of a clash the later one would take precedence over the earlier one.
3. A letter with a *clausula* overriding not only past but future papal letters which did not make special mention of it and quote it.
4. A letter subsequent to one in one of the last-mentioned two categories and making special mention of it.
5. A letter overriding all existing legal obstacles, including papal letters which could not be abrogated without special mention being made of them, even though the letter overridden is not specially mentioned or quoted.[129]

Here we have, so far as letters of grace are concerned, the beginning of an answer to 'Hageneder's question': 'how were the Church and Christendom to be ruled without an administration equal to the task?' It is in fact Hageneder's own answer, with respect to the problem of unregistered outgoing letters.

'Notwithstanding/*Non obstante*' clauses need to be read with care. Take the document printed at *1255, March 20,[130] which lists four dioceses to which Peter of Aigueblanche, bishop of Hereford, had a right to confer seven benefices to seven clerics. On a quick reading it looks like one of the highest categories in the 'notwithstanding' hierarchy, close to the Ace of Spades. On closer examination it is not so high. Firstly, it overrides any objection on the grounds that the number of canons is fixed, even if that had been by papal authority. Next comes the clause 'or if papal documents should have been sent there to others', which seems to put this on the level of number 2 in the hierarchy: letters with *non obstantibus*

---

[129] I quote from *Medieval Religious Rationalities*, 145, which goes on, 145–146, to give more detail about ranking. (On p. 146, note 92 I give a wrong reference: for 'Sext 3.1.7' read 'Sext 3.4.7'.) My analysis was based especially on Hageneder, 'Päpstliche Reskripttechnik'; other relevant studies by Hageneder are listed in *Medieval Religious Rationalities*, 178–179; these findings by Hageneder suggested a central theme of the present book; see also H. Dondorp, 'Review of Papal Rescripts in Canonists' Teaching', *Zeitschrift der Savigny-Stiftung für Rechtsgeschichte, Kanonistische Abteilung*, 76 (1990), 172–253.

[130] BL Harley Ch 111. A. 21.

clauses. The phrase 'to whom [recipients of earlier papal letters] we do not wish prejudice to be generated on account of this' presumably means that the force of their letters remains, except when up against the present one. The next clause overrides any rights not to be excommunicated, suspended or put under interdict without a papal letter making specific mention of the privilege. This is to ensure that the enforcement mechanism behind the current letter cannot be blocked by a previous privilege, but it does not say (as a rapid reading might suggest), that no subsequent papal letter can override this one without making specific mention of it.

Executors of papal letters, and bishops, would know how to construe such clauses strictly. A more straightforward case is ***1281, October 7** (ANF J.683.4), a bull sealed on silk granting to Philip III of France the privilege of immunity from any excommunication which does not mention specially and expressly the document itself (i.e. J.683.4). This would be no. 3 in our ranking: a letter with a *clausula* overriding not only past but future papal letters which did not make special mention of it and quote it.

The language of 'notwithstanding' clauses will seem elaborate and highly complex to anyone unfamiliar with legal documents, medieval or for that matter modern. ***1354, January 21**[131] is an example:

… **notwithstanding** the fact that some people may have obtained special or general letters from the apostolic see or its legates concerning provisions to be made for them from this[132] or other ecclesiastical benefices, even if, through these [letters], procedures have been started[133] for inhibiting [i.e. disposal of the benefice], reservation, or reaching a decision,[134] before all of which people with claims on these benefices, **except if by our authority** [exercised subsequently to the current document],[135] we wish you to take precedence in the pursuit of this benefice; but that no prejudice to them be generated by this with regard to their pursuit of other benefices; **or [notwithstanding] if it has been granted at a privilege by the said see [i.e. the papacy] to the same bishop or any others whatsoever, jointly or severally, that they are by no means bound to receive or provide for anyone and cannot be compelled to do so, and that from those or other benefices pertaining, jointly or severally, to their collation, provision, presentation or any other kind of power to dispose, nobody should be able to be provided with a benefice by an apostolic letter which does not make full and explicit reference, with verbatim**

---

[131] AAV Reg. Vat. 226, fo. 1v.   [132] 'huiusmodi'.   [133] 'sit processum'.
[134] 'decretum'.
[135] I.e.: the current document overrides all previous ones but could be overriden by a subsequent one. The acute suggestion made by Michael Haren, that 'preterquam …' be taken with 'expectantibus': i.e., 'except those with an expectation by our authority to the benefice', makes excellent sense of the Latin, but would seem to contradict the previous notwithstanding clauses that explicitly 'bump' candidates with earlier papal expectatives.

quotation, of such a privilege; and [notwithstanding] any other general or special privilege[136] of the said see, whatever its contents, through which, not being made explicit or inserted in its entirety in the present letter, the effect of this grace might be impeded in any way or delayed ...

These clauses make the letter something like the Ace of Spades, outranking any other letter except a later one of the same kind: number 5 in the ranking listed above.

Rationalisation under the Avignon papacy

The last example has taken us far into the period of the Avignon papacy. It should be said that under the Avignon papacy the administration became generally more efficient, at least relatively speaking.[137] Once at Avignon, the curia was no longer itinerant, which must have made governance more convenient for all concerned. Papal government had settled down. An expression of this was the Avignon palace, completed by 1350.[138] In the early Middle Ages it had made sense to move around the papal state, living off food rents from papal estates, but in the monetarised economy of the fourteenth century it was no longer necessary. The administration now had a stable base, just as did the French monarchy in Paris and the English monarchy at Westminster. Plaintiffs and petitioners no longer had to chase after the curia. Provisions were routinely registered,[139] which would have made it possible to find out if the same benefice had been granted twice – though whether it was easy to do so,[140] how often anyone took the trouble, and whether application

---

[136] 'indulgentia'.
[137] P. Zutshi, 'Changes in the Registration of Papal Letters under the Avignon Popes (1305–1378)', in Broser, Fischer, and Thumser, *Kuriale Briefkultur im späteren Mittelalter*, 237–261, esp. 259 (also in Zutshi, *The Avignon Popes and Their Chancery*, 107–138, esp. 135). On registration generally see R. von Heckel, 'Das päpstliche und sicilische Registerwesen in vergleichender Darstellung mit besonderer Berücksichtigung der Ursprünge', *Archiv für Urkundenforschung*, 1 (1908), 371–511 (wide ranging, fascinating comparative survey) and O. Hageneder, 'Die päpstlichen Register des 13. und 14. Jahrhunderts', *Annali della Scuola Speciale per Archivisti e Bibliotecari dell' Università de Roma*, 12 (1972), 45–76. On the Diplomatics of the Avignon papacy generally see the authoritative studies of Zutshi, *The Avignon Popes and their Chancery: Collected Essays*: for registration, a key article (already discussed above) in the same volume 'Changes in the Registration'.
[138] E.g. J. Rollo-Koster, *Avignon and its Papacy, 1309–1417. Popes, Institutions and Society* (Lanham, MD, 2015), 201.
[139] G. Mollat and C. Samaran, *La fiscalité pontificale en France au XIV siècle (période d'Avignon et Grand Schisme d'Occident)* (Bibliothèque des Écoles Françaises d'Athènes et de Rome, 96; Paris, 1905), 88.
[140] From *ibid.*, especially 88–93, where Mollat and Samaran examine the efforts to implement the benefice-Annates system.

and enforcement became more efficient, are further questions.[141] If the matter was important enough, they could: in 1318 John XXII was able to tell the king of England that he could not find an entry in the registers for a disputed fact – the implication being that he could be sure that it had never happened. Again, it has been suggested (though mistakenly I think) that Benedict XII claimed to the French king in 1341 that all letters were registered.[142] Benedict XII probably meant 'all letters to anyone who was anyone', for it would seem that *gratis* provisions for poor clerics (*in forma pauperum*) were not registered;[143] nor were simple letters of grace or simple letters of justice.[144] Nonetheless, the curia followed the track towards systematic record keeping beaten by the English monarchy, albeit at a distance and on a smaller scale. More was registered and the process became less haphazard. An important innovation was the registration of incoming petitions ('supplications'), 'likely to have been an innovation of the pontificate of John XXII or Benedict XII'.[145] Patrick

---

[141] Hageneder, 'Die päpstlichen Register', 75–76, seems to play down the difference between the thirteenth and the fourteenth centuries. Since, however, provision of benefices was now linked to papal income, my guess is that Hageneder's path-breaking assessment is much less applicable to the Avignon period.

[142] S. Zanke, *Johannes XXII., Avignon und Europa. Das politische Papsttum im Spiegel der kurialen Register (1316–1334)* (Leiden, 2013), 5 note 22, quotes the following: 'omnes et singule littere, quas regibus et principibus ac quibusvis personis aliis [...] destinavimus et nos destinare contingit, registrare [..] et registrantur de verbo ad verbum continue', following Hageneder, 'Die päpstlichen Register', 70. As Hageneder notes, at 74, Benedict XII says elsewhere that all letters that went through *nostram cameram* – only a small proportion of letters *tout court*, however one understands the phrase – were registered. Zanke's statment that 'Aus einer selektiven wurde eine umfassende Archivierung' (*Johannes XXII.*, 5) is a misinterpretation, despite the 'quibusvis personis aliis' of the passage he quotes, if he really intended to say that all outgoing mail was recorded. In a personal communication Patrick Zutshi puts it that the passages quoted by Zanke in this footnote refer to letters in the secret registers and per cameram registers.

[143] Zutshi, 'Changes in the Registration', 136.

[144] *Ibid.*, 123. Note Peter Herde's comment that '... über den zahlenmäßigen Umfang der päpstlichen Delegationsgerichtsbarkeit ... nicht informiert sind' ('Zur päpstlichen Delegationsgerichtsbarkeit im Mittelalter und in der frühen Neuzeit', *Zeitschrift der Savigny Stiftung für Rechtsgeschichte*, 119, *Kanonistische Abteilung*, 88 (2002), 20–43, at 37). Simple letters of justice were still not registered as a matter of course in the Renaissance period: see Frenz, *Die Kanzlei*, 68 – but I have found commissions to judges delegate in the AAV *Reg. Lat.* series (an example is Reg. Lat. 823, fo. 300r–v), so this generalisation may be qualified by future research, which is a desideratum. One possibility to be investigated is that only particularly important commissions to judges delegate were registered. See also P. Zutshi, 'Unpublished Fragments of the Registers of Common Letters of Pope Urban VI (1378)', in B. Flug, M. Matheus and A. Rehberg, eds., *Kurie und Region. Festschrift für Brigide Schwarz zum 65. Geburtstag* (Stuttgart, 2005), 41–61, at 45.

[145] Zutshi, 'Changes in the Registration', 133. (In the Vatican Archives this is AAV *Reg. Suppl.*) Note too Zutshi's important article 'The Origins of the Registration of Petitions in the Papal Chancery in the First Half of the Fourteenth Century', in H. Millet, ed.

Zutshi's tentative chronology is that we do not have enough evidence for
any conclusions about the pontificate of Clement V but that

Under John XXII more than one source indicates that some form of registration
of petitions occurred. It is unlikely that the registers were of the same type as the
series of registers which survives for Clement VI. ... Then, in the pontificate of
Benedict XII or, at the latest, that of Clement VI, official registers of petitions
maintained by special registers were introduced.[146]

There was a staff for the registration of supplications: 'three clerics, two
magistri, and eight, later twelve, register scribes'.[147]

The Avignon popes were thus better equipped than their predecessors
to meet the crushing demand for papal services.[148] Even with all this
administrative rationalisation, however, the pressure of business was still
colossal for a government with only a fraction of the resources that
secular rulers might have at their disposal. Therefore more must be said
about how the curia coped. Formularies are part of the explanation.

Prefabrication

Formularies like those studied by Ute Pfeiffer and her mentor Peter
Herde, taken together with a clause in John XXII's reform constitutions,
Pater familias, give us a clue to another part of the answer to 'Hageneder's
question'. These formularies were discussed above as evidence for the
expanding range of types of papal documents; but they are also evidence
for how the papacy coped with the burden of business – evidence of their
own role. The function of a formulary is to economise on thinking
time.[149]

Suppliques et requêtes. Le gouvernement par la grâce en Occident (XIIe–XVe siècle)
(Collection de l'École Française de Rome, 310; Rome, 2003), 177–191 (reprinted in
his *The Avignon Popes and their Chancery*, 69–83). Millet, *Suppliques* contains a number
of other papers relevant to the history of supplications to the pope, notably: P.
Montaubin, 'L'administration pontificale de la grâce au XIIIe siècle: l'exemple de la
politique bénéficiale', 321–342; A.-M. Hayez, 'Les demandes de bénefices présentées à
Urbain V: une approche géographico-politique', 121–150; N. Gorochov, 'Le recours
aux intercesseurs. L'exemple des universitaires parisiens en quête de bénéfices
ecclésiastiques (vers 1340–vers 1420)', 151–164. For reproductions (with
transcriptions) from the registers over many centuries, see B. Katterbach, *Specimina
Supplicationum ex Registris Vaticanis* (Subsidiorum Tabularii Vaticani, ii; Rome, 1927).
[146] Zutshi, 'The Origins', 186.
[147] Frenz, *Die Kanzlei*, 100: 'Dort sind drei Kleriker ... zwölf Registerschreiber tätig.'
[148] See *Aux origines de l'état moderne, passim*.
[149] I have not tried to answer 'Hageneder's question' with respect to financial
administration, but note the following authoritative assessment, converging with the
present book's interpretation of Avignon administration generally, of Stefan Weiß: 'Wir

The following analysis of how formularies were used in this period highlights surprising similarities with the early Middle Ages – *mutatis mutandis*, obviously. It will be remembered that in the early Middle Ages a combination of a formulary (the *Liber Diurnus*) and contributions by the beneficiary reduced the need for cerebral effort at the centre. The formulary was available outside the papal writing office. To be fair to the centre, the formulary must have been compiled largely from documents actually dispatched.

The parallels in the period from the early thirteenth century are not exact but are nonetheless telling. The *Audientia* formularies were surely based on real communications (as is common with formularies). One of the thirteenth-century formularies edited by Uta Pfeiffer has an indulgence to all those who visit a convent of Franciscan nuns in Lisbon on specified feast days, and who are truly penitent and have confessed their sins, of 100 days of the penance enjoined on them.[150] A very similar document was produced for a community of English nuns at the end of the twelfth century (edited and translated at *1195, January 21, TNA SC 7/9/35). This need not have been the model for the formulary text but if not there was surely a common source.

Like the *Liber Diurnus*, the *Audientia* formulae were available outside the curia. British Library Lansdowne MS 397, fo. 147r–168v, closely related to the *Audientia* formulary, is written in an English hand (late thirteenth or very early fourteenth century) and travels with Durham texts. Its setting in life was clearly Durham cathedral priory, where there were doubtless one or two monks capable of picking the formula they needed.[151] For those without such a resource there were proctors at Rome who would find the right formula before the papal administration was even approached. We know that it was possible to make an unofficial copy of the *Audientia* formulary: a colophon in one of the manuscripts described in Peter Herde's edition says so.[152] Herde thinks that another

---

haben die Apostolische Kammer als eine Institution kennengelernt, die mit geringem Personalaufwand und primitiven Methoden die katholische Christenheit des 14. Jahrhunders gleichwohl überraschen effektiv besteuert hat' (*Rechnungswesen und Buchhaltung des Avignoneser Papsttums (1316–1378). Eine Quellenkunde* (*MGH* Hilfsmittel, 20; Hanover, 2003), 200.

[150] Pfeiffer, *Untersuchungen*, Trier, Stadtbibliothek NR. 859/1097, no. 60, pp. 186–187.

[151] Durham cathedral priory had a substantial collection of papal documents, some of which survive. Sayers, *Original Papal Documents*, xliv, which goes up to 1304, describes Durham as 'the pearl among the Benedictine houses with fifty-eight originals'; note her good comments, at xlv, on the almost aggressive legal culture of the house. P. Zutshi, dealing with the subsequent period (1305–1415), points out that it is 'the largest English collection of original papal documents of the period [1305–1415] in a cathedral archive': see Zutshi, *Original Papal Letters in England*, XXI–XXII.

[152] Herde, *Audientia*, i, 80: '... transscribi feci de quaterno cancellarie'.

manuscript was a copy made by a proctor from a Chancery exemplar.[153] He rejects the possibility that Leipzig, Universitätsbibl. lat. 937 is a Chancery exemplar and raises the possibility that the copyist was a proctor.[154] With the help of a proctor or someone familiar with the right models, one could have the document drafted before one even approached the curia, saving administrative time.

The document that follows the letter to Lisbon in the manuscript is also to nuns, this time at Urbino. It is a classic grant of papal protection, with *arenga* at the beginning and a 'Nulli ergo omnino hominum ... Si quis autem ...' clause at the end, and standard formulaic language in between.[155] Probably a draft would have been presented to the papal Chancery and waved through unchanged, winning for the pope the good will of the nuns, at almost no cost since the administration paid for itself, as we shall see,[156] and perhaps giving the nuns some protection against evil men who might come after their property.

Both the cases from the formulary edited by Pfeiffer fall clearly under the 'letter of grace' category. Letters modelled on them would have been sealed with silk thread, and there would have been tittles and long ligatures. The formularies edited by Pfeiffer and Herde are usually, and rightly, associated with letters of justice, but as already noted they also contained form letters of grace.[157] In other formulae, long since edited but never closely studied for their content to my knowledge, models for silk-thread letters are plentiful.[158]

The long route through the system – not the norm?

The fact that much of the thinking and drafting was done with the aid of formulae by petitioners, litigants, or their proctors before the curial administrators even started work is part of the answer to Hageneder's question, but when one looks at standard accounts of the elaborate procedures that then ensued, the question comes back again. Textbook presentations, rightly exploring the luxuriant details of the most complex processes, can easily leave the impression that every letter of grace or of

---

[153] Herde, *Audientia*, i, 105.   [154] Herde, *Audientia*, i, 132–133.

[155] Pfeiffer, *Untersuchungen*, no. 61, p. 187.

[156] And have already seen with respect to the *scriptores*.

[157] Note (in a formulary closely related to the one edited by Herde) in BL Lansdowne MS 397, fo. 162r–v, incipit 'Clemens episcopus etc. Dilecto filio Roberto de la Rey, subdiacono, rectori ecclesie de Winston' curam animarum habentis Dunolmensis diocesis, salutem. Devotionis ac probitatis tue meritis...', that the rubric is 'Dispensatio gratiosa'.

[158] Tangl, *Die päpstlichen Kanzleiordnungen*, 228–360.

justice followed a winding path through many stages and received the personal attention of the pope or the vice-chancellor.[159] In this spirit, Fernando De Lasala and Emanuele Boaga provide a splendid overview in the form of a table of the stages through which a letter could pass in the thirteenth century.[160] Let us follow the twists and turns before identifying the short cuts.

Stage A in the table begins with 'preliminary business' ('Negotia praevia'):[161] in the beginning is the supplication, possibly through a proctor; then comes the reception in the *data communis* or, from the end of the century, by a *referendarius* who gets it to the pope by a cardinal or another; it goes to the pope if it deals with something important; if it deals with something routine (*de normalibus*), to the vice-chancellor; before the late thirteenth century, it is dealt with orally; in the late thirteenth century, the pope either writes *Fiat*, which leads to the grant of a grace, or *Audiat*, if a judge is to be appointed; the judge will either be in the curia, quite probably a papal chaplain as *auditor* (later perhaps the Rota, once that court had come into being)[162] or a judge delegate in the locality; then the document is sent into production, with a written indication of the *abbreviator* who will take charge of drafting it. Stage B is the production of the document (*Confectio documenti*). A draft is written according to the Chancery formularies, either by a notary or an *abbreviator*. Then the minute is examined.[163] After that it is read before the pope (in exceptional cases) or returned to the petitioner or proctor to be taken on to be copied. A fee is paid. A *rescribendarius* allocates it to a member of the college of *scriptores*. A fair copy is made. The *rescribendarius* or a *taxator* writes on it (under what will be the fold) the fee to be paid. It goes to be inspected in the chamber of a notary, or by the vice-chancellor if it is very important. After that, it is inspected by the *corrector litterarum apostolicarum*, and returned to the Chancery. Now we enter the final stage – after this long and complicated gestation the document is almost born. If it is of great importance (such as a privilege),

---

[159] Rabikauskas, *Diplomatica Pontificia*, 76–77; De Lasala, *Il Documento* 214–215; A. Paravicini Bagliani, *La Cour des papes au XIIIe siècle* (Paris, 1995), 92–94.

[160] De Lasala, *Il Documento, Tavole Sussidiarie,* Tav. II (done by Boaga).

[161] German translations are provided – a tribute presumably to the prominence of German scholars in the field.

[162] On the Rota, whose normal business was not mainly matrimonial as now, see K. Salonen, *Papal Justice in the Late Middle Ages. The Sacra Romana Rota* (London, 2016) and P. Ingesman, *Provisioner og Processer. Den romerske Rota og dens behandling auf danske sager in middelalteren* (Aarhus, 2003); there is an English summary at 523–550. See below, Chapter 5.

[163] 'examinatio et siglatio minutae': but Patrick Zutshi informs me that minutes were not sealed (personal communication).

it is read by the vice-chancellor in the pope's presence, to be then signed by the pope and cardinals, and dated; alternatively, it can be read in the *Audientia publica*, where there will be the vice-chancellor, the *auditor litterarum contradictarum*, some notaries, *abbreviatores*, and proctors. If it passes that stage, it is taken on to the *bullaria* to be sealed, whether with hemp or silk thread, by lay brothers.[164] Another fee is paid, then yet another fee is paid for registration. Finally, the document is given to the person who started the process, or to the proctor. Getting through all these stages demanded a lot of administrative time and effort.

It is easier to understand how the curia coped if one realises that the full elaborate procedure was only for a subset of 'elite' documents. For routine documents there were short cuts through the system, much more economical of time and effort (and consequently of money). The following paragraphs deal with the minimalist route. For if one reads the small print of the textbook presentations and bears in mind some common-sense considerations, one is lead to look for 'quick service' pathways for the bulk of the business.[165]

A short cut for simple letters

As a thought experiment, let us see how easily a straightforward letter might be produced, without pope or vice-chancellor needing to be bothered with it at all.

To start with the pope: it is clear that he could be and in fact had to be spared large classes of routine business.[166] That letters of grace were not all read to the pope becomes clear if we put the constitutions of John XXII together with the Chancery ordinance of Nicholas III and the

---

[164] Note that the idea that the *bullatores* had to be illiterate is refuted by P. Herde, 'Der Geschäftsgang', 238 note 486 (my thanks to Patrick Zutshi for the *fiche*).

[165] Patrick Zutshi points out that one could look at it the other way round: 'More and more controls were introduced for the more important letters (e.g. registration of petitions, and then of the resultant letters, examination *in litteratura* of provisors present in curia, recording of provisions in chamber registers, letters re honorary chaplains sent on to the Chamber), but the quick service route was available for certain categories' (personal communication). This makes perfect sense: a principle of proportionality can be discerned.

[166] Herde, 'Der Geschäftsgang', 150, writes of 'der Versuch der Päpste, die weniger wichtigen Sachen bei dem größer werdenden Geschäftsanfall untergebenen Beamten zur selbständigen Bearbeitung zu übergeben und sich dadurch auf die wichtigen Angelegenheiten zu konzentrieren'. For a list of the categories of business dispatched without involving the pope, see G. Barraclough, 'The Chancery Ordinance of Nicholas III. A Study of the Sources', *Quellen und Forschungen aus italienischen Archiven und Bibliotheken*, 25 (1933–1934), 192–250, at 237–250. Different kinds of letter are listed. When '- Dentur' is written after a category, that type of letter did not need to be read to the pope.

formulae for the Chancery edited by Tangl. Those letters designated as *litterae dandae* in Nicholas III's Chancery ordinance were not read to the pope.

In Nicholas III's Chancery ordinance the vice-chancellor and/or the notaries are sometimes specified[167] but often not. It is in fact clear that senior Chancery officials, the notaries and the vice-chancellor, did not always need to be involved, any more than the pope, unless serious expertise in re-drafting was required. This applies to letters of grace as well as to letters of justice, as a close reading of the 1331 reform constitutions makes clear.[168]

If we read between the lines of John XXII's reform constitutions more of the answer to 'Hageneder's question' begins to emerge. This attention to the unobvious is required because the John XXII's reform regulations are above all an elaborate price list for Chancery services, and an attempt to prevent conflicts of interest, rather than a user's guide to the system. It should be said that they are not introducing a completely new system, since elements of it go back to the thirteenth century.

Important for answering 'Hageneder's question' is what we learn from the 1331 constitutions about the class of officials called '*abbreviatores*', who were definitely a prominent element in the system before the constitutions.[169] After a detour to explicate the role of the *abbreviatores* it will be possible to show another relatively simple route through the system (in addition to the *per viam correctoris* route), without all the arabesques of the elaborate procedure described on the basis of De Lasala and Boaga and other standard accounts. For much of the routine business could be done through the *abbreviatores*, and without great expense. The following pages will give an impression of complexity – readers need not feel impelled to master all the details. The short-cut pathways are not necessarily easier for the modern student to follow than the long route as presented in the handbooks of Diplomatics. Short cuts can require a lot

---

[167] E.g. Barraclough, 'The Chancery Ordinance', no. 6. (46), p. 238: 'Legantur per vicecancellarium'; no. 21 (54), p. 240 'Legantur per notarios et vicecancellarium'; nos. 30 (57) and 31 (58), p. 242: 'Legatur per notarios'.

[168] Tangl, *Die päpstlichen Kanzleiordnungen*, 94 item 12 explicitly states that *abbreviatores* not on the staff of a notary could deal with both letters of grace and letters of justice (Patrick Zutshi explained to me that at this point John XXII is talking about the checking of fair copies). I see nothing that unambiguously bars *abbreviatores* attached to a notary from dealing with both kinds. See also items 115 and 116 (note especially the words 'gratiam vel iustitiam'), *ibid.*, p. 101, where no distinction between the two kinds of *abbreviatores* appears to be drawn.

[169] '... non v'è alcun dubbio che ai tempi di Giovanni XXII l'impiego degli abbreviatori della Cancelleria sia stato in pieno vigore' (P. Rabikauskas, 'Abbreviatori della Cancelleria Pontificia nella prima metà del secolo XIV', *Annali della Scuola Speciale per Archivisti e Bibliotecari dell' Università di Roma*, 12 (1972), 153–165, at 153.

of local knowledge. Nonetheless, they must have drastically reduced the expense, the time, and above all the need to apply high-level intellect. What all the details of the short cuts ultimately reveal is a set of procedures that saved time and effort both for the curia and those who sought its services.

Middle-level administrators take the strain off the top men

The *abbreviatores* were a kind of middle management capable of handling a lot of relatively routine business. One may assume that they took on the easier assignments: e.g. checking drafts submitted by the proctor (the legal representative) of a petitioner. If the proctor was competent, the *abbreviator* might only need to sign off on the draft. For more delicate drafting recourse could be had to the notaries. The *abbreviator* class emerged in the same kind of way as that of the new class of *scriptores*, in that an initially quite unofficial role came to be formalised. As with the *scriptores*, this development probably goes back to the second half of the twelfth century. The role was regularised later than that of the *scriptores*: the first oath of office is from the mid-thirteenth century. In the later part of the century some became attached to the vice-chancellor and swore an oath to him.[170]

Under Innocent III, according to Brigide Schwarz, they were paid by the notaries for whom they worked, rather than receiving fees for work.[171] If so, that changed, because the 1331 reform constitutions of John XXII list their fees for correcting different kinds of letter.[172] Like the *scriptores*, they were paid by the piece.

There are some unresolved technical questions about their role, but enough of it for present purposes is understood: in a nutshell, they were responsible for the drafts of the more routine papal letters (in addition, some of them at least had a role in the checking of the fair copies of letters near the end of the process).[173] Already in the thirteenth century there were *abbreviatores* who worked for the seven notaries,[174] senior officials in

---

[170] Katterbach, *Referendarii*, XI.
[171] For the foregoing, Schwarz, *Die Organisation*, 21–22.
[172] Tangl, *Die päpstlichen Kanzleiordnungen*, 94–101.
[173] 'Alcuni degli abbreviatori della Cancelleria, oltre alla scrittura delle lettere de grazia, venivano chiamati a presiedere, assieme con il vicecancelliere, l'esame dei documenti prima della spedizione' (De Lasala, *Il Documento*, 233); 'l'ispezione del documento ha luogo più spesso (e dal XIV sec. in poi esclusivamente) in una riunione del capo della cancelleria con i notai e alcuni abbreviatori scelti' (Frenz and Pagano, *I Documenti*, 80).
[174] Or six, when the vice-chancellor took the place of one.

the Chancery.[175] The vice-chancellor, head of the Chancery, could probably call on the services of the *abbreviatores* of the notaries, but, probably later, he also acquired his own *abbreviatores* (perhaps only around the start of the fourteenth century).[176] Scholars generally assume that there was a clear division of labour between the two kinds of *abbreviatores* but that may be too simple: the only compelling evidence is that there is a separate 'distributor' of 'de iustitia' work for the *abbreviatores* attached to the notaries;[177] on the other hand, however, it is clear that the *abbreviatores* attached to the vice-chancellor could deal with both letters of justice and letters of grace,[178] and John XXII's 1331 reform constitutions themselves do not suggest much differentiation.[179] My suspicion is that the *abbreviatores* of the notaries were in practice allowed to pick up routine sealed-with-silk-thread letter-of-grace business if it was simple and stereotyped. This would fit the fact that *Audientia* formularies do include some formulae for letters of grace, as already noted.[180]

The technical question of whether notaries' *abbreviatores* could handle some letters of grace is, however, not especially important for the present argument, which is that there was a quick and relatively easy route through the system for 'simple' (but for those involved not trivial) business involving both silk- and hemp-sealed letters. The key fact is that the

[175] On the notaries see the important study by P. Zutshi, 'The Office of Notary in the Papal Chancery in the Mid-Fourteenth Century', in *idem*, *The Avignon Popes and their Chancery*, 155–178. See also Paravicini Bagliani, *La Cour*, 89–90.
[176] Rabikauskas, 'Abbreviatori', 157.
[177] Schwarz, *Die Organisation*, 246–248; Schwarz, 'Der Corrector litterarum apostolicarum', at 150, note 188; cf. notes 186 and 191. Bresslau, *Hanbuch*, i, 296 says that the *abbreviatores* not connected with notaries dealt with 'die Hauptmasse der *litterae gratiosae*' but does not footnote this particular point. A propos of a letter of Clement VI of 1348 Zutshi comments, in 'The Office of Notary', 164, that apparently 'the pope is not concerned here ... with specifying which type of *abbreviatores* carried out the notaries' duties, merely with recording that generally even when present in the curia the notaries did not carry out their duties in person'.
[178] Schwarz, 'Der Corrector litterarum apostolicarum', 155, accepts that *abbreviatores* attached to the vice-chancellor could take responsibility for letters of justice as well as letters of grace; cf. the comment at the end of her note 217, pp. 155–156: 'Auch aus [Tangl] KO 94 #13 und 98 #58 ist nicht zu entnehmen, daß die Abbreviatoren zur Zeit von *Pater familias* in zwei sich ausschließenen Kategorien zerfielen.' Patrick Zutshi drew my attention to this.
[179] Frenz, *Die Kanzlei*, 142 and note 14, prints 'existat, [...] formis communibus de iusticia'. The words he omits are important though: 'simplicibus ac legendis et gratiosis aliisque' (Tangl, *Die päpstlichen Kanzleiordnungen*, 92, item 3).
[180] See above, note 000. I do not know if the formulae for letters of grace printed by Tangl, *Die päpstlichen Kanzleiordnungen*, between 229–303, were similarly available, but it seems likely that proctors could get access to them, as it seems they could to the main *Audientia* formulary.

abbreviatores formed a layer of responsible officials between the level under the pope (notaries and vice-chancellor) and the *scriptores*, a class of senior/middle management men who could relieve the top men of much of the quantitative burden and speed relatively routine business along a more rapid route than the elaborate one described above.

It should be added that 'the way in which much of the low-grade business was able to get through and be issued was by impetrants' simply having a head start on rival interests in their localities, so that a game of perpetual catch up was in course'.[181] Although there were controls, at least from the time of Innocent III, it was system that tended to favour petitioners.

From the point of view of the petitioner

If we now look at curial process from the point of the petitioner, whether for a letter of grace or a letter of justice (or *litterae executoriae*), we see that in uncomplicated cases it might not be too difficult to draft a petition. A set of simple models was produced with papal approval by Cardinal Guala Bichieri.[182] The forms could be as straightforward as this: 'A., a cleric, makes it known to your holiness that V., a cleric or a layman of diocese N. [*talis diocesis*] has without cause [*temere*], putting aside all fear of God, laid violent hands on him. Therefore he petitions for judges';[183] or 'A., the master, and the brothers of the hospital of blessed Mary of N. petition your Holiness that, with the customary clemency of the apostolic see, taking their persons under the protection of St. Peter and of yourself, you may deign to confirm to it the said hospital[184] the other goods which they justly possess in the present or which they will with the Lord's help by just means acquire in the future.'[185]

---

[181] Wise comment by Michael Haren.

[182] von Heckel, 'Das päpstliche und sicilische Registerwesen', Beilage 'Der Libellus petitionum des Kardinals Guala Bichieri', 500–511; 'Explicit libellus petitionum curie Romane a magistro Gualas cardinali compilatus et a papa comprobatus ...' is the colophon (p. 510).

[183] 'Significat s. v. A. clericus, quod V. clericus vel laicus talis diocesis manus in eum iniecit dei timore postposito temere violentas. Unde petit iudices' (Guala, 'Libellus petitionum', in von Heckel, 'Das päpstliche und sicilische Registerwesen', 500–510, at 502, paragraph 2).

[184] 'dictum hospitale ... eidem'; one should probably understand this awkward sentence as a confirmation to the hospital of its physical plant and other goods past and present.

[185] 'Supplicat s. v. A. magister et fratres hospitalis beate Marie de N., quatenus ex consueta sedis apostolice clementia personas eorum sub protectione beati Petri et vestra suscipientes dictum hospitale et alia bona, que in presenti iuste possident vel in futuro iustis modis prestante domino potuerint adipisci, eidem confirmare dignemini'

Getting a draft of the letter to be sent might not be that complicated either. As already suggested, if you wanted a letter of grace (or letter of justice) that did not deviate from a common form, you or probably your proctor would approach an *abbreviator* – whether or not on the staff of a notary. The wording of item 8 of the 1331 reform constitutions – 'expediting the business of the parties who come to them' (*partium ad eos provenientium*)[186] – might suggest that the proctors approached the *abbreviatores* directly, but in fact the vice-chancellor assigned petitions to *abbreviatores* who did drafts and then passed them on to the relevant proctors.[187] Probably the contact man would be the *distributor* (a rotating function), who would dole out tasks to *abbreviatores*. *Abbreviatores* on the staff of notaries were told to be easy to find, in or near chambers of notaries (one of which was interestingly called the 'general chamber' (item 6 of the 1331 reform constitutions).[188] Brigide Schwarz has rightly shown that we should not think of papal administration in terms of office buildings,[189] but proctors did have to know how to contact *abbreviatores*. The Chancery, *cancellaria*, which one could translate as 'the residence'[190] of the vice-chancellor, would be another place, even though we should not imagine it as the place of work of papal scribes, *scriptores*.[191] Perhaps that is where *abbreviatores* not attached to a notary collected assignments.

If the assignments were of the formulaic sort we are considering, they would probably be in good shape anyway. The 1331 constitutions state that

That nobody should dare to compose a draft, unless he has been commissioned to do it under the supervision of the vice-chancellor or a notary or whichever,[192] exceptions[193] being made, however, for simple[194] letters and 'letters to be read'[195]

(Guala, 'Libellus petitionum', in von Heckel, 'Das päpstliche und sicilische Registerwesen', 506, para. 19).
[186] Tangl, *Die päpstlichen Kanzleiordnungen*, 63.
[187] 'The procedure is evident from original petitions: R(ecipe) followed by the abbreviator's name and the signature of the vice-chancellor' (Patrick Zutshi, personal communication).
[188] Tangl, *Die päpstlichen Kanzleiordnungen*, 93.   [189] Schwarz, *Die Organisation*, 67–71.
[190] Word suggested to me by Patrick Zutshi. Brigide Schwarz uses the correct but less comprehensible 'Livree'; Schwarz, *Die Organisation*, 68.
[191] Schwarz, *Die Organisation*, 68–69.
[192] 'nullus audeat formare notam, nisi abbreviator per vicecancellarium vel notarium seu quemvis eorum factus existat'; Tangl, *Die päpstlichen Kanzleiordnungen*, 92, no. 3 (the free translation is necessary to bring out the overcompressed meaning).
[193] Bresslau, *Handbuch*, i, 300–301.   [194] Cf. Herde, 'Die Urkundenarten', 69–70.
[195] 'legendis' – to the pope: cf. Herde, 'Die Urkundenarten', 62. From context, this must have been for formulaic documents important enough to be read to the pope but so straightforward in their wording as not to need expert composition. Possibly one should

and letters of grace and other common form letters of justice, [none of] which require fresh composition.[196]

That implies that the proctor could do the draft in straightforward cases,[197] perhaps on the basis of a private copy of an earlier similar document or of the relevant formulary. Even the client might have such a formulary, for instance if the client was a substantial monastery (like Durham, which had British Library Lansdowne MS 397).[198] If so, the drafting could be done in house, and the proctor's labour and cost would be reduced. Even if the institutional client did not have a copy of the *Audientia* formulary, they might be able to access a similar letter to use as a model. The formulary is orientated towards letters of justice, though by no means exclusively.[199] The formulary for petitioners composed by Cardinal Guala Bichieri included (1226/1227) some petitions for letters of grace as well as for letters of justice.[200] Thus the *abbreviator* might not need to do much: in fact item 3 of John XXII's reform constitutions, just discussed, suggests that he might not do any actual rewriting at all.

The *abbreviator* would check this quite possibly ready-made draft, collecting a fee for doing so.[201] The fee was not outrageous: for instance, the fee for checking a draft of a formal letter of protection was not to be more than 1 Turonensis Grossus (*Gros Tournois*) according to the 1331 reform constitution of John XXII.[202] Thomas Frenz characterises fees of between 2 and 5 *grossi* as 'extraordinarily low'.[203] To get an idea of what that could buy, in 1299 Boniface VIII spent 40 *Turonenses Grossi* on a pair of strong boxes to hold documents of the *Camera apostolica*, 9 *Turonenses Grossi* for 'Jordan who was sent to Anagni for three days', so for his travel and subsistence presumably, and 16 Turonenses Grossi to

---

emend to 'simplicibus legendis' rather than 'simplicibus et legendis' – the editor has to make another emendation two words later ('grossis' to 'gratiosis').

[196] 'simplicibus ac legendis et gratiosis aliisque formis communibus de iusticia, que non mutantur, dumtaxat exceptis'; Tangl, *Die päpstlichen Kanzleiordnungen*, 92, item 3.

[197] Patrick Zutshi drew my attention to the implication. Cf. also Rabikauskas, *Diplomatica Pontificia*, 134 note 45 (late medieval example).

[198] For original papal letters still in the Dean and Chapter Muniments at Durham see P. Zutshi, *Original Papal Letters in England*, nos. 118, 119, pp. 59–60, and 305, p. 155.

[199] British Library MS Lansdowne 397, fo. 162r–v is a 'dispensatio gratiosa'; Herde, *Audientia*, i, 413–429.

[200] Herde, *Audientia*, i, 33–34.

[201] On the fees for the *abbreviatores* see Tangl, *Das Mittelalter in Quellenkunde und Diplomatik*, ii, 'Taxwesen der päpstlichen Kanzlei', 780–784. He implies, at 783, that the detailed provisions of the 1331 reform constitutions for an 'Abbreviatorentaxe' may have fallen into desuetude and that an older fee system may have been revived: see '... hat die Abbreviatorentaxe seit Johann XXII ... Vergessenheit gekommen sein'.

[202] Tangl, *Die päpstlichen Kanzleiordnungen*, 92–101, at 95, item 25.

[203] Frenz, *Die Kanzlei*, 146.

the laundress 'for sewing up four sheets for the lord' (for the pope presumably).[204] In 1338, 12 large sheepskins were purchased for 2 *Turonenses Grossi*.[205] If the *abbreviator* was sloppy and missed something and the letter had to be rewritten after the fair copy had been made, he would have to bear the cost of the rewriting.

Such mistakes could be picked up by the *Corrector litterarum contradictarum* once the fair copy had been produced by a Chancery *scriptor*, who would write it out with the features of a letter of grace: tittles, ligatures, etc. If it was not done well, it would be sent back, but if the fair copy passed the inspection, it would be sent on to be sealed with silk thread. The beneficiary or his/its proctor could take away a letter of grace. Compared with the elaborate sequence of moves described earlier, what we see here is a short and cheap way through the system. The actual process was more user-friendly than the description of it will have been to the reader.

Letters of justice, the delegation system and the *Audientia litterarum contradictarum*

The foregoing has been about letters of grace. What about letters of justice? Much the same applies, if these were of the 'simple' sort, for which ready made models could be employed, but it is worth dwelling on some extra aspects which are a tribute to administrative ingenuity in making good the lack of a well-funded bureaucracy.[206] These elements are at the beginning and at the end of the documents' journey through the system, the *Geschäftsgang*. The middle part is very similar to the path taken by a simple letter of grace.

First, the litigant or his lawyer would look for the right kind of model. In England in the same period, the litigant and his man of law would look for an appropriate writ. In both cases, you needed a form letter which

<hr/>

[204] '1034 eidem pro uno pari cophinorum ad tenendum acta camere 40 tur. gross' (T. Schmidt, ed., *Libri Rationum Camerae Bonifatii Papae VIII (Archivum Secretum Vaticanum, Collect. 446 necnon Intr. et ex.* 5 (Littera Antiqua, 2; Vatican City, 1984), p. 144); '1285. Item Jordano qui fuit missus Anagniam pro 3. diebus 9 tur. gross' (Ibid., 175); '1966. Item eidem [*the* lotrix] pro sutura 4 linteaminum pro domino 16 tur. gross' (*Ibid.*, 262). There would be other fees down the line – see Lunt, *Papal Revenues in the Middle Ages*, i, 125–129 – not to mention 'gifts'. All things considered, however, it is likely that routine judicial business at the papal court was inexpensive by comparison with almost any civil litigation in the modern English or American legal systems, and was predominantly demand-driven; *a fortiori*, letters of grace were responses to demand.
[205] K. H. Schäfer, ed., *Die Ausgaben der apostolischen Kammer unter Benedikt XII., Klemens VI. und Innocenz VI. (1335–1362)* (Paderborn, 1914), 71: 7 January 1338.
[206] Rabikauskas, *Diplomatica Pontificia*, 77–79; d'Avray, *Medieval Religious Rationalities*, 136–142.

would start a legal process. There were registers of royal writs in
England, and for papal justice there was the formulary of the *Audientia*,
which could be obtained in unofficial copies. British Library Lansdowne
MS 397 is the case just mentioned: it seems to be a formulary for the use
of the Benedictine community at Durham, closely related to the
Audientia formulary edited by Peter Herde.[207]

*1281, August 23 (TNA SC 7/64/40) uses the standard *Audientia*
formula 'super terris, debitis, possessionibus, et rebus aliis iniuriantur
eisdem'.[208] That formula or similar formulae were still being used in the
fifteenth century.[209] As with a letter of grace, probably almost as good as
a model in a formulary would be a minute in the institution's archives of
a letter starting the same sort of lawsuit. The litigant would have the
opportunity to propose the names of judges delegate.

The judge delegate system enabled the papacy to stretch its judicial
arm all over Latin Europe with some efficacy and at little financial cost. It
has been well studied on a regional basis, notably by Jane Sayers for
England[210] and by Harald Müller.[211] More interregional comparison
would be desirable. In England, notably, disputes about secular land
would go to the royal courts, even if the litigants were a bishop and a
monastery. The underlying reason was surely the relatively efficacious
and rational character of English royal justice, at least where land disputes were concerned. That level of rationality was not reached by
secular courts in Germany, and I suspect that comparison would reveal
an inverse correlation with the reach of ecclesiastical justice.[212] *1281,
August 23 (TNA SC 7/64/40) appoints judges delegate to hear a case
between the abbot and community of Prüm and various citizens, apparently lay, of Cologne, Laon (*Landunensis*) and Metz. Although we do not

---

[207] Here I should thank Peter Herde, who long ago passed on to me a handwritten
description of the manuscript's contents done by one of his pupils.

[208] Cf. Herde, *Audientia*, ii, 96.

[209] British Library Add Chart 19553: 15 March 1496. Alexander IV to the abbots of the
Schottenstift of Erfurt and of St. Giles of Brunswick. Here the version of the formula is
'super nonnullis pecuniarum summis, bonis, et rebus aliis iniuriantur eidem'.

[210] Sayers, *Papal Judges Delegate in the Province of Canterbury*. See also Brentano, *York
Metropolitan Jurisdiction and Papal Judges Delegate*.

[211] H. Müller, *Päpstliche Delegationsgerichtsbarkeit in der Normandie (12. und frühes 13.
Jahrhundert)*, 2 vols. (Studien und Dokumente zur Gallia Pontificia; 4, 1 & 2; Bonn,
1997). Note that for most if not all the period covered the *Audientia litterarum
contradictarum* system which we find under Innocent III and after would not have
been in operation, so that it would have been easier for a plaintiff to get
biased judges.

[212] W. Trusen, *Anfänge des gelehrten Rechts in Deutschland. Ein Beitrag zur Geschichte der
Frührezeption* (Wiesbaden, 1962), argues that canon law was a principal carrier of
Roman law to Germany.

know what kind of property was involved, it is hard to imagine that in England such a case would have been settled anywhere but in a royal court. But the comparison is misleading: there was nothing like the English monarchy to resolve disputes from these three towns.

Judges delegate were men in the localities appointed by letters of justice – in the case just mentioned, **1281, August 23** (TNA SC 7/64/40), the judge appointed was the *primicerius* (a leading official in the episcopal administration) of Metz. The papacy did not pay them. They were *honoratiores*, to use Max Weber's term – men who were more-or-less obliged by their position and status to do responsible work without adequate, or perhaps any, remuneration. (Possibly they could collect expenses from the litigants.)[213] Usually the letter of justice nominated two or three, allowing one or two of them to send apologies at least on that occasion. They had the advantage of local knowledge, combined with delegated papal authority for the case in question.

Armed with an appropriate draft, the litigant, or more probably the proctor, would go to a notary's chambers or to the vice-chancellor's residence to find an *abbreviator* to check the document. Probably a *distributor* would assign one. The *abbreviator* would check that the document was in the right form. If so, the proctor would take it on to be copied. There was no Chancery office in which all the scribes worked, for they worked from their homes, but there would be a man in charge of assigning work, another *distributor*:[214] once again it was a short-tenure office passed between the scribes.[215]

After the fair copy was ready it would be checked by the *corrector*[216] (who would leave a mark when something had to be corrected),[217] and then, only then, would it be read aloud at the *Audientia litterarum contradictarum*, where it could be challenged.[218] This extra stage was introduced by Innocent III, and it was a crucial one. This reading was the opportunity for anyone or their proctor to speak up and contradict the document. That could be unfortunate for the litigant because it could easily result in a revision, of content or judges proposed, which would mean making a fresh fair copy. Making a new fair copy was expensive, bothersome and time consuming. But it was especially likely to happen if the litigant had proposed judges unacceptable to the other party. To propose biased judges was asking for trouble and expense.

---

[213] Suggested to me by Patrick Zutshi.   [214] Rabikauskas, *Diplomatica Pontificia*, 78
[215] *Ibid.*, 71.   [216] *Ibid.*, 78.   [217] *Ibid.*, 61.
[218] On the *Audientia litterarum contradictarum* see e.g. Rabikauskas, *Diplomatica Pontificia*, 73; on the sequence – fair copy before the reading in the *Audientia* – *ibid.*, 78.

The significance of the sequence – reading in the *Audientia* not before but *after* the fair copy had been made ('engrossed') – was missed by most scholars, but not by Peter Herde, the greatest expert on the judge delegate system:

> In the case of letters of justice it is likely ... that negotiations about who to have as judges delegate, where the case should be heard, and about certain clauses of the letter took place at the initial stage of the process of getting a letter sent, in order to avoid the eventuality of an objection being levelled against the fair copy, which might in some circumstances lead to the preparation of a fresh letter, at considerable expense.[219]

It was thus in the interest of even the most litigious party to treat the judge delegate system as a system of arbitration. It was a rational choice to agree on the judges and the parameters of the dispute with the opposing party. If one did not, there was a good chance one would regret it.

The creation of the *Audientia litterarum contradictarum* was a stroke of genius on Innocent III's part. If the parties could compromise in advance on the choice of judges, the judgment was much more likely to be accepted as fair. This was the one aspect of the judge delegate system that F. W. Maitland failed to appreciate in his path-breaking paper on 'William of Drogheda and the Universal Ordinary'.[220]

Expeditio per viam correctoris

An even more streamlined variant been analysed by Thomas Frenz: the *expeditio per viam correctoris*.[221] The proctor of the plaintiff – he implicitly associates the procedure with letters of justice – does a draft, has a fair copy made by a papal scribe, and gets it checked by the *corrector* who was at the end of the copying chain (it is possible he was also involved before the fair copy was made). We should think of proctors as rather like English solicitors or Continental European notaries, not cheap, but still a sensible choice for anything with a legal aspect; although with simple

---

[219] P. Herde, 'Zur päpstlichen Delegationsgerichtsbarkeit', 37: 'Vermutlich wurden ... führen konnte'; cf. d'Avray, *Medieval Religious Rationalities*, 140 note 73.

[220] Reprint in Maitland, *Roman Canon Law in the Church of England*, 100–131, at 114–115. His remark (114) that a defendant could 'recuse' obviously biased judges is probably not a reference to the *Audientia*, which had not at that time been investigated.

[221] Frenz and Pagano, *I Documenti*, 84–86; Frenz, *Die Kanzlei*, 140–148; cf. B. Schwarz, 'The Roman Curia', 210. Patrick Zutshi points out that even though the Latin name comes in late there are hints of the procedure much earlier, under Innocent III: he points to the Decretals of Gregory IX, X.5.20.8, A. Friedberg, *Corpus Iuris Canonici*, 2 vols. (Leipzig, 1922 edn.), i, col. 821.

form letters it might have been possible to follow a model and save the cost of a proctor. Finally the document would be signed by a protonotary and in many cases (Frenz estimates approximately 50 per cent)[222] read aloud at the *Audientia litterarum contradictarum*. It was Frenz's view that this procedure begins with John XXII's reform constitutions.[223] There are reasons to think, however, that it may go back to the thirteenth century.[224] Compared with the labyrinthine route charted by De Lasala and Boaga (for instance) it was a strikingly time-, cost-, and labour-saving system.

The Apostolic Penitentiary

Simpler still, because uncontentious and unlikely to trespass on the rights of others, were the procedures of the Apostolic Penitentiary. The Penitentiary has been the object of intense historiographical interest since the registers were made available a generation ago, but they do not survive from before the fifteenth century.[225] Registration goes back earlier, though not all petitions were registered.[226]

Even so, we know a great deal about the earlier history of the institution, thanks above all to Arnaud Fossier,[227] who has made good use of such documents as Benedict XII's bull of 1338 on Penitentiary procedures and, above all, of formularies. *1330s gives an idea of the fascinating material they contain.

---

[222] But Patrick Zutshi comments that this is speculative: 'I can see no means of estimating the quantity of non-registered business. We can only give figures for the registered letters; and the registers of petitions are too fragmentary to allow any conclusion' (personal communication).

[223] Frenz, *Die Kanzlei*, 142–143. I have failed to find in the document the sharp separation between procedures for letters of justice and for letters of grace that Frenz seems to assert, but the question is not important for present purposes.

[224] d'Avray, *Medieval Religious Rationalities*, 141 and note 78.

[225] Bibliography in the following chapter.

[226] E. Goeller, *Die Päpstliche Pönitentiarie von ihrem Ursprung bis zu ihrer Umgestaltung unter Pius V* (Bibliothek des Königlich Preussischen Historischen Instituts in Rom, 3, 4, 7, 8 [4 vols. in 2]; Rome, 1907–1911) I, i, 187–188. According to Ludwig Schmugge, doyen of penitentiary research, 'As to your question: Murner refers here to *litteris confessionalibus* (which where obviously not registered during the schism) "and some other letters". Normally all supplications, for which a positive answer has been given by the penitentiary, in the XV. c. are registered. Not to be found in the registers are the *litterae ecclesiae* of the *penitentiarii minores* and the *sola signatura* decisions, where the positive answer is given on the supplication-sheet sent back to the petitioner. As far as I know also some decisions *in foro conscientie* are not registered or at least should not be registered. In some archives you may find such letters' (personal communication).

[227] Fossier, *Le Bureau*, especially 84–86 and 96–100 for the *Geschäftsgang*; see also Schwarz, *Die Organisation*, 115–125.

Much of the work of the Penitentiary was oral, the forgiveness in confession of very grave sins, for which no payment was allowed; letters of absolution were issued where required, but the procedure seems to have been streamlined;[228] the long-term survival chances of these letters must have been minimal. Part of the business of the Penitentiary was public, however. It was responsible for release from excommunication and, increasingly, for dispensations. One would probably need a proctor, to frame the petition to the Penitentiary in the proper form.[229] The proctor would have a formulary to work from (perhaps petitioners too could get access to one, as with the *Audientia* formulary, in which case they could probably save themselves time and keep the proctor's fee down). If the petition was in the proper form, and the case uncontroversial, the *regens* of the Penitentiary would sign the petition and return it to the proctor, who would pass it on to a *distributor*, who may have given it to the *corrector* to be turned into a draft latter,[230] and allocated it to a scribe to be copied in accordance with the Penitentiary's Diplomatics.[231] The Penitentiary had its own *scriptores*.[232] The *corrector* who drafted the minute was recruited from the Penitentiary *scriptores*. He also checked the finished letter, combining roles that were distinct in the Chancery. The Penitentiaries themselves were friars, lived in convents with their brethren, and were paid a modest salary,[233] so did not need to live off fees – indeed they had to make an oath not to benefit financially from the production of letters.[234] The *scriptores* got a living from fees for copying letters, as the *scriptores* of the Chancery did, but their rates were reasonable.[235] Scribes were supposed to waive fees for poor petitioners, and if they refused they could be deprived of their revenues.[236] In the period covered by this chapter, the Penitentiary system was relatively inexpensive and administratively lean.

Most of the letters of grace sent by the Penitentiary could also be sent by the Chancery.[237] Which route to choose may have been a judgment call by the petitioner or the proctor: presumably the Chancery way was

---

[228] Fossier, *Le Bureau*, 84, 96.
[229] *Ibid.*, 92–96; Goeller, *Die Päpstliche Pönitentiarie*, I, i, 186.
[230] '[The proctor] pouvait alors la remettre au "distributeur" qui la donnait au "correcteur", chargé, on s'en souvient, de composer la "minute" de la lettre' (Fossier, *Le Bureau*, 96): Patrick Zutshi suggests to me, however, the possibility that 'penitentiary letters were produced on the basis of petitions', without the intermediate stage of a draft.
[231] For the form, see Goeller, *Die Päpstliche Pönitentiarie*, I, i, 190–200.
[232] Fossier, *Le Bureau*, 106–107, noting, at 107, a tendency for the title of scribe to become honorific.
[233] Paravicini Bagliani, *La Cour*, 109   [234] Fossier, *Le Bureau*, 91.   [235] *Ibid.*, 86–91.
[236] *Ibid.*, 86.   [237] *Ibid.*, 99.

more expensive but perhaps smoother for important people? Sometimes the same business would be dealt with jointly or successively by the Penitentiary and Chancery, for instance if the business turned out to be more serious than originally thought and a second petition requiring a new letter of grace was needed.[238]

Simplicity and complexity

There is no contradiction between the relative simplicity of the routes through the curia just outlined and the mass of complex detail one meets in textbooks that deal with papal Diplomatics.[239] These handbooks are quite right to take us through all the stages through which the most important letters might need to pass. Nevertheless, it is important to remember that the enormous mass of documents calendared in the great series of the École Française de Rome seldom belonged to that subset of exceptionally important letters, though of course they mattered to those who asked for them. Then, in addition to this mass of letters recorded in the registers, there were all the simple letters of justice that, in this period, appear to have by-passed the registration system altogether.[240] (An implication is that the papal administration was doing much more business even than scholars have thought. It may be noted that routine English royal writs were also unregistered – but the sheriff who dealt with them was supposed to return them to the centre, and we have bunches of these returned writs. With papal government there was no equivalent to that.) We only know about them when they turn up in the localities, and their survival rate was low since nobody had any particular interest in keeping them after the trials they brought about. The bias of survival is likely to lead us to underestimate grossly the output of papal government.

Then (as now, in England or the USA at least), determination and good legal advice were keys to success in the system, and then, as now, the higher the quality of the legal advice, the higher the fee, but the system was more user-friendly for ordinary petitioners and litigants than it can easily appear. From the users' point of view, it offered to relatively unimportant people and institutions relatively easy access to supreme

---

[238] *Ibid.*, 99.

[239] E.g. Frenz and Pagano, *I Documenti*, 76–82, and the path analysis by De Lasala – Boaga reported above.

[240] Herde, 'Zur Audientia', 68.

judicial authority,[241] by contrast with modern jurisdictions where inter-mediate stages are inescapable (and costly in the extreme). At the other chronological end, Roman emperors had offered, in principle, the same direct access to ultimate authority,[242] but without developing a routine equivalent to the judge delegate system which provided papal justice on one's doorstep.

Solution of a paradox

The main focus of the foregoing has been on the paradox of papal power at its zenith (say from Innocent III to the Great Schism), namely, that the pope's personal authority attracted much more business than one man and his vice-chancellor could cope with, and lacked anything like a modern bureaucracy to process it. It was not as if popes had nothing else to do but expedite day-to-day business. He was at the centre of high-level disputes such as the confrontation of the friars with the secular clergy, and of international relations such as relations between the crowns of Aragon, Naples and Sicily,[243] or of England and France;[244] he was frequently asked to intervene in the religious life of kings, espe-cially the French monarchy, to whom popes granted so many favours;[245] he had to handle highly complex annulment proceedings (again with the French monarchy to the fore);[246] frequently he was trying to give direc-tion to wars to keep the papal states in Italy independent of great powers or, in the fourteenth century, to recover control of them; if he was wise, he gave attention to ways of balancing the books.[247] That was enough to monopolise the time and attention of any workaholic. But meanwhile the volume of routine business had swelled to enormous proportions, far beyond his powers to handle even in the most perfunctory way, even if there had been no great affairs to attend to. A glance at the array of volumes of *lettres communes* of John XXII succinctly summarised under the aegis of the École Française de Rome is enough to bring this home,

---

[241] Parallels with Fatimid Egypt need to be explored: see Rustow, 'Fatimid State Documents', 244.

[242] F. Millar, *The Emperor in the Roman World (31 BC–AD 337)* (London, 1977).

[243] G. Le Bras, 'Boniface VIII, symphoniste et modérateur', in *Mélanges d'histoire du Moyen Âge, dédiés à la mémoire de Louis Halphen* (Paris, 1951), 383–394.

[244] Bombi, *Anglo-Papal Relations*.

[245] A. Tardif, *Privilèges accordés à la couronne de France par le Saint-Siège. Publiés d'après les originaux conservés aux Archives de l'Empire et à la Bibliothèque impériale* [1224–1622] (Paris, 1855).

[246] d'Avray, *Dissolving Royal Marriages* and *Papacy, Monarchy and Marriage*.

[247] C. Bauer, 'Die Epochen der Papstfinanz: Ein Versuch', *Historische Zeitschrift*, 138 (1928), 457–503, especially at 459–503.

and as we have just these, there is a whole class of outgoing communications, letters of simple justice, which they do not record. So we come back to Hageneder's question: how did popes manage? We have seen that the judge delegate system in combination with a formulary provides part of the answer, and that another part is the creation of systems and of a layer of officials, the *abbreviatores*, that took the bulk of routine business off the hands of the pope and vice-chancellor.

Functional equivalence with the English royal writ system

A little comparative analysis is illuminating. It is worth looking at how another government coped. English kings faced a similar problem: how to combine royal duties requiring personal attention with the staggering expansion of government business.[248] The functional equivalent of the judge delegate system, and the common forms and *Audientia* formulary that came to underpin it, was the system of 'writs of course'. The English system was developed a generation or more before its papal equivalent. Registers of writs were the equivalent of the *Audientia* formulary. The 'writs of course' were the counterpart of standardised letters of justice. Registers of writs contained a large set of templates from which a plaintiff could get the Chancery at Westminster to generate, for only a modest fee, a letter setting in motion a lawsuit to be organised by the sheriff of the county in question, in which a jury of neighbours would be asked a straightforward question requiring only local knowledge, the answer of which would settle the suit. *Novel disseisin* is the simplest case. The plaintiff claims to have been dispossessed of his land without a court judgment. The writ tells the sheriff to get neighbours to view the disputed land, then report to the county court when the royal justice next comes round to hear cases. If they say that the plaintiff possessed the land at a defined recent date, he got it back. If the dispossessor thought he had a better claim, the onus was on him to bring a lawsuit, which would be much messier and more complicated. These procedures proved very popular, and Magna Carta, against the generally anti-royal grain of the document, wanted more of them even though they meant an expansion of royal power.[249]

The papacy could not organise juries of neighbours and did not have justices who toured regularly around Christendom, which was much too vast, but the judge delegate system performed an analogous function.

---

[248] The classic study is M. Clanchy, *From Memory to Written Record* (3rd edition, Oxford 2012).

[249] W. Stubbs, *Select Charters* (Oxford, 1888), clauses 18 and 19, p. 299.

Clever rules instead of a tax-salary system

There were two layers of papal government, one where the judgment of the pope was in play, and another, quantitatively much more considerable, where communication was shaped by stereotyped forms. In a sense it had been thus in the early Middle Ages too: there were high-level papal communications of the kind collected in the *Codex Carolinus*, and the more routine kind represented by the *Liber Diurnus*, on the other. But the comparison is qualitative not quantitative: the production of papal privileges along *Liber Diurnus* lines is a trickle compared with the great flood of letters of grace and justice from the papal curia of the thirteenth or fourteenth century. Quantitatively, the papacy after Innocent III looks forwards towards the early modern and modern state rather than backwards towards the *Liber Diurnus* era. By 1300 the difference between the papacy and modern governments, so far as the researcher's predicament – too much material! – is concerned, is only one of degree. Nobody will ever edit, let alone study and translate, all the papal records of the last two medieval centuries, for there is just too much, so the historians *modus operandi* becomes more like that of a modern historian who cannot hope to 'read all the sources' for anything but a very specific topic.

The crucial difference between double-layered papal government and the analogous structure in the modern state is that with the medieval papacy the layers were not linked by money or by bureaucratic hierarchy in the Weberian sense – Brigide Schwarz's great insight in her 1972 study.[250] (The picture she revealed for *scriptores* applies also, *mutatis mutandis*, to the *abbreviatores* discussed above.) Anyone who has taught the papal history of this period knows that students (and some scholars) have in mind – simply take for granted – a model of a modern state bureaucracy: it is funded by taxation, direct or indirect, which cascades down to departments, situated in an office building, with a managerial hierarchy, with pay corresponding to position in the hierarchy, and the possibility of promotion. It is already a generation since Brigide Schwarz demolished this assumption in her brilliant dissertation, which does not mean that her findings have reached everyone interested in the medieval papacy.

To bring together some of Schwarz's findings, already discretely discussed: By contrast with a modern bureaucracy, much curial administration was self-funding. *Abbreviatores* and, further down the line, *scriptores* were paid directly by the clients for their work. There were

---

[250] Schwarz, *Die Organisation, passim.*

further fees for sealing and registration, and of course there were tips.[251] As the system became settled, these transactions were recorded by marks on the documents themselves,[252] as were other stages of the process: experts work out from the marks and notes on original documents the names of the scribes and sometimes other administrators involved.[253]

Work was allocated by one of the group, in the case of the *scriptores* a *distributor* selected by vice-chancellor and notaries to be in charge for a limited term of six months.[254] He allocated work with a view to equalising the work-load and corresponding income. There was no hierarchy.

The link with the man at the top was made not by money but by rules,[255] like those of the 1331 reform constitutions of John XXII, or the oaths that the *abbreviatores, scriptores,* and other cogs in the administrative machine had to swear. These rules regulated prices and professional behaviour and in general established a quasi-legal framework for the administrative machine. The link between the pope and routine administration consisted of words, not money. The money came from people and institutions from all over Europe who chose – for more often than

---

[251] Frenz and Pagano, *I Documenti*, 91. Frenz points out that 'tips' were required in practice to ensure that the service was good; perhaps restaurants or very high-end hotels provide analogies. Note too though his comment that 'Troviamo spesso tassazioni eccessive, vale a dire l'uso scorretto del sistema delle tasse' (*ibid.*). Patrick Zutshi comments that 'sealing tax did not go to the bullatores (rather than to the *Camera apostolica*), which doesn't mean that the latter weren't paid by petitioners, but is there any evidence about this?' and adds that 'the register tax went to the vice-chancellor, not to the people who did the work' (personal communication).

[252] Rabikauskas, *Diplomatica Pontificia*, 60–63.

[253] *Ibid.*, 60–64, as is done for example by Sayers, *Original Papal Documents*, 492–595, and Zutshi, *Original Papal Letters in England*, 271–324 (and 325–326 for 'Unidentified Annotations' and 'Table of Figures'). For details of the various marks indicating scribe, *corrector*, proctor, etc., and stages of the process and other officials, match the numbers on the list in Frenz and Pagano, *I Documenti*, 76–78, with the corresponding numbers on the table showing the schema of the face and dorse of a document at 86. For more detailed analyses see for instance the very helpful pages of Sayers, *Original Papal Documents*, lx–lxi, and Zutshi, *Original Papal Letters in England*, LXV–LXXXI.

[254] Schwarz, *Die Organisation*, 86. From the mid-thirteenth century we have the new office of *rescribendarius* (*ibid.*, 90). (This seems to be the gist of Brigide Schwarz's circumlocutory 'Da die Eiden der anderen Chargen, des Reskribendars [and another office] ... nicht erkennen lassen, daß diese Ämter schon vor der Mitte des 13. Jahrhunderts bestanden hätten ...'; Schwarz, *Die Organisation*, 90). He was appointed by the vice-chancellor alone (*ibid.*, 91). The name implies that his principal remit was to oversee the distribution of letters that had to be copied afresh (*ibid.*, 91). From the time of the Chancery reform of John XXII there was a rearrangement: the *rescribendarius* ceased to oversee letters to be recopied and took over the oversight of letters of grace, while the *distributor* looked after letters of justice (Frenz and Pagano, *I Documenti*, 78).

[255] Tangl, *Die päpstlichen Kanzleiordnungen, passim*; Barraclough, 'The Chancery Ordinance'; E. von Ottenthal, *Regulae Cancellariae Apostolicae. Die päpstlichen Kanzleiregeln von Johannes XXII. bis Nicolaus V.* (Innsbruck, 1888).

not they surely had a choice[256] – to deal with the papal system rather than ecclesiastical authority closer to home, and most of it went directly to the administrators who did the work without passing through a papal kitty.

No need to think?

It would be an exaggeration to say that the men who kept the papal machine going at the lower, routine level had no need at all to think, but it would be true to say that most of the thinking could be done for them. It could be done by the client or client's proctor who picked the form letter from a copy of the *Audientia* formulary or from a model following an appropriate stereotyped form. The *abbreviator* did not have to compose a letter, only to check the minute presented to him. The scribe would copy the minute without needing to think about the content, and the *corrector* would look it over to make sure that it was in the proper form, but would not need to change anything if no mistakes had been made earlier – and it was a nuisance for both the client and the abbreviator if they had been. With litigation, we can guess that the litigant often came to an agreement with the defendant about the terms of the dispute and the judges, to avoid trouble and expense at the *Audientia litterarum contradictarum*. It was certainly in the litigant's rational interest to do this. That would have saved the *auditor litterarum contradictarum* a lot of thought. With letters of justice or *litterae executoriae*, sealed normally with hemp, but with silk thread if they functioned like a charter to establish a right, the thinking would be done in the localities by the judge or judges delegate who heard the case. The whole procedure required remarkably little mental activity in Rome, except on the part of the clients' men of law, the proctors – just as the English writ system required remarkably little mental activity on the part of the royal administrators in Westminster. Much cerebral activity had gone into designing these systems, which were like good computer software packages that minimise case-by-case decision-making. Whatever one may think of thirteenth- and fourteenth-century popes and cardinals, they had to be very able – like the graduates of the École Nationale d'Administration in modern France or top British civil servants. But they could use their gifts on the tougher decisions where their brains were needed, and let the system do the routine business for them.

---

[256] They did not have a choice if a legal case was between parties from two different ecclesiastical provinces, and as Patrick Zutshi reminds me (personal communication), some business was a papal monopoly.

Conclusion

How to rule the religious world without a bureaucracy worthy of the name? This chapter has attempted to answer the question, concentrating above all on the simplified procedures that enabled the curia to handle a quantitatively staggering burden of business. The Diplomatics of high-level documents dispatched through the pope's personal chamber or through the (quite distinct) apostolic chamber have been given their due, and the lengthy 'bureaucratic journey' which a subset of letters took though the system, and which handbooks of papal Diplomatics present in such intricate detail, has been re-described as it deserves to be, but the principal aim has been to understand the mass production. Though it is good to dwell lovingly on the complex construction of Lamborghinis and Rolls Royces, one must not forget the production-line cars, the over-whelming majority of the total produced. New categories of official took on much of the burden. New genres of documents met the increasingly variegated demand. There were new formal and external manifestations of this variety, but to understand them properly the contents of the document must be penetrated also. Ingenious systems were devised that left much of the burden of work to the petitioner or litigant, as in the early Middle Ages but on a vastly greater scale. Formularies might provide a short cut, as they certainly did for the curial officials. Furthermore, instead of the salaried and tax-funded officials that make a modern bureaucracy run, the papacy relied on self-funding guilds controlled by oaths, on remuneration of *scriptores* 'horizontally', for piece work, rather than 'vertically' through salaries; on rules for ranking potentially conflict-ing letters; and on a delegation system for which there is no precise parallel in world history.

5   From Schism to Counter-Reformation, c. 1378–c. 1600

The Schism of 1378–1417, and the conciliar challenge to papal authority that continued after the Schism, amount to what was surely the greatest crisis in papal history except perhaps the Reformation. One might have expected it to have cut papal documentary production down to size. Far from it. Though fewer of the documents have been edited or calendared, and nobody has tried to measure the shelf space occupied by fifteenth-century records in the Vatican Archives, there can be no doubt about the astonishing scale of the fifteenth-century curial administrative operation.[1] A monument to the scale of the system is the *Repertorium Germanicum*, a stately series of (highly compressed) biographies of individuals who crop up in late medieval papal records.[2] Another indication: Arnold Esch could write what is practically a social history of late medieval Europe almost entirely on the basis of the Registers of the *Penitenzieria Ap.* series (until recently in the Vatican Archives, now in the *Penitenzieria Apostolica*'s own archive).[3] Those registers do not survive from before the fifteenth century and it is not clear whether they were kept before then. In terms of scale and even (it will be argued) in terms of system rationality, there was no 'decline of the medieval papacy' where letter production and record keeping were concerned. It can be regarded as a further stage in a slow process of governmental

---

[1] My thanks to Werner Maleczek for pointing out this elephant in the room of late medieval research. It has been calculated that about a-million-and-a-half documents were dispatched in response to petitions in the period 1471–1527; see Frenz, *Die Kanzlei*, 38, 83. But I suspect that this is a gross underestimate. Letters sent *per viam correctoris* were not registered, so Frenz estimates the total sent in this way on the basis of the total that survive in relation to the total of other categories surviving (*ibid.*, 82). But probably documents emanating from the *per viam correctoris* procedure had a lower chance of survival. Frenz himself stresses that the margin of error around his estimates is very large (*ibid.*, 83).

[2] For an introduction to recent volumes and the history of the series see d'Avray, 'Germany and the Papacy'.

[3] A. Esch, *Die Lebenswelt des europäischen Spätmittelalters. Kleine Schicksale selbst erzählt in Schreiben an den Papst* (Munich, 2014). See my review in *English Historical Review*, 131 (2016), 166–168.

rationalisation – understood here in a value-free sense as the capacity to absorb complexity.[4]

The Schism and papal Diplomatics

Thirteenth-century papal governmental systems relieved the senior men of routine bureaucratic tasks and found ways of compensating for administrative irrationalities such as ignorance of outgoing mail. A curious mixture of administrative rationality and irrationality characterises medieval papal government generally. This survey has not dealt with financial administration, but the thirteenth-century system was a bizarre continuation of the early medieval method of moving around estates and letting the court live off them for a limited time. In the thirteenth century, senior officials were still remunerated in kind: fodder for horses, food, drink.[5] It was not for a common table, but to take away for their own households. By contrast with the early Middle Ages, it had to be purchased, and much of it doubtless went to waste. On the other hand, some fiscal administration was outsourced to Italian bankers on the cutting edge of financial technique.[6] As for remuneration in kind, by John XXII's time money had replaced payment in kind, cutting down on court expenses.[7] Much of the administrative irrationality was ironed out of the papal system under the Avignon popes, John XXII and his successors.

Thus by the time the papacy moved back from Avignon to Rome, more orderly administrative systems than had obtained in the thirteenth century were in place. There was even a steady income stream, thanks to the taxes on those benefices to which the pope had appointed. Expenditure was still a problem, however, for several reasons. Military operations to make Rome safe for the pope's return had been a terrible drain on papal finances. In Rome the curia lacked the credit network that

[4] Cf. N. Luhmann, *Einführung in die Systemtheorie* (Heidelberg, 2002), 184.

[5] Astonishingly, something like that system seems to have been back in place in the later fifteenth century (Ugo Baldini, personal communication), though there is to my knowledge no study of the long-term evolution.

[6] Paravicini Bagliani, *La Cour*, 85–87; A. Jamme, 'De Rome à Florence, la curie et ses banquiers aux XIIe et XIIIe siècles', in Maleczek, *Die römische Kurie und das Geld*, 167–205.

[7] L. Dehio, 'Der Übergang von Natural- zu Geldbesoldung an der Kurie', *Vierteljahrschrift für Social- und Wirtschaftsgeschichte*, 8 (1910), 56–78; F. Baethgen, 'Quellen und Untersuchungen zur Geschichte der päpstlichen Hof- und Finanzverwaltung unter Bonifaz VIII', *Quellen und Forschungen aus Italienischen Archiven und Bibliotheken*, 20 (1928–1929), 114–237; B. Guillemain, *Les recettes et les dépenses de la Chambre Apostolique pour la quatrième année du pontificat de Clement V (1308–1309) (Introitus et Exitus 75)* (Rome, 1978).

it depended on in Avignon.[8] The cardinals took a big bite out of papal income. When Urban VI tried to get them to contribute more, they reacted badly: it is surely a key cause of the Schism[9] which began soon after the definitive return to Rome. The Schism threw everything into confusion. The cardinals who rejected Urban VI, who had threatened to reform them and whose anger-management problems aggravated the situation, chose their own pope and returned to Avignon. It had only recently been vacated, which facilitated the return. At Avignon, old administrative traditions were resumed. The *Reg. Aven.* (*Registra Avenionensia*) series was simply continued by the Chancery of the Avignon obedience. At Rome, the procedures had to be recreated almost from scratch and a new series had to be started under Boniface IX. This is the *Reg. Lat.* series in the Vatican Archives. The name *Registra Lateranensia* has nothing to do with its Schism origins: the volumes were kept for a time in the Lateran palace centuries later. So this series was the continuation in the Roman obedience of the pre-Schism *Registra Avenionensia*. As with the latter, the *Reg. Lat.* 'support' was paper, but unlike the Avignon registers no subsequent copy on parchment was made.[10] The *Reg. Lat.* series of the late medieval period and after has been relatively little explored, and its scope may have expanded to include more letters appointing judges delegate, as will be discussed below, but if so this is evolution rather than revolution in government.

Expeditio per cameram

Evolution rather than revolution also characterises the history of another system that bridges the caesura of the Schism: *expeditio per cameram*, discussed in the previous chapter. As explained there, scholars do not agree about what *camera* stands for. The following – provisionally – follows Frenz.[11] 'Dispatched through the camera' means that the work was done in the pope's private quarters, and the document authorised by the pope, not by the head of the Chancery. The latter's mark is omitted. Instead there is a mark of one of the pope's personal secretaries. They were sent as letters close, *litterae clausae*, sealed so that nobody could read

---

[8] See the important thesis of I. Polancec, 'The Domestic Papal Court between Avignon and Rome in the Pontificate of Urban V (1362–1370)' (PhD thesis, University College London, 2008).

[9] Weiß, *Rechnungswesen und Buchhaltung des Avignoneser Papsttums*, 201–202: 'Daß der Ausbruch des Großen Abendländischen Schismas … auf Gegenliebe stieß'.

[10] De Lasala, *Il Documento*, 260–262; Frenz and Pagano, *I Documenti*, 56–57. Both give details of the features of the content and layout of these registers.

[11] Frenz, *Die Kanzlei*, 132–140.

them without breaking the seal. One reason for sending a letter *per cameram* was that the Chancery was not a particularly secure environment.[12] Another was to allow a letter to be sent even if it broke some of the strict rules of the Chancery's own Diplomatics.[13] When a letter had been blocked because of a defect, it could still be sent *per cameram* for an extra fee, which helped support the secretaries (important since some were lay humanists who could not be remunerated with benefices); as time went by, this provided a solution not only for small defects such as an erasure or deviation from the required formula, but also for conscious contradictions of Chancery rules.[14] So *expeditio per cameram* brought some perhaps needed flexibility into the overall system. In these procedures the *Secretarius domesticus* seems to have played a key role.[15] Key points for Vatican Archives users to take away from this are that letters sent through the *Camera* are registered in the following series: *Reg. Vat.*, initially, then also in *Cam. Ap.*, *Sec. Cam.* and *Sec. Brev.*[16] As Frenz points out, the latter series is virgin territory for research.[17]

The 'brief'

Expeditio per cameram goes back before the Schism and gradually evolves. Another procedure, one with a great future ahead of it, seems to be a product of the Schism crisis. Secretaries were also used for a new form of document, the brief, *breve* (plural *brevia*).[18] Secretaries qua secretaries were not Chancery officials, and had not been since Benedict XII,[19] though he had not stopped them from holding Chancery offices – a different administrative hat and handy income stream. The importance of secretaries grew in the fifteenth and sixteenth centuries: in the later fifteenth century secretaries came to be responsible for much routine business, with those that dealt with it differentiated from secretaries working with the pope on high-level matters.[20]

---

[12] *Ibid.*, 132; on the need for confidentiality as a reason for this evolution, see C. Egger, 'Vertraulichkeit und Geheimhaltung in der hochmittelalterlichen päpstlichen Kanzlei', *Archiv für Diplomatik, Schriftgeschichte, Siegel- und Wappenkunde*, 63 (2017), 253–271.

[13] Frenz, *Die Kanzlei*, 124.   [14] *Ibid.*, 133–135.   [15] *Ibid.*, 137–139.

[16] *Ibid.*, 138–139. Letters that brought the pope an Annate (tax on a benefice) were registered in a different way from other *per cameram* letters. Now, however, both kinds of registers are probably to be found in subseries of the *Reg. Vat.* series, at least until the *Cam. Ap.*, *Sec. Cam.* and *Sec. Brev.* series took over.

[17] Frenz, *Die Kanzlei*, 139. This series does not include only letters sent 'per cameram'.

[18] Frenz, *Die Kanzlei*, 165; Frenz and Pagano, *I Documenti*, 32–35.

[19] Zutshi, 'The Papal Chancery: Avignon and Beyond', 10.

[20] Good account in P. Partner, *The Pope's Men. The Papal Civil Service in the Renaissance* (Oxford, 1990), 26–28. See Meyer, 'Regieren', 82, for a compressed, insightful analysis of what he calls an 'innere päpstliche Kanzlei'.

An increased reliance on secretaries together with the new form of communication by brief helped the Roman popes to handle the haemorrhage of Chancery staff. Their role would later be held by some famous humanists, notably Lorenzo Valla, who had earlier exposed the Donation of Constantine as a forgery, and Poggio Bracciolini. They were well equipped for the delicate diplomatic correspondence for which briefs were a favoured tool.

The model was at hand, in Italy. The word translated as 'brief', *breve* (plural *brevia*), is translated in a medieval English context as 'writ', but the latter is probably not an ancestor of the papal *breve*.[21] A much more probable model is a type of 'secret letter', also called *breve*, used by Giovanna I of Naples and her predecessors; when cardinals and the Chancery decamped to Avignon, a new curia had to be created at Rome, and with it this new documentary practice, under the pressure of the need to improvise.[22] Everything suggests that desperate situation led to this break with tradition.

Briefs differed in a number of ways from traditional papal letters.[23] Their format is 'landscape' as opposed to 'portrait' to a greater extent than had been customary. Their parchment is thin and prepared, on both sides, to make it look 'virgin', white and blemish-free. The script was not different at first, but from the fourth decade of the fifteenth century a humanistic script, *cancelleresca italica*, became the norm for briefs.[24] Whereas the *intitulatio* (sender's name) of a traditional papal letter took the form '[Pope's name] *episcopus servus servorum dei*', starting in the left hand margin, in a brief the name stands on its own at the head of the document, in the middle, in the form '[Pope's name] *papa* [number]'. In a traditional letter the *inscriptio* (recipient's name) would be in the form '*Dilecto filio* [Name in dative]' or equivalent according to status (e.g. *Venerabili fratri*), but in a brief the vocative replaces the dative, so: *Dilecte fili*, or *Venerabilis frater*. Both types, however, can use the same standard salutation: *Salutem et apostolicam benedictionem*, and both can begin with *Ad perpetuam rei memoriam* when the nature of the document called for it. In the dating clause, both kinds have the unexpanded *Dat'* (which could be *Datum* or *Data*) the A.D. year, and the year of the pontificate, but in briefs there is in addition the phrase *sub anulo piscatoris*,

[21] Frenz and Pagano, *I Documenti*, 33.
[22] K. A. Fink, 'L'Origine dei Brevi Apostolici', *Annali della Scuola Speciale per Archivisti e Bibliotcari dell' Università di Roma*, 11 (1971), 75–81, at 78.
[23] The following comparison is based on Rabikauskas, *Diplomatica Pontificia*, 96, and Frenz and Pagano, *I Documenti*, 32–33; see also Schmitz-Kallenberg, *Papsturkunden*, 111.
[24] Frenz and Pagano, *I Documenti*, 34.

sealed with the fisherman's ring. Traditional papal letters used the Roman calendar, while briefs use the calendar system current today. Whereas in traditional papal letters the year begins nearly three months later than it does today, on 25 March, the feast of the Annunciation, briefs of the fifteenth and sixteenth centuries take the year to start from 25 December, a week earlier than the start of the modern year. In briefs, the secretary always wrote his own name under the text, to the right.[25]

Though at first the briefs were used mostly for high-level material, in the second half of the fifteenth century the scope of the genre enlarged enormously to include routine petitions.[26] The Vatican documentary series AAV *Dataria ap., Brev. Lat.* reflects a range covering the issues traditionally dealt with by both letters of grace and letters of justice.[27] This insufficiently explored series shows the papal system of government by delegation in action, though the details are not always given. In some cases the register appoints the delegates and instructs them to act in accordance with the supplication enclosed in the brief: such a brief is called a *breve supplicatione introclusa*.[28] To discover what these were about, one would need to find the corresponding entry in the Register of Supplications.[29] According to the guide edited by Blouin et al. 'In the *Brev. Lat.* registers, at the end of each brief, there is a reference to the *Registra supplicationum* in which the relevant supplication has been transcribed';[30] the source for this must be Lajos Pásztor.[31] For the period from 1523 to 1678 this can be done via the 'Minuta Brevium in Forma Gratiosa' series (AAV *Dataria Ap., Min. Brev. Lat.*). Pásztor describes the elaborate series of steps required to match up a brief in the *Brev. Lat.* series with the supplication in the *Reg. Suppl.* series, via the minute in the *Min. Brev. Lat.* series, on the verso of which there is the data required to make the match(!).[32] For the period before 1523 this method is not available,[33] and even after it is, one cannot assume that there is a supplication corresponding to every brief.[34] The key point, however, is

---

[25] *Ibid.*, 89.   [26] Schmitz-Kallenberg, *Papsturkunden*, 110.

[27] Blouin et al., *Vatican Archives*, **3.2.7.5**, pp. 146–147; Pásztor, *Guida*, 54–56 (which could leave the impression, misleading I think, that only 'grace' material is included).

[28] Frenz, *Die Kanzlei*, 168–169.

[29] On the Register of Supplications see Diener, 'Die grossen Registerserien', 339–343.

[30] Blouin et al., *Vatican Archives*, 146.

[31] Pásztor, *Guida*, 54–55, 72–73. (The first page extent makes the process look simpler than it is revealed to be in the second one.)

[32] *Ibid.*, 73.

[33] If one were desperate, it might be worth following up Pásztor, *Guida*, 55 note 2.

[34] '*Spesso* si può trovare …', Pásztor, *Guida*, 72 (italics added).

that the judge delegate system continued.[35] The *Brev. Lat.* series continued into modern times.[36]

As noted above, in the Roman obedience during the Schism, and after the Schism, the series of registers known as the *Registra Lateranensia* took over the function of the *Registra Avenionensia* (which were continued in Avignon during the Schism).[37] A feature of the *Registra Lateranensia* – one which has not received as much attention as it deserves – is the inclusion of commissions to judges delegate.[38] This is further evidence that the system of papal delegation was still going strong in the late Middle Ages. I do not know if the *Registra Lateranensia* records appointments of judges delegate in the early modern period, and we do not know what proportion of judge delegate commissions were registered.

Much continuity can also be found in the *Geschäftsgang*, the passage of a document through the system. As with the thirteenth century, it looks a complicated process if one counts all the possible stages.[39] In the previous chapter, the stages through which a thirteenth-century papal letter could pass were listed on the basis of the Tavola II attached to De Lasala's *Il Documento*. Leonard Boyle has conducted a similar exercise for the fifteenth century. Boyle's account is so well done that there is no need to rehearse all the details, especially since it it relatively accessible,[40] but once again one is struck by the sheer complexity: Boyle includes 15 or so stages (depending on what one counts as a discrete stage). He has in mind the procedures leading up to the conferral of a benefice, which involved an income for life, so a serious matter.

Did the pope have to know?

We should note, however, that Boyle assumes the direct involvement of the pope – signing or speaking – as a matter of course: the *referendarius* 'examined the petition and, if satisfied that it complied with due form

[35] Examples at AAV Dataria Ap., Brev. Lat., 10, fo. 76r–v, 12 March 1528.
[36] Blouin et al., *Vatican Archives*, 146, gives its dates as 1490–1809, 1814–1908.
[37] *Ibid.*, **3.2.6.7**, pp. 133–135.
[38] An example is AAV Reg. Lat. 823, fo. 300r–v (modern foliation), 1 June 1482: a judge delegate case between the abbot of St. Martial of Limoges and bishop of Limoges, regarding exemption.
[39] Cf. P. Zutshi, '*Inextricabilis curie labyrinthus* – The Presentation of Petitions to the Pope in the Chancery and the Penitentiary during the Fourteenth and First Half of the Fifteenth Century', in A. Meyer, C. Rendtel and M. Wittmer-Butsch, eds., *Päpste, Pilger, Pönitentiarie. Festschrift für Ludwig Schmugge zum 65. Geburtstag* (Tübingen, 2004), 393–410. A key finding is that it was the petitioners and their proctors who decided whether a petition should go to the Chancery or to the Penitentiary.
[40] Boyle in M. J. Haren (ed.), *Calendar of Papal Letters Relating to Great Britain and Ireland*, xv, *Innocent VIII. Lateran Registers 1484–1492* (Dublin, 1978), xvi–xvii.

and was not making any false claims, "referrred" its contents to the pope who … either signed the petition himself or told the Referendary to sign his own name'.[41] Boyle may have been mistaken in this, or misleading in his choice of words. *A priori*, it is unlikely that the pope could have spared the time for even perfunctory attention to so many letters, and it looks as though he did not have to do so, when one looks at the genesis of a document under a microscope.

Such an examination shows that the pope did not need to be involved. The first stage of the process requiring thought was for a *referendarius* to decide where a petition should go. The *referendarii* collectively constituted the *Signatura*. It was was split by Alexander VI (and perhaps de facto earlier) into a *Signatura gratiae* and a *Signatura iustitiae*, though the personnel of the two parts was largely the same.[42] After passing through the *Signatura*, the petition had to be dated (important for priority when there was competition for a benefice), then registered in the Register of Supplications (now AAV *Reg. Suppl.*, one of the largest and longest series in the Vatican Archives). It would be checked for accuracy, then taken to the *abbreviator* to whom it had been assigned, who would do a draft for the final letter. He would take the draft to the *rescribendarius* who was taking his turn to be in charge of the writing office, and would assign a *scriptor* to make a fair copy (perhaps under the proctor's supervision to help with unfamiliar proper names). There would follow two checks by two kinds of *abbreviatores*, perhaps a final check against the draft by the *abbreviator* who did it, and a check for erasures by the *custos* of the Chancery. The vice-chancellor would sign off on it. It would still need to be sealed and registered. At frequent stages along the way fees would need to be paid, and there were elaborate arrangements for rewriting if a document failed the checks.[43] They would have encouraged due care.

Hageneder's question again

Even if the pope did not have to be personally involved, we are still, once again, faced with 'Hageneder's question': how did the papal

---

[41] Boyle in Haren, *Calendar*, xvi.   [42] Frenz, *Die Kanzlei*, 96–97, and note 27.

[43] L. Schmitz-Kallenberg, ed., *Practica Cancellariae Apostolicae saeculi XV. exeuntis* (Münster i. Westfalen, 1904), especially 16–35, compared with Frenz and Pagano, *I Documenti*, 75–82. The *Practica* had been earlier studied and edited by J. Haller: see C. Märtl, 'Modus expediendi litteras apostolicas: Pragmatische Schriftlichkeit und *stilus curiae* am Ende des 15. Jahrhunderts', in J. Nowak and G. Strack, eds., *Stilus – Modus – Usus. Regeln der Konflikt-und Verhandlungsführung am Papsthof des Mittelalters* (Turnhout, 2019), 335–351 (my thanks to Patrick Zutshi for the reference), at 336 note 2 and 346 note 40. Märtl renames the work 'Anleitung', since Schmitz-Kallenberg's title does not appear in any known manuscript (Märtl, 'Modus', 338), and she reconstructs its setting in life and tradition.

administration cope with the deluge of business? The administration had plenty of defects, as Leo X's effort to remedy them before and through the Fifth Lateran Council show.[44] Both contemporary would-be reformers and modern historians can easily slip into moralising mode, the latter drawing data from the former – should we not judge them by their own standards?

Paradoxically, to judge the people we study by their own standards may not be such a good idea (unless we are in the 'praise and blame' business, like most ancient and some modern historians). It is easy to forget that the people we study did not necessarily possess a sociological understanding of the systems of which they were a part. We do not expect medieval people to have understood the economics of the money supply, so why should we expect them to have understood the sociology of social systems? However that may be, and moralising aside, the papal curia did manage to cope with a huge volume of demand for its services, and as with the preceding period we need to ask *how* the system coped.

Cascading down the task of copying

When the intended set of recipients was large, the pope could outsource the copying to public notaries, and those who wanted the document diffused would pay the bill. In the document transcribed at *1455[45] Calixtus II writes that

... since it would be difficult to take the present letter to all the places where they would be needed, we wish and also decree that, inside and outside a judicial setting, the same credence should be attached to a copy signed by the hand of a notary public and guaranteed[46] by the seal of any prelate whatsoever, and the same weight given to it, as to the said original letter if it were to be produced or shown.

The same formula and system that it indicates is found in the same pope's bull of 30 December 1455 granting a crusade indulgence:

For the rest, since it would be difficult to bring this present letter to all the places in which they would be required, we wish and ... decree, that absolutely the same credence should be attached to a copy or it signed by the hand of some public notary and furnished with the seal of some churchman, and in all respects and in every way the same status should be accorded to it in the judicial forum and outside it, as to the aforesaid original letter, were it to be presented or shown.[47]

---

[44] N. H. Minnich, 'Lateran V and the Reform of the Curia', *Bulletin of Medieval Canon Law*, 37 (2020), 135–196.

[45] BL Add Ch 13331.   [46] 'munito'.

[47] 'Ceterum, quia difficile foret, presentes nostras litteras ad singula, in quibus ille necesse forent, loca transferre, volumus et ... decernimus, quod illarum transumpto manu

An indulgence to those who financially support the same crusade is to be cascaded down in the same way, but this time by verbatim inclusion in the letters of archbishops and bishops:

Commanding the said archbishops and bishops that as soon as they have the present letter or one of them has, they should without delay transmit its contents, inserted verbatim into their letters, to the other aforesaid archbishops and bishops, and we decree that the same credence should be attached to the letters containing the aforesaid contents as would be attached to the original letter were it to be presented or shown.[48]

This seems to be a standard formula in the documents ably edited by Jenks.

One may note in passing that this technique of the papacy had a past and a future. It will be remembered that in 404 Innocent I asked Victricius of Rouen to make his 'book of rules known … throughout the neighbouring dioceses' (*404), while in the seventeenth century (1628) the Congregation of the Council would write to a dozen nuncios telling them to pass on to the prelates of their regions some new draconian measures against non-residence.[49] The pope himself was at the origin of such ramifying lines of communication continued by hands outside the curia.

Managing without the pope

At a more routine level, at least in the second half of the fifteenth century, it appears the pope himself did not need to be involved, even in the production of letters about serious matters like a benefice. The vice-chancellor could sign instead, though there were rules limiting the value

---

alicujus notarii publici subscripto ac sigillo alicujus ecclesiastici prelati munito ea prorsus fides adhibeatur, ac illi in judicio et extra in omnibus et per omnia stetur, sicut originalibus litteris predictis si forent exhibite vel ostense'; S. Jenks (ed.), *Documents on the Papal Plenary Indulgences 1300–1517 Preached in the* Regnum Teutonicum (Later Medieval Europe, 16; Leiden, 2018), 136. 'illi' or 'illis': my thanks to Michael Haren for correcting a misunderstanding of the Latin on my part here.

[48] 'Mandantes prefatis archiepiscopis et episcopis, quatinus presentes litteras, quamprimum illas habuerint seu aliquis eorum habuerit, tenorem earum de verbo ad verbum in suis litteris insertum aliis archiepiscopis et episcopis prefatis transmittere non postponant, decernentes quod litteris premissum tenorem continentibus illa fides adhibeatur, que adhiberetur ipsis originalibus litteris, si forent exhibite vel ostense'; Jenks, *Documents*, 139.

[49] AAV 19 Nov Congr. Concil. Libri Litterarum 12, fo. 147r–149v. There is a dossier of replies (starting with one dated June 1628), from the nuncios and sick-notes etc. from men who gave reasons for non-residence: AAV Congr. Concilio, Congregatio Super Residentia Episcoporum Positiones (aa. 1631–1651), 1.

and terms of what he could approve.[50] Furthermore, a *rescribendarius* could sign on the pope's behalf, at least in the second half of the fifteenth century. The formula used implies that he did so in the presence of the pope, but even if this was literally true initially, that probably ceased to be the case.[51]

A key piece of evidence suggests that a *referendarius* could sign without the pope knowing anything about it. A late fifteenth-century treatise on how to navigate the production of a papal provision to a benefice asks about precedence in a conflict of letters when the pope, a *referendarius*, and the vice chancellor have all signed one – presumably the same request or there would be no clash. The ranking is: first pope, then *referendarius*, then vice-chancellor. One may infer from this that the latter two could sign without the pope's knowledge. The treatise suggests that there is no particular difficulty in getting the *referendarius* in charge to sign.[52]

As noted above, in the second half of the fifteenth century the *secretarii* began to take on routine business in addition to the high level of correspondence that had been their remit from the Schism days. Is it not likely that when their business ballooned quantitatively, the pope ceased to be involved in the production of every letter? There is no direct evidence known to me, but the parallel chronology suggests the connection.

As with the thirteenth-century *Geschäftsgang*, it is worth emphasising that there were other pathways through the system which did not involve the pope. The *per viam correctoris* pathway mapped by Frenz was discussed in the previous chapter. As already argued there, when one reads the relevant regulation by John XXII as a whole, it seems that Frenz's analysis can apply to some letters of grace, as well as to letters of justice.[53]

Earlier, the Chancery ordinance of Nicholas III had made it clear that a whole series of letters of grace – whenever the category listed ends with *Dentur*, without qualification – could go through without being read to pope, vice-chancellor, or notary. There is no reason to think that popes personally shouldered a greater burden of this kind of routine business in the fifteenth than in the thirteenth or fourteenth century.

Another late medieval short cut did involve the pope but otherwise drastically streamlined the process: viz., the pope's signature on the

---

[50] Schmitz-Kallenberg, *Practica*, 18; Frenz, *Die Kanzlei*, 95–96.
[51] Frenz, *Die Kanzlei*, 96–97 (note the word 'zunächst', 96).
[52] '... suadeo, ut principalem referendarium accedas et presentes huiusmodi supplicacionem sibi ad manum et sine dubio signabitur tibi ...' (Schmitz-Kallenberg, *Practica*, 17).
[53] Cf. Frenz, *Die Kanzlei*, 142, with Tangl, *Die päpstlichen Kanzleiordnungen*, 92 item 3. As noted earlier, Frenz's abridged version omits the word *gratiosis*.

petition. It was originally against the rules to cut so many corners, but it was de facto acceptable from the pontificate of Sixtus IV (1471–1484). The procedure was to treat a supplication signed by the pope as sufficient to obtain the result, without going through all the subsequent stages elaborately analysed by the *Practica*. This was the *breve supplicatione introclusa*: the brief in which the original supplication was enclosed.[54] The covering letter, or rather brief, was indeed brief and it was formulaic.

Another short cut that became a beaten track in the course of the fifteenth century was to treat a letter of supplication that the pope had approved in writing on the petition itself as a sufficient legal title, without a separate letter being issued. Initially the Chancery and indeed popes tried to prevent this, but from the pontificate of Sixtus IV it was accepted, though not for contentious litigation or grants of benefices. Sixtus IV, Innocent VIII, and Alexander VI allowed it, however, for such graces as permission to use a portable altar and dispensations from fasting. The Chancery regulations against this short cut were overcome by adding at the end of the petition a formula to the effect that the 'signature alone' would be sufficent to give it force, without the issue of any other letter being required: 'Et quod presentis supplicationis sola signatura sufficiat absque aliarum litterarum desuper expeditione'.[55] (A facsimile of a splendid example may be found as a table at the front of Schmitz-Kallenberg's *Practica*.) Parchment instead of the normal paper was the support for these 'quod sola signatura' petitions.[56] This fast-track procedure must have cut down the volume of business conducted by the Chancery *scriptores* as well as saving petitioners trouble and expense.

The Penitentiary

The 'signature on the petition' method was also sometimes used by the Apostolic Penitentiary, though not so often.[57] In any case, by the second half of the fifteenth century the pope would seldom deal with penitential cases personally, as he had delegated the necessary powers to the cardinal penitentiary, the *penitentiarius maior*, and his staff. The pope was not even

---

[54] Frenz, *Die Kanzlei*, 66, 168–169. To obtain a brief *supplicatione inclusa* (as opposed to a Chancery route letter), to get an appeal judgment by a judge delegate with papal authority, reasons, such as poverty, had to be given in the supplication: see *Ibid.*, 84. For examples of letters *supplicatione inclusa* in the *Brev. Lat.* register see AAV, Dataria Ap., Brev. Lat., 10, fo. 76r–v, 12 March 1528.

[55] For the foregoing, Schmitz-Kallenberg, *Practica*, pp. XX–XXI.   [56] *Ibid.*, p. XX.

[57] Salonen and Schmugge, *Sip*, 73. Salonen and Schmugge have helped me with this section though personal communications, as well, of course, as through their publications.

formally the issuer of documents emanating from this rather crucial organ of later medieval papal government.

The Penitentiary has been well studied by a galaxy of scholars, of whom we may single out here Kirsi Salonen and Ludwig Schmugge, joint authors of a magisterial study of the Diplomatics of the Penitentiary[58] as well as of many other individual studies too numerous to list here. Thanks to their work, it would be superfluous to give a detailed treatment to Penitentiary Diplomatics, which in many respects mirrors the Diplomatics of the Chancery, though the Chancery had no equivalent to the *litterae ecclesiae* which 'minor penitentiaries could issue to those who confessed their sins to them in the main basilicas in Rome', as evidence of absolution.[59] They are on relatively small pieces of parchment and sealed with the red wax seal of the Penitentiary, attached by hemp string.[60] The *narratio* tells the reader nothing about the actual sins confessed. The *dispositio* absolves them by the authority of the pope. Of course the pope would have no personal involvement.[61]

In fact nearly all the Apostolic Penitentiary's work was done without the personal involvement of the pope. In some cases he might be called upon to give oral authority to decisions otherwise outside the competence of the Penitentiary.[62] As noted, the pope could also sign petitions and have them expedited through the Penitentiary to be turned into a papal letter, in which case the phrase 'Fiat ut petitur' is used in the register record. The phrase 'Fiat de speciali',[63] on the other hand, indicates that this is the kind of decision that is technically reserved to the pope but which he has by a special oral commission delegated – as a

---

[58] Salonen and Schmugge, *Sip*, especially 68–105. The bibliography gives an indication of the wealth of scholarship on the Apostolic Penitentiary since its archive was opened in 1983. When *Sip* was published, the archive was accessible through the Archivio Apostolico Vaticano, but it has since been moved back to the Penitentiary itself (the office continues) in the Piazza della Cancellaria, where scholars are made most welcome: www.penitenzieria.va/content/penitenzieriaapostolica/it/archivio-storico.html. For the period before we have surviving registers, see Fossier, *Le Bureau*. For Leo X's attempt to reform the Penitentiary (and the curia generally) in the second decade of the sixteenth century, see the important article by Minnich, 'Lateran V', 176–188. This casts a light – harsh, as is the way with reform efforts – on many details of the practical working of the institution.

[59] Salonen and Schmugge, *Sip*, 86.   [60] *Ibid.*, 87.   [61] *Ibid.*, 86, 88.

[62] *Ibid.*, 102: in such cases the phrase, if there had been an 'expressed mandate' from the pope, is: 'et de eius speciali et expresso mandato super hoc vive vocis oraculo nobis facto'; the phrase 'et de eius speciali mandato super hoc vivae vocis oraculo nobis facto' (*ibid.*) meant according to *ibid.*, 102, that 'the decision ... was made by a special faculty from the pope': he had orally given the Penitentiary permission to deal with a category of cases outside its competence. But see at n. 65 below.

[63] Ludwig Schmugge, personal communication, suggests that this is short for 'Fiat de speciali facultate papae'.

category, not just in that individual case – to the *penitentiarius maior*, and in practice also his deputy, the *regens*, could make the decision.[64] The technical terminology used is tricky but a leading specialist summarises it thus:

Fiat in forma – that is a decision by-the-book. Sometimes this is used when the petitioner is asking something that the Penitentiary cannot/does not want to grant, but wants to grant at least something. (Thus a kind of downgraded decision in respect of what was asked.) *Fiat de speciali* – that is a decision within the powers granted by the pope for each new cardinal penitentiary when he was appointed. *Fiat de speciali et expresso* – this is a decision by extended powers given to the cardinal (and his staff) by the pope. I understand this as a long-lasting delegation of powers which the pope did not have to renew every time, although I have occasionally seen it presented so by some scholars.[65]

There could be more than one *regens* at a time, though probably not in the same place.[66] In practice the *regens* and his staff probably handled most of the business. As with letters that went through the Chancery, the Penitentiary was a responsive form of authority: driven by demand. As with the Chancery, it would receive a supplication addressed to the pope, probably prepared by a proctor who knew the ropes. (We may guess that those who had no proctor communicated through their bishop who might have one on retainer, perhaps shared with neighbouring bishops, or who would know how to obtain the services of one.) The proctor would take it to one of the two *auditores* in the Penitentiary, both canon lawyers. If it was in order, they would put a summary of the contents on the left-hand corner of the petition and take it to be signed by the *penitentiarius maior* or the *regens*. The signature obtained, the proctor took it to a *distributor* who brought it to one of the men who could write up a draft response (a 'yes' by that stage though in some cases with qualifications). The *distributor* then passed the draft to one of the Penitentiary *scriptores*. The finished letter was then checked, elaborately in some cases, but in routine cases just by the Penitentiary's *corrector*, the namesake and approximate counterpart of the Chancery *corrector*. It was then sealed and registered, in one of the many volumes that have kept scholars busy in recent decades.

---

[64] Salonen and Schmugge, *Sip*, 75–76. Kirsi Salonen tells me that in her (very extensive) experience of the Penitentiary registers there is no difference between decisions made by the cardinal penitentiary and by the *regens* (personal communication). In her paper on 'Cardinals and the Apostolic Penitentiary', in M. Hollingsworth, M. Pattenden and A. Witte, eds., *A Companion to the Early Modern Cardinal* (Leiden, 2020), 144–153, at 151–153, Salonen gives statistics for the relative proportion of petitions signed by the cardinal penitentiary.

[65] Kirsi Salonen (personal communication).   [66] Salonen and Schmugge, *Sip*, 15.

So rich is their evidence that (as noted earlier) it has proved possible to write a full and good social history of late medieval Europe just on the basis of them![67]

Examples of entries in the Penitentiary registers are supplied in the 'Documents' section of the synthesis by Salonen and Schmugge.[68] They are drops in an ocean of documentation. The office dealt with 2,800–3,600 petitions a year[69] – all of it papal business but not much of it demanding the pope's personal attention. Office charisma had been delegated and routinised. One has the impression of an office that got through a heavy burden of business with a fair degree of professionalism and efficiency.[70] That said, it was not like just any other efficient bureaucracy. The huge demand presupposes a belief in the office charisma. As Ludwig Schmugge puts it, 'In late medieval Christianity the papal curia was not regarded so much as the *radix omnium malorum* (as antiroman polemic of the fifteenth oor sixteenth century would have it), as, rather, an inexaustible fountain of grace.'[71]

---

[67] Esch, *Die Lebenswelt.*

[68] For some intriguing texts from my own Penitentiary researches, cf. d'Avray, *Medieval Marriage*, 267–270, 285–287, and 'Authentication of Marital Status: A Thirteenth-Century English Annulment Process and Late Medieval Cases from the Papal Penitentiary', *English Historical Review*, 120 (2005), 987–1013, at 1009–1013.

[69] Salonen and Schmugge, *Sip*, 16. Schmugge suggest that '2,800–3,600 may be too small a number for the Holy Years' (personal communication).

[70] L. Schmugge, P. Herspeger and B. Wiggenhauser, *Die Supplikenregister der päpstlichen Pönitentiarie aus der Zeit Pius' II. (1458–1464)* (Tübingen, 1996), 19: 'Diese knappe Frist … Dutzend Hände'; Schwarz, *Die Organisation*, 149–150. For a thoroughly critical view of the Penitentiary, presenting it as a primarily profit-generating organ after the middle decades of fifteenth century, see W. Müller, 'The Price of Papal Pardon – New Fifteenth-Century Evidence', in Meyer et al., *Päpste, Pilger, Pönitentiarie*, 457–481, especially 466, 470–471, and W. Müller's earlier fuller paper on 'Die Gebühren der päpstlichen Pönitentiarie (1338–1569)', *Quellen und Forschungen aus italienischen Bibliotheken und Archiven*, 78 (1998), 189–261, especially 230 (increases in charges linked with sale of offices), 231 (charges 'pro sigillo' absent from the 1338 rules of Benedict XII), 233 (Calixtus II's pontificate as turning point). He shows moral disapproval because even in the 1338 rules the compositions paid by corporations were higher than for individuals (216), and because in the second half of the century there were higher compositions for deliberate violations of canon law than for inadvertent ones (217–218). What remains to be done is a comparison between increases in fees and inflation, and to focus on how much in real terms the composition for, say, a standard pre-marriage dispensation for a fourth-degree kinship relationship changed – the equivalent of the foregoing analyses of quick, simple and relatively cheap routes through the papal curia.

[71] L. Schmugge, 'Suppliche e diritto canonico. Il caso della Penitenzieria', in Millet, *Suppliques*, 207–231, at 207: 'Nella christianità tardomedioevale la curia papale non veniva considerata tanto come *radix omnium malorum* (come vorebbe la polemica antiromana del Quattro e Cinquecento) ma piuttost come la inesauribile fonte di grazia'.

Self-funding administration, again

Another part of the answer to 'Hageneder's question', for this period as for the thirteenth and fourteenth centuries, is that the production of papal letters did not need to be funded by any kind of direct taxation, because the fees paid at each stage paid the cost of administration. References to fees punctuate a long section of the chapter on the 'way of expediting apostolic letters' in the *Practica*.[72] This must have been irksome for petitioners – though British academics should remember that we make graduands pay quite a lot for graduation ceremonies, and American academics should remember how much undergraduates are expected to lay out on course books – but it simplified administration from the pope's point of view. The centre did not have to actually organise the administration, only to make rules for it. The colleges of scribes organised themselves, though they had to take an oath.

The corporate self-organisation of scribes was underpinned until quite late in the period by a strong sense of religious solidarity. This was another of the insights of Brigide Schwarz. The colleges of scribes of the Chancery and of the Apostolic Penitentiary were confraternities: they had a commitment to attend mass together every day and to attend each other's funerals.[73]

Sale of offices

According to Schwarz, the togetherness diminished in the fifteenth century because of the sale of offices.[74] In general, the sale of offices system has met with disapproval from historians. It may seem surprising, therefore, to suggest that the system might be part of the answer to 'Hageneder's question', so far as the late medieval papacy is concerned.

Granted: on the surface the sale of offices looks instead more like a key symptom of the 'decline and fall of the medieval papacy', to quote the title of a forgotten but once remarkably popular book by Leonard Elliott-Binns.[75] Had the papacy which fought simony in the eleventh century really come to this? It is true that the offices to be sold were relatively minor administrative or clerical offices, not bishoprics or abbacies. Historians of mentalities have not yet fully elucidated the distinction in the minds of medieval clerics between a spiritual office and a source of

[72] Schmitz-Kallenberg, *Practica*, 21–40.
[73] Schwarz, *Die Organisation*, 161–166; daily mass and burials, 163.   [74] *Ibid.*, 182.
[75] According to Worldcat, http://worldcat.org/identities/lccn-n50–11807/ (accessed 16 June 2022), 33 editions were published between 1934 and 1967.

income. Moralising aside, however, the system looks like a recipe for medium-term financial disaster and for immediate inefficiency.

If, as will be argued, the system was functional, this was more by accident than design. It was not part of a strategic plan of social control, though it may have functioned in that way. Its function, intention, and origins all need to be distinguished. Its origin was a financial predicament and its aim to acquire cash.

The roots of the sale of offices system lay in the conception of the office of *scriptor* as a benefice, one without sacramental duties attached, and in the practice of giving a present when it was conferred.[76] A new phase began with Boniface IX and his desperate need for more income during the papal Schism.[77] Both claimants to the papacy wanted to try to keep up appearances and their governments were running on income now split two ways. Then after the end of the Schism the system of sale of offices continued and it was expanded in the course of the fifteenth century to include *abbreviatores* and then new 'colleges' of venal offices.[78]

The very word 'venal' has distinctly pejorative connotations and indeed the sale of offices is indeed usually presented in an entirely negative light.[79] The need for money up front was certainly the motive for the system, but historians and anthropologists have learned to distinguish motives from functions, and to realise that some practices survive because they have consequences, perhaps unintended, conducive to the working of the broader system to which they belong. That insight may be applicable here. The survival for a lengthy period of the sale of offices system not only at the papal curia but in other European governments[80] should lead one to ask whether it was really as absurd as it seems on the surface.

Crucially, the system helped to build up an implicit alliance between the papacy and notable families in Italy.[81] In the fourteenth century, the papal curia had left for Avignon because Italy had become too hot for it to

---

[76] Schwarz, *Die Organisation*, 167–185; for descriptions of the system see also Frenz, *Die Kanzlei*, 193–198, Frenz and Pagano, *I Documenti*, 69; Partner, *The Pope's Men*, index s. v. 'offices, venal'.

[77] Schwarz, *Die Organisation*, 181.   [78] Partner, *The Pope's Men*, 12.

[79] For a recent assessment, see M. Pattenden, *Electing the Pope in Early Modern Italy, 1450–1700* (Oxford, 2017), 221–228. The elision from venal office to 'benefices' on p. 228 might need re-thinking, if only in terms of clarity of language. According to Pattenden (223) interest was paid on the capital 'invested' in the office; if so, this was a change from the system of sale of offices described by Frenz, *Die Kanzlei*, 184. Pattenden's book is much broader in scope than its title suggests: it argues for a (very negative) interpretation of the papacy in the period covered.

[80] Frenz, *Die Kanzlei*, 193 note 1, with further references.

[81] Partner, *The Pope's Men*, 17–18; Pattenden, *Electing*, 224–225. Note his pertinent comment, at 225, that 'by increasing the proportion of elites who were net financial

handle, after a couple of centuries of shaky relations. Over the course of the period from the fifteenth to the eighteenth centuries, by contrast, a multitude of capillary connections between the curia and Italian families had developed. This surely helped to cement a stable socio-political base in an uncertain world of reformations and religious wars – a base perhaps more stable than at any point since the disruptions of the 'papal turn'.[82]

If sale of offices was absurd, so too are the national debts accumulated by modern governments when they issue bonds. Almost unimaginable amounts of debt were created in this way during the Covid crisis of 2020. Yet government borrowing was generally regarded as the only responsible course of action. Furthermore, if we regard venal offices as quasi-bonds, they did have an advantage over modern government bonds. If not sold within 20 days of the holder's death,[83] they reverted to the papacy and could be sold again. Frenz gives some statistics: 38 per cent of offices vacated by death against 62 per cent by 'resignation'.[84] The latter included promotions.[85] If you were made a bishop or cardinal, you had to surrender benefices, though not every category (notably, you could remain a *secretarius*); the popes seem to have been able to resell benefices vacated by promotion.[86] The proportion returning to the pope is actually rather high. Moreover, even if the office was resold, the pope took a fee.[87]

Another advantage over bonds as we know them is that some of the holders of most categories of office did actually do some work, unlike modern bond investors. Sale of offices may have created a superfluity of civil servants, but that did mean that the administration did not need to be understaffed. Furthermore, even if office holders were under-employed,[88] the fact that they had a job with status must have been a non-negligible attraction to most. To be one of 'the pope's men', with a role in the world, and to be part of a college with the sociability that this implied, must have been preferable, for many, to hanging around in the parental home and looking like a waste of space. As noted above, colleges were religious confraternities, with their own chaplains; a certain

---

beneficiaries of papal activity, they [i.e. popes] simuiltaneously reduced the incentives for those elites to resist the exercise of papal prerogatives'.

[82] 'Vista nell'ottica tutta cittadina, l'età della riforma rappresenta indubbiamente un lungo momento di difficoltà … La turbolenza e il disordine misero in discussione istituzioni e pratiche consolidate … La nascita del comune è una sorta di risposta a questa perdurante fase di instabilità.' S. Tognetti review of C. Wickham, *Roma medievale. Crisi e stabilità di una città, 900–1150*, transl. A. Fiore and L. Provero (Rome, 2013) in *Archivio Storico Italiano* 172 (2014), 355–359, at 358.

[83] Frenz and Pagano, *I Documenti*, 69   [84] Frenz, *Die Kanzlei*, 195.
[85] *Ibid.*, 195 note 16.   [86] *Ibid.*, 194.   [87] Partner, *The Pope's Men*, 199.
[88] Frenz, *Die Kanzlei*, 184 at note 7, 191.

solidarity was part of the system, and there was all the comfort of belonging to a status group; members heard mass together and attended each other's funerals. They wore prescribed clothing. Within reason, most people are happier with some work to do and a sense of belonging. We will see that the college of the *scriptores brevium* established in 1503, with its 81 'saleable vacatable (i.e. re-saleable) offices' was one of the engines of the administration after Trent.

Early modern papal documents

While nobody would pretend that medieval papal Diplomatics is a subject for those who 'require to be tempted to the study of truth',[89] it is impressively well researched. The preceding pages are studded with footnotes to works on the highest level of scholarship, and other studies equally impressive have been omitted because there is simply too much to pack in. It is not that the last word has been said even by the excellent textbooks and other studies; in the present volume I have tried to add something by clarifying the distinction between what was routine and relatively simple, on the one hand, and, on the other, the elaborate procedures for documents where more was at stake. The foregoing analyses have aimed to give a fuller answer to 'Hageneder's question', and to explain how the institution coped with the pressure of business. But the answers were for the most part already to be found, even if sometimes well hidden, within the existing scholarly literature.

All that changes when we turn to the post-medieval period. For that period there seems to be a shortage of scholarship on the path of a document through the system – the *Geschäftsgang* – and its relation to the existing records of the Vatican Archives. Spadework that a medievalist takes for granted has hardly even been attempted. A few scholars such as K. A. Fink, Thomas Frenz, and Lajos Pásztor have broken some of the ground. But over large areas the surface has barely been scratched. In general, the state of research is sad when compared with the immense achievements of medieval scholars working on papal documents and Diplomatics.

The scale of the task yet to be tackled is revealed by a glance at the list of 'Series Containing Records Created from 1501–1600' in a guide to the

---

[89] 'The History of Institutions cannot be mastered, – can scarcely be approached, – without an effort. It affords little of the romantic incident or of the picturesque grouping which constitute the charm of History in general, and holds out small temptation to the mind that requires to be tempted to the study of Truth' (W. Stubbs, *The Constitutional History of England. Its Origin and Development*, i (Oxford, 1875), iii).

Vatican Archives.[90] It is very long, though it includes older series that continued to generate documents. There can be no question of doing justice to this wealth of material. Consequently, the final sections of this survey will be both more original and at the same time more provisional, and indeed less secure – for want of good guides and maps of the territory. For sure, this initial sketch map will be replaced eventually by precision cartography; but a start has to be made. The analyses that will follow get technical, and not every reader, even early modernists, will want or need to follow all the details. Two things may be said in defence of the technicality. First, if you want to assess a car, observing the road-handling and bodywork is not enough: you need to look under the bonnet and understand the engine. Secondly, the huge scale on which early modern records were generated by the papacy was in part a result of continued demand for responses, and the Diplomatics of these records shows how the *curia* coped.

One may begin with the series of documents linked to the consistory of cardinals,[91] since it straddles the late medieval and post-medieval periods. *Arch. Concist., Acta Camerarii* contains 'official notes of questions treated in secret, public or semi-public meetings of the Consistory, and in "general" or "particular" assemblies'.[92] 'Much of the business is financial and relates to the provision of major benefices controlled by the College of Cardinals and the allotment of pensions or subventions.'[93] *Arch. Concist., Acta Misc.* give information on provisions to benefices and 'sometimes serve as a diary of the curia'.[94] *Arch. Concist., Acta Vicecanc.* 'consists of the vice-chancellor's minutes of consistorial business'.[95] These series are important for understanding the movers and shakers of papal policy.

Segreteria di Stato and Epistolae ad principes

What would eventually become the most powerful instrument of papal policy, the *Segreteria di Stato*, seems to have its origin in the creation by Leo X in 1513 of the *secretarius intimus*, later called the *secretarius status*,[96]

---

[90] Blouin et al., *Vatican Archives*, 546–551.

[91] *Indice dei Fondi … dell'Archivio Apostolico Vaticano*, 20–21, with subseries listed; Boyle, *Survey*, 80–83; Pásztor, *Guida*, 130–133, 135–136 (very important for the prosopography of the episcopate), 136–142.

[92] Boyle, *Survey*, 81.

[93] Blouin et al., *Vatican Archives*, 30, with a reference to B. M. Hallman, *Italian Cardinals, Reform, and the Church as Property* (Berkeley, CA, 1985).

[94] Boyle, *Survey*, 82.   [95] Blouin et al., *Vatican Archives*, 31.

[96] Frenz, *Die Kanzlei*, 180; Boyle, *Survey*, 69; P. Richard, 'Origines et développement de la Secrétairerie d'État Apostolique (1417–1823) (Suite) (1)', *Revue d'histoire ecclésiastique*, 11 (1910), 505–529, at 505–507.

a secretary with special responsibility for diplomatic relations conducted in Italian. Latin was used, however, for an administrative organ that was formally part of the *Segreteria di Stato* until 1678, when it was formally devolved from it, namely the Secretariate *Epistolae ad principes*.[97] The letters emanating from it are addressed to cardinals, bishops and nuncios as well as to princes, and the series also contains incoming mail. The series is important for the history of ecclesiastical politics and has been much studied.[98]

A vast range of subseries in the Vatican Archives are associated with the *Segreteria di Stato* (many of them of course relating to periods later than the one that concerns us).[99] Among them are records of nunciatures.

Nunciature

Nunciature documents are among the most important (and well studied). They are at the opposite end of the spectrum of papal Diplomatics from the routine procedures with which we have been principally concerned. In 1513 Leo X set up what was in effect a permanent embassy, 'nunciature', in Vienna, and others followed in the sixteenth and seventeenth centuries.[100] Nuncios corresponded regularly with the 'Secretariate of State';[101] records deriving from this Secretariate, those relating to nuncios and much more, are voluminous and of key importance for the post-medieval history of the papacy in its more political

---

[97] Fink, *Das Vatikanische Archiv*, 79: 'Es entwickelte sich im Zusammenhang mit dem Staatssekretariat, von dem es aber im Jahre 1678 durch Innozenz XI. getrennt wurde unter Erhebung zu einer selfständigen Behörde'. In the Vatican Archives their designation for purposes of ordering documents is *Ep. ad Princ.* According to Boyle, *Survey*, 67, 'This Secretariate was founded in the pontificate of Paul IV (1559–1565).' Boyle notes, *ibid.*, that the series is to be distinguished from the '*Brevia ad Principes et alios viros* (*Arm.* XLIV–XLV) instituted by Leo X in the Apostolic Secretariate, in that their style is less pompous than that of the *Brevia*, and that, unlike Briefs in general, they were not sealed with the Ring of the Fisherman. They did not ... replace the *Brevia ad Principes*, but rather ran parallel to them. In effect, the *Epistolae* were used for routine letters in Latin, while the *Brevia* were reserved for special occasions.'

[98] Fink, *Das Vatikanische Archiv*, 79.

[99] *Indice dei Fondi ... dell'Archivio Apostolico Vaticano*. Page numbers are liable to change as the electronic version is updated on the AAV website, but the main series can be easily identified by the title written first in the normal way and then vertically from top to bottom in the left-hand margin, while the subseries have their own indented headings in heavy red type. They are called up under 'Secr. Stato', followed by the subseries name and document: e.g. *Secr. Stato, Cardinali,* [then the relevant document number].

[100] Boyle, *Survey*, 75, with bibliography. For *nuntii* in the later Middle Ages see the recent thesis by A. Zielinska, 'Territorialization, the Papacy, and the Institutions of the Polish Church, 1198–1357' (PhD thesis, University College London, 2021).

[101] Boyle, *Survey*, 76.

aspects.[102] This was arguably a spin off from the fifteenth-century system of *secretarii*,[103] but if so it evolved into a distinct institution staffed by men who did not belong to the college of secretaries and were adept at drafting documents in Italian, which became the normal language for diplomatic correspondence with nuncios.[104]

The system relying on Italian takes off under Leo X (1513–1521), who put a cousin in charge of vernacular diplomatic correspondence.[105] Peter Partner argues that this system

> pointed towards the development, later in the century, of the secretariat of the papal cardinal-nephew ... These discontinuities in the history of the papal secretariat are minimized by its historians, but they are of the first importance in assessing its early modern growth. If there was a revolution in government in the papal secretariat of the sixteenth century, it is to be connected, not with the impersonal power of the papacy, but with the change to the use of Italian in papal political correspondence, and with the power assumed by the papal relatives in controlling this correspondence ... In the end the history of the papal secretariat illustrates the flexibility of monarchic power, and its ability to transform institutions according to its needs, and not the steady growth of a modernising institution.[106]

The system of putting the Secretariate of State in the hands of a cardinal-nephew means that the family papers of great Roman families also have much relevant material.[107] The Vatican Archives has a rich collection of such papers, which show the cardinal-nephews in action.[108]

---

[102] For archival series deriving from the Secretatiate of State's activity, see Archivio Apostolico Vaticano, *Indice dei Fondi ... dell'Archivio Apostolico Vaticano* (2022), main headings in red *Armadio XLVI–XLIX*; *Armadio LX–LXI*; *Miscellanea [Armadi I–XV]*; *Segreteria di Stato* (heading written, as noted above, both in the normal way at the head of the list of indented subseries, and then also vertically in the left-hand margin of the *Indice*; the *Indice de Fondi* should be supplemented by Pásztor, *Guida*, especially 73–87, 94–95, Boyle, *Survey*, 70–78, and Blouin et al., *Vatican Archives*, 178–212, for some idea of their rich contents, including nuncio material (198–207). For specific treatment of nuncio records see L. E. Halkin, *Les Archives de Nonciatures* (Bibliothèque de l'Institut Historique Belge de Rome, 14; Brussels, 1968). Halkin gives a fine bibliography which shows that 'les nonciatures du XVIe siècle ont fait l'objet d'études nombreuses et copieuses', though subsequent records are not well explored (*ibid.*, 26). He cautions against any idea of publishing all the documents *in extenso* (80). Halkin notes that his survey does not take account of the records of the Congregations (27 note 1).

[103] Frenz and Pagano, *I Documenti*, 34.

[104] Partner, *The Pope's Men*, 43; Boyle, *Survey*, 69.   [105] Partner, *The Pope's Men*, 43–44.

[106] Partner, *The Pope's Men*, 44 – perhaps an implicit criticism of P. Prodi, *Il Sovrano Pontefice: un corpo e due anime: la monarchia papale nella prima età moderna* (Bologna, 1982)?

[107] Which I confess I have not explored.

[108] See Boyle, *Survey*, section on 'Archives of Cardinal-Nephews and of Former Papal Families', 73–74, and *Indice dei Fondi ... dell'Archivio Apostolico Vaticano*, main headings in red, in the alphabetical list, *Carte Farnesiane* and *Fondo Borghese, Serie I–V*.

Focus on the foregoing series can leave the impression that the early modern papacy was all about politics and emoluments of office. The impression is corrected by attention to more routine governance, but the latter remains to a remarkable extent *terra incognita* for the 'post-Renaissance' period. A key innovation during and after the Council of Trent was the creation of a system of Congregations. There was overlap between the cardinals on the various Congregations – 'Congregation' could almost be translated as 'Committee' – and some overlap between their areas of competence also. For instance there was a Congregation for 'bishops and religious orders', Congr. Vescovi e Regolari, with numerous subseries,[109] but the Congregation of the Council too dealt with exemption issues. The relation between the many sub-systems of early modern papal government is one of the many topics requiring investigation. I would suggest that the hypothesis holding the field should be that we have an interesting mixture between Weber's three types of government: patrimonial, bureaucratic, and charismatic. The 'office charisma' of the pope kept everything together. The systems respected canon law, as anyone who has looked inside the massive *buste* of documents knows, and aimed at consistency, so to that extent they approximate to the bureaucratic model. But the patrimonial authority of the pope meant that the division of labour between different congregations, and the congregations and the Apostolic Penitentiary come to that, was far from clear cut.

These two key Congregations, of the Council and of the Inquisition, will be discussed in more detail below. Scholars are well aware of the creation of the Congregations as a revolution in papal administration, though how they actually worked in practice or what they did in detail is not easy to discover in standard works.

There is a lot of uncertainty about the administrative staffing of these Congregations. My own guess would be that the cardinal in charge paid his personal staff. From this point of view, and generally, the Congregation of the Inquisition[110] and the Congregation of the Council are the best studied, and these have a special claim on the attention of historians. The work done so far is of high quality but it is only a beginning and has not yet found its way into the general scholarly consciousness.

[109] *Indice dei Fondi ... dell'Archivio Apostolico Vaticano*, main heading in the alphabetical list (written in red vertically in left-hand margin) *Congregazioni Romani*, subheading *Vescovi e Regolari*; Pásztor, *Guida*, 156–161.
[110] Ugo Baldini informs me that the Congregation of the Inquisition had income from property (personal communication). I do not know how the property was acquired.

Routine administration outside the Congregations

Standard works have even less to say, however, on the early modern continuation of themes whose medieval history has been sketched above: the *Geschäftsgang*, the passage of a document through the administration, and the relation of those processes to the record series in the Vatican Archives.[111] To reconstruct this on the basis of records as now arranged would be near impossible, but if inferences from the current series in the Vatican Archives are combined with early modern treatises on curial systems, some clarity begins to emerge. For the analysis which follows, the following have proved particularly helpful:[112]

- British Library MS Egerton 2210: Instruttioni di Dataria e Cancellaria, fo. 1r–106r (index fo. 107r–111v); fo. 112r–163r 'Relatione della corte di Roma et del suo governo con riti, ordini, e precedenze che in essa si osservano'; fo. 163v–182r: long lists of offices and prices (perhaps part of the 'Relatione');
- British Library MS Stowe 379: 'Tractatus de praxi Romanæ Curiæ';
- Johannes Baptista De Luca, *Relatio Curiae Romanae* (Cologne, 1683) British Library call number 5051. aa. 26 (henceforth De Luca, *Relatio*).

A key to the complexity is this: apart from the Congregations (which appear to have had their own scribes – paid for by the relevant cardinal?), documents were written either by the Chancery *scriptores* or by the *scriptores brevium*: so there are thinking departments serviced by two writing departments, with a complicated division of labour, to produce the actual letters. Whether emanating from the *Dataria*, or from the *Secretaria Brevium*, letters to be sent as briefs would be actually written by the college of the *scriptores brevium*. There seems to have been a lot of overlap between the *Dataria* and the *Secretaria Brevium*, and also

---

[111] I have looked in vain in M. Rosa, *La Curia Romana nell'età moderna. Istituzioni, cultura, carriere* (Rome, 2013), though it is a good general history of the curia. Very useful though is T. Frenz, 'Die "Computi" in der Serie der Brevia Lateranensia im Vatikanischem Archiv', *Quellen und Forschungen aus Italienischen Archiven und Bibliotheken*, 55/56 (1976), 251–275.

[112] Other sources worth exploring are BL Add MS 8468 Treatise on the Sacra Rota Romana, late seventeenth century, by Jacob Eimerix de Mathiis (1626–1696), 'who was auditor of the Rota from 1668 ...' (BL electronic catalogue); BL Add MS 8466, c. 1611: excerpts from Rules of Apostolic Chancery; Hunobaldus Plettenbergius, *Notitia Congregationum et Tribunalium Curiae Romanae* (Hildesheim, 1693) (available online); Thomas De Rosa, *Tractatus De executoribus litterarum apostolicarum* (Venice, 1697)(available online); Octavianus Vestrius, *In Romanae Aulae Actionem ... Introductio* (Venice, 1573), BL call number 1606/1424; Theodor van Meyden, *Tractatus de officio et jurisdictione Datarii, et de sylo Datarii* (Venice, 1654).

uncertainty over which the *magister brevium* belonged to (perhaps his primary role was to represent the college of *scriptores brevium* to both the *Secretaria Brevium* and the *Dataria*).[113] But the business of those two organs ended up with the *scriptores brevium*.

The Chancery was doing less thinking than its output might lead one to imagine. From the mid-sixteenth century in fact the Chancery's importance diminished considerably: it expedited only a modest proportion of papal letters, including those that it sent as a 'front' for the Penitentiary.[114] That arrangement can only be investigated here in a preliminary way but, to put it in a nutshell, there is reason to think that, for a range of business, the writing was done in the Chancery after the thinking had been done in the Penitentiary, the continuing, behind-the-scenes role of which in this area easily passes unnoticed.

The Penitentiary after Trent

What existing 'maps' of post-Trent papal governance tell us is that in 1569 the personnel of the Penitentiary was drastically cut – e.g. from 24 *scriptores* to two, and that all 'external forum' business (e.g. marriage dispensations when there was no need for secrecy) was removed from the Penitentiary, theoretically leaving it to concentrate only on the internal forum – confessional matters.[115] It is possible to add something to this understanding of both external and internal forum business.

In accordance with the decision to restrict the Penitentiary to internal forum business, proctors and *scriptores* previously belonging to the Penitentiary were transferred to the Chancery, as was the power to grant graces with implications for both *fora*, i.e. relating to the external forum of public ecclesiastical law as well as the internal forum of conscience: *in utroque foro*.[116] In the Middle Ages, the Penitentiary's dispensations to marry within forbidden degrees, or to become a priest despite

---

[113] Cf. Frenz, *Die Kanzlei*, 179. In the eighteenth century Benedict XIV attempted to rationalise the divison of labour between them: see Pásztor, *Guida*, 113–114.

[114] 'Ipso saec. XV momentum cancellariae decrescere coepit, ita ut a secunda medietate saec. XVI cancellaria ad merum officium technicum expeditionis exiguae partis documentorum pontificiorum reduceretur' (Rabikauskas, *Diplomatica Pontificia*, 102).

[115] A. Saraco, *La Penitenzieria Apostolica. Storia di un Tribunale di misericordia e di pietà* (Vatican City, 2011), 31. The opening of the post-Trent archive of the *Penitenzieria* has been a great stimulus to historical research: see notably A. Saraco, ed., *La Penitenzieria Apostolica e il suo Archivio. Atti della Giornata di Studio ... 18 novembre 2011* (Vatican City, 2012), and K. Nykiel and U. Taraborrelli, eds., *L'Archivio della Penitenzieria Apostolica. Stato Attuale e Prospettive Future* (Vatican City, 2017).

[116] This probably increased the administrative cost, as Chancery letters were more expensive: cf. Müller, 'Price of a Papal Pardon', 474.

'irregularities' such as a bodily deformity, would hold up with bishops or in ecclesiastical courts. So would its absolutions from excommunication.

Did the Penitentiary have nothing more to do with any of this after the big reform? Would it be the pope's own job from then on to make many of the decisions previously taken by the Penitentiary?[117] If that was the intention, it was surely quite unrealistic, so we should question whether that really was the plan. Those who have worked on the vast series of huge volumes of Penitentiary registers from the pre-Trent period may well wonder how the pope could possibly have handled all the extra work.

Theoretically, the workload should have been drastically reduced by the Council of Trent's legislation. Trent tried to reduce access to dispensations for marriage within forbidden degrees. They could be granted *gratis* to those who entered into marriage in the proper form and subsequently discovered an impediment. Otherwise, they should not be granted at all, or only rarely and for a reason.[118] So there may have been a hope that the flood of dispensations would turn into a trickle and not take up too much of the Chancery's time. As with Lateran IV's rules, this was unrealistically rigorous. Nobody by this time thought that the forbidden degree rules were theological absolutes, and practical considerations pressed hard. So the path to dispensations continued to be well-trodden.

That brings us back to the question of whether the pope actually did attempt this impossible task. Probably not. We do not know for sure, but there are indications that there was nothing so simple as a lock, stock and barrel transfer of business from Penitentiary to Chancery and pope. The evidence is partly inference from the eighteenth century. The next big reform of the Penitentiary was in 1744, by Benedict XIV. The good short history of the Penitentiary by a former archivist, Alessandro Saraco, tells us that Benedict XIV wanted to limited the Penitentiary to the internal forum.[119] But that had supposedly happened with the 1569 reform! The inference is that there must have been external forum business in the period between the two reforms. That may have been because of a partial reversal by Urban VIII in 1634 of the 1569 change.[120] In any case, the 1744 reform left (rather than gave, one may assume) the *Penitentiarius maior* a significant amount of jurisdiction *in utroque foro*.

---

[117] Saraco, *La Penitenzieria Apostolica. Storia*, 32–33.

[118] Council of Trent, Sessio XXIV, De Reform. Matrimonii, C. V, F. Von Schulte and E. L. Richter, eds., *Canones et Decreta Concilii Tridentini … accedunt S. Congr. Card. Conc. Trid. Interpretum Declarationes ac Resolutiones* (Leipzig, 1853), 219.

[119] Saraco, *La Penitenzieria Apostolica. Storia*, 37.

[120] H. C. Lea, *A Formulary of the Papal Penitentiary in the Thirteenth Century* (Philadelphia, PA, 1892), xxix.

An early modern account of how the *curia* worked (De Luca's *Relatio*) gives further and more direct evidence that the Penitentiary continued to do external as well as internal forum business: absolutions from censures and from some irregularities (irregularities were defects which were not sins but nevertheless normally a bar to the priesthood – a major disfigurement of blindness in one eye for instance), alongside strictly internal forum (confessional) business. Furthermore, some briefs, *brevia*, which dealt with confessional and some external forum business may have been dispatched by the *scriptores* of the Penitentiary itself, since they had a different form, and seal, from other briefs.[121]

That is only part of the story, however, for there is also reason to think that, as suggested above, the Penitentiary did the thinking part of some of the kind of business which it had conducted before the 1569 reform, while the Chancery took care of the mechanical task of expediting the documents. I think it possible that this was the case even before Urban VIII's intervention in 1634, though the whole subject needs more research. There are strong indications that the Penitentiary continued to be involved behind the scenes in external forum marriage dispensations in remote degrees (i.e. in the more routine cases). It looks as though Penitentiary proctors dealt with such dispensations intellectually, so to speak, but did not actually issue them formally. The agency that received documents, drafted or at least assessed by Penitentiary proctors, but not formally within the Penitentiary's purview, would be the Chancery. Thus, the documents and the registers of them are formally speaking Chancery not Penitentiary – though, and this is important, the fees go to the Penitentiary. This half-responsibility for some dispensations produced an income stream that helped support the Penitentiary staff.[122]

---

[121] 'Adhibetur etiam in Curia vocabulum brevium in illis expeditionibus, quas ut plurimum pro foro interno, ac etiam pro externo pro absolutionibus, a censuris, & ab aliquibus irregularitatibus, concedit Tribunal Poenitentiariae, sed istae expeditiones longe diversam habent formam [from other briefs], diversumque sigillum, adeo ut redoleant diversitatem notoriam *infra. disc.* 12' (Johannes Baptista De Luca, Relatio Curiae Romanae (Cologne, 1683), Disc VII.12, p. 59).

[122] For the foregoing see De Luca, *Relatio*: he suggests that the Penitentiary did do the thinking for letters which would be dispatched by the Chancery: '... circa minores dispensationes matrimoniales, super remotioribus gradibus, quae expediuntur in Cancellaria Apostolica, per illos Procuratores Poenitentiariae, quorum officium quoque ad instar aliorum, est venale, illaque modica emolumenta, quae pro huiusmodi dispensationibus solvuntur, destinata sunt sustentationi ipsius Poenitentiarii, eiusque ministrorum, et officialium, de quibus infra, qui regunt hoc Tribunale fori interni seu poenitentialis' (De Luca, *Relatio*, Disc. XII: 5–6, p. 86); also British Library MS Stowe 379, Tractatus de praxi Romanae Curiae: 'Magnus Poenitentiarius cognovit de materiis quae spectant ad forum poenitentiale, veluti de quibusdam absolutionibus, et aliis materiis quae ad poenitentiarium mittuntur; absolutiones tamen quae a Papa obtinentur, quamvis sint tantum sub simplici

To unpack this: on the one hand, one may infer that the fees for copying now went to the Chancery *scriptores*, so that the *Registra matrimonialium* now in Penitentiary archive would be, accordingly, formally speaking Chancery records or, if not, at least a record of minutes sent on to the Chancery. (That remains to be verified.) The fees, however, that – with other kinds of business – would go to remunerate the *abbreviatores* for their labour[123] would be passed on instead to Penitentiary staff. An analogy which may help explain how these fees were reconciled with the Council of Trent's requirement that dispensations be granted *gratis* is the system of court costs in modern Common Law jurisdictions, which do not sell justice but do routinely expect the litigants to pick up the cost of administering it, not to mention paying their lawyers, the counterparts of proctors at the curia. For the end user, it does not feel as if justice is free.

After the 1569 reform the harder-to-get dispensations for closer degrees, e.g. between uncle and niece, may have by-passed the Penitentiary altogether. Even in these cases the substantive change cannot have been so great as first appears. In the Middle Ages also, in really close forbidden degree cases, the *penitentiarius maior* would have had to consult the pope. At any time, dispensations normally[124] belonged to the public world of the external forum.

What of the internal forum proper in the post-Trent period? It has been possible to find out much more about the Penitentiary's internal forum thanks to the opening of the post-Trent part of the Penitentiary archive in 2011.[125] The evidence is a little later than one would like.[126] There was a box in which petitions would be placed. They would be identified by a motto, not by the supplicant's name. If you (or, presumably, your proctor) wanted to find out what progress had been made, there was a place and times (Monday and Friday after lunch) where the Penitentiary proctors (to be distinguished from proctors of penitents)

signatura expeditae, sunt tamen potiores ipsis quae ab ipso poenitentiario conceduntur, licet in charta mem-//fo. 2r/-brana, et cum sigillo expediantur' (fo. 1v–2r).
[123] Tangl, *Die päpstlichen Kanzleiordnungen*, 94–101.
[124] If for some reason the marriage or the impediment could not be made public, that might take the case out of the external forum.
[125] I am extremely grateful to the then Archivist Mons. Alessandro Saraco and to Dr. Ugo Taraborrelli for making this new archive an ideal space for research.
[126] A key source is V. Mangioni, S.J. (1573–1660), 'Methodus expedita Supplicandi in Sacra Poenitentiaria', Archivio della Penitenzieria Apostolica, Miscellanea 'Mangioni', ed. D. L. d'Avray, 'La Penitenzieria nel Seicento: Attività e Prassi', in Nykiel and Taraborrelli, *L'Archivio della Penitenzieria Apostolica*, 165–172, at 170–172. It complements the account, printed in *ibid.*, 168–170, in Plettenberg, *Notitia*: see below.

could be found, and a book where one could find the name of the
Penitentiary proctor handling one's case. A complementary source (in
print, not from the archive) tells us what a penitent and his or her
confessor needed to do, giving a diplomatic of the letter to the
Penitentiary – the assumption is that the petitioner is far from Rome.[127]

The *iter* of marriage dispensations

As just noted, the Penitentiary had nothing to do even behind the scenes
with dispensations for marriages within close degrees, nor was the
Chancery the relevant writing office. These dispensations were dispatched by the *Secretaria apostolica* – with *scriptores brevium* doing the
writing. They were sent closed, as briefs, whereas dispensations for more
remote degrees were sent by the Chancery as letters patent – open
letters.[128] There is a logic here. More discretion might be called for when
close relatives were getting married – their relation would not necessarily
be public knowledge where they lived.

One may imagine that the sequence was this: a supplication for a
marriage dispensation would go to the *Signatura gratiae*,[129] which had
been turned into a Congregation of Cardinals by Sixtus V;[130] then it
would be sent to the *Dataria* to be dated, and then registered in the
Register of Supplications, which had its own administrative personnel
including scribes.[131] At that point it is possible that its future path would
be determined by an official in the *Dataria* called the *Revisore di
matrimoniali*;[132] alternatively, the decision may have been made by a
referendarius in the *Signatura gratiae*.

---

[127] Plettenberg, *Notitia*, in d'Avray, 'La Penitenzieria', 168–170.
[128] Frenz, 'Die "Computi"', 260.
[129] On the *Signatura gratiae* see De Luca, *Relatio*, Discursus XXX, pp. 155–165.
[130] Frenz, 'Die "Computi"', 260.   [131] Frenz, *Die Kanzlei*, 100.
[132] 'Della Dataria. Vi e anco la Dataria la quale si bene e officio ammovibile non di meno
stimatissimo fra tutti gli altri, essendo solito darsi dal papa a prelati di valore et alle volte
da molti anni inqua si da a Cardinali per le mani del quale passono le vacanze di tutti li
beneficii che non esprimono di maggior valore //fo. 133v/ che di 24 ducati annui ...'
(British Library Egerton MS 2210, fo. 133r–v). More follows on his (considerable)
power over benefices, then more on day to day activity, but note the following passage
'Ha un altro officiale detto Revisore di matrimoniali //fo. 135r/ il quale non ha altra cura
che di fare segnare tutte le suppliche sopra dispense in gradi di consanguinità e d'affinità
et di scommuniche ad revelationes chiamati "Significavit"' (British Library Egerton MS
2210, fo. 134v–135r). Then on the office as a whole: 'Di tutti li sopradetti officiali che
ha ha sotto di se il datario, non ci è alcuno, che compri il suo officio, senon quello delle
componende, essendo gli altri eletti dal Datario, eccetto il Sotto datario che si elegge da
sua Santita ...' (British Library Egerton MS 2210, fo. 135r).

If the request was for a routine marriage dispensation, it would be passed semi-informally to the Penitentiary, whose officials would draft a dispensation and send it on to the Chancery, which would produce the letter. It would be registered either in the *Reg. Lat.* series[133] or in the series of registers currently held in the Archive of the Penitentiary, or perhaps in both. (I suggested above that the *Registra matrimonialium* now in Penitentiary archive were of the minutes sent on to the Chancery, but all this remains to be elucidated. Nobody has investigated whether the same cases appear in both.) If the petition was for a hard-to-get dispensation, for marriage within close degrees, it would go back to the *Signatura gratiae* where it would be discussed; the pope would need to approve the decision or give one; then the dispensation would be sent to the *Secretaria apostolica* to be written as a closed brief, and registered in what is now the *Sec. Brev., Reg.* series in the Vatican Archives (or so a cursory sounding suggests to me).

The *Sec. Brev., Reg.* series and the *Dataria Ap., Brev Lat.* series

The relation of the *Sec. Brev., Reg.*, series and the *Dataria Ap., Brev Lat.* series has not been worked out, so far as I can discover. If so this is yet another example of the pitiful state[134] of early modern papal Diplomatics. There is the usual problem of relating archival series to institutions. I tentatively propose the following hypothesis, invoking the distinction between thinking departments and 'writing pools'. The thinking department behind the *Sec. Brev., Reg.* would be the *Secretaria brevium*, Secretariat of Briefs, while the thinking department behind the *Dataria Ap., Brev Lat.* department would be, obviously, the Datary. The content of the letters emerging from both 'thinking departments' overlaps. Furthermore the archival series in which both were registered were the work of the same 'writing pool' of secretaries, who had also written the letters sent out. Rather as with the Carabinieri and the Polizia in modern Italy, this writing pool co-existed in a complicated division of labour with the other great writing pool, the Chancery. An example of the complication is that the Datary could send letters to either writing pool, depending on content and function.

---

[133] Frenz, 'Die "Computi"', 260.
[134] Again one would need to single out a few honourable exceptions, notably Thomas Frenz.

The division of labour between Chancery and *Secretaria apostolica*

The desirability of confidentiality may explain why the *scriptores brevium* were assigned dispensations for close degrees. Perhaps it was more customary for them to write closed letters. Another reason might be that such dispensations tended to be granted to important people.[135] For letters on major matters to important people, the *secretarius brevium* and his *scriptores* seem to have been preferred, and especial care was taken to ensure that the genuineness of such letters was verifiable by checking in the archives.[136]

When it came to other less sensitive matters, however, it looks as though the order was reversed and that it was the Chancery that got the more important business. We know that the officials of the Chancery met three times a week in the vice-chancellor's palace, presumably to discuss these weighter matters.[137] They included provisions to metropolitan and episcopal sees, benefices of the secular clergy and some pertaining to religious orders (perhaps abbacies etc.), the sale of offices in the Roman curia, dispensations to allow men who were 'irregular' (because twice married or married to a widow or illegitimate)[138] to hold benefices and offices and other revenue-producing ecclesiastical posts, and

---

[135] For the rationality behind this, see d'Avray, *Papacy, Monarchy, and Marriage*, 215–216.

[136] 'Cumque (ut praemissum est) per dictum Secretarium Brevium maiora, et graviora negotia Papalia expediantur, ipsaque brevia, aliud non habent signum authentici, nisi subscriptionem Secretarii et impressionem dicti sigilli piscatorii in cera rubea, de facili delebili, vel amovibili; Hinc, pro certitudine expeditionis, bene provisum est, non solum cum registratione in libris seu registris, diligenter tentis, & custoditis (ut etiam fit de aliis literis Cancellariae, sub plumbo), sed //p. 60/ cum minutis seu matricibus subscriptis manu ipsius Papae, quae per Secretarium conservantur, pro eius indemnitate, ac etiam pro certificatione veritatis gratiae, atque pariter suis statutis temporibus, in Archivio Apostolico diligenter custodiuntur' (De Luca, *Relatio*, Disc. VII.15, pp. 59–60). If I understand this correctly, a 'belt and braces' approach was adopted: the letters were registered like those of the Chancery, but the drafts (*minutis*) of the letters too were kept in the Apostolic Archive, which here seems to be treated as distinct from the registers.

[137] 'Hoggi l'officio di V Cancelliere [Cancelliero *ms.?*] frutta da 1400 in 1600 scudi l'anno, la giurisdittione del quale e sopra lespiditioni delle lettere Apostoliche di tutte le materie, le suppliche delle quali //fo. 122r/ sono signate dal Papa, eccetto quelle che si-/-spediscono per breve sub anulo Piscatoris, et nel suo Palazzo tre volte la settimana ... si radunano gli officiali della Cancellaria Apostolica ...' (Relatione, British Library Egerton MS 2210, fo. 121v–122r). Further on we read that 'L'officio degl' Abbreviatori e di fare le minute delle Bolle sopra le suppliche gia segnate dal Papa e revidere [reudere *ms.?*] le bolle doppo che sono scritte' (British Library Egerton MS 2210, fo. 122v). For styles of *Dataria* and Chancery and the difficulty of summarising their features, see De Luca, *Relatio*, Discursus IX: 28–29, pp. 71–72.

[138] I suspect that a Chancery dispensation might not be needed if the irregularity was not in the public domain – probably in that case the Penitentiary dealt with it.

'alienations' of Church goods and other property matters worth more than ten gold ducats.[139] The *secretarius brevium* and his college of *scriptores brevium* could deal with alienations worth less than ten ducats in revenue, and dispensations for age, for shortening the prescribed time gaps between different minor and major orders of priesthood, and for illegitimacy so long as the permission was just to receive orders, not a benefice; for that a letter with a leaden seal needed to be dispatched by the Chancery; the office of the *secretarius brevium* could, however, grant indulgences and similar graces.[140] It seems, though, to have dealt with a

[139] 'Per organum huius Secretarii Brevium expediuntur illae literae Apostolicae, quae dicuntur in forma brevis, signatae, cum alias insinuato adeo fiduciario annulo piscatorio, *supra disc. 3*, qui per ipsummet Pontificem, sive per magis intimum, probataeque fidei familiarem cum summa diligentia custoditur, istaque dicuntur literae in forma Brevis, ad differentiam aliarum literarum, quae sub plumbo expediuntur, per organum Cancellariae, ut infra, istaeque vocantur Bullae, pro diversa negotiorum qualitate, quoniam per Cancellariam sub plumbo expediuntur literae provisionum ecclesiarum Metropolitanarum, & Cathedralium, aliarumque dignitatum, & beneficiorum saecularium, & aliquorum Regularium, ac etiam nonnullorum officiorum vacabilium, vel non vacabilium Romanae Curiae; Prout etiam dispensationes matrimoniales, & beneplacita Apostolica super alienationibus, aliisque conventionibus bonorum, & iurium Ecclesiae, quando valor excedat summam seu redditum decem ducatorum auri de camera, & aliquae dispensationes puta super bigamia, vel super publica irregularitate seu legitimis natalibus pro beneficiis, & dignitatibus, aut super pensionibus ecclesiasticis, cum similibus' (De Luca, *Relatio*, Disc. VII.8, p. 58).

[140] 'Per hanc vero Secretariam [brevium], atque per has literas in diversa forma brevis expediuntur dicta beneplacita super alienationibus bonorum Ecclesiae infra dictam summam, decem ducatorum Camerae in reddito, necnon dispensationes super aetate, vel super interstitiis, aut super defectu natalium, promovendorum ad ordines, non autem ad dignitates, & beneficia, cum istae dispensationes super defectu natalium vel ratione bigamiae, aut alterius irregularitatis vel incapacitatis, ut supra, expediri soleant, pariter //col. b/ per cancellariam sub plumbo; Nec non per hanc viam brevis expediuntur indulgentiae & et aliae similes gratiae' (De Luca, *Relatio*, Disc. VII.8, p. 58). Later, after explaining how minutes of briefs dealing with high-level business were kept in the Archives, as well as registered, for purposes of verification and security (De Luca, *Relatio*, Disc. VII.14–15, pp. 59–60), De Luca goes on to clarify that this was not necessary for briefs dealing with minor routine matters: i.e the routine matters which were *less* important than those which the Chancery dealt with: 'Illis forsan gratiis vel brevibus exceptis, quae concedantur super rebus consuetis, modicique momenti, adeo ut pene nemini negentur, unde propterea, generalis commissio seu probata fides Secretarii, ac impressio dicti annuli piscatorii sufficientes videntur, Ut (ex gr.) sunt, brevia super dispensatione interstitiorum pro suscipiendis sacris ordinibus in tribus diebus festivis, aut super dispensatione aetatis tredecim mensium ad suscipiendum ordines sacros, sive quaedam species indulgentiarum quae sub certa forma omnibus conceduntur; Puta pro altari privilegiato in una die hebdomadae, & in octava mortuorum; Aut pro indulgentia plenaria in una tantum solemnitate totius anni alicuius Eccleiae, cum similibus gratiis quae, sub certa & generali formula inalterabili, cuique petenti conceduntur, quoniam, cum fraudis seu falsitatis timor desuper verisimiliter non cadat, idcirco superfluae videntur dictae maiores diligentiae; Potissime ob huiusmodi expeditionum multiplicitatem, magnamque copiam, unde propterea , quando desideretur aliquid speciale & alterativum formulae consuetae,

lower class of business than the Chancery, with the striking exception (as we have just seen) that it dealt with the most important business involving religious politics and diplomacy and (as just noted) the dispensations for close marriages which were traditionally used to end wars and political tensions.[141]

A 'sandwich' system

One can think of the complex relation between the Chancery and its *scriptores*, on the one hand, and the *scriptores brevium* under the *secretarius brevium*, on the other, as a 'sandwich system'. On top, there is delicate high-level business, conducted by closed letters. This came under the *secretarius brevium*. Then there was the upper end of business involving a whole range of matters: property above a certain value, dispensations for illegitimate men to receive benefices, etc. That was Chancery business. Finally, on the lowest tier, the *scriptores brevium* came into their own again, writing letters about property matters below the ten ducat mark, or for dispensations not to hold benefices, but to receive holy orders.

The 'sandwich' pattern sounds strange but it is explicable in the light of the history of papal briefs. The top layer of the 'sandwich' goes back to the early history of briefs, when they were written by secretaries close to the pope for high-level communications on matters of major importance. They seem to have started doing this systematically as a result of the Schism which started in 1378[142] – perhaps too many senior administrators had left Rome with the cardinals who started the Avignon observance.

The bottom layer of the 'sandwich' has its origins around the middle of the fifteenth century, with *brevia communia*, common briefs, which were used for lesser matters and which were attractive because less entangled with red tape than Chancery products.[143] Key milestones are 1487, when 'apostolic secretary' offices were made saleable, and 1503, when *scriptores brevium* were made into a college of saleable offices.[144] The innovations in 1487 and 1503 were motivated of course by the need to raise money, but had the effect of creating an administrative system which had some real advantages for matters not important enough to go through the Chancery, though similar in kind.

---

tunc dictae diligentiae intrant, pro diversa negotiorum qualitate, diversisque stylis, quibus in his materiis deferendum est. / Circa vero emolumenta ...' (De Luca, *Relatio*, Discursus VII.[paragraph number missing], p. 60).

[141] For the records of the Secretariate of Briefs in the Vatican Archives see Blouin et al., *Vatican Archives*, **3.2.11.23**, pp. 173–175.

[142] Frenz, *Die Kanzlei*, 165.   [143] *Ibid.*, 166.   [144] *Ibid.*, 223.

One looks in vain in the scholarly literature for a straightforward analysis of how the administrative structures just described map on to existing series in the Vatican Archives.[145] One should probably think of two 'writing pools': on the one hand, the Chancery scribes continuing a very long tradition and also doing some of the writing that used to be done by Penitentiary scribes, and on the other, a pool of *secretarii*, periodically restructured, the types and stages of whose work is represented by different AAV series. Series revealing the 'work in progress' stage include *Arm. XL–XLIII*, which contain 'corrected drafts of briefs'.[146] The 'outbox' of the *secretarii* would be represented by series like *Dataria Ap., Brev. Lat.* Similarly the *Reg. Lat.* series represents the 'outbox' of the work of the Chancery *scriptores*.

This very tentative rough sketch of the structure needs to be filled out and corrected by more precise research. Were this about the Middle Ages, the work would have been done long ago. The preceding summary is not only provisional but incomplete. For instance, De Luca, *Relatio*, also discusses other kinds of curial letters which are thought to be briefs, but are not actually papal briefs,[147] and other kinds of secretaries.[148] Again, as we have seen, some documents sent by the Penitentiary were called briefs though they were very different from papal briefs proper and probably written by a different set of scribes.[149] These refinements of diplomatic detail should not distract us from the key fact that there were two main 'writing pools', not necessarily responsible for the decision-making behind the documents they wrote.

The material products of the two 'writing pools' certainly differ in appearance. There is a sensible analysis of the physical contrasts between the two types in De Luca's *Relatio*. Letters written by the secretaries are sealed with the fisherman's ring (impressed on red wax)[150] whereas Chancery letters are sealed closed by a leaden seal or have a leaden seal hanging from cords. Briefs are on parchment that is whiter and smoother

---

[145] Boyle, *Survey*, 62–67, makes an attempt, but even from him one does not take away a clear picture.

[146] *Ibid.*, 64.

[147] 'Aliae vero expeditiones Curiae, quae ratione qualitatis chartae de corio, generaliter ab exteris in Curia non versatis, brevia Apostolica creduntur, & nuncupantur (& utinam istam credulitatem ac nuncupationem non imprimerent illi mali causidici, qui exteros non informatos decipiunt, supponendo esse brevia Apostolica), sunt monitoria Auditoris Camerae, sive inibitiones Rotae, aliorumque Tribunalium, aut processus fulminati, & similes expeditiones Judicum & Tribunalium' (De Luca, *Relatio*, Discursus VII.11, p. 59).

[148] De Luca goes on, *Relatio*, VII.18–19, pp. 60–61.

[149] *Ibid.*, Disc. VII.12, p. 59), and above note 000.

[150] De Luca, *Relatio*, Disc. VII.15, p. 59.

than the parchment used for Chancery documents. Chancery documents are written in the script that De Luca calls 'gallican' (he must mean what we would call 'Gothic'), whereas briefs are in 'Latin', i.e. humanistic script: elegant and easy to read![151] Early modern examples of a Chancery letter and of a brief (representative also of a contrast going back to the fifteenth century) can be seen at *1587/8 (BL Add MS 6878 (9)) and *1588 (BL Add Ch 12811) respectively, transcribed in the documents section and reproduced in Plates 5 and 6.

The two writing offices could collaborate. Briefs might be written by secretaries for business for which the definitive document should come from the Chancery, but where a provisional letter was needed, regarding possession for instance: 'writs for taking possession in the name of the Chamber'.[152]

Justice

Not only did demand for papal graces and favours but also demand for papal justice continue after the Council of Trent. Here again the researcher seems to be in uncharted territory by comparison with the relatively healthy state of medieval scholarship. The most familiar landmark is the Roman Rota, still a tribunal today though principally for marriage cases. It has been well studied up to the eve of the Reformation by Per Ingesman[153] and Kirsi

---

[151] He describes the physical difference between briefs and Chancery bulls: 'Aliud enim genus literarum Apostolicarum, quae expediuntur per Cancellariam, non sub dicto anulo, sed sub plumbo seu sigillo plumbeo pendente ex cordulis, diversum habet nomen seu vocabulum, quoniam, ad differentiam istorum brevium, Bullae nuncupantur, diversam habent formam, tam circa species membranarum, quoniam pro brevibus in usu sunt membranae subtiles, & albae, pro bullis autem membranae magis nigrae, & rudes seu grossae, quam etiam in charactere, quoniam brevia inscribuntur in charactere latino, nitido, & eleganti, ac intelligibili; in bullis //59/ autem retinetur antiquus stylus characteris gallici ...' (De Luca, *Relatio*, Disc. VII.9, pp. 58–59).

[152] 'Etiam in provisionibus Cathedralium, et Metropolitanarum, vel dignitatum, & beneficiorum super quibus expediri solent, ac debent, literae sub plumbo per Cancellariam, expediri solent istae literae in forma brevis sub anulo piscatorio, ad certum effectum provisionalem, adipiscendi scilicet possessionem, etiam literis non expeditis, quia nempe expediat, ex pluribus respectibus, pro //col. b/ casuum qualitate, illarum expeditionem, per aliquod tempus differre; Eaque dicuntur brevia de capienda possessione nomine Camerae, quae tamen non eximunt ab obligatione expediendi dictas alias literas, sed potius expresse ad id obligant, sub decreto annullativo gratiae, infra terminum sex mensium; ...' (De Luca, *Relatio*, Disc. VII, 13, p. 59).

[153] Ingesman, *Provisioner*. Ingesman develops an important argument. From the second half of the fifteenth century links between the Danish Church and Rome intensified. In particular, there was a major expension of provisions to Denmark, and there was a trend in the second half of the fifteenth century 'to use suits for the Rota as a means of

Salonen,[154] though its subsequent history needs more work. Salonen found that the 'majority of processes, circa 80 per cent concerned benefice issues,[155] while the percentages of property litigation (14 per cent) and marriage litigation (1 per cent) were much smaller' – but still it was not 'only a tribunal for resolving benefice litigation',[156] and dealt with a broad range of matters including jurisdictional powers and founding parishes.[157] It could take civil cases from the papal states.[158] The court was a lot more efficient than scholars thought before Salonen's study; if only about 30 per cent of cases were taken to their conclusion,[159] the reasons are to be sought in the behaviour of the litigants (forcing opponents to reach a compromise, etc).[160] It seems likely that the patterns Salonen has elucidated would also be found after Trent.

In the early modern period the Rota seems to have taken business away from the *Audientia litterarum contradictarum*,[161] which continued to function but in a diminished way. The *per viam correctoris* procedure described in the previous chapter must have kept costs down. But its business seems to have declined in importance since its great medieval days, losing ground not only to the Rota but also, for delegated justice, to the *Signatura iustitiae*.[162]

---

obtaining Danish benefices or pensions from them'; 'with regard to Denmark the curial market of prebends had its heyday very late, from around 1475 to 1525, compared to central areas of Western Europe where it flourished in the fourteenth or in the first half of the fifteenth century'; 'the appearance of the curialists on the Danish scene and the expansion in the papal system of provisions created an insecure legal situation within the field of benefices, with an increase in litigation in consequence' (545). In a manner familiar to historians of medieval England, the Danish king used papal provisions to reward clerical royal servants, using lawsuits to this end when it suited (546). Litigants who were already at the curia had a considerable advantage (548), so it could be argued that the Rota system was less fair than the judge delegate system. The relation between Rota justice and delegated justice needs more research. Ingesman suggests that the remit of the Rota was (a) benefice cases 'almost on a production line basis', (b) 'cases of great importance which often involved matters of principle', and (c) cases where the parties could afford a Roman trial and were very determined to win (549).

[154] Salonen, *Papal Justice*. See also Minnich, 'Lateran V', 166–176: rich detail.
[155] Cf. Ingesman, *Provisioner*, 547: 'Right from its beginning the Rota seems to have been a court that specialized in benefice cases.'
[156] Salonen, *Papal Justice*, 178.   [157] *Ibid.*, 179.   [158] *Ibid.*, 180.   [159] *Ibid.*, 180.
[160] *Ibid.*, 181–182.
[161] P. Herde, 'Zur päpstlichen Delegationsgerichtsbarkeit', 41: 'Gegen Ende des 17. Jahrhunderts hat … Johannes Ciampini … in seinem Werk über den Vizekanzler der Römischen Kirche berichtet, daß von der einstigen Delegationsgerichtsbarkeit nur noch ein Schatten übriggeblieben sei … die Rota viele Prozesse entschied, die früher delegiert worden waren …'.
[162] *Ibid.*, 40: 'Bereits seit dem 15. Jahrhundert ist ein starker Abbau der Funktionen dieser Behörde festzustellen. Die durch die zahlreichen "Konkordate" des 15. Jahrhunderts und dann durch das Konzil von Trient vorgenommene Dezentralisierung der

The *Signatura justitiae*,[163] working between or alongside the Rota and the *Audientia litterarum contradictarum*, seems not to have written its own letters but to have sent them to one or other of the writing pools, and in the case of contentious litigation this would seem to have been the *Secretaria brevium*. Thus the documents now in the *Dataria ap., Brev. Lat.* series of the Vatican Archives started with the *Dataria* but were written up by scribes of the *Secretaria brevium*; among the letters sent, our sources tell us, were *commissiones* to judges delegate, an indication that this system did not atrophy after Trent.[164]

The system of congregations

The post-Trent systems just described evolved from medieval institutions. Alongside them, we find after Trent an entirely new system of Congregations, involving different types of papal document and different procedures. 'Congregation' means in effect a committee of cardinals meeting regularly, doing much of the work previously done by the cardinals together, in Consistory. Congregations too answered to the pope, but he would not necessarily be present. The Diplomatics of the post-Trent Congregations needs much more work. For instance, how were the staff who serviced the congregations remunerated? I suspect that the Secretaries had benefices and great expectations of promotions, and that the scribes were paid out of the pockets of the cardinals. But these are guesses. Something more than guesswork can, however, be attempted to elucidate the systems of at least

---

kirchlichen Rechtsprechung führte an der päpstlichen Kurie zu einem Rückgang der Justizsachen. Dazu wurde ein Teil der einfachen Justizbriefe seit Innocenz VIII. (1484–92) in der Form des Breve expediert und der *audientia* entzogen. Auch der *signatura iustitiae* zog immer mehr Fälle an sich ...'. Herde goes on list elements of continuity but then returns, at 41, to the theme of decline. As just noted, he gives evidence that the Rota was draining business from the *Audientia*, and he makes the important observation that for delegated justice briefs as covering letters for the original supplication were doing some of the work formally done through the *audientia* process. 'Immer mehr ging die *signatura iustitiae* dazu über, bei Reskripten mit gemischter Rechtsmaterie (Justiz-und Gnadensachen) von der Ausstellung der früher durch die *audientia* gehenden Urkunden abzusehen und die Angelegenheiten durch Breven mit Einschluß der Supplik (*per breve supplicatione introclusa*) zu expedieren ... Aus diesen und vielen anderen Gründen verfiel das Urkundenwesen der *audientia* ...' (at 41).

[163] De Luca, *Relatio*, Disc. XXXI, pp. 165–181.

[164] See note at the end of the chapter on the justice delegate system in the early modern period. See also Blouin et al., *Vatican Archives*, under Brevia Lateranensia, **3.2.7.5**, pp. 146–147. On the Brevia Lateranensia series see Diener, 'Die grossen Registerserien', 344, 346.

the two most important Congregations, the Inquisition and the Congregation of the Council.[165]

The Congregation of the Inquisition

The opening of the Inquisition archive in 1998 attracted much interest[166] and understandably stimulated much scholarship. The Diplomatics of its documents has not been the focus of much of this research, but a good study of the archive by Francesco Beretta provides some handrails, along the way pointing out the parallels with the 'notary Diplomatics' of the day.[167] From 1550 a key figure in the day-to-day running of the Inquisition (founded in 1542) was the notary,[168] who headed an

---

[165] For the Congregation of Rites, set up in 1588, J. Nemec provides a starting point by presenting the main surviving documentary sources ('L'Archivio della Congregazione per le Cause dei Santi (ex-S.Congregazione dei Riti', in *Miscellanea in Occasione del IV Centenario della Congregazione per le Cause dei Santi (1588–1988)* (Vatican City, 1988), 339–352).

[166] A. Cifres, ed., *L'Iinquisizione Romana e I suoi Archivi. A vent'anni dall'apertura dell'ACDF* (Rome, 2018). Note the moving intervento, at 81–82, to open the 'round table', by Carlo Ginsburg, a letter from whom led to the opening of the archive. See also A. Prosperi, 'Una Esperienza di Ricerca al S. Uffizio', in idem, *L'Inquisizione Romana. Letture e Ricerche* (Rome, 2003), 221–261. It is impossible not to surmise that Antonio Gramsci provides a theoretical framework and inspiration to Prosperi. For the historiographical tradition in which Prosperi is writing and which he in his has much influenced, see S. Ditchfield, 'In Sarpi's Shadow: Coping with Trent the Italian Way', in *Studi in Memoria di Cesare Mozzarelli i* (Milan, 2008), 585–606; also, for a fine survey of the field, Ditchfield's 'In Search of Local Knowledge. Rewriting Early Modern Italian Religious History', *Cristianesimo nella Storia*, 19 (1998), 255–296. For balanced treatment of the Inquisition, see also the essays of J. Tedeschi, in his *Il Giudice e l'eretico. Studi sull'Inquisizione romana* (Milan, 1997).

[167] F. Beretta, 'L'archivio della Congregazione del Sant'Ufficio: bilancio provvisorio della storia e natura dei fondi d'antico regime', *Rivista di Storia e letteratura religiosa*, 37 (2001), 29–58; I read this in a pre-publication pdf when the libraries were closed during a Covid lockdown and I am very grateful to Dr. Daniel Ponziani, of the archive, for making it available to me. See the comments on the paper in T. F. Mayer, *The Roman Inquisition. A Papal Bureaucracy and its Laws in the Age of Galileo* (Philadelphia, PA, 2013), 245 note 159. What follows is based on Beretta, and is close to a translation of sections of his original: this note takes the place of quotation marks. I am also much indebted to Ponziani for correcting my understanding of Beretta. Thus the credit for this section goes to Ponziani and Beretta, though any faults are mine. See also the balanced treatment by Mayer, *The Roman Inquisition*, especially 26–37; on 28–34 Mayer explores the weaknesses of the Decree Registers as records of what happened. A. Del Col, 'Vent'anni di studi sull'Inquisizione romana: risultati e attese', in Cifres, ed., *L'Iinquisizione Romana e I suoi Archivi*, 45–80, at 53–56, picks up the theme of the unreliability of the record keeping and the records.

[168] Mayer, *Roman Inquisition*, 28–32, 34, and 142–144 thinks that the shortcomings of the notaries – he writes of laziness, incompetence and uncertain remuneration – go far towards explaining the defects of the records, quite apart from later losses thanks to Napoleon (*ibid.*, 36).

administrative staff. The notary registered the administrative and judicial decisions (*decreta*) of the Congregation,[169] now to be found in the Registers: 'Regestra Decretorum S[acrae] Cong[regationis]; for example ACDF, S.O., 1616, c. 1. These are more revealing for the sixteenth century than for the following period,[170] and for the sixteenth century we also have notes taken during sittings of the court:[171] these are now ACDF, S.O., St. St. P 4 b; for a detailed list of them in the 1745 inventory see ACDF, S.O., St. St. P 1 a, c. 122r–v. ('S.O.' stands for 'Stanza Storica'.) The notes informally recording sessions could be taken on loose sheets or in a small book called 'Broliardellus'.[172] A modern inventory distinguishing between *Decreta* and notes is a major desideratum.

In addition to the notes and the registered decrees, there were formal documents based on the decrees. These were signed by the notary and bore the seal of the Congregation, and registers of them were kept, the so-called *Libri extensorum*:[173] St. st. L 3 a for the period 1582–1600.[174] One may also mention documents relating to the administration of the Holy Office: ACDF, S.O., St. St. L 3 c–d (*Instrumenta* 1583–1609), and ST. st. T 6 a–i (*Instrumenta* 1610, etc.).

ACDF, S.O., St. St. LL 5 a contains the acts of the visits to or inspections of the Holy Office by cardinals (*Acta visitationis S.O. Urbis*) for the period 1701–1737. The archive was included in the inspections.[175]

In addition to these series there are the dossiers relating to individuals, books or theological topics, rich sources for historical research. They are normally made up of sheets of paper of roughly A3, folded in two to form a quire.[176] Then the quires could be inserted within quires to make a dossier of the size needed. Letters or other relevant sheets could be added as required. Large dossiers could be indexed, with reference to pagination at the foot of sheets on the right-hand side.[177] An example of such a dossier is ACDF, S.O., D.B. (*De Baptismate*) 1 (1618–1698), n. 1, the case of a Capuchin who denied the validity of Calvinist baptism. This was contrary to a recent decision by the Congregation of the Council,[178] but it is unclear how well that was known.[179] As the extract transcribed at

---

[169] Beretta, 'L'archivio', 32.   [170] *Ibid.*, 32 note 12.   [171] *Ibid.*, 32.   [172] *Ibid.*, 34.
[173] *Ibid.*, 41; cf. 35.   [174] *Ibid.*, 35.   [175] Information from Dr. Daniel Ponziani.
[176] 'piegandoli a metà per formare un quaderno di due pagine'; Beretta, 'L'archivio', 35. Beretta must be using 'pagina' where one would write 'folio' in English, since there would be four pages counting the recto and the verso.
[177] Beretta, 'L'archivio', 36.
[178] *Congr. Concilio, Positiones (Sess.)*, 16, fo. 116r (modern pencil foliation).
[179] P. Fagnani, *Commentaria in Secundam Partem Tertii Libri Decretalium* (Cologne, 1681), 317–321, on c. *Si quis puerum*, makes no mention that I can find of the Congregation of

*1618–1620[180] suggests, the case was started by his own doubts about the validity of his own baptism and consequently of his priestly orders. He wrote a treatise to show the sevenfold erroneousness of Calvinist baptism. Reading between the lines, he was badgering the Inquisition and the pope to be allowed to be rebaptised and re-ordained, at least conditionally. The pope obliged, as the document transcribed shows, but the friar was told not to continue his researches into the validity of Calvinist baptism.

In the Congregation of the Inquisition documents seem to have been filed pragmatically: i.e. a document relating to a local inquisition rather than an individual would be classified with that office, some censures not leading to a trial would be collected in miscellaneous collections, and there would be separate dossiers for license to read prohibited books, requests for graces and dispensations, etc.[181] There were also volumes of 'sentences', which include abjurations by the accused,[182] but nearly all of these are lost, possibly when the archive was being brought back from Paris, after the defeat of Napoleon, who had taken it there![183]

There was a major reorganisation at the end of the sixteenth century, when a proper archive was created. In the early seventeenth century the office of archivist was established on a permanent basis. Once a year, as trials were completed, the documents would be filed by diocese, or religious order, or type of crime, in volumes bound or simply tied together. Some of these dossiers were vast, sometimes with over a thousand pages. The pages would be given new numbers, at the head on the right. Thus the user of the dossier will see both the 'working' numeration at the foot of the page and the 'archival' foliation at its head.[184]

Another reorganisation, in the later eighteenth century, complicates life for the historian who wants to establish the original context of documents.[185] On highly rational principles from the point of view of the living institution and its reference needs – by contrast with today's archival best practice with its emphasis on retaining original structures – the archivist Guiseppe Maria Lugani extracted sections of dossiers to compile new ones. These included series for the censure of books and propositions, doubts relating to the administration of the sacraments, and other doctrinal and jurisdictional questions. Thus, for example, he put together a volume on heretics condemned in contumacy, St. St. M 4

---

the Council's decision, which is curious because he had been its secretary and on other matters shows knowledge of its decisions.

[180] ACDF, S.O., D.B. (*De Baptismate*) 1 (1618–1698), n. 1 fo. 1v.
[181] Beretta, 'L'archivio', 36–37.   [182] *Ibid.*, 40.   [183] *Ibid.*, 53.   [184] *Ibid.*, 37–38.
[185] *Ibid.*, 46–49, for what follows.

f., and five volumes on doubtful points relating to baptism: St. st. M 6 n–r.[186] While disastrous from the point of view of a modern trained archivist, this could be useful to historians investigating particular themes that map on to Lugani's classification.

The Congregation of the Council

Less well known than the Congregation of the Inquisition is the Congregation of the Council,[187] though research at the Max-Planck-Institut für Rechtsgeschichte und Rechtstheorie, formerly Max-Planck-Institut für Rechtsgeschichte in Frankfurt, under Benedetta Albani, the leader in the whole field, is putting it on the map. The Congregation was founded in 1564 by Pius IV.[188] Under Pius V its powers were extended: it could make legally binding decisions,[189] and Sixtus V laid out its powers in terms that opened the door for it to become the supreme authority under the pope for everything other than matters of faith (the remit of the Inquisition).[190] A proper appreciation of its importance, which can hardly be overstated, will re-balance historians' understanding of the early modern papacy.

The documentation it has left is enormous. Unlike the Inquisition, its archive is not independent, but integrated into the Vatican Archives. There are no problems of access, only of scale. We know less about the Congregation's inner workings than with the Inquisition. By the seventeenth century the meetings were on Thursdays or Saturdays[191] – serviced

---

[186] *Ibid.*, 48 note 83.
[187] For bibliography up to c. 2009, see D. L. d'Avray, *Rationalities in History. A Weberian Essay in Comparison* (Cambridge, 2010), 195–196. R. Parayre, *La S. Congrégation du Concile. Son Histoire – sa procédure – son autorité. Thèse présentée à la Faculté de Théologie de Lyon* (Paris, 1897), though old, is the work of a member of the 'Studio' of the Congregation (still going strong then) – the group of young canon legal eagles who helped to service its administration – which enhances its value. On the 'Studio' see F. Romita 'Lo "Studio" della Sacra Congregazione del Concilio e gli "Studi" della Curia Romana', in F. Romita, ed., *La Sacra Congregazione del Concilio. Quarto Centenario della Fondazione (1564–1964)* (Vatican City, 1964), 633–677.
[188] For the context of the Congregation's creation, see F. Romita, 'Le Origini della S. C. del Concilio', in Romita, *La Sacra Congregazione del Concilio*, 13–50. Parayre, *La S. Congrégation*, 12.
[189] Parayre, *La S. Congrégation*, 22–23.
[190] *Ibid.*, 31; the contents of the *Positiones* series, on which more below, is the best evidence of the wide extent of the Congregation's powers.
[191] 'Vi e la Congregatione del Concilio per interpretrare [*sic*] il testo del Sacro Concilio Tridentino facendosi ogni settimana una volta, il sabbato ò il giovedi ad libitum del signore Cardinale capo di quella(?)' (Relatio, British Library Egerton MS 2210, fo. 125v). Anne Jacobson Schutte, *By Force and Fear. Taking and Breaking Monastic Vows in Early Modern Europe* (Ithaca, 2011), 90 is categorical that the meetings were 'held once or twice a month on Saturday afternoons in the Quirinal palace', rejecting as

by a staff which managed the paperwork and records, a secretary[192] (presumably some assistants) and consultants[193] – but we have few details about the Congregation of the Council's staff or procedure. Those who have worked on its records see the same manuscript hands recurring, but are so far unable to put names to them.

A whole range of subseries come under the umbrella of the *Congr. Concilio* series in the Vatican Archives, but the following seem the most important for the history of papal history in general, as opposed to local Church history.[194] Bound volumes of 'Decreta' – *Congr. Concilio, Libri Decret.* – record important decisions of the Congregation. In effect, these were so to speak 'in-house' laws, to guide the Congregation in subsequent judgments and ensure consistency, not to be made public. Only in the eighteenth century were the Congregation's judgments printed for the public domain. Volumes of letters bound in a similar way record outgoing correspondence, though almost certainly only the most important communications. This is the *Congr. Concilio, Libri Litter.* series. The aforementioned two series are both relatively small in format and easy to handle.

That cannot be said of the third series, the *Congr. Concilio, Positiones,* and *Positiones (Sess.)*, which are vast folders or *buste*, each of which can contain many hundreds of loose quires. The *Positiones* series is also the most fascinating series for historians because it is full of concrete cases and because it enables one to follow in detail the reasoning behind the Congregation's decisions.[195] Substantial extracts from the dossier on the validity of Calvinist baptism are printed at *1570 – showing that its remit cannot be sharply separated from that of the Congregation of the Inquisition, which also had to think about Calvinist baptism, as we have seen. Presumably the Congregation of the Council dealt with the problem because of the major implications of the question of Calvinist baptism for ecclesiastical practice. Should converted Calvinists be baptised?

based on no evidence the assertion of A. Menniti Ippolito that the Congregation also met on Thursdays, but the statement in the Egerton manuscript reopens the possibility, and also indicates weekly meetings. Perhaps the routine changed over time.

[192] Parayre, *La S. Congrégation*, 20; at one early point a secretary for each cardinal on the Congregation seems to have been envisaged: *ibid.*, 41–42. For the role of the secretary a little later than the period that mainly concerns us, see Schutte, *By Force and Fear*, 111–112.

[193] Parayre, *La S. Congrégation*, 41–42.

[194] For the latter, note especially *Congr. Concilio, Relat. Dioec.*, and *Congr. Concilio, Libri Litter. Visit. SS. Liminum.*

[195] This is seldom possible for the Middle Ages. As noted earlier, an exception is the pontificate of John XXII: see *1333, **September 6 and** 7, and, more generally, P. Nold, *John XXII and his Franciscan Cardinal* and *idem, Marriage Advice for a Pope.*

Did a mixed marriage with a Calvinist have the same status as marriage with a pagan?

Dossiers on given questions within the *buste* included the expert theological and canon legal arguments for and against by the consultants.[196] I know of no source so important for the history of papal Christianity that has been so little exploited by historians.[197] An up-to-date inventory is being prepared by Albani and her team, a searchlight in the darkness still shrouding this extraordinary archival series.

For the years 1564–1625 the volumes are organised thematically, roughly according to decrees of the Council of Trent. The call number for these is *Congr. Concilio, Positiones (Sess.)*. There is a useful unpublished catalogue of volumes 1–75 by Domenico Troiani, *Indici 910–924*, in the catalogue room of the Vatican Archives. Subsequent volumes are ordered chronologically and by diocese within a volume.[198] For the time being at least there is also a third series consisting of volumes that should really be integrated within one or other of the first two. These are the *Congr. Concilio, Positiones (Carte Sciolte)*, also called *Buste marroni*.[199]

On the basis of this documentation one can roughly reconstruct the journey of a piece of business through the system – the *Geschäftsgang* – in the Congregation of the Council. A letter would arrive with a problem case or sometimes with a list of questions (reminiscent of the lists sent to popes from the fourth century on). The letter might come from anywhere in the Catholic world, including the New World. Dioceses in Italy naturally come up a lot, followed by Spanish correspondents (enough to relativise the picture of a national Church entirely run by the king and the Spanish Inquisition). The secretary of the Congregation would open a dossier, inserting the initial communication and, probably, having extra copies made. With the most complex cases, on which the cardinals, after discussion, felt that external opinions would be helpful, the question would be sent out to the theologians or canon lawyers for their expert assessments,[200] though in the majority of cases the decisions would be taken internally within the Congregation, or sometimes by sub-

---

[196] For a later seventeenth-century example see d'Avray, *Rationalities in History*, 188–195.

[197] Schütte, *By Force and Fear*, 9–10 on the *Positiones* series, and *passim*.

[198] For the foregoing, see P. Caiazza, 'L'Archivio Storico della Sacra Congregazione del Concilio. (Primi appunti per un problema di riordinamento)', *Ricerche di Storia Sociale e Religiosa. N.S.*, 42 (1992), 7–24, at 12–13.

[199] *Ibid.*, 14–15. For other subseries see AAV *Indice dei Fondi*, under main heading *Congregazioni Romani* (written at the head of the list in capitals, in the normal way, then also vertically in left-hand margin), subheading *Concilio (ora Clero)*, then list of sub-sub-headings.

[200] Dr. Benedetta Albani advised me in a personal communication on the role of external experts.

congregations. There must have been a list of consultants but probably
others could be asked if the need was felt. They would write their
opinions, giving their arguments and authorities. These expert opinions
are impressive documents. The dossiers would be presented to the
cardinals who composed the Congregation, though not all of them would
be present for every session. They would reach a decision, or if they could
not, they would ask the pope to make the call. Presumably a letter would
be sent out as a reply in all cases, but only some of them were be copied
into the current *Libri Litter.* volume. In the *Positiones* series we find traces
of many other letters.[201] As noted, the *Libri Decret.* volumes recorded
important decisions. According to an attractive theory proposed by
Benedetta Albani, the secretary of the Congregation personally kept a
record of the decisions and later on copied them, or the most important
of them, into a register.[202] Alphabetical indices of decisions were made
so that the Congregation could consult precedents internally, an in-
house way to avoid contradicting earlier decisions. These are currently
on the open shelves of the search room of the Vatican Archives – a
primary source functioning as a finding aid.

The Congregation of the Council was not only a source of solutions to
uncertainties: it also acted as a tribunal. It could judge annulment cases,
for instance. A closely related category of cases, applications for release
from monastic vows on grounds that they had been taken under duress,
has been thoroughly investigated by Anne Jacobson Schutte. The
Council of Trent had shown awareness that some men and women might
want to leave religious life, and allowed them to approach the local
bishop and monastic superior to ask for this; given, however, the family
pressure that had pushed them into an order in the first place, and the
amour propre of their community, it was uncommon to get through this
five-year window, so that a petition to the pope was the only legal route
left. The petitioner would usually want a local proctor to frame the
petition.[203] If the Congregation of the Council thought the case had
sufficient merit, they would appoint a delegate in the locality to produce
a dossier. The delegate would normally be the bishop, but if there was
reason to think he was biased (say because he was related to the family
members who had used 'force and fear') another suitable delegate would
be appointed.[204] In the localities, the investigation would follow the form

---

[201] '... non tutte le lettere della SCC sono registrate nei Libri Litterarum, ma c'è traccia di
molte lettere inviate anche nella serie Positiones' (Benedetta Albani, personal
communication).
[202] Personal communication from Dr. Benedetta Albani.
[203] Schütte, *By Force and Fear*, 90–91.   [204] *Ibid.*, 91–92.

invented in the late twelfth century and regularly used after that: each party would break down what it sought to prove into a series of succinct propositions, each party would list witnesses, and the delegate would get the testimony of each witness on each of the propositions about which they had knowledge.[205] A dossier of the answers would be compiled and sent to Rome. Those who could afford it would then prepare their case with the costly help of professional canon lawyers and proctors,[206] though poor petitioners could ask for the case to be heard by the secretary rather than the cardinals of the Congregation; for these, legal aid was provided.[207]

As with so much papal government, the business of the Congregation of the Council was demand-driven.[208] The demand for legally binding answers was met by a lean administrative mechanism over which a committee presided. The functionality of the Congregation of the Council helps us answer 'Hageneder's question' – how did popes exercise authority over such a vast area without commensurate financial or military resources? – for the post-Trent period?

Conclusion

Though the 1378–1417 Schism marks a watershed, there are important continuities. The *Reg. Lat.* series takes over the role of the *Reg. Aven.* series. Curial letters continue to deal with high-level affairs. Secretaries continue to write them. But there are changes. Increasingly, papal secretaries are humanists writing in humanist script. They take on responsibility for producing a new kind of papal letter, the brief. Initially briefs are for high-level business or for special reasons of one sort or another, but in the later fifteenth century they become a routine vehicle of business. A 'sandwich structure' can be discerned by which the most delicate letters were briefs written by secretaries, as were low-level routine letters, while an intermediate layer was the business of Chancery scribes. The 'journey' of letters through the system, the *Geschäftsgang*, has apparently never been worked out for the post-Trent period. I have made an attempt to do so, and it need not be rehearsed here. The various organs all had

---

[205] *Ibid.*, 94–95. For this powerful procedure, not so much 'inquisitorial' as adversarial, though in a way unfamiliar to the Common Law tradition, see d'Avray, *Papacy, Monarchy and Marriage*, 86–93. Most scholars seem hardly to be aware of how different this procedure was from 'inquisitorial procedure' in the sense of judge-led questioning.

[206] Schütte, *By Force and Fear*, 96–105.   [207] *Ibid.*, 96; cf. 104–105.

[208] The Inquisition was an exception, in that those who came before its tribunals obviously did not want to be there.

their letters copied by one of the two bodies of writers, Chancery *scriptores* or secretaries. Thus the Apostolic Penitentiary probably maintained more of its old role than has been apparent: it did the thinking for many letters now produced by the Chancery, and received some income in return. It was argued that the sale of offices, apparently a financial lunacy, had a social function in keeping the elite of the papal states invested (literally) in the papacy, so that the hostilities of the post-papal turn period were never resumed. The funding of the administrative staff of the cardinals remains mysterious: probably a cardinal paid for his own staff, which might explain why cardinals were so greedy for benefices. The cardinals and, presumably, members of their entourages, administered the Congregations which took over so much papal business after Trent. Exploration of that business has only just begun, especially where the crucial Congregation of the Council is concerned, but it appears to have been administratively economical and inexpensive for people who sought papal clarification on a vast range of points. Understanding the contents of what this Congregation did yields answers to 'Hageneder's question' for the post-Trent period.

Note on the justice delegate system in the early modern period.

The following extracts, too bulky to fit in a footnote, illustrate the survival of the judge delegate system after the Council of Trent.

De Luca, *Relatio,* Disc. VII.14, p. 59: 'Datur quoque, circa forensia contentiosa, quaedam species brevium Apostolicorum, per organum cuiusdam officialis, qui Secretarius brevium dicitur, sed est officium venale, extra Palatium, & sine assistentia apud Papam, pro illis brevibus, seu literis, quas expedire oportet, pro commissionibus vel delegationibus causarum appellationis vel restitutionis in integrum quae extra Curiam, seu in partibus, diriguntur Episcopis vicinioribus vel Iudicibus synodalibus, aut aliis personis in ecclesiastica dignitate constitutis. Sed huius officialis inspectio cadit potius sub Tribunali Signaturae *infra. disc.* 30 & 31.'; Instruttioni, British Library Egerton MS 2210, fo. 93r (I put the headings in italics): *'Dell' Appellatione al Nuntio.* Si dall' ordinario o vero dal Metropolitano, o Giudice delegato dalla sede apostolica si appella e si ricorre al nuntio, vi sono in questo quattro modi per poter giudicare. *Delle Commissioni in partibus.* Il primo modo e per via de Commissione domandando che si commetta la causa a qualche giudice in partibus, secundo se domandara se la parte adversa non haverá fatto 'Nihil transeat' nel libro del Registratore dell' Abbreviatore che per ponerlo si paga due reali de derrito [*despite letter forms sic for* denaro? – suggestion of Miles Pattenden] che li da termine tre mese, il che havendo cosiposto sara necessario citare la parte adversa accio si eliggano il giudice li quali non concordandosi doppo' l'Abbreviatore nomina ex officio quello che li parera, la qual commissione si paga di denari 33 reali solidi(?)'; note also the reference to delegated justice and 'commissioni' in Relatione, British Library Egerton MS 2210, fo. 123v–124r: 'Del Prefetto della Signatura di Giustitia. Il prefetto della signatura di Giustitia il quale e Cardinale ha di provisione 100 ducati di Camera il mese la giurisdittione del quale, a fare li rescritti a tutte le suppliche et commissioni di cause le quale si delegano per giustizia, et per ogni Giovedi eccetto le vacanze avanti di S. E. [= Sua Eminenza] nel proprio suo Palazzo si fa la signatura di Giustizia per quelle commissioni e rescritti, li quali sono contentiosi frale parte, et intervenendoli 12 Prelati votanti Referendarii de piu antichi che vengono informati dalle parti come anco se informa il signore Cardinale Prefetto, e si lascia a ciascheduno l'informatione in scriptis, in facto et in Jure [Juris ms.?], et inoltre intervengono tutti gli altri Prelati Referendarii quali possono in ogni signatura proporre due commissioni per ciascheduno //fo. 124r/ intervenedoci tanto quelli che propongono come quelli che non propongono, e di piu v'interviene un Auditore di Rota Monsignore luogotenente civile del signore cardinale vicario per difendere la loro giurisdittione. Ma questi non votono, e perche molte delle cause che si delegano vanno spedite per lettera del signore Cardinale Prefetto sottoscritta et altre vanno per Breve. Pero sopra questo vi sono due officiali, uno chiamato il Prefetto delle minute de Brevi il quale, fatto che ha la minuta, le consegna all'altro officiale chiamato il Maestro di Brevi il quale conforme alle minute dategli et sottoscritte da quello che fa li brevi li quali poi consegna accio che li facci sigillare al segretario delli brevi che vanno sotto tassa. Il primo officio vale m/12 scudi et il secondo m/13 et il denaro dell' uno é dell' altro frutta da otto o diece procento, et questo è quanto occurre nell signatura di Giustizia.' Hunobaldus Plettenbergius, Notitia Congregationum et Tribunalium Curiae Romanae (Hildesheim, 1693), pp. 308–309, writing about the Signatura iustitiae, seems to assume delegation of justice outside as well as within Italy – he specifies that either a brief or a bull is possible if the destination is outside Italy, but only a brief if within Italy; Thomas De Rosa, Tractatus De executoribus litterarum apostolicarum, Partis II Cap. VI, pp. 364–365. T. Frenz, 'Die "Computi" in der Serie der Brevia Lateranensia im Vatikanischem Archiv', Quellen und Forschungen aus Italienischen Archiven und Bibliotheken, 55/56 (1976), 251–275, at 260, implies that justice delegated to the localities declined from around 1600, but the source extracts quoted above are certainly evidence that the judge delegate system survived.

De Luca, *Relatio*, had referred to 'iudicibus synodalibus' (Disc. VII.14, p. 59). This is a reference to a system set up by the Council of Trent, Sessio XXV, De Reformatione, C. X.[209] An example of the system in action shortly after the Council is AAV Dataria Ap., Brev. Lat. 123, fo. 74v–77v. In this letter of 1590, December 13, Gregory XIV writes to judges appointed by a diocesan synod. Historians should be on the lookout for more such examples. The casual reference to synodal judges by De Luca, writing in the later seventeenth century, suggests that the system was still functioning at least in principle. Nonetheless the eighteenth-century classic treatise by Benedict XIV on 'The Diocesan Synod' implies that it was not working but that the judge delegate system continued even so:

... in Sacrae Congregationis Concilii Archivo nullus extat catalogus Iudicum Synodalium, qui ab Episcopis fuerit ad Sedem Apostolicam unquam transmissus, neque aliud huius rei invenimus exemplum, praeter unicum adnotatum a Cardinali Bellarmino *ad cap. 10 sess.25.Concil. Trident.* Ex hoc porro Episcoporum incuria fit, ut Sedes Apostolica causas in partibus personis committat in dignitate constitutis, ad solam normam *citat. cap. Statutum*,[210] nulla habita ratione Iudicum Synodalium, quorum nomina ignorat, sicuti ad rem perpendit Barbosa *ad dictum cap. 10 Triden. num 25*, scribens: *Decretum hoc de committendis causis solis Iudicibus Synodalibus respectu Papae in usu non est, cum adeo frequenter ipse committere soleat causas aliis personis tam in Dignitate Ecclesiastica constitutis, quam deputatis in Synodo: sed id verisimiliter ex eo procedit, sive quia sit supra Concilium, sive quod Dioecesani Episcopi ex sua parte etiam non curent ad Summum Pontificem transmitti denominationes, et designationes Iudicum a Synodo factas, quod tamen iuxta hoc decretum facere tenentur, et sic Papa ex quadam quasi necessitate iustitiae administrandae decretum non observat.* Et tamen saepius Episcopi conquesti sunt apud Sacram Congregationem Concilii, quod a Sede Apostolica delegationes fierent personis minus idoneis, perinde ac si ipsimet non essent huius abusus praecipua causa. Id autem dissimulavit Sacra Congregatio, et ne muneri suo deesset, monuit Officiales, ad quos pertinet, ut in causis in partibus committendis, omnino morem gererent Tridentino. Ita a Sacra Congregatione rescriptum fuisse ad Turritanum Antistitem die 3. Februarii 1635. legimus *(lib. 15 decretor. pag 162. a tergo) Significatum est Ministris huius Sanctae Sedis pro commissione causarum in partibus, ut eas nonnisi ab Archiepiscopo in Sy-//*p. 107/*nodo ad praescriptum cap. 10.Sess.25. de reform. designatis, et notificandis committunt.* Idemque et Nos fieri curavimus, dum eiusdem Sacrae Congregationis Secretarii munere fungebamur. Etenim cum Episcopus Portallegren. Postulasset, ut causae solis committerentur Iudicibus in Synodo electis, nequaquam autem, ut antea fieri solebat, Protonotariis Apostolicis, inter quos multi reperiebantur indocti et imperiti, et hanc instantiam Nos retulerimus ad Sacram Congregationem, haec die 17. Novembris 1725. Rescripsit, a

---

[209] Von Schulte and Richter, *Canones et Decreta*, 457–458.
[210] VI.I.3.11, Friedberg, *Corpus*, ii, cols. 941–942.

D. Cardinali Praefecto serio agendum esse cum Cardinali Pro-Datario, ut a suis Administris adamussim servari mandaret Tridenti sanctionem. Sed si Episcopi nomina Iudicum in Synodo deputatorum Sedi Apostolicae non manifestant, sibi imputare debent, quod commissiones ad minus peritos quandoque dirigantur. Officiales enim Sanctae Sedis divinare non possunt, quinam in hac, aut illa Dioecesi idonei [idoneni *edn.*] sint ad Apostolicas commissiones rite subeundas, ac propterea Apostolicas litteras ad eos dirigunt, quos audiunt, aliquo specioso titulo condecoratos, quamvis non ignorent sub specioso tituli cortice homines aliquando latere satis rudes et crassos.[211]

Benedict XIV tried to breath new life into the 'synodal judges' system,[212] but that takes us beyond the period covered by this volume.

---

[211] Benedict XIV De Synod. Dioeces. Rome 1747 lib 4 cap. 5 num. 6, pp. 106–107 (note that the pagination differs in different editions of this important work, so the easiest way to trace references is though the Book ('Lib.)->Chapter (Cap.)->Section number structure).

[212] Benedict XIV De Synod. Dioeces., lib 4 cap. 5 num. 9, p. 108.

6   Retrospective: Some Long-Term Continuities

The periodisation of the preceding chapters is somewhat arbitrary, like all periodisation. Furthermore all periodisation also tends to obscure underlying continuities. Continuities there were indeed, and readers will have noticed certain themes that recur in each chapter. To draw some of the threads together, it is worth putting the spotlight on some of these long-term features of papal document production and its wider setting.

Registration

In the history of written records there may be nothing to compare with the papal tradition of registering documents. As already noted, it goes back to Late Antiquity,[1] and has an unbroken tradition to the present day, though we have only sporadic survivals[2] from the period before Gregory VII; nor do we have the actual registers for the popes between Gregory VII (d. 1085) and 1198, the start of Innocent III's pontificate.[3] They may not have existed in the form which is familiar to us from the end of the twelfth century on, to judge by a careful analysis of the ninth century by Veronica Unger.[4] The proliferation of papal registers has been discussed in successive chapters. The chronological sequence may be

---

[1] C. Pietri, *Roma Christiana. Recherches sur l'Église de Rome, son organisation, son politique, son idéologie de Miltiade à Sixte III, 311–440*, 2 vols. (Bibliothèque des Écoles Françaises d'Athènes et de Rome, 224; Rome, 1976), i, 672–676, especially 273. Cf. d'Avray, *Papal Jurisprudence, c. 400*, 91: 'In nostris ... scriniis'; *ibid.*, 121: 'chartarum'.

[2] The so-called 'Collectio Britannica', British Library Add MS 8873, is a source of a significant number but it is difficult to disentangle what is genuine: K. Herbers, *Leo IV. und das Papsttum in der Mitte des 9. Jahrhundert. Möglichkeiten und Grenzen päpstlicher Herrschaft in der späten Karolingerzeit* (Päpste und Papsttum, 27; Stuttgart, 1996), 49–91.

[3] Frenz and Pagano, *I Documenti*, 52–53.

[4] Unger, *Päpstliche Schriftlichkeit*, 289: on the register of John VIII (which survives in a later copy in Beneventan script), she writes: 'es handelt sich nicht um ein klassisches Kanzleiregister. Es gibt keine Spuren, dass es als solches benutzt wurde.'

traced conveniently in one of the indices to the guide edited by Blouin et al.[5]

Responsive government

Another inheritance from the empire was a responsive government system. A Late Antique precedent was the 'rescript government' of Roman emperors. The phrase has been used also for the papacy and other medieval institutions, and is especially to the fore in the many works of Ernst Pitz. His thesis extends to the whole of the medieval period, ranging from a monograph on Gregory I (d. 604)[6] to Calixtus III (d. 1458). Pitz took a basically sound insight too far and argued for it in a way that aroused the antagonism of experts. He presented his theories in an extreme, almost caricatural form, seemed not to have absorbed enough of the relevant scholarly literature, appeared arbitrary and self-contradictory, and dismissed the ideas of past and present specialists in Diplomatics, notably the work of Peter Herde, to whose findings constant and grateful reference has repeatedly been made in the previous pages. This drew strong reactions, from Peter Herde and others.[7]

While Herde's specific criticisms of Pitz are well founded, the reaction against Pitz in the early 1970s was exaggerated insofar as it could appear to dismiss the very concept of rescript government. If one defines rescript government as government, much of which takes the form of responses to initiatives from the governed, whether to obtain favours or start litigation, the concept should not be controversial. Herde gives an account of rescript government as applied to Roman emperors which would seem to work well also for the papacy, and to fit well with his own findings, though, as he points out, it is a broader concept than Pitz's. Rather than be drawn back into this debate, which generated a lot of heat and only a

---

[5] Blouin et al., *Vatican Archives*, 541–559 (for series up to the eighteenth century).

[6] Pitz, *Papstreskripte*.

[7] P. Herde, 'Ernst Pitz, Supplikensignatur und Briefexpedition an der Römischen Kurie im Pontifikat Papst Calixts III. (Bibliothek des Deutschen Historischen Instituts in Rom 42)', *Zeitschrift der Savigny-Stiftung für Rechtsgeschichte: Kanonistische Abteilung*, 60.1 (1974), 414–424. Cf. Pferschy-Maleczek, 'Rechtsbildung durch Reskripte unter Gregor dem Großen?'; other critics are listed by Werner, *Papsturkunden*. Particularly fierce is Herde, 'Zur Audientia'. The unremitting polemic against Pitz aside, this is full of important findings about thirteenth- and fourteenth-century papal Diplomatics and government. For more positive views see T. F. X. Noble, *Speculum* 68 (1993), 1195–1197, and Müller, 'Price of a Papal Pardon', 472. The criticism of Pitz calls to mind the sharp reaction of the 'Zunft' (Werner Maleczek's term) to Pflugk-Harttung's work on early medieval papal Diplomatics, over a century ago.

little light, it seems better to stick to 'responsive' government. In fact the general thesis about the responsive character of papal government now seems to be a commonplace with medieval historians. Naturally it does not exclude papal agency. Of course popes took the initiative from time to time, and a Gregory VII or John XXII did so on a massive scale. They are exceptional, but it was always open to the pope to decide how to respond if he thought the matter warranted his attention. The key point is that so much of the initiative came, so to speak, from 'below'. Herde, Hageneder and the other experts also took that for granted, and the pattern goes back to the first decretals.

The definition of a papal decretal offered by Detlev Jasper when writing about Late Antiquity and the early Middle Ages[8] could apply to any century from the fourth on. He contrasts the 'brotherly pastoral style' (he is quoting an earlier writer) of letters from the first four centuries with the new style normal from the fifth century: 'they appeared in the form of a "responsum", objective and purely factual information modelled on Roman imperial decrees and official documents'.[9]

A structure that stretches from the pagan Roman empire into the early modern period (and after for that matter) is not a trivial historical phenomenon. An implication of this resemblance to imperial rescripts is that these papal decretals were indeed mostly responses. The addressee of the imperial rescript or papal decretal initiated the epistolary exchange. That immediately tells us that both the imperial and papal systems were as much or in fact more reactive than 'pro-active'. With decretals, the 'genesis of the document', in the language of Diplomatics, is more often than not a letter from a bishop. The process was demand-led. That keyword has been repeated so often as to be wearisome, but it is crucial for understanding papal history.

That points us to the key question: how to explain the demand, which in turn brings us to consider the complexities and uncertainties of the Church in Late Antiquity.[10] Often the questions involved the possibility that there was a principle at stake: in fact, the problem might precisely be whether or not, or how far, absolute principle was involved, and how far the question was a matter of man-made law. This kind of jurisprudence goes back to the late fourth century, but continued throughout the Middle Ages, though there was not much of it from the late ninth to late eleventh centuries, and it diminished again after the thirteenth. The Council of Trent threw up new issues, as is normal with new laws that

---

[8] Jasper and Fuhrmann, *Papal Letters*, 12–13.   [9] *Ibid.*, 18 and 19.
[10] d'Avray, *Papal Jurisprudence, c. 400*, 1 and *passim*. In this book and in *Papal Jurisprudence, 385–1234*, I try to explain the demand.

create systems imperfectly compatible with existing ones, and the Congregation of the Council continued the work of resolving uncertainties and complexities.

Letters from bishops with lists of questions

An interesting sub-genre of papal rescripts consists of replies to bishops who send not one but a list of questions. The first papal decretal, of Siricius to Himerius of Tarragona, 385 C.E., deals with such a list.[11] There are strong structural similarities between the lists of questions sent in Late Antiquity and in the twelfth century.[12] F. W. Maitland pointed out that

The English bishops seem to have been peculiarly fond of submitting such questions to the pope. What, they ask, are we to do about this or that matter? In 1204 the bishop of Ely sent a whole legal catechism to Innocent III. The answering epistle has been cut up into no less than thirteen capitula [in the *Decretals of Gregory IX*, or *Liber Extra*].[13]

But the history of this interesting genre goes far beyond the thirteenth century. Soundings in the astonishingly rich *Positiones* and *Positiones (Sess.)* series of the Vatican Archives would surely reveal many such lists of 'dubia' put to the Congregation of the Council established shortly after the Council of Trent. As in the Middle Ages, they could go up to the pope. As a random instance from a still later period, in 1746 Benedict XIV wrote to the archbishop of Florence in reply to three questions relating to ecclesiastical patronage.[14]

Judges delegate

The judge delegate system is another structure transcending periods. It enabled popes to exercise power over areas and issues where they had no local knowledge. The system is already in operation under Gregory I, as

[11] K. Zechiel-Eckes, *Die erste Decretale: Der Brief Papst Siricius' an Bischof Hmerius von Tarragona vom Jahr 385 (JK 255)* (MGH Studien und Texte; Hanover, 2013); d'Avray, *Papal Jurisprudence, c. 400, passim* (the decretal constantly recurs in the thematic chapters).

[12] Very important is A. Duggan, '*De consultationibus*. The Role of Episcopal Consultation in the Shaping of Canon Law in the Twelfth Century', in B. C. Brasington and K. G. Cushing, eds., *Bishops, Texts and the Use of Canon Law around 1100. Essays in Honour of Martin Brett* (Aldershot, 2008), 191–214, especially 201–211.

[13] Maitland, 'William of Drogheda and the Universal Ordinary', in *idem*, *Roman Canon Law in the Church of England*, 124.

[14] *Benedicti Papae XIV. Bullarium*, tomus secundus, vol. 4 (Malines, 1826 edition), 52–66.

we can see thanks to the partial survival of his register. According to
Ernst Pitz, there are 65 papal letters in which we see the delegation
system in action.[15] Pitz comments that: 'All in all ... one can say that
the delegation of justice with full power to pass judgment can be classified among classical forms of papal rescripts in contested litigation.'[16] It
is not quite clear if this is meant to indicate continuity with the later
system, and as in so many respects we do not know how much was going
on in the early Middle Ages.[17]

In one case at least (in 598) it seems that it was left to the opposed
parties to pick the judges.[18] Though this did not to my knowledge
become a formal part of the judge delegate system in its thirteenth-
century heyday, as reformed by Innocent III the system was likely to
turn into de facto arbitration acceptable to both parties: close attention to
the *Geschäftsgang* gives reason to think that it was in the interests of the
parties to come to an understanding about the judges. It was argued
earlier on the basis of the Diplomatics of judges delegate (as elucidated
by Herde, Hageneder, and others) that the papal judicial system could be
run with notable economy of money and effort in the thirteenth century.

In a sense the judge delegate system was even bound up with the
provision of benefices by letters of grace. Delegates were commissioned
to carry out the provision, and doing so was a legal judgment, in that they
had to judge whether the facts on the ground fitted what the document of
conferral asserted. There were a variety of legitimate grounds – e.g.
blatant unsuitability of the person put forward – for opposing a provision
without defying papal authority, and the *executor* had to judge their
strength.[19] An *executor* might also have to face other executors enforcing

[15] Pitz, *Papstreskripte*, 189.
[16] 'Insgesamt ... kann man sagen, daß die Richterdelegation mit Urteilsvollmacht zu den
klassischen Formen des Papstreskripts in Parteisachen gehört'; Pitz, *Papstreskripte*, 190.
[17] An entry in the early medieval *Liber Diurnus* may indicate a need for a ready-made
formula to start a letter commissioning a judge delegate. The heading itself does not
suggest that: 'PROLOGUM IUDICATUM PRIVILEGIUM', hard to translate. The
contents of the formula does, however, suggest the settlement of a dispute, and if it was
being judged at Rome it is not clear why a letter would be needed: but perhaps one party
managed to obtain it without the other's presence. 'Dum pro exsequendis iustitiae
profectibus et altercantium sopiendis tergiversationibus pastoralis nos uehementer
prouocare dinoscitur sollicitudo curae. idcirco vigilantiori insistimus ut si qua inter
partes deceptio exoritur. liquida protinus indagine perscrutari & equitatis moderamine
quae ad congruendae limari et quoniam constat'; Foerster, *Liber Diurnus Romanorum
Pontificum*, C 79 = V 94 = A 74, p. 252.
[18] Letter to Victor, bishop of Palermo, 'Sicut Iudaeis', June, 598: *MGH (Epp), Gregorii
I Papae Registrum Epistolarum*, ed. L. M. Hartmann, *Libri VIII–XIV*, VIII, 25, p. 27, line
15: 'iudices a partibus eligantur'.
[19] Barraclough, *Papal Provisions*, 52–53 and (with insightful comparisons to the English
royal writ system) 92–97. See too his 'The Executors of Papal Provisions in the

other provisions to the same benefice. So the *executores* too were a sub-species of judge delegate.[20] Consequently, it may be that the letters appointing them went through the *Audientia litterarum contradictarum*,[21] where a third party's proctor would be able to have them sent back – perhaps because the *executor* was not trusted to be fair.

All this executive work was done by *honoratiores* – unsalaried agents of high status. Presumably the would-be recipient of the benefice had to pick up the administration fees for the letters appointing executors, as well as for the letter of provision, thus saving the papacy money. Money to run a world government was in shorter supply than one might think. There were a few periods when the papacy had a large and secure income: in the age of Gregory the Great thanks to Sicilian estates, in the earlier ninth century because they had acquired new lands,[22] and under John XXII and his immediate successors in the Avignon period, because of benefice taxes. At other times the income was hardly com-mensurate with the task. The details of papal Diplomatics, when under-pinned by the wider historical work on the judge delegate system, go a long way to explaining how governance nonetheless continued.[23]

There seems to be a 'folk assumption' among scholars that the judge delegate system went into decline after the thirteenth century; later

Canonical Theory of the Thirteenth and Fourteenth Centuries', *Excerptum ex Actis Congressus Iuridici Internationalis Romae 12–17 Novembris 1934*, iii, 109–153. For an up-to-date treatment correcting some of Barraclough's findings see Hitzbleck, *Exekutoren*.

[20] 'the commissioning of an executor … implied a judicial cognizance of the facts of the case and of the legal issues which a papal provision involved' (Barraclough, *Papal Provisions*, 138, and see previous note).

[21] Personal communication from Prof. Herde. This may require more investigation. The reference to Frenz, *Die Kanzlei*, 72 that I give in *Medieval Religious Rationalities*, 143 does not actually confirm Herde's hunch, tempting though that is. Frenz, *Die Kanzlei*, 151, identifies a Chancery mark indicating that a letter had passed through the *Audientia*. It is something like a *q* with two cross-bars, in a different ink, below the descender. (The cross-bars indicate that the letter had indeed been read: Frenz, *Die Kanzlei*, 153.) Is this mark found on letters appointing *executores*? That might be harder to verify than it sounds, as there was no particular reason for anyone to keep original *litterae executoriae*.

[22] Wickham, *Medieval Rome*, 21–22.

[23] P. Herde, 'Zur päpstlichen Delegationsgerichtsbarkeit'; H. Müller. 'Entscheidung auf Nachfrage: Die delegierten Richter als Verbindungsglieder zwischen Kurie und Region sowie als Gradmesser päpstlicher Autorität', in J. Johrendt and H. Müller, eds., *Römisches Zentrum und kirchliche Peripherie: Das universale Papsttum als Bezugspunkt der Kirchen von den Reformpäpsten bis zu Innozenz III* (Neue Abhandlungen der Akademie der Wissenschaften zu Göttingen, Philologisch-Historische Klasse, NS 2, Studien zu Papstgeschichte und Papsturkunden; Berlin, 2008), 109–131; d'Avray, *Medieval Religious Rationalities*, 139–142; K. Herbers, F. López Alsina and F. Engel, eds., *Das begrenzte Papsttum. Spielräume päpstlichen Handelns. Legaten – delegierte Richter – Grenzen* (Abhandlungen der Akademie der Wissenschaften zu Göttingen, NS, 25; Berlin, 2013), 237–309 (contibutions by Santiago Domínguez Sánchez, Daniel Berger, and Frank Engel).

periods certainly get much less scholarly attention. It is not easy to test this 'folk assumption'. The survival of documents commissioning judges delegate seems to be largely a matter of chance. Two turned up in the British Library's enormous collection of charters.[24] Exploration of the electronic database that goes with the great *Repertorium Germanicum* project could reveal many more cases. The technique would be to conduct online searches under 'committ. partibus'.

In this poorly charted territory researchers would do well to exploit to the full the evidence of papal registers. Harald Müller's study of Normandy only goes up to the early thirteenth century, while Jane Sayers excellent monograph quite legitimately concentrates more on local sources, and finishes at 1254. She hints, without quite asserting, that the system she has presented decayed from the later thirteenth century.[25] If we fast forward to the fifteenth century, however, we find rich material for the history of judges delegate in the *Registra Lateranensia* series.[26] An example is Reg. Lat. 823 fo. 300r–v (1482, June 1). A preliminary sounding[27] suggests that the *Dataria Apostolica, Brev. Lat.* series too is relevant: i.e. that commissions to judges delegate could be sent by brief, via the college of secretaries, under the aegis of the *Dataria*, as well as by the Chancery with its *Reg. Lat.* series of registers.

In the early modern period we are in territory still less well explored;[28] the provisional results in the present volume will surely be overtaken by future scholarship. I have stressed the chasm between the impressive body of knowledge built up by a century-and-a-half of research on medieval papal Diplomatics and the sketchy state of the field of post-Trent papal Diplomatics, where there is good 'micro-surgery'[29] on parts of the system but only the most general idea (creation of the Congregations, etc.) of how it worked as a whole. The field is wide open.

It is hard for instance to find scholarly bibliography on a new system set up by the Council of Trent. It laid down that provincial or diocesan synods should choose men (at least four) who were suitable to act as judges delegate when required. Should one of these die, the bishop after consultation with his cathedral chapter was to appoint a replacement to

---

[24] British Library Harley Charter 111 A 34, 17 August 1425. Cf. British Library Add Ch 19553 (1496, March 15).

[25] Sayers, *Papal Judges Delegate*, 276–277.

[26] For the series, see Blouin et al., *Vatican Archives*, **3.2.6.7**, pp. 133–135.

[27] AAV Dataria Ap., Brev. Lat., 10, fo. 76r–v, 12 March 1528 (also discussed above).

[28] Useful leads for the pre-Tridentine period in Frenz, *Die Kanzlei*, 94–95, especially notes 11 and 13. R. Puza, 'Signatura iustitiae und commissio. Ein Beitrag zum Prozeßgang an der römischen Kurie in der Neuzeit', *Zeitschrift der Savigny Stiftung für Rechtsgeschichte, kanonistische Abteilung*, 95 (1978), 95–115, is less relevant than its title suggests.

[29] The phrase is Miles Pattenden's (personal communication).

act until the next provincial or diocesan synod.[30] For the period after Trent a key *fondo* in the Vatican Archives for delegated justice is likely to be a source to whose importance attention was drawn earlier: *Dataria Ap., Brev. Lat.*,[31] an ill-explored series that started in 1490.[32] A document sent by Gregory XIV on 8 December 1590 is an example.[33] The Congregation of the Council also commissioned delegates – usually but not necessarily the local bishop – to collect the facts on the ground and send them back as a dossier.

Hageneder's question

'How were the Church and Christendom to be ruled without an administration equal to the task?' Hageneder's question has been a *Leitmotif* running through the detailed discussions above. Papal Diplomatics is not only a precondition for understanding papal documents, but also has the elements for solutions to the problem Hageneder posed, and partly answered, with the help of Diplomatics.

Hageneder's answer related above all to thirteenth-century letters of grace, but the phrase 'Hageneder's question' has been extended in this book to a much wider period. A general argument of this book is that 'applied Diplomatics' helps answer the question for the whole period from Late Antiquity to the early modern world, and for a wide range of documentary production, not just for the period and documentary genre that especially interested Hageneder.

In Late Antiquity the papacy had no means of enforcing legal decisions. Yet it was on the receiving end of many requests to resolve uncertainties, often arising from the incompatibilities between autonomous Christian systems which tended to occur as the latter evolved. The popes developed a 'software' based on Roman imperial rescripts to meet the demand for responses. Furthermore, the *arengae* or *prooemia* of their

---

[30] See above, note on the justice delegate system in the early modern period at the end of Chapter 5, citing Schulte and Richter, *Canones et Decreta*, 457; *ibid.*, 457–458 for resolution by the Congregation of the Council of problems arising from this new legislation. Nonetheless the system does not seem to have worked, so that popes went on appointing judges delegate as best they could. Again, see note at the end of Chapter 5.

[31] As noted above: Blouin et al., *Vatican Archives*, 3.2.7.5., pp. 146–147. Note the comment on p. 146, second column: 'one finds in this series many commissiones or assignments of tasks, pertaining to judicial matters ... These kinds of delegations of authority carry a special formula, "Mittimus vobis supplicationem presentibus introclusam ... volumusque et vobis committimus ac mandamus quatenus ... ad illius executionem procedatis ..."'.

[32] Blouin et al., *Vatican Archives*, 146, with detail and further references on the series' relation to the *Registra Supplicationum*.

[33] AAV Dataria Ap., Brev. Lat. 123, fo. 68v–71v.

responses could serve to transmit to the recipients ideas about the Petrine legitimation of the apostolic see. This Petrine ideology was then further transmitted in canon law collections from Late Antiquity on, into the Carolingian period, when the Pseudo-Isidorian forgeries also transmitted genuine papal decretals from Late Antiquity to an extensive clerical public.

Then, in the post-Carolingian period, a version of 'Hageneder's question' needs to be asked to explain how the papacy was able to meet the demand for documents despite the woeful inadequacies of papal administrators when it came to basic Latin. The quantity of demand for papal letters was a tiny fraction of what it was to become, but, to compare small things with large, there was an analogous asymmetry between demand and the capacity to produce. Diplomatics provided an answer: papal privileges were written in an ancient script so hard to read that the beneficiaries were unlikely to be able to check the Latin, whereas the materiality of the documents – papyrus – and their extraordinary length did the work of enhancing papal prestige. Moreover, those lousy Latinists did not need to do much prose composition: they could take the formulae for the beginnings and ends of the documents from the *Liber Diurnus* formulary (the Latin of which was also shaky), and the substantive part from drafts brought by the representatives of the beneficiaries (the Latin of which was interestingly local).

For all the vast difference in scale, there are analogies with the later production of papal documents. In the later period, too, papal government was predominantly demand-driven. Then, too, much of the work was done by the people who wanted the documents. Those who sought papal justice, graces or the resolution of uncertainties were prepared to share much of the burden of its production. They could do much of the drafting of the letters they sought. Just as with the early Middle Ages, we have seen how people came to the papal court with prepared texts that might only need to be tweaked, or (this was a difference) who got an experienced proctor to do their draft. The formularies used by the papal administrators to save thinking case-by-case were available outside the curia (as the *Liber Diurnus* had been). The curial officials were likely to find that the petitioner or litigant, or their proctor, had saved them the trouble of finding the relevant formula. As the pressure of business mounted in the twelfth century and afterwards, the main bill for producing documents was picked up by the petitioners and litigants, who paid directly the *scriptores* and others (notably *abbreviatores*, from the thirteenth century) involved in the documents' journey through the system.

Agents in the locality cost the papacy little. We have seen that in Late Antiquity papal jurisprudence predominantly took the form of replies to questions from bishops. When they received the answers of the apostolic see it was up to the bishops to enforce them if they chose to do so.

Later on, perhaps even under Gregory I, but above all from the twelfth century on, the delegation system must be a key element in any answer to 'Hageneder's question'. Papal judges delegate and executors of papal decisions in the localities did not so far as we know get paid by the papacy. Acting with papal authority enhanced their status, and to say 'yes' when asked to do so was a duty that went with their status. It was not easy to say 'no' to the occasional papal request to take on full papal authority.

After Trent, day-to-day jurisprudence was handled inexpensively by the Congregation of the Council, run by a committee of cardinals whose income came from elsewhere, and serviced by a secretary with a small staff. We may surmise – it is just a guess – that the canon law and theology consultants may have given their services for nothing except the status of being at the centre of religious decision-making. To maintain consistency, in-house records of previous decisions were kept. It is true that in contested cases between clients with means the parties would employ expensive lawyers, but that was not the papacy's problem, any more than the cost of legal counsel for well-heeled litigants is a problem for the modern state. There was a procedure for indigent litigants.

A general conclusion

All of these papal systems were controlled by rules. Hageneder put his question in the context of the papacy's problem in keeping track of the letters of grace it had already issued. His convincing answer was that there was a system of ranking rules to enable local bishops and papal executors to decide on priorities of competing letters. One may generalise from this example. The papacy lacked the resources to fund a 'Weberian' bureaucracy but was adept at devising standardised sets of rules governing its communications and enabling it to run systems that circumvented its own shortcomings, and thus it was able to meet the expanding demand for its services. The mechanics of how this was done can only be uncovered with the help of the discipline of applied Diplomatics, and this book has tried to apply the discipline to explain the how. Why there was the demand remains to be explained, a different story.

Transcriptions

*404. Innocent I to Victricius of Rouen: the *arenga*.

J^3.665 = Old Jaffé 286 (85)

The base manuscript is BAV Vat. Lat. 5845, fo. 83ra–b, siglum *Db*. For the status of this manuscript and a description see d'Avray, *Papal Jurisprudence, c. 400*, 4, 30–42. Readings or lemmata are from *Db* unless otherwise stated. Cues to textual variants are before the lemma, cues to sources after the lemma.

Db is collated against BAV Vat. Lat. 630, siglum *V630*, fo. 207ra–b. It is a key manuscript of Pseudo-Isidore and the base manuscript for the edition being prepared by Eric Knibbs. Where they diverge, I have collated the other main (though generally inferior) manuscript of the Late Antique *Dionysiana*, Paris, BNF 3837, fo. 107vb–108vb, siglum *Da* (cf. d'Avray, *Papal Jurisprudence, c. 400*, 27, description 44–45) and a good manuscript (probably) of the *Quesnelliana* collection, Arras Bibliothèque Municipale 572 (744), fo. 53r–v, siglum *Qa* (cf. d'Avray, *Papal Jurisprudence, c. 400*, 26–27, 48; description 42–44). I note their readings when they agree with *V630* against *Db*.

For present purposes this *arenga* is of interest as a carrier of Petrine papal ideology: hence the emphasis on the close match between the Late Antique transmission by the *Dionysiana* and *Quesnelliana*, on the one hand, and the Pseudo-Isidore transmission which magnified it. What Pseudo-Isidore transmitted was substantially the genuine article in this case. The influence may be inferred from the wide diffusion of Pseudo-Isidore. The *arenga* also influenced the forged part of Pseudo-Isidore: Ps. Felix II JK =230 c. 12 'adjuvante deo et sancto apostolo Petro apostolo, per quem et apostolatus et episcopatus in Christo cepit exordium' (BAV Vat. Lat. 130, siglum *V130*, fo. 194ra; *PL* 130 col. 645; J^3.†505 = Old Jaffé †230 (clviii)).[1]

---

[1] Pending the critical edition which is in the hands of Eric Knibbs, and rather than cite an electronic edition whose future cannot be guaranteed, the Patrologia Latina edition is

Important too is direct evidence of its influence. This is picked up in the following works (and very likely others too):

- Letter Pope Gregory I to Boniface-Wynfrith, *MGH* Epp. Sel. 1, letter 26, pp. 44–45.
- Hincmar of Laon, *Rotula prolixa*, *MGH* Conc. 4, Suppl. 2: 'Die Streitschriften Hinkmars von Reims und Hinkmars von Laon 869–871': 'Sed dicam vobis, quod tacere nec debeo nec audeo: Non putavi ad dehonorationem vestri pertinuisse, quod Romam misi, quod Romam ire volui et volo, quod a Roma auxilium expetivi, unde omnis episcopatus sumpsit exordium et retinet processionis et successionis incrementum'; p. 374. Cf. p. 380 at note 92.
- 'Epistolae Gregorii IV. Papae', *MGH* Epp. 5 *Epistolae Karolini Aevi (III)*: '... omnis sanctae religionis relatio ad sedem apostolicam, quasi ad capud ecclesiarum debet referri, et inde *normam* sumere, unde sumpsit *exordium* ...'; p. 79 (my italics).
- 'Nicolai I. Papae Epistolae De Causis Rothadi et Wulfadi', in *MGH* Epp., *Epistolae Karolini Aevi (IV)*: 'Dispensationem quippe redemptionis humani generis ante tempora saecularia Deus omnipotens penes se ordinatam custodiens, tempore carnis ostendens, ascensurus ad caelos in apostoli Petri, per quem et apostolatus et episcopatus sumpsit exordium, confessione curaque praecipue collocavit'; p. 399.

'<INTITULATIO>Innocentius <INSCRIPTIO> [2]Victori episcopo Rotomagensi <SALUTATIO> salutem.

<ARENGA> Etsi [3]tamen, [4]frater, pro merito et honore sacerdotii, quo plurimum polles vivendi et docendi [5]ecclesiasticae regulae nota sunt omnia, neque est aliquid **(Db, fo. 83rb)** quod de sacris lectionibus tibi minus [6]esse videatur, tamen quia Romanae ecclesiae normam atque auctoritatem magnopere [7]postulastis, voluntati tuae [8]morem admodum gerens [9]de gestis vitae et morum probabilium disciplinas annexas litteris meis misi, per quas [10]advertunt ecclesiarum regionis vestrae populi, quibus rebus et regulis christianorum vita in sua [11]cuiusque professione debeat contineri, qualisque servetur in urbis

preferable to the edition by Hinschius: see H. Fuhrmann, *Einfluß und Verbreitung der pseudoisidorischen Fälschungen*, 3 vols. (*MGH* Schriften, XXIV, 1–3; Stuttgart, 1972–1974), vol. i, p. 174.
[2] Victoritio *Da:* Victricio *Qa:* Victorico *V630.*   [3] tibi *Da, Qa, V630.*
[4] frater karissime *Da, Qa (cor. from* karissimae), *V630.*
[5] ecclesiasticae regulae] *Db, Da, V630,* secundum ecclesiasticas regulas *Qa (making better sense).*
[6] collectum esse *Da, Qa, V630.*   [7] postulasti *Da, Qa, V630.*
[8] *cor. from* morum *in V630.*   [9] de gestis] *after correction in Qa:* digestas *V630.*
[10] advertant *Da, Qa, V630.*   [11] cuiuscumque *V630.*

Romae ecclesiis [12]disciplina. Erit dilectionis tuae per plebes finitimas et consacerdotes nostros, qui in illis regionibus propriis ecclesiis praesident, regularum hunc librum quasi [13]didascalicum atque monitorem sedulo insinuare, ut et nostros cognoscere et [14]in fidem confluentium mores valeant docendi sedulitate [15]reformare. (**V630, fo 207rb**) Aut enim propositum suum ex hac nostra congruenti lectione cognoscent aut, si quid adhuc desideratur, facile poterunt ex [16]bona imitatione supplere. [17]Incipiamus igitur, (**Db, fo. 83va**) adiuvante [18]sancto apostolo Petro, per quem et apostolatus et aepiscopatus in Christo caepit exordium, ut, quoniam plures saepe [19]emerserunt causae, quae in aliquantis non erant causae, sed crimina, ut de caetero sollicitudo sit unicuique sacerdoti in [20]suam ecclesiam curam huiusmodi habere, sicut [21]apostolus praedicat Paulus, talem ecclesiam deo exhibendam non habentem maculam aut rugam, [22]nec alicuius morbidae ovis afflatu conscientia nostra contaminata violetur. Propter eos igitur, qui vel ignorantia vel [23]desidia [24]pigritia ignavia non [25]tenent ecclesiasticam disciplinam [26]et multa non praesumenda praesumunt, recte postulasti, ut in illis partibus istiusmodi, quam tenet ecclesia Romana, forma servetur: non quod nova praecepta aliqua [27]inpenderentur, sed ea, quae per desidiam aliquorum neglecta sunt, ab omnibus observari cupiamus, quae tamen apostolica et patrum traditione sunt constituta. (**Db, fo. 83vb**) Scriptum est namque [28]ad Timotheum [29]Paulo monente: State et tenete traditiones nostras, [30]quas didicistis sive per verbum sive per epistolam. Illud certe tuam debet mentem vehementius excitare, ut ab omni labe saeculi istius inmunis ante dei conspectum [31]securus inveniaris. [32]Cui multum enim creditur, plus ab eo exigitur. Ergo quoniam non pro nobis tantum, sed pro populo Christi cogimur praestare rationem, [33]disciplina deifica populum erudire debemus. [34]Extiterunt enim nonnulli qui statuta maiorum non tenentes castitatem ecclesiae [35]sua praesumptione [36]violarent, populi favorem sequentes et dei

---

[12] *The ';' mark following* disciplina *in V630 is probably punctuation, not an abbreviation mark. Is it possible that it could derive from the semi-colon-like word separation mark in* Qa, *fo. 53, seven lines up?*

[13] magisterium *added in margin after* didascalicum *in Db.*   [14] ad *Da, Qa, V630.*

[15] formare *Da, Qa:* formari *V630.*   [16] his bona *V630.*   [17] Incipiamur *V630.*

[18] sancto apostolo] deo et sancto dei apostolo *V630.*

[19] emersesunt *Db?:* emerserint *Da: cor. from* merserunt *in V630.*

[20] suam ecclesiam] sua ecclesia *Da, Qa, V630.*   [21] beatus apostolus *V630.*

[22] aut *Da, Qa:* ne *V630.*   [23] dissidia *Da.*

[24] pigritia ignavia *(clearly an incorporated gloss)*] om. *Da, Qa, V630.*

[25] *cor. from* tenerit *in V630.*

[26] et multa non praesumenda praesumunt, recte] ut multa non presumenda quae sunt rectae *Da.*

[27] imperentur *Da, Qa, V630.*

[28] ad Thessalonicenses secunda et ad *V630: Qa interlines* Thessolonicenses.

[29] apostolo Paulo *V630.*   [30] quas didicistis] om. *Da, Qa:* quas tradidi vobis *V630.*

[31] et securus *V630.*   [32] Cum *V630.*

[33] disciplina deifica populum] *probably corrected from clear* disciplinam deificam populum *in Qa:* idcirco disciplina dei sanctificare populum et *V630.*

[34] Extiterunt enim nonnulli] *cor. between lines to* Quosdam enim asseris exstitisse *Qa:* Quosdam enim asseris exstitisse *V630.*

[35] suam *Da:* suae *V630: cor. from* suae *Qa.*   [36] violant *V630.*

iudicium non timentes. Ergo ne silentio nostro existimemur his praebere consensum, [37]dicente domino: Videbas furem et currebas cum eo, haec sunt, quae deinceps intuitu divini iudicii omnem catholicum episcopum expedit custodire.'

*1195, January 21. TNA SC 7/9/35.

Celestine III indulgence for alms for nuns. National Archives, Kew, online catalogue entry notes that the document is sealed with silk thread.

'<INTITULATIO> Celestinus episcopus servus servorum dei, <INSCRIPTIO> venerabilibus fratribus archiepiscopis, episcopis, abbatibus, prioribus et aliis ecclesiarum prelatis ad quos /1// littere iste pervenerint, <SALUTATIO> salutem et apostolicam benedictionem. <ARENGA> Quoniam, ut ait Apostolus, omnes stabimus ante tribunal Christi recepturi prout gessimus /2// in corpore, sive bonum sive malum, oportet nos diem messionis extreme misericordie operibus prevenire, et eternorum in-/3//-tuitu seminare in terris quod reddente Domino cum multiplicato fructu colligere valeamus in celis, certam spem fi-/4//-duciamque tenentes, quoniam qui parce seminat parce et metet, et qui seminat in benedictionibus, de benedictio-/5//-nibus et metet vitam eternam. <NARRATIO> Cum itaque dilecte in Christo filie priorissa et moniales ecclesie sancte Marie de Wika ea /6// dicantur inopia laborare, quod redditus sui ad earum sustentionem sufficere minime dinoscantur, tali con-/7//-sideratione inducti et illarum maximis necessitatibus provocati, <DISPOSITIO> fraternitatem vestram presentibus litteris exhor-/8//-tamur, et attentius commonemus, quatinus unde earum suppleatur inopia, populum vobis a deo commissum /9// ad beneficia prescripte ecclesie sancte Marie de Wika conferenda, exemplo inducatis et verbo. Nos vero de bea-/10//torum apostolorum Petri et Pauli meritis confisi omnibus qui a festo nativitatis beate Marie virginis usque ad festum /11// sancti Michaelis et per Octabas eius eiusdem, prenominatum locum visitaverint, et sanctimonialibus ibidem deo servientibus ali-/12//-qua beneficia erogaverint, centum dies vere penitentibus et confessis indulgemus: rogantes et commonentes vos in Christo /13// quatinus divini intuitu et pro caritate beati Petri et nostra sepedictis monialibus gratiam aliquam conferatis. <DATATIO> Datum Lat-/14//-ran' xii Kal. Februarii pontificatus nostri anno quinto.'

*1200, March 8. TNA SC 7/19/16.

Innocent tells prelates to protect the Templars. Though it is sealed with silk thread, it does not have the other features of a letter of grace: no ligatures, no 'tittles' instead of straight-line superscript abbreviations. In content, it is a mandate, a command to the prelates. Nonetheless it functions as a privilege

---

[37] dicente domino] domino dicente per prophetam *V630*.

which would explain the silk thread. Sayers, Original Papal Documents, *p. 7, no. 12, calendars the document as follows: 'Mandate to the archbishops, bishops, abbots, priors, and other prelates of churches, to whom these letters shall come, to cause full justice to be shown to the brothers of the order of Knights of the Temple, when they request it, against all evil-doers, both clerks and laymen, within their jurisdiction.'*

'<INTITULATIO> Innocentius episcopus servus servorum dei, <INSCRIPTIO> venerabilibus fratribus archiepiscopis, episcopis et dilectis filiis abbatibus prioribus et aliis /1// ecclesiarum prelatis ad quos littere iste pervenerint, <SALUTATIO> salutem et apostolicam benedictionem. <NARRATIO> Non absque dolore cordis et plurima turbatione di-/2//-dicimus quod ita in plerisque partibus ecclesiastica censura dissolvitur, et canonice sententie severitas enervatur, /3// ut viri religiosi, et hii maxime qui per sedis apostolice privilegia maiori donati sunt libertate, passim a male-4//-factoribus suis iniurias sustineant et rapinas, dum vix invenitur qui congrua illis protectione subveni-/5//-at, et pro fovenda pauperum innocentia se murum defensionis opponat. Specialiter autem dilecti filii nostri /6// fratres militie Templi tam de frequentibus iniuriis quam de cotidiano defectu iustitie conquerentes, /7// universitatem vestram litteris petierunt apostolicis excitari, ut ab iniuriis quas sustinent et pressuris vestro /8// possint presidio respirare. <DISPOSITIO> Eapropter, universitati vestre per apostolica scripta mandamus firmiterque precipimus /9// quatinus, cum predicti fratres, qui pro singulis iniuriis sibi illatis ad sedem apostolicam sine gravi dif-/10//-ficultate recursum habere non possunt, ad vos venerint iustitiam postulantes, de omnibus malefa-/11//-ctoribus suis tam clericis quam laicis vestre iurisditioni subiectis faciatis per censuram ecclesiastiam re-/12//-moto appellationis et dilationis obstaculo eisdem iustitie plentitudinem exhiberi, ita quod pro defectu /13// iustitie suam ad nos deferre querimoniam non cogantur. <DATATIO> Datum Lateran' viii / Id' martii pontificatus nostri anno tertio.'

*1212, February 24. BL Add Ch 1542. Monastic exemption dispute.

There had been a long-running dispute between this daughter house of Cluny and the local bishop. It had been entrusted to judges delegate, and then come to Rome, but had not been decided because the house did not have the requisite documents at hand. It was finally settled at another hearing, on the previous feast of St. Martin. The document shows the complexities that could arise out of exemption, especially when the exempt house has parishes. The document looks at first sight like an original letter of grace but not when one examines it more closely. It seems to be a copy made to look like a letter of grace, not for purposes of forgery but, more probably, for archival purposes, to show at a glance that this was a document granting privileges to the monastery.

Most of the letter matches the Litterae executoriae *sent on 24 February 1212 to the abbot of Saint-Sulpice of Bourges and to the dean and archdeacon of Bourges, who were charged with ensuring that the settlement was activated: see* F. *Villard,* Recueil des documents relativs à l'abbaye de Montierneuf de Poitiers (1076–1319) *(Archives Historiques de Poitou, LIX; Poitiers, 1973), no. 117, pp. 191–194: details of other copies/near copies ibid., 192.*

'<INTITULATIO> INNOCENTIUS Episcopus servus servorum dei <INSCRIPTIO> Dilectis filiis Cluniacen' et monasterii Novi Pictavensis Abbatibus et Conventibus <SALUTATIO> Salutem et apostolicam benedictionem. <NARRATIO, COMBINED WITH NOTIFICATIO> Causam que /1// vertebatur inter vos ex parte una et venerabilem fratrem nostrum episcopum et dilectos filios capitulum Pictavense ex altera super exemptione Monasterii Novi Pictavensis diversis iudicibus nos recolimus commisisse, su-/2//-per qua, licet diversis temporibus fuerit multipliciter laboratum, testes tamen ex mandato nostro ab utraque parte recepti fuerunt, et demum depositiones eorum*n*dem apud sedem apostolicam publicate. Verum, quia /3// pars vestra privilegia sua tunc pre manibus non habebat, partibus postmodum nostris dedimus litteris in mandatis, ut super eadem causa munite privilegiis, et aliis rationibus que ad ipsius decisionem spectabant /4// per se vel sufficientes procuratores in festo beati Martini proxime preterito nostro se conspectui presentarent, tam super predicta causa quam super aliis articulis equitatis iudicium dante Domino recepture. Demum /5// igitur dilectis filiis Petro Salathiele ac Iohanne monachis vestris, et magistro Iohanne et Hugone canonico Sancte Radegunde Pict' predictorum episcopi et capituli procuratoribus in nostra presentia constitutis /6// audivimus diligenter que voluerunt proponere coram nobis, et cum hincinde super premissis fuisset diutius disputatum, tandem idem negotium de consensu partium nobis mediantibus taliter /7// est sopitum, <DISPOSITIO> quod Abbas et conventus Monasterii Novi ut Pictavensis episcopus favorabilior sit eis et efficacior ad iustitiam de suis malefactoribus faciendam, semel in anno per diem unum cum /8// moderato equitaturarum numero prout in Lateranensi concilio est statutum[38] eundem exibeant et procurent; in ceteris vero idem monasterium ab eius iurisdictione sit liberum et exemptum, nisi quod crisma / 9// oleum sanctum, consecrationes altarium, dedicationes basilicarum, ordinationes monachorum seu clericorum, qui ad sacros ordines fuerint promovendi, necnon et benedictionem abbatis, sine professione aliqua, [39]recipi-/10//-ent ab episcopo memorato, si quidem catholicus fuerit et gratiam apostolice sedis [40]habuerit, ac ea ipsis gratis et sine pravitate aliqua voluerit exibere; alioquin liceat eis quemcumque maluerint catholicum /11// adire antistitem, gratiam et communionem apostolice sedis habentem, qui nostra fretus auctoritate, ipsis quod postulatur impendat, sicut in autenticis privilegiis continetur, que nos ipsi perspeximus /12// et examinavimus diligenter. Cum

---

[38] Summerlin, *The Canons of the Third Lateran Council*, 112 and index *s.v.* '1179, Lateran Council, canons of … c. 4'.

[39] recipient] *sic ms., probably error for* recipiant *as in the papal register.*   [40] hui't *ms.*

autem Pictavensis episcopus in civitate Pictavensi generale posuerit interdictum, iidem illud servabunt, ita quod illo durante non celebrabunt divina nisi clausis / 13// ianuis, non pulsatis companis, suppressa voce, interdictis et excommunicatis exclusis, quos caute vitare curabunt. Ad sinodum quoque Pictavensis episcopi abbas monasterii Novi, secundum generalem consuetudinem /14// regionis accedet ratione capellarum, vel ecclesiarum suarum, que ipsi episcopo sunt subiecte, sed si forsitan capellani ea que statuta fuerint in synodo neglexerint aut contempserint observare /15// non in abbatem vel monasterium, set in ipsos cappellanos, episcopus poterit canonicam exercere censuram. Ne igitur quod nobis mediantibus est statutum valeat ab aliquo temere violari, illud auctoritate /16// apostolica confirmamus et presentis scripti patrocinio communimus. <PROHIBITIO> Nulli ergo omnino hominum liceat hanc paginam nostre confirmationis infringere vel ei ausu temerario contraire. <SANCTIO> Si quis autem hoc attemp-/17//-tare presumpserit, indignationem omnipotentis dei et beatorum Petri et Pauli apostolorum eius se noverit incursurum. <DATATIO> Datum Lat. vi. kl. Martii pontificatus nostri anno quintodecimo.' Nos vero abbas et conventus mo-/18//-nasterii Novi predicti huiusmodi privilegium sicuti de verbo ad verbum superius continetur penes nos reservamus, et eius transcriptum sanctissimo patri nostro in Christo . . abbati Cluniacensi sigillis nostris si-/19//-gillatum nos tradidimus reservandum in testimonium veritatis[41] /20//.'

Corresponding entry in the papal register, Innocent III Reg Vat 8, fo. 84v: '... Datum Lateran' vi. kal. martii. pontificatus nostri anno quinto decimo. In eodem modo scriptum est Clunian' et monasterii Novi Pictavensis abbatibus et conventibus: 'Causam que vertebatur, etc', usque in finem. # In eodem modo scriptum est super hoc abbati Sancti Supplicii, .. decano et archidiacono Bituricen': 'Causam que vertebatur, etc.', usque 'ab aliquo temere violari, districte vobis per apostolica scripta precipientes mandamus quatinus id observari per censuram ecclesiasticam appellatione [42]postposita firmiter nunc faciatis, contradictores censura simili compescendo, quod si non omnes, etc., duo vestrum', usque 'exequantur'. Datum Lateran' vi. kal. martii pontificatus nostri anno quinto decimo.'

*1243, July 10. AAV Reg. Vat. 21i, fo. 4r

Innocent IV prevents Agen falling under interdict because of the misdemeanours of the count of Toulouse or his officials.

---

[41] The passage from 'Nos vero abbas ...' to 'testimonium veritatis' states that a verbatim copy of the document was sent to the mother house; BL Add Ch 1542 is in fact the copy in question. It is one of a number of Cluny documents acquired by the British Library.

[42] postposita firmiter]?: postfir *or* postfu *ms. without the expected point after* postposita *and with the* firmiter *oddly placed stylistically.*

'xxi. [INSCRIPTIO] *Episcopo Agennensi.* [NARRATIO] Ex parte tua nobis extitit intimatum quod cum Civitas Agennensis excepta medietate iustitie tempor/alis ad te pertineat pleno iure, multotiens accidit quod pro delicto Comitis Tholosani vel suorum / officialium ecclesiastico supponitur interdicto in gravem Agennensis ecclesie lesionem. Quare nobis hu/militer supplicasti, ut providere super hoc de benignitate sedis apostolice curaremus. [DISPOSITIO] Fraternitatis itaque tue / supplicationibus inclinati volentes tibi facere gratiam specialem, auctoritate presentium inhibemus ne aliquis / tuo ad id vel Capituli Agennensis non accedente consensu, in civitatem predictam occasione dictorum / Comitis vel Officialium interdicti sententiam nisi de mandato sedis apostolice speciali audeat pro/mulgare. [PROHIBITIO & SANCTIO] Nulli ergo nostre inhibitionis etc. Siquis autem etc. Datum Anagn. vi. id. Iulii anno primo./'

*1244, March 7. Innocent IV. BL Add Ch 17857.

The pope prohibits excommunication or interdict by ecclesiastical authorities against Foucarmont abbey or its servants.

This is a letter of grace – conferring a favour and to be kept – in form as well as content. The whole of the pope's name is in capitals, there are long ct and st ligatures, and tittles instead of plain superscripts. The initial letters of Dilectis, Cum [a nobis], Ex [parte], Nos [autem], Nulli, and Si [quis] are in bold. The only deviation from the standard appearance is that the ascenders of the top line are lower and more sober than one might expect from a classic letter of grace.

Sayers, Original Papal Documents, *no. 260, p. 120, catalogues it as follows: 'Grant to the abbot and convent of Foucarmont, Cistercian Order, diocese of Rouen, that ecclesiastical authorities may not excommunicate or pass sentence of interdict upon members of their household (familiares), servants, benefactors, or any others who grind in their mills or cook in their ovens.' Sealed on silk ('extat ser.', Sayers). Cf. Morgan, 'Religious Dimensions', 192, Sayer,* Original Papal Documents, *no. 279, pp. 127–128, and the formula in* Tangl, Die päpstlichen Kanzleiordnungen, *p. 256, no. XV.*

'<INTITULATIO> INNOCENTIUS episcopus servus servorum dei <INSCRIPTIO> Dilectis filiis .. abbati et conventui monasterii Fulcardimontis Cisterciensis ordinis Ro-/1//-thomagensis diocesis, <SALUTATIO> salutem et apostolicam benedictionem. <ARENGA> Cum a nobis petitur quod iustum est et honestum, tam vigor equitatis quam ordo exigit / 2// rationis ut id per sollicitudinem officii nostri ad debitum perducatur effectum. <NARRATIO> Ex parte siquidem vestra fuit propositum coram nobis quod /3// nonnulli ecclesiarum prelati vestris libertatibus invidentes cum eis non liceat ex apostolice sedis indulto in vos excomunicationis vel interdicti /4// sententias promulgare, in familiares servientes et benefactores ac illos qui molunt in molendinis vel coquunt in furnis vestris quique ven-/5//-dendo seu emendo vel alias vobis comunicant sententias proferunt memoratas, sicque non vim et potestatem privilegiorum vestrorum sed sola /6// verba servantes vos quodammodo excommunicant, dum vobis alios [43]comunicare non sinunt, et ex hoc iudicari videmini iudicio iudeorum, et qui /7// vobis comunicant in predictis illud evenit inconveniens quod maiorem excomunicationem incurrant quam excomunicatis [44]excomuni-/8//-cando fuerant incursuri. Quare nobis humiliter supplicastis ut providere quieti vestre super hoc paterna sollicitudine curaremus. <DISPOSITIO> Nos autem /9// vestris supplicationibus inclinati, ne quis [45]predictorum huiusmodi sententias in fraudem privilegiorum apostolice sedis decetero promulgare pres[sumat] /10// auctoritate presentium inhibemus, decernentes eas si per presumptionem cuiuspiam taliter promulgari contigerit irritas et inanes. /11// <PROHIBITIO> Nulli ergo omnino hominum liceat hanc paginam nostre inhibitionis infringere vel ei ausu temerario contraire. <SANCTIO> Si quis autem hoc at-/12//-temtare presumpserit, indignationem omnipotentis dei et beatorum Petri et Pauli apostolorum eius se noverit incursurum. Datum Lateran' /13// non. martii pontificatus nostri anno primo.'

*1255, March 20. BL Harley Ch 111. A. 21.

'*Faculty to the bishop of Hereford to appoint seven clerks to benefices in the cities and dioceses of Worcester, London, Winchester and Hereford; if prebendal, they are to be admitted as canons notwithstanding any statute limiting numbers.*'[46] 'On 9 April 1255 Alexander issued the fatal bull setting out the terms on which Henry III could sign up for Sicily: Foedera, 316–318. Aigueblanche was Henry's envoy at the papal court and closely involved in it all. Doubtless this concession was his reward. No wonder Matthew Paris fulminated about the papal use of 'notwith-standing'. At the same time Aigueblanche was devising the scheme whereby English religious houses took out fictional loans from Italian merchants, their repayments being set against the money they owed for the crusading tax. The payments in fact went to the pope or to pay off papal debts. No wonder the hostility to Aigueblanche in England was sulpherous.[47] Calendar in Sayers, Original Papal Documents, no. 480, p. 217. Sayers identifies the scribe as '*ra': written on the fold on the right-hand side: cf. her list of scribes p. 527.

'<INTITULATIO> Alexander episcopus servus servorum dei [INSCRIPTIO] venerabili fratri [48].. episcopo Herefordensi <SALUTATIO> salutem et apostolicam benedictionem. <ARENGA-NARRATIO> Honestum esse /1// censemus et quasi debitum, nec indignum, ut favor apostolice gratie quo digne personam tuam prosequimur, tuis cedat interdum dome-/2//-sticis gratiosus. <DISPOSITIO> Devotis igitur fraternitatis tue precibus inclinati, providendi

---

[43] *After erasure, probably of* 'ex'?   [44] *Error for* 'communicando'.

[45] *It is tempting to emend to* 'prelatorum' *but other similar letters have* 'predictorum'.

[46] Sayers, *Original Papal Documents*, no. 480, p. 217.

[47] David Carpenter, personal communication, 25 November 2020.

[48] *Dots on either side of erasure.*

septem clericis cuilibet eorum de unico ec-/3//-clesiastico beneficio competenti
vel alio etiam si curam habeat animarum si vacat vel quamcito se facultas
obtulerit, ad cuiuscumque collationem /4// vel presentationem pertineat, cui
super iure suo preiudicari per hoc in posterum nolumus, in civitatibus vel
diocesibus Wigorniensi Lon-/5//-doniensi Wintoniensi et Herefordensi et
eorum singulos inducendi per te vel alium in corporalem beneficii
possessionem huiusmodi /6// ac faciendi eos in ecclesiis in quibus eis duxeris
providendum, si prebendales existunt, in canonicos et in fratres admitti cum /7//
plenitudine iuris canonici stallo sibi in choro et loco in capitulo assignatis, necnon
contradictores – monitione premissa – per cen-/8//-suram ecclesiasticam,
appellatione postposita, compescendi, non obstante certo canonicorum numero
vel contraria consuetudine aut statuto /9// iuramento, confirmatione apostolica
vel alia quacumque firmitate vallatis, vel si pro aliis apostolica sint ibi scripta
directa quibus nolumus huius-/10//-modi obtentu rescripti preiudicium generari,
seu si eccclesiarum ipsarum personis ab apostolica sede indultum existat quod
interdici suspendi /11/ vel excommunicari non possint per litteras sedis eiusdem
plenam de ipso indulto et expressam de tenore ipsius de verbo ad verbum
mentionem /12// minime facientes, liberam tibi auctoritate presentium
concedimus facultatem. <PROHIBITIO> Nulli ergo omnino hominum liceat
hanc pa-/13//-ginam nostre concessionis infringere vel ei ausu temerario
contraire. <SANCTIO> Si quis autem hoc attemptare presumpserit,
indignationem omnipotentis /14// dei et beatorum Petri et Pauli apostolorum
eius se noverit incursurum. <DATATIO> Datum Neapoli xiii kal. aprilis /15//
pontificatus nostri anno primo.'

*1268 June 1. BL Add Ch 6306.

*Clement IV approves the appropriation of a parish to the cathedral chapter of
Worms. Calendar in Sayers,* Original Papal Documents, *no. 732, p. 330.*

'<INTITULATIO> Clemens episcopus servus servorum dei, <INSCRIPTIO>
dilectis filiis .. decano et capitulo ecclesie sancti Andree Warmaciensis,
<SALUTATIO> salutem et apostolicam benedictionem. <ARENGA> Iustis
pete-/1//-entium desideriis dignum est nos facilem prebere consensum, et vota
que a rationis tramite non discordant effectu prosequente complere.
<NARRATIO> Sane /2// petitio vestra nobis exhibita continebat quod
venerabilis frater noster .. Warmaciensis episcopus, attendens quod redditus et
proventus prebendarum vestrarum erant /3// adeo tenues et exiles quod ex illis
sustentationem nequibatis assequi congruentem, ecclesiam in [49]Bentherscim
Warmaciensis diocesis in qua ius habebatis /4// patronatus diligenti
deliberatione prehabita vobis in prebendarum ipsarum augmentum auctoritate
ordinaria duxit in usus proprios concedendam, /5// ita quod quamcito illam per
eiusdem rectoris obitum vacare contingeret, possetis eam usibus huiusmodi
applicare, de ipsius ecclesie proventibus vicario /6// inibi perpetuo servituro pro

---

[49] *For* Bentersheim.

sustentatione sua et supportandis eiusdem ecclesie oneribus portione congrua reservata capituli Wormaciensis ad id /7// accedente consensu prout in litteris inde confectis plenius dicitur contineri. <DISPOSITIO> Nos itaque vestris supplicationibus inclinati quod per eundem episcopum /8// super hoc provide factum est ratum habentes et firmum illud auctoritate apostolica confirmamus et presentis scripti patrocinio communimus. /9// <PROHIBITIO> Nulli ergo omnino hominum liceat hanc paginam nostre confirmationis infringere vel ei ausu temerario contraire. <SANCTIO> Si quis autem hoc attemptare /10// presumpserit, indignationem omnipotentis dei et beatorum Petri et Pauli apostolorum eius se noverit incursurum. <DATATIO> Dat. Viterbii /11// kal. iunii pontificatus nostri anno quarto.'

*1277, Jan 18. BL Add Ch 1548.

Judge delegate given right to investigate property which Cluny and its dependencies wrongly alienated (according to the current abbot) and to restore them where appropriate. Calendar in Sayers, Original Papal Documents, *no. 791, p. 357.*

*This is a mandate, so its appearance is identical to that of a letter of justice. Only the first letter of the pope's name is a capital, the ascenders in the first line are of moderate size, the normal horizontal superscript line is used as an abbreviation rather than the superscript, and there are no extended ligatures. Note the use of clauses (*clausulae*).*

'<INTITULATIO> Johannes episcopus servus servorum dei, <INSCRIPTIO> dilecto filio .. abbati sancti Cornelii de Compendio Suessionensis diocesis <SALUTATIO> salutem et apostolicam benedictionem. <NARRATIO> Ex parte /1// dilecti filii .. abbatis Cluniacensis nobis extitit intimatum quod tam abbates et priores qui fuerunt pro tempore ac conventus Cluniacenses /2// quam priores et conventus prioratuum Cluniacensis ordinis monasterio Cluniacensi pleno iure subiectorum domos grangias prata nemora /3// molendina possessiones redditus vineas iura iurisdictiones et quedam alia bona eorumdem monasterii et prioratuum datis super hoc litteris et in-/4//-strumentis confectis publicis, interpositis iuramentis et penis adiectis nonnullis clericis et laicis aliquibus eorum ad vitam, quibusdam vero ad non /5// modicum tempus et aliis perpetuo ad firmam vel sub censu annuo pro sue voluntatis arbitrio in ipsorum monasterii et prioratuum lesionem enor-/6//-mem concedere presumpserunt, quorum aliqui litteras confirmationis in forma communi a sede apostolica impetrasse dicuntur. Quare /7// idem abbas nobis humiliter supplicavit ut ipsis monasterio Cluniacensi et prioratibus super hoc providere paterna sollicitudine curaremus. /8// <DISPOSITIO> Nos itaque ipsius precibus inclinati discretioni tue per apostolica scripta mandamus quatinus non obstantibus iuramentis instrumentis et /9// litteris, penis ac confirmationibus supradictis vel si aliquibus ex predictis qui bona huiusmodi taliter detinere noscuntur a predicta /10// sede indultum existat quod per litteras apostolicas interdici suspendi aut excommunicari non possint, nisi in eis de indulgentia huiusmodi /11/ expressa mentio habeatur, et constitutione de duabus dietis edita in concilio generali dummodo ultra tertiam vel quartam aliquis ex-/12//-tra suam diocesim auctoritate presentium ad iudicium non trahatur, ea que de bonis predictorum monasterii et prioratuum per concessiones /13// huiusmodi alienata inveneris illicite vel distracta ad ius et proprietatem eorumdem monasterii et prioratuum legitime revocare pro-/14//-cures, <SANCTIO> contradictores per censuram ecclesiasticam appellatione postposita compescendo. Testes autem qui fuerint nominati si se gratia, odio, vel timore /15// subtraxerint, censura simili appellatione cessante compellas veritati testimonium perhibere. <DATATIO> Datum Viterbii /16// xv kal. Februarii pontificatus nostri anno primo.'

*1278, September 19. ANF J.709.296.5.

Letter of justice or rather litterae executoriae. French prelates instructed not to stop the French king's men for punishing with death clerks who have committed a capital offence if they have already been deprived of their clerical status for some other reason.

Only the first letter of the pope's name is enlarged, and it is hardly decorated; the ascenders in the top line are medium sized, not greatly exaggerated; the abbreviation marks are normal superscript lines, not tittles; there are no extended ligatures. The only large black letter apart from the N for Nicolas is E for 'Ex parte'. Calendar in Barbiche, Les actes pontificaux originaux, *ii: 1261–1304, p. 227, no. 1599.*

'<INTITULATIO> Nicolaus episcopus servus servorum dei, <INSCRIPTIO> venerabilibus fratribus archiepiscopis et episcopis et dilectis filiis aliis /1// ecclesiarum prelatis per regnum Francie constitutis, <SALUTATIO> salutem et apostolicam benedictionem. <NARRATIO> Ex parte carissimi in Christo fi-/2//-lii nostri Philippi regis Francorum illustris fuit propositum coram nobis quod nonnulli clerici bigami et vi-/3//-duarum mariti ac alii etiam clerici uxorati regni sui diversa maleficia committere non verentur, que oculos /4//divine maiestatis offendunt, et homines scandalizant. <DISPOSITIO> Quocirca universitati vestre per apostolica scripta manda-/5//-mus, quatinus non impediatis quominus idem rex, comites et barones ipsius regni sub quorum iuris-/6//-dictione malefactores ipsi consistunt, ipsos in enormibus dumtaxat criminibus deprehensos, que sanguinis pe-/7//nam requirunt, eis primitus clericali gradu previa ratione privatis, puniant secundum quod iustitia suade-/8//-bit, consuetudine contraria que eos rationabiliter non eximat a pena sanguinis non obstante. <DATATIO> Datum Viterbii /9// xiii kal. Octobris pontificatus nostri anno primo.'

*1279, January 23. BL Add Ch 1551.

The document illustrates the tensions between Cluniacs and bishops. Calendar in Sayers, Original Papal Documents, *no. 808, p. 367. Duplicate of BL Add*

Ch 1550 = *Sayers, no. 807. Cf. A. Bernard and A. Bruel, eds.*, Recueil des Chartes de l'abbaye de Cluny, *vi (1211–1300) (Paris, 1903), no. 5245, p. 673, and* Bullarium Cluniacense *p. 143 col. 2, no. 1, available through database* Cartae Cluniacenses Electronicae: *www.cn-telma.fr/chartae-galliae/ charte261440/ Nicolas 3 pape Numéro B06699. Sayers,* Original Documents, *p. 367, comments that it is in the same hand as her no. 807, but she doesn't note a scribe's name. She does say, p. 554 note 6, that the proctor must be the same as in 808, though the document has been clipped where his name would be.*

'<INTITULATIO> Nicolaus episcopus servus servorum dei <INSCRIPTIO> dilectis filiis .. abbati et conventui Cluniacensi <SALUTATIO> salutem et apostolicam benedictionem. <ARENGA> Cum a no-/1//-bis petitur quod iustum est et honestum tam vigor equitatis quam ordo exigit rationis ut id per sollicitudinem offficii nostri /2// ad debitum perducatur effectum. <NARRATIO> Sane ad audientiam apostolatus nostri pervenit quod archiepiscopi episcopi decani archidiaconi et alii ecclesiarum /3// prelati tam vos quam priores et presbiteros vestros talliis exactionibus et procurationibus quas extra domos sibi postulant exhibe-/4//-ri, domos etiam ipsas contra Lateranense concilium equitaturarum et personarum numerum excedentes immisericorditer ag-/5//-gravare presumunt. Insuper, ecclesias ad vos spectantes subiciunt interdicto et presbiteros ipsos suspendunt, nullam /6// rationabilem causamsicut diciturpretendentes, sed tantum proprie voluntatis arbitrium prosecuti. <DISPOSITIO> Volentes igitur vo-/7//-bis in hoc patrocinium apostolicum impertiri, ad instar felicis recordationis Celestini papae iii predecessoris nostri / 8// auctoritate vobis apostolica indulgemus ut eisdem [50][in] talliis et procurationibus indebitis non teneamini de /9// cetero respondere. Sententiam vero quam in ecclesias aut presbiteros vestros nisi pro manifesta et rationabili causa /10// et ordine debito ventilata duxerint promulgandam decernimus non tenere. <PROHIBITIO> Nulli ergo omnino hominum lice-/11//-at hanc paginam nostre concessionis et constitutionis infringere vel ei ausu temerario contraire. <SANCTIO> Si quis /12// autem hoc attemptare presumpserit, indignationem omnipotentis dei et beatorum Petri et Pauli apostolorum /13// eius se noverit incursurum. Datum Rome apud sanctum Petrum x kal. Februarii / 14// pontificatus nostri anno secundo.'

*1281, August 23. TNA SC 7/64/40.

Martin IV to primicerius of the church of Metz, appointing him judge delegate in a property case. The good TNA catalogue entry is as follows: 'Order to the primicerius of the church of Metz to hear and determine the complaint of injury to their lands, etc., brought by the abbot and convent of Prüm against Conon

---

[50] *Damaged.*

*and Reyner de Entwelt brothers, knights, Dankel [son of] Walter de Entwelf,
Henry de Rurdorf, Lewis and Clement [sons of] Lewis the huckster (institor),
brothers, and Peter called "Aurilles laici" and Yda his wife, of the cities and
dioceses of Cologne, Laon and Metz. Conquesti sunt ... Orvieto. 10 Kal. Sep.,
1 Martin [IV.]. Bulla missing.'*

The document is based on the Audientia *formulary. In this area, including
Cologne and Metz, and, it appears, Laon, there was no secular authority
superior to all parties and capable of giving rationally based justice. The
thought is that more property cases may have come before judges delegate in
Continental Europe than in England, where royal justice was highly developed
and rational, though there is no way to verify this quantitatively. But we do not
know what kind of property was at issue and the plaintiff is ecclesiastical, so
even in England it might have been a matter for ecclesiastical justice.*

'<INTITULATIO> Martinus episcopus servus servorum dei, <INSCRIPTIO>
dilecto filio .. primicerio ecclesie Metensis, <SALUTATIO> salutem et /1//
apostolicam benedictionem. Conquesti sunt nobis .. abbas et conventus
monasterii Prumiensis ordinis sancti Be-/2//-nedicti quod Conon et Reynerus de
Entwelt, fratres, milites, Dankel Walteri de Entwelt, /3// Henricus de Rurdorf,
Ludewicus et Clemens Ludowici institoris, fratres, et Petrus dictus /4// Aurilles
laici, et Yda uxor predicti Petri, Coloniensis, Laudunensis[51] et Metensis
civitatum, et /5//[hole in parchment]c [= etc.?] super terris debitis, possessionibus,
et rebus aliis iniuriantur eisdem. Ideoque discretioni /6// tue [*from sense: illegible in
document*] per apostolica scripta mandamus quatinus, partibus convocatis, audias
causam et, appellatio-/7//-ne remota, debito fine decidas, faciens quod decreveris
per censuram ecclesiasticam /8// firmiter observari. Testes autem qui fuerint
nominati, si se gratia, odio vel timore sub-/9//-traxerint, censura simili appellatione
cessante compellas veritati testimonium perhibere. Datum /10// apud
Urbemveterem x kal. Septembris pontificatus nostri anno primo.'

*1281, October 7. ANF J.683.4.

*King Philip III of France is not to be excommunicated without a special
command of the papacy overriding the present document.*

Calender by Barbiche, Les Actes Pontificaux originaux, *ii, no. 1663,
p. 254.*

'<INTITULATIO> MARTINUS episcopus, servus servorum dei,
<INSCRIPTIO> carissimo in Christo filio Philippo regi Francie illustri /1//
salutem et apostolicam benedictionem. <NARRATIO> Celsitudinis regie

---

[51] Probably rather than 'Landunensis'. If this is indeed Laon, it is quite a distance from the
other cities, but they are also quite a distance from each other.

gratificari volentes, tuis devotis supplicationibus inclinati /2// <DISPOSITIO> auctoritate tibi presentium indulgemus ut in personam tuam nullus auctoritate ordinaria, /3// vel etiam delegata possit excommunicationis sententiam promulgare, absque speciali sedis predicte /4// mandato faciente plenam et expressam de persona tua, et toto tenore indulgentie huiusmodi /5// mentionem. <PROHIBITIO> Nulli ergo omnino hominum liceat hanc paginam nostre concessionis infringe-/6//-re, vel ei ausu temerario contraire. <SANCTIO> Siquis autem hoc attemptare presumpserit, indignationem /7// omnipotentis dei et beatorum Petri et Pauli apostolorum eius se noverit incursurum. Datum /8// apud Urbemveterem non. Octobris pontificatus nostri anno primo.'

*1330s Penitentiary Formulary. BL Add MS 24057, fo. 9r.

This extract from a penitentiary formulary is an example of the genre's potential as a source for social and religious life. The manuscript is undated. It bears a resemblance to Manuscrits datés VI, *dealing with Burgundy and central and southern France,*[52] *Plate XLIV, 1323, or ibid., II, Pl. XLV, 1324.*

'2. De symonia commissa cum aliquis promittat adversario petenti pecuniam ut eum non vexet in ecclesia.

<INSCRIPTIO> Dilecto in Christo N. <NARRATIO> Tua nobis petitione monstrasti quod cum tu olim ecclesie canonice tibi collate possessionem habere non posses propter potentiam illiciti detentoris, tu, ea intentione ut tuam vexationem redimeres, eidem detentori, intervenientibus amicis communibus promisisti, et iuramento proprio promissionem huiusmodi roborasti, te sibi C. solid' Turon' pensionis nomine annis singulis [53]solutorum, et sic possessionem ipsius ecclesie pacificam habuisti. Sed [quia] antequam ex ea aliquos proventus reciperes, per quendam qui plenum ius habebat in ea, fuisti ipsa ecclesia totaliter spoliatus, promissam pensionem solvere non curasti. Et licet inde tua conscientia sit secura, tamen ne quis emulus in te ex hoc [54]symonie vitium vel periurii notam inpingat, supplicasti tibi super hiis ad cautelam per apostolice sedis providentiam subveniri. <DISPOSITIO> Nos igitur attendentes [55]quod tres habere debet comites iuramentum, veritatem scilicet, iudicium et iustitiam, quodque iusiurandi non affert vinculum iuratio talibus destituta, ne tibi in hac parte desit cautele remedium auctoritate domini pape, cuius penitentiarie curam gerimus, te ab excessu huiusmodi et iuramenti tanquam [56]illiciti et temerarii,

---

[52] M. Mabille, M.-C. Garand, and J. Metman, under the general editorship of C. Samaran and R. Marichal, *Catalogue des manuscrits en écriture latine. Portant des indications de date, de lieu ou de copiste*, tome VI [2] *Planches. Bourgogne, Centre, Sud-Est et Sud-Ouest de la France* (Paris, 1968).

[53] *corr. from* soluctorum.   • [54] *End of word too faint to read and supplied from sense.*

[55] quod tres ... iustitiam] *supplied in lower margin, with cues.*   [56] illiti *corr. from* illiti.

observantia duximus absolvendum, iniuncta inde tibi penitentia quam vidimus iniungendum.'

*1333, September 6 and 7. AAV Armadio XXXIV 2.

John XXII's consultative decision-making process: a rare glimpse of the genesis of papal thinking.

Following a list of experts present in person: '... predictus dominus [57]Tusculanus episcopus, ex parte et de mandato prefati domini nostri vive / vocis oraculo, ut dixit, sibi facto, precepit eisdem magistris simul ut premittitur / congregatis in virtute sancte obedientie et sub pena excommunicationis ut certis articulis infrascriptis / secundum scientiam ipsis magistris a deo datam omni fictione et affectione postpositis, prout senti-/-ebant veraciter responderent, qui quidem domini magistri dixerunt quod mandato predicto volebant / prout possent et scirent deo dante plenarie obedire, protestantes et expresse / dicentes quod se et eorum dicta atque dicenda in et super articulis infrascriptis et circa / ipsos articulos supponebant correctioni et declarationi sancte Romane ecclesie ac domini nostri pape / predicti.' (fo. 115r, lower, stamped, foliation)

... 'Ad .xii. / Articulum, qui talis est: "Utrum catholicum an hereticum vel erroneum sit dicere quod anime sancte / nolunt modo habere, set in die iudicii, [58]gloriam corporis", dictorum dominorum magistrorum fuerunt / diverse oppiniones discordes, quibusdam dicentibus articulum istum erroneum, aliis falsum / et temerarium, aliis dicentibus ipsum articulum verum, aliis distinguentibus de appetitu / naturali et de appetitu relato ad ordinationem divinam, et verum in ultimo [59]sensu.' (fo. 116r, lower, stamped foliation).

*1350 circa. BL Harley MS 273, fo. 7r.

Forged papal indulgence. This is a probably typical example of indulgences attributed to John XXII and attached to prayers and is found in a blank leaf in BL Harley MS 273, fo. 7r (note that as usual sincere confession and contrition are required).

'Urbanus p[apa] quartus et Iohannes vicesimus secundus concesserunt / omnibus vere confessis et contritis, dicentibus in fine saluta-/-tionis beate Marie 'Iesus', lx dies indulgentie, videlicet quilibet / xxx dies. Et si quis dixerit psalterium beate Marie habebit / quolibet die xxiiiii annos, xxxiii septimanas, et tres dies / indulgentie: hoc est in septimana clxxii annos, xxv / septimanas et tres dies. Et qui in fine ewangelii Iohannis, / videlicet 'In principio erat verbum', etc, cum dicitur 'verbum caro / factum est' genuflexerit, vel devote inclinaverit, vel terram, / parietem, seu scabellum osculatus fuerit, unum annum/ et xl dies indulgentie habebit.'

---

[57] *After* episcopus *deleted.*   [58] *With otiose abbreviation sign.*   [59] *After erasure.*

*1354, January 21. AAV Reg. Vat. 226, fo. 1v.[60]

This text illustrates use of 'clauses' (clausulae) in a letter of Innocent VI.

'<INSCRIPTIO> Dilecto filio Iohanni de Malaceyo minori canonico ecclesie sancti Marcelli de Premeriaco Nivernensis /1// diocesis salutem etc. <RATIO> Vite ac morum [61]honestate et alia tuarum probitatis et virtutum merita super quibus apud /2// nos fidedigno commendatur testimonio, nos inducunt ut tibi reddamur ad gratiam liberales. Volentes /3// itaque tibi in presbiteratus ordine constituto premissorum meritorum tuorum intuitu gratiam facere specialem, <DISPOSITIO> beneficium /4// ecclesiasticum, cum cura vel sine cura, cuius fructus, redditus, et proventus – si cum cura: sexaginta, si [62]vero sine /5// cura fuerit, quadraginta librarum Turonensium parvorum – secundum taxationem decime valorem annuum – non ex-/6//-cedant, [63va]siquod vacat ad presens vel cum vacaverit, quod tu per te vel procuratorem tuum ad hoc legitime con-/7//-stitutum infra unius mensis spatium postquam tibi vel eidem procuratori de illius vacatione constiterit, dux-/8//-eris acceptandum, conferendum[cat] ad venerabilis fratris nostri .. episcopi Eduensis[64] collationem provisionem presentationem seu quamvis /9// aliam dispositionem pertinens, si quod vacat ad presens, vel cum vacaverit, quod tu per te vel procuratorem tuum ad hoc /10// legitime constitutum, infra unius mensis spatium, postquam tibi vel eidem procuratori de illius vacatione /11// constiterit, duxeris acceptandum, conferendum tibi post acceptationem huiusmodi, cum omnibus iuribus et pertinentiis /12// suis donationi [65][sedis] apostolice reservamus, districtius inhibentes [66]eidem episcopo ne de huiusmodi beneficio interim, etiam /13// ante acceptationem predictam, nisi postquam [67]ei constiterit quod tu vel procurator predictus illud nolueritis ac-/14//-ceptare, disponere quoquomodo [68]presumant; ac decernentes ex nunc irritum et inane si secus super hiis a /15// quoquam quavis auctoritate scienter vel ignoranter contigerit attemptari, non obstantibus si aliqui super /16// provisionibus sibi faciendis de huiusmodi vel aliis beneficiis ecclesiasticis in illis partibus speciales vel generales apostolice /17// sedis vel legatorum eius litteras impetrarint, etiam si per eas ad inhibitionem reservationem et decretum vel alias quomodo-/18//-libet sit processum, quibus omnibus, preterquam auctoritate nostra, huiusmodi beneficia expectantibus, te in ipsius beneficii /19// assecutione volumus anteferri, sed nullum per hoc eis quo ad assecutionem aliorum beneficiorum preiudi-/20//-cium generari, seu si eidem episcopo vel quibusvis aliis communiter vel divisim a dicta sit sede indultum /21// quod ad receptionem vel provisionem alicuius minime teneantur et ad id compelli non possint quodque de /22// huiusmodi vel aliis beneficiis ecclesiasticis ad eorum collationem provisionem presentationem seu quamvis aliam dispositionem, coniunctim /23// vel separatim spectantibus, nulli valeat provideri per litteras apostolicas non facientes plenam et expressam ac de verbo /24// ad verbum de

---

[60] My thanks to Michael Haren for correcting two mistakes in my initial transcription.
[61] honestate] *error for* honestas.   [62] vero] *after* cum *deleted.*
[63] *The* ᵛᵃ ... ᶜᵃᵗ *indicates that the words from* 'siquod' *to* 'conferendum' *are to be deleted.*
[64] I.e. Autun.   [65] sedis] *om. ms.*   [66] eidem] *corr. from* eisdem.
[67] ei] *corr. from* eis.   [68] presumant] *sic.*

indulto huiusmodi mentionem; et [nonobstante] qualibet alia dicte sedis indulgentia generali vel /25// speciali, cuiuscumque tenoris existat, per quam presentibus non expressam vel totaliter non insertam effectus /26// huiusmodi gratie impediri valeat quolibet vel differri et de qua cuiusque toto tenore habenda fit in /27// nostris litteris mentio specialis; seu quod in ecclesia sancti Marcelli de Premeriaco canonicatum et /28// prebendam ac in domo sancti Lazari de Hubento Nivernensis diocesis quamdam perpetuam capellaniam /29// quorum fructus propter eorum tenuitatem ad decimam non taxantur nosceris obtinere. <PROHIBITIO & SANCTIO> Nulli ergo etc. /30// nostre reservationis inhibitionis et constitutionis infringere etc. <DATATIO> Datum Avinion' xii Kal Februarii /31// anno secundo.'

*1363, May 30. AAV Reg. Vat. 245, fo. 174v–175r.

Urban V writes submissively to monarchs.

The letter closes the section containing litterae secretae for May 1363. This volume of the register is structured by alternating 'secret letter' and 'cameral letter' sections for each month.

'Eidem [Joanna Queen of Sicily]

Dilectus filius nobilis vir Dominicus Lercarius de Janua / fidelis tuus, lator presentium, prout nobis asseruit, pro certis suis / negotiis ad tue serenitatis presentiam dirigit gressus suos. Rogamus / igitur serenitatem eandem [69]quot dictum Dominicum nostrarum precum intui-/-tu regiis habeas favoribus commendatum. Datum Avinion' v Kal Iunii / anno primo./

Carissimo in Christo filio Iohanni Regi Francie illustri, salutem. / Recolimus quod ad instantiam nostram per serenitatem tuam con-/-cessum fuit dilectis filiis .. consulibus et universitati Castri Sancti / Ambrosii, Uticensis diocesis, spectan*tis* ad ecclesiam Uticensem, quod possent apud / eundem locum, qui est aptus ad nundinas et mercatum, semel / in septimana mercatum, et bis in anno nundinas retinere, tuaque / celsitudo commisit duobus [70]suis consiliariis quod de predictis, si forsan in ali-/-enum preiudicium vergerent, se diligentius informarent, per eorumque / relationem tibi cognito quod non solum non vergerent in alienum / preiudicium, sed in utilitatem magnam rei publice redunda-/-rent huiusmodi nundinas bis in anno et mercatum semel in edo-/-mata fieri, concessit de gratia speciali, prout in litteris regiis inde / **(fo. 175r)** confectis dicitur plenius contineri. Cum autem ut dicitur Comes / Bellifortis et consules de Alesto, asserentes huiusmodi regiam gratiam / in eorum preiudicium esse factam, cum tamen sit longa viarum distan-/-tia a loco de Alesto ad Castrum Sancti Ambrosii predictum, obtinue-/-rint a cancellario tuo per litteras regias causam super hiis in par-/-lamento poni, ex quo dicti episcopus ac consules et

---

[69] *Orthographic variant for* quod.
[70] *Definitely the manuscript reading, but Michael Haren suggests that it is an error for* 'tuis', *and that the scribe might have been error prone.*

universitas, / quos sincere diligimus, multiplicibus expensis et laboribus grava-/-rentur, serenitatem eandem rogamus attente quatinus de re-/-gia benignitate dictam gratiam velit ex certa scientia approbare, / ratificare, ac decernere obtinere perpetuam roboris firmitatem / non obstantibus huiusmodi litteris in contrarium impetratis. Datum / Avinion' iii kal. Iunii anno primo.'

*1455. Calixtus III. BL Add Ch 13331.

Knights of St. John not to be taxed for war against Turks.

Idris Bell, 'A List of Original Papal Bulls and Briefs in the Department of Manuscripts, British Museum', English Historical Review, *36 (1921), 393–418, 556–582, no. 229, p. 418, summarises it thus: 'Rome, St Peter's, 25 September 1455. Exemption of brethren of the hospital of St. John of Jerusalem from payment of tenth levied by Nicholas V to resist the Turk. First Line. Ad futuram rei memoriam. Bulla lost. "Spetiali gratia et".'*

The document has a good set of Chancery marks:
fold closed, above the plica, top right:

> [71]*Pro Ie de Vicen^a dupp^{ta}*
>
> [72]*B. de Piscia*
>
> [73]*solvit*
>
> *Collata et concordat*

Under the plica, left-hand side when plica open:

> *L*
> [74]*Sep.*   [75]*M. (?) Amici*

---

[71] *Frenz position 7 '(a destra sulla plica, completamente sul margine superiore) annotazioni circa la ripartizione della tassa degli scrittori, la riscrittura, la sostiuzione nel caso di bella copia, la nota gratis, ecc.*

[72] *Preceded by a distinctive mark, resembling a notarial sign. Frenz position 8: the scriptor/ grossator.*

[73] *Frenz position 9: '(sulla plica, nel margine destro)
nota della tassa della bullaria expressa in floreni.*

[74] *Frenz position 10 '(sotto la plica, nel margine sinistro)
nota del rescribendario circa il mese del computo'.*

[75] *Frenz position 11 '(sotto la plica a sinistra)
quietanza della tassa (in grossi) oppore nota Visa degli scrittori (posta dal rescribendario e dal computator)
prima del 1479 in aggiunta ad a0: sottoscrizione del controllo degli abbreviatori (?)*

On dorse, lower left-hand corner above plica: '*Exemptio fratrum hopsitalis sancti Iohannis / Ierosolem a decima imposita per papam / pro cruciata contra Theucros*[76] *facta*'

'<INTITULATIO> Calistus episcopus servus servorum dei, ad futuram rei memoriam /1// <ARENGA> Speciali gratia et favore illa de causa magistrum et fratres ac personas hospitalis sancti Iohannis [77]Ierosolemitan' dignos fore existimamus quia sicut accepimus ad hoc semper intendunt ut atrocissimorum /2// hostium fidei christiane nephanda conteratur iniquitas ac eadem christiana fides constans et firma remaneat ac continuum suscipiat incrementum. <NARRATIO> Dudum siquidem felicis recordationis /3// Nicolaus Papa V, predecessor noster, ut sevitie atrocissimi Mahometi Turcorum principis, qui civitatem Constantinopolitan' durissima obsidione et debellatione [78]seperatam in suam ditionem /4// cum magna christiani populi strage transtulerat et de toto orbe terrarum nomen delere christianum gloriabatur, celeriter [79]resistere posset per suas litteras inter cetera omnium beneficiorum /5// ecclesiasticorum in toto orbe terrarum patriarchatuum, archiepiscopatuum, episcopatuum, abbatiarum et quorumcunque aliorum beneficiorum regularium vel non regularium, exemptorum vel non exemptorum /6// cuiuscunque ordinis, status, gradus vel conditionis forent omnium fructuum decimam secundum verum valorem sine ulla [80]deceptione ex plenitudine apostolice potestatis tam sancto /7// operi integram reservavit, et deinde nos qui ipso Nicolao predecessore sicut Domino placuit rebus humanis exempto fuimus divina disponente clementia ad apicem summi apostolatus assumpti, /8// cum ex litteris prefati Nicolai predecessoris nonnulla dubia exorta fuissent, que ad faciliorem rerum agendarum executionem partim additione videbantur indigere, de venerabilium fratrum /9// nostrorum sancte Romane ecclesie [81]cardinalium inter cetera voluimus, statuimus pariter et decrevimus ad solutionem decime universalis [82]pro infra primum, videlicet Septembris, et pro /10// alia infra secundum Octobris ac pro reliqua tertia partibus infra tertium Novembris menses presentis anni, preter comprehensos in predictis litteris Nicolai predecessoris omnes et /11// singulos Grandimonensis, Camaldulensis, Vallisumbrose, Cruciferorum, Humiliatorum necnon beate Marie Theotonicorum, Sancti Iacobi de Spata, Calatrave, Alcantaren', Montesie et quorum-/12//-cumque aliorum ordinum seu militiarum regulares vel religiosas personas, exemptas et non exemptas, cuiuscunque preeminentie status, gradus, ordinis, sexus vel conditionis forent quoscunque fructus /13// redditus et proventus ecclesiasticos ubilibet obtinentes, personis dicti hospitalis sancti Iohannis Ierosolemitan', illis videlicet ex eis qui ad

---

[76] I.e. Turks: see Du Cange, *Glossarium, s.v.* Teucri.   [77] Ierl'mitan'.   [78] *Sic.*
[79] *Sic.*
[80] Michael Haren points out in a personal communication that 'in the (partial) text as printed by Baronius, *Annales Ecclesiastici*, 28 (Bar-le-Duc, 1874), p. 601 (a), of Nicholas V's bull, *Ad perpetuam rei memoriam. Fuit jam olim ecclesiae* ..., which I take to be the point of reference of the present, the corresponding word is "exceptione".'
[81] *Michael Haren points out that after this word* 'consilio et assensu' *must have dropped out of the text (they are certainly missing).*
[82] *eyeskip error: read:* pro prima?

insulam Rodi [83]personaliter se conferrent, quos tantummodo /14// a prestatione huiusmodi exemptos esse voluimus, duntaxat exceptis ad eandem solutionem decime integre et cum effectu, nuntiis nostris seu deputandis ab eis faciendam teneri, prout in singulis /15// litteris predictis quarum tenores, ac si de verbo ad verbum insererentur, presentibus haberi volumus pro sufficienter expressis, plenius continetur.<DISPOSITIO> Nos igitur attendentes quod persone dicti hospitalis /16// magnis expensarum oneribus sunt pregravate, adeo quod eis incommodum valde foret decimam ipsam persolvere, de dictorum fratrum consilio, auctoritate apostolica tenore presentium tam predictas que ut /17// prefertur ad insulam Rodi [84]personaliter se contulerint, quam omnes et singulas alias personas dicti hospitalis utriusque sexus ubicunque commorantes, etiam si ad [85]insulam predictam personaliter non /18// accesserint, a prestatione decime huiusmodi excipimus ac exemptos esse ac ad illius solutionem non teneri decernimus pariter et declaramus. Ceterum, quia difficile foret presentes litteras ad singula /19// ubi ille necessarie forent loca deferre, volumus et etiam decernimus quod earum transumpto manu notarii publici subscripto et sigillo [86]cuiuscunque prelati munito illa prorsus fides in iudicio et extra adhibea-/20//-tur et ei stetur sicuti dictis originalibus litteris si forent exhibite vel ostense.< PROHIBITIO> Nulli ergo omnino hominum liceat hanc paginam nostre declarationis et constitutionis infringere vel ei ausu temera-/21//-rario contraire. <SANCTIO> Si quis autem hoc attemptare presumpserit, indignationem omnipotentis dei et beatorum Petri et Pauli apostolorum eius se noverit incursurum. <DATATIO> Datum Rome apud Sanctum Petrum /22// anno incarnationis dominice millesimo quadringentesimo quinquagesimo quinto septimo kal. Octobris pontificatus nostri anno primo.'

*1570. AAV Congr. Concilio, Positiones (Sess.) 16, fo. 6r–116r. All folio references below to this 'busta' are to the new foliation.

The Congregatio Concili *addresses the problem of Calvinist baptism. The Council of Trent (preoccupied with Lutherans rather than Calvinists) had declared that 'If anyone says that baptism, which is given by heretics too in the name of the Father, Son, and Holy Spirit, with the intention of doing what the Church does, is not true baptism, let him be an anathema.*[87] *The theology of predestination that developed within Calvinism was much more explicit than Luther's, and it raised the question: if salvation and damnation are preordained, what difference does baptism make? The question perhaps lurked below the surface of Luther's theology and even Augustine's, but predestination was to*

[83] *underlined.*   [84] personaliter ... commorantes] *underlined.*
[85] insulam ... ac exemptos] *underlined.*   [86] cuiuscunque] cuuscunque *ms.*
[87] 'Si quis dixerit, baptismum, qui etiam datur ab haereticis in nomine Patris, et Filii et Spiritus Sancti, cum intentione faciendi quod facit ecclesia, non esse verum baptismum: anathema sit' (Schulte and Richter, *Canones et Decreta,* p. 41, Sessio VII De Baptismo Can. IV.

the forefront of the Calvinist world-view. The validity of Calvinist baptism was not just a theoretical question: if it was invalid, converts from Calvinism had to be baptised, and Calvinist marriages were not entirely indissoluble.

Underlining in the transcription indicates underlining in the manuscript. I have not tried to transcribe the numerous and barely legible marginal comments, some of which are cued to the text.

'**/fo. 6r/** Quoniam ex Concilii Tridentii Decreto habetur Canone iiii, sectio-/-nis septimae, quod si quis dixerit baptismum, qui etiam ab heraeticis datur, In nomine Patris et Filii et Spiritus sancti, <u>cum intentione faciendi / quod facit Ecclesia, non esse verum baptismum, anathema sit,</u> maxi-/-me videtur ambiguum pluribus Catholicis doctoribus <u>an heraeticorum / Calvinistarum</u> modernorum Baptismus sit verus, et an vere baptizant, / <u>cum eis desit intentio etiam universalis, faciendi quod facit Ecclesia, nullam / etenim vim efficaciam et virtutem tribuunt baptismo, ut asserunt</u> / Libro iiii° Institutionis Christiane C. xiiii et xv[88] ex Ioanne Calvino, ubi / <u>negant baptismum esse sacramentum efficax gratiae collativum et peccatorum remis-/-ivum in puero, quem puerum credunt in utero materno esse iustificatum,</u> / modo a parentibus Christianis procreetur, ita quod si decedat sine / baptismo, non minus ingreditur regnum. Cum itaque <u>intentio saltem / universalis</u> requiratur ad integritatem baptismi, quam <u>non habent, / nec particularem, nec universalem, nec formalem, nec virtualem,</u> [89]heraetici / moderni Calviniste, verisimile habetur quod <u>vere non baptizantur,</u> id / quod humillime peroptant <u>Catholici quidam doctores</u> plenius in-/-telligere et suam sanctitatem, reverendissimosque cardinales obnixe supplicant / super hac re decernere, <u>an liberum sit evangelizantibus</u> / <u>verbum Domini docere populum fidelem quod baptizati ab ipsis / Calvinistis heraeticis sint denuo baptizandi,</u> an non? [90]– Quia, ut / iam dictum est, illis deest tertia pars baptismi integralis, sci-/-licet intentio.'

The next page is mainly blank, with a few notes.

 # Camillo Capilupi[91] reports on the instructions given him by Cardinal Michele Bonelli (the 'cardinale Alessandrino' to get the reports of the theologians to Cardinal Francesco Alciati).

'**/fo. 8r/** Illustrissimo et reverendissimo signore mio patrone osservandissimo. /

Il signore cardinale Alessandrino mi ha mandato le qui alligate scritture sopra quel dubio de haere-/-ticorum babtismo le quali io stesso haverei portato a vostra

---

[88] J. Allen, ed., *Institutes of the Christian Religion by John Calvin*, iii (Philadelphia, PA, 1816), Book IV, chs. 14 and 15, pp. 298–346.

[89] *In left-hand margin, scarcely legible, a gloss which seems to indicate that the pope agreed with the Congregation that Calvinist baptisms were valid: it includes the words* 'Sanctitas sua ... censuit ... eos vere baptizare'.

[90] *At foot of page, barely legible:* 'Facta relatione __ __ __ __ quod ist_ Calvinista?rum baptismus verus sit et ideo baptizati ab eis non sint iterum baptizandi __ __ Calvinistae discesser__ ab ecclesia'.

[91] See *Dizionario Biografico degli Italiani, s.v.*

signoria illustrissima se non fossi tanto occu-/-pato quanto io sono nel proveder alle cose necessarie per la venuta del Granduca / come sua Santita mi ha ordinato, pero si degnera havermi per iscusato, et di tenermi / nella sua felice gratia, nella quale humilmente mi raccomando. Di Casa il xiiii / di Febraro MDLXX /

Di vostra signoria illustrissima et reverendissima /

[92]Humilissimo servitore / Camillo Capilupi.'

'**/fo. 9r/** [*Same script*] Hae sunt sententiae sex thologorum super baptismo / Calvinistarum / quas cum ad Congregationem Concilii referre voluissem, / dictum fuit, ut eas prius per manus singulorum[93] / transmitterem. / Videantur ergo quam primum, et deinde ad me /remittantur, ut postea ad Congregationem / referre possim.'

/fo. 10v/ [*In the same hand, at centre of page (on which there are also a number of scribbled notes, including* 'Votum 6 theologorum quod C. Alessandrinus(?) / transmittendum habuit (*supplied above line*) per manus ex Decreto / Congregationis')]

All' illustrissimo et reverendissimo signore mio patrone / osservandissimo il signore Cardinale Alciati.'

Opinion of the Servite friar Benedictus a Burgo Sancti Sepulcri.[94]

'**/fo. 12r/** Articulus propositus. / Quoniam ex concilii Tridentini decreto habetur Canon. 4° sessionis sep-/-timae, quod si quis dixerit baptismum qui etiam ab hereticis datur In nomine Pa-/-tris, et filii, et Spiritus sancti cum intentione faciendi quod facit ecclesia non esse verum / baptismum, anathema sit, maxime videtur ambiguum pluribus catholicis doctoribus / an hereticorum Calvinistarum Baptismus sit verus, et an vere baptizant, cum eis / desit intentio universalis faciendi quod facit ecclesia, nullam etenim vim, effica-/-ciam et virtutem tribuunt baptismo, ut asserunt Libro 4 Institutionis Christiane, c. 14 / et 15, ex Joanne Calvino ubi negant baptismi sacramentum esse gratie collativum / et peccatorum remissivum in puero, quem puerum credunt in utero materno esse

---

[92] *At foot of page, right-hand side.*

[93] I am unclear as to what this means: possibly that the opinions should be sent to individual members of the Congregation before being submitted to the secretary.

[94] Personal communication from Benedetta Albani: 'Mi ha risposto Lorenzo Sinisi con alcune interessanti informazioni su Benedetto da San Sepolcro. Ecco cosa mi ha scritto: "… Quanto al personaggio di cui mi chiede notizie non sono purtroppo in grado di dirLe molto. Le uniche notizie reperite sono relative alla carica di Provinciale del suo ordine che rivestì nella provincia "Romandiolae (Ravenna e Romagna) e ad un suo insegnamento teologico a Bologna e alla Sapienza Romana dove dovrebbe aver tenuto lezioni sul I libro delle Sentenze di Pietro Lombardo (cfr. A. Gianio, Annalium Sacri Ordinis Fratrum Servorum B. Mariae Virginis, t. II, Lucae, Marescandoli, 1721, pp. 176, 195, 203, 211; G. Marini, Lettera … a Giuseppe Muti Papazurri nella quale si illustra il ruolo de' professori dell'Archiginnasio romano, Roma, 1797); per ulteriori ricerche si potrebbe magari dare un'occhiata al Sarti-Fattorini per i maestri bolognesi (oltre ai rotuli dello stesso ateneo pubblicati dal Dallari a fine 800) mentre per Roma guarderei il Carafa e il più recente libro di E. Conte sui maestri della Sapienza.'

iustifi-/-catum, modo a parentibus christianis procreetur. Itaque si decedat vir sine baptismo / non minus ingreditur regnum, [95]etc. Cum itaque intentio saltem universalis requira-/tur ad integritatem baptismi, quam non habent, nec particularem, nec universalem, / nec formalem, nec virtualem, heretici moderni Calviniste verisimile habetur / quod vere non baptizant, id quod humillime peroptant catholici quidam doctores / plenius intelligere et suam Sanctitatem, reverendissimosque cardinales obnixe supplicant super hac re / decernere, an liberum sit evangelizantibus verbum Domini docere populum fidelem / quod baptizati ab ipsis Calvinistis hereticis sint denuo baptizandi, an non, quia ut / iam dictum est illis deest tertia pars baptismi integralis, scilicet intentio. /

Ex articulo igitur isto mihi proposito elicitur / ista questio examinanda, videlicet: /

An heretici Calviniste vere baptizent, itaque baptizati ab illis sint vere bap-/-tizati, an denuo sint baptizandi? /

Et primo videtur quod verisimile sit eos non vere baptizare et per consequens quod ab illis / baptizati sint denuo baptizandi.

Ratio autem huius dicti est quia qui non habet intentionem baptizandi et faciendi / quod facit ecclesia non vere baptizant. Sed Calvinistae heretici sunt huiusmodi. Igitur/ Maior propositio patet quia ad integritatem baptismi, ut omnes theologi fatentur, oportet ut / adsit intentio baptizantis. Minor etiam apparet vera quia ut dicitur in arti-/-culo suprascripto et proposito, heretici Calvinistae nullam vim et efficaciam / tribuunt baptismo, sicuti patet, inquit articulus propositus Libro 4 Institutionis Christiane / cap 14 et 15 ex Joanne Calvino ubi [96]negant baptismi sacramentum esse gratiae colla-/-tivum et peccatorum remissivum in puero. At ecclesia catholica tribuit baptismo vim / et efficaciam quam isti negant. Igitur non videntur habere intentionem faciendi quod facit / ecclesia, et per consquens non vere baptizant.

//fo. 12v/ Secunda ratio: Ab hereticis non potest conferri baptismus. Sed Calvinistae sunt heretici. Igitur non baptizant. / Minor propositio est verissima, et maior probatur, quia qui immundus est alium mundare nequaquam / potest. Sed heretici sunt immundi. Igitur mundare alios non possunt. Igitur neque baptizare, quia qui / baptizat mundat. Minor est clara et maior probatur per divum Ciprianum dicentem: / Quomodo (loquens de heretico) [97]santificare aquam potest cum ipse immundus est, et apud quem Spiritus sanctus / non est, cum Dominus dicat in lege: quecumque tetigerit immundus immunda erunt. / Quis potest dare quod ipse non habet? Igitur qui immundus est mundare non potest. Igitur heretici / non vere baptizant. /

Sed contra: Qui <u>utitur forma baptismi a Christo instituta, et ab ecclesia / recepta cum intentione conferendi, sacramentum baptismi,</u> [98]<u>et faciendi quod facit ecclesia, vere baptizat.</u> Calviniste sunt / huiusmodi. Igitur Calviniste baptizant. /

---

[95] etc.] *this might instead be punctuation.*   [96] negat *could be read.*   [97] *Sic.*
[98] *Supplied in margin with omission marks.*

\# Respondeo igitur ad questionem, et pro responsione et eius dilucidatione/ sunt aliqua annotatione digna. /

Primo notandum est quod ea quae integrant sacramentum baptismi tria sunt, videlicet, materia, / forma, et intentio: quae omnia necessaria sunt ad collationem baptismi, itaque al-/-tero istorum deficiente sacramentum baptismi esset nullum. In hoc autem quesito non est dif-/-ficultas de materia, nec disparitas inter hereticos et catholicos, nec etiam est / difficultas de forma, que est invocatio sanctissimae Trinitatis sub nomine trium / personarum expressa, quam formam presuppono istos hereticos servare, tanquam veram, / sicuti vera est teste divo Augustino, Beda et Magistro Sententiarum. Divus namque Augustinus / ad questiones Orosii – et habetur De consecratione Dist 4. c. *Quamvis*: inquit: 'Quamvis unum / sit baptisma et hereticorum, scilicet eorum qui in nomine Patris, et Filii, et Spiritus sancti baptizant, et Ecclesiae catholicae, tamen qui foris ecclesiam baptizantur, non sumunt ad salutem bap-/-tismum, sed ad perniciem; habentes formam sacramenti, virtutem autem eius abnegantes, et ideo / ecclesia eos non rebaptizat, quia in nomine Trinitatis baptizati sunt; et ipsa est forma / sacramenti.' Hec Augustinus.[99] Beda vero ita inquit: 'Sive hereticus sive schismaticus sive / [100]facinorosus, quisque in confessione [101]sanctissimae Trinitatis baptizet: non valet ille qui baptiza-/-tus est a nobis catholicis rebaptizari, ne confessio et trinitatis invocatio videatur / annullari'.[102] At Magister Sententiarum habet hec verba libro 4 Dist. 6. De illis vero qui ab here-/-ticis baptizantur utrum baptizandi sint queri solet, ad quod breviter dicimus quia quicumque / sit qui baptizet, si servatur forma a Christo tradita verum baptismum dat, et ideo qui illum sumit / non debet rebaptizari.[103] Quare concluditur quod si Calviniste utantur forma a Christo tradita / quod non errant in forma. Tota igitur difficultas est de intentione: pro qua:[104] /

2° Notandum [est] [105]quod intentio cum sit de integritate baptismi quod ipsa est necessaria ad hoc ut confe-/-ratur vere baptismus. Nam quando aliquid se habet ad multa indeterminate, si illud / debet perfici, oportet quod se*m*per per aliquod determinetur ad unum.[106] At ea que in baptismo aguntur / diversimode agi possunt, quia ablutio aque in baptismo potest fieri ad ludum, ad munditiam / corporalem, et ad munditiam seu sanctificationem spiritualem. Igitur oportet ut ista actio determi-//13r/-netur ad unum effectum, hoc autem fieri debet per intentionem lavantis et abluentis, quae intentio / exprimitur per verba que in

---

[99] He must be taking these references from Peter Lombard: see *Magistri Petri Lombardi ... Sententiae in IV Libris Distinctae* [ed. Ignatius Brady], ii, Liber III et IV (Spicilegium Bonavernturianum, V; Grottaferrata, 1981), Liber IV, Dist. VI, Cap. 2 (37), p. 269. Brady gives references in the notes.

[100] *After deletion.*   [101] s'iae *ms. (though* 'sanctae' *is in the source).*

[102] *Petri Lombardi ... Sententiae,* Liber IV, Dist. VI, Cap. 2 (37), p. 269.

[103] *Ibid.,* pp. 268–269.

[104] Note that syntactically links up with '2° Notandum ...' below, despite the clearly marked paragraph break.

[105] 'quod ... quod': *the repetition may simply be lax language.*

[106] Cf. *Sancti Thomae Aquinatis ... Opera Omnia,* ed. Commissio Leonina, xii (Rome, 1906), Quaestio LXIV, Articulus VIII, pp. 51–52.

baptismo dicuntur. Propterea Magister Sententiarum loco supra allegato /
loquens de illis qui ioco et ludo baptizantur, inquit in fine: [107]'Videtur / tamen
sapientibus non fuisse baptisma, ut cum aliqui in balneum vel flumen merguntur
in no-/-mine Trinitatis, non est tamen baptismus quia non intentione baptizandi
illud geritur. Nam in hoc et in aliis sacramentis sicut forma est servanda, ita et
intentio illud cele-/-brandi est habenda.' Hec Magister.[108] Quare luce clarius
apparet quod intentio est de integritate / baptismi et per consequens necessaria
iis qui baptizant. Attamen: /

3° Notandum est quod aliquem habere intentionem faciendi quod facit ecclesia
potest bifariam / intelligi, primo modo explicite, secundo modo [109]implicite.
Explicite in-/-telligo quando quis cum catholica ecclesia non solum credit ea
vera esse que sunt / de substantia baptismi, verum etiam ea que faciunt ad
effectum ipsius, itaque nullomodo discre-/-pat ab ecclesia, sed ei in omnibus
conformatur. Implicite intelligo quando quis, etiam [110]quod dis-/-sentiat ab
ecclesia in multis et presertim circa ea que non sunt de substantia, de
integrita-/-te, et de necessitate baptismi, licet sint de pertinentibus ad eius
effectum, non tamen discrepat / ab ea in collatione baptismi, creditque in his
que pertinent ad necessitatem baptismi / omnia ea que ecclesia credit. Et sic
Calviniste implicite habent intentionem faciendi / quod facit ecclesia, id est
conferre baptismum in ea materia quam confitetur ecclesia et in ea / forma
quam Christus instituit, que quidem forma, quoniam ab ecclesia est approbata,
/ et ea catholici utuntur, propterea Calviniste dicuntur habere intentionem
implicite facien-/-di quod facit ecclesia, quia ista forma, a Christo instituta et ab
ecclesia approba-/-ta, est ab eis recepta, et ipsa utuntur.[111] /

4° Notandum est quod aliud est loqui de natura et substantia ipsius baptismi,
aliud est loqui / de consequentibus ipsum. Esse namque seu substantia baptismi
integratur illis tribus partibus iam dictis / videlicet materia, forma, et intentione.
Consequentia vero baptismum seu effectus / ipsius sunt collatio gratiae, remissio
culpae et huiusmodi. Potest igitur quis errare / circa effectum baptismi qui non
errabit circa ipsius substantiam, et ita poterit talis / conferre baptismum vere, et
baptizatus ab illo non erit de novo baptizandus./

5° est notandum pro maiori expressione eorum que dicta sunt, quod aliud est
dicere heretici-/-cum vere baptizare, aliud est dicere hereticum baptizare
efficaciter ad salu-/-tem. Nam prima pars est vera, secunda vero falsa. Veritas
primae partis / probatur authoritate [112]divi Augustini Lib. 2 Contra epistulam
Parmeniani c. 13 dicentis[113] ut bap-/-tismum non amittit qui recedit ab ecclesia,

---

[107] *After deletion.*
[108] *Petri Lombardi ... Sententiae,* Liber IV, Dist. VI, Cap. 5 (40), p. 273.
[109] *After deletion.*   [110] *Sic for* qui?
[111] My thanks to Michael Haren for drawing attention to a mistake in my
    original punctuation.
[112] *With* S. Augustini *in margin.*
[113] *Petri Lombardi ... Sententiae,* Liber IV, Dist. XXV, cap 1, p. 410 (with references to
    Augustine editions, *PL* 43, 70 s. and M. Petschenig, ed., *Sancti Aureli Augustini Scripta
    Contra Donatistas,* PARS I (Corpus Scriptorum Ecclesiasticorum Latinorum [= CSEL],
    p. 79 – but the Lombard is almost certainly the direct source).

neque ordinem, characterem, etc., ita nec / ius dandi, utrumque enim sacramentum est et quadam consecratione, scilicet verbi dei, utrumque homini / datur: Illud cum baptizatur, istud cum ordinatur. Ideo utrumque in ecclesia catholica / cum schismatici redierint non licet iterari. Ipsa unim unitas confert ecclesiae catholicae quod / schisma abstulerat. Item <u>Libro 3 De Baptismo contra</u> Donatistas, c. ii,[114] inquit: Ideo catho-/-lica ecclesia non rebaptizat a schismaticis baptizatos ne videatur sibi tribuere / quod Christi est, aut eos non habere intus cum acciperent amittere utique foras exeundo non possent.[115]

//fo. 13v/ At secundae partis falsitas per eundem divum Augustinum probatur qui Libro 3 De Baptismo contra Donatistas / c. 13, inquit: Quamvis idem sit apud hereticos aut schismaticos baptismus Christi, non tamen ibi / operatur remissionem peccatorum, propter discordiae foeditatem et dissensionis iniquitatem, tunc autem / incipit valere idem baptismus ad remittenda peccata cum ad ecclesiae unitatem redierint sive / pacem.[116] Non quod defectus sit in sacramento baptismi, sed quod idem sacramentum baptismi quod foris propter / discordiae foeditatem operabatur mortem, propter pacem et unitatem intus operetur salutem. / Et c. 10 eiusdem libri inquit: Aliud est non habere aliquid, aliud est non iure habere vel illici-/-te usurpare. Non propterea sacramenta non sunt sacramenta quia eis illicite quidam utuntur,[117] sic schisma-/-tici habent quidem baptismum sed illicite utuntur. Et Libro 6 c. 9: Quod baptismus extra unitatem / ecclesie nullum habeat salutis effectum verum esse credo.[118] Et Lib. 4 c. 17: Aliud est non habere, / et aliud non utiliter habere: qui non habet, baptizandus est ut habeat, qui autem non utiliter / habet corrigendus est, id est, veniat ad ecclesiam ut utiliter habeat.[119] /

Ultimo notandum quod licet ab hereticis et presertim Calvinistis baptizatus non debeat / iterum baptizari, est tamen per *im*positionem manus reconciliandus, tum ut accipiat Spiritum sanctum, tum / in signum detestationis hereticorum: et per haec patet solutio ad argumenta principalia. /

Ad primum negatur minor. Ad probationem dicitur quod collatio gratiae et remissio pec-/-catorum in baptismo non sunt de substantia baptismi sed sunt effectus. Nam ab illo ta*m*quam a causa / (eo modo quo sacramenta dicuntur causa) provenit iste effectus collationis gratiae et remis-/-sionis peccati. Et propterea licet Calvinistae non habeant hanc intentionem circa effectum / baptismi quam habet ecclesia, cum <u>hoc tamen stat quod habeant intentionem</u>

[114] *Recte* Book 3 c. 11.
[115] Augustine, 'De baptismo contra Donatistas', Lib. 3 c. 11, M. Petschenig, ed., CSEL, 51, p. 206 *PL* 43, col. 145 (quotation not quite verbatim).
[116] Augustine, 'De baptismo contra Donatistas', Lib. 3 c. 13, *PL* 43, col. 146, M. Petschenig, ed., CSEL 51, p. 208.
[117] Augustine, 'De baptismo contra Donatistas', Lib. 3 c. 10, *PL* 43, 144, M. Petschenig, ed., CSEL 51, p. 205, *Petri Lombardi ... Sententiae*, Liber IV, Dist. XXV, cap 1, p. 411 at note 3.
[118] Augustine, 'De baptismo contra Donatistas', Lib. 6 c. 9, *PL* 43, col. 204., M. Petschenig, ed., CSEL 51, p. 308.
[119] Augustine, 'De baptismo contra Donatistas', Lib. 4 c. 17, *PL* 43, col. 170, M. Petschenig, ed., CSEL 51, pp. 250–251.

circa illa que pertinent ad / substantiam, scilicet circa materiam, formam, et intentionem, quam intentionem saltem implicite habent. /

Ad secundum negatur maior. Ad probationem dicitur quod i*m*mundum conferre alteri munditiam / [120]dupliciter potest intelligi, unomodo principaliter, aliomodo ministerialiter. Primomodo verum est quod i*m*mundus / munditiam alteri conferre non potest, non autem secundomodo quia malitia ministri non aufert / neque i*m*pedit sacramentum. Ad illud vero quod pro hac re dicitur de <u>divo Cipriano</u> responditur quod vel / ille est intelligendus de his hereticis qui extra formam ecclesie baptizant, vel si ipse / intelligit de his qui iuxta formam ecclesiae et cum intentione faciendi quod facit ecclesia baptizant / non est tenendum, quia illud dixit nimio zelo, divo Augustino teste qui inquit: martirem Ci-/-prianum gloriosum qui apud hereticos vel schismaticos datum baptismum nolebat cognoscere / dum eos nimis detestaretur, tanta eius merita usque ad triu*m*phum martirii secuta sunt / ut et charitatis qua excellebat luce obumbratio illa fugaretur. Et siquid pur-/-gandum erat passionis falce tolleretur.[121] Et sic patet ad questionem.

Quamobrem pauca haec litteris mandare volui non ut huic arduae difficultati ac diffi-/-cillime quaestioni finem i*m*ponerem, verum potius ut maioribus meis quibus non potui non / summopere moremgerere aliqua in parte satisfacerem. Non igitur haec vitio temeritatis / erunt mihi ascripta quoniam hoc mei muneris, hae meae erant partes, quid ani-/-mus meus certe quadam modestia circa propositam difficultatem gratia consultatio-/-nis senserit in medium afferre: qua in re, ut etiam in omnibus aliis, se*m*per feci, saniori ac sanc-/-tiori iudicio tum doctorum pietissimorum, tum sanctae matris ecclesiae Romanae me subiicio, in quam omnes vere / catholici et fideles iugi ac pari intentione recurrere illi coherere atque inseri [122]debent. /

Frater Benedictus a Burgo Sancti Sepulcri Ordinis Servorum./'

Antonio Posii a Monteilicino, O.M.

This Franciscan is known as the author of a Thesaurus ... in omnes Aristotelis et Auerrois libros copiosissimus (Venice, 1562).

'**/fo. 14r/** Responsio fratris Antonii Posii a Montilicino Ordinis Minorum / Con [ventualium] ad dubium per illustrissimum dominum cardinalem Alexandrinum propositum. /

Dubium /

An Calvinistarum hereticorum baptismus sit verus et / vere baptizent pueros, ita ut non sint rebaptizandi / cum tamen ipsi intentionem neque generalem, / neque

---

[120] 2[r].
[121] Augustine, *De Unico Baptismo*, cap. 13.22, *PL* 43, col. 606, M. Petschenig, ed., CSEL 53, p. 22; *Petri Lombardi ... Sententiae*, Liber IV, Dist. VI, cap. 2, p. 270.
[122] *After deletion.*

particularem, neque virtualem, neque forma-/-lem habeant faciendi quod facit ecclesia, credant-/-que pueros in utero esse iustificatos, modo sint / ex fidelibus parentibus procreati, nec baptis-/-mum collativum esse gratie velint, etc. /

Responsio /

Si Calviniste formam baptismi integram ecclesiae ser-/-vent in baptizandis pueros atque aqua utantur, ita / ut ibi sit partes essentiales sacramenti, verus / est baptismus, nec rebaptizandi aliquomodo sunt. /

Ut autem veritas prepositae conclusionis eluceat magis, / brevibus annotabo qualem ipse baptismus / [123]debeat habere intentionem. Mox dubitationes / dubitantium rescindam. Divus Bonaventura (ut primum / aggrediar) 4 Sent. Dist. 6. q. 1 ar. 2[124] hoc scri-/-ptum [125]reliquit: Necessarium est intervenire intent-/-tionem ministri qua intendat illo actu et ver-/-bo talem effectum dare, vel saltem facere quod

/fo. 14v/ facit ecclesia, vel saltem quod instituit Christus dispen-/-sare. In iis verbis certe Seraphicus hic doctor / videtur innuere ministrum sub triplici disposi-/-tione quando vere baptizat, videlicet quod interdum / specialem habeat intentionem quam habent actu / vel virtualiter catholici, vel generalem, pari / modo actu vel virtualiter quam habent quan-/-doque ministri, qui de effectu speciali sacramenti / non sunt imbuti, aut quia non sunt fideles, aut / quia rudes. Vel saltem habeat faciendi quod / fecit Christus – quod verbum (ni fallor) tangit here-/-ticos qui ecclesiam nolunt agnoscere vel satha-/-nicam sequuntur [126]eam que vera est et firma-/-mentum veritatis persequentes omnibus conatibus. / [127]Divus etiam Thomas 3 Part. q. 64 art. 8 Ad primum ar-/-gumentum[128] respondens habet haec verba: Et ideo requi-/-ritur eius intentio qua se subiiciat principali / agenti, ut scilicet intendat facere quod facit / Christus et ecclesia. Verum circa ecclesiae intentionem / quam habent baptizantes ar. X.[129] sanctus doctor notat duo, / quorum alterum est sacramenti collatio et alterum / est effectus sacramenti collati. Primum certe adest / unicuique operanti vel ministranti sacramentum / ut opus Christi humano modo, hoc est dictu / non iocando cum fictione, vel a casu ut ebrius in actu,

/fo. 15r/ ita quod animus neque ad effectum sacramenti, neque / ad collationem sacramenti, neque ad opus Christi quod-/-cumque sit illud neque ad ecclesiam [130]tendat, sed si rationabili-/-ter ministretur saltem ut ceremonia Christi et / opus evangelicum est semper ibi sufficiens inten-/-tio, licet alterum desit, nempe gratie collationem / actualemque iustificationem mediante sacramento intendere. Ex iis

---

[123] *After deletion.*
[124] S. Bonaventurae Opera Omnia, ed. Quaracchi Fathers, iv (Quaracchi, 1889), iv, Dist. VI, P. II. Art. II. Quaest. I, Conclusio, p. 153.
[125] *In margin, in the 'decision hand':* S. Bonaventura.   [126] *After deletion.*
[127] *In margin, in the 'decision hand':* S. Thomas.
[128] *Sancti Thomae Aquinatis … Opera Omnia,* Quaestio LXIV, Articulus VIII, p. 52.
[129] Ibid., Quaestio LXIV, Articulus X, p. 54 (not a verbatim quotation but the substance of the 'Respondeo' section fits).
[130] *Supplied in margin.*

patet veritas conclusionis, in / qua asserebamus Calvinistarum baptismum esse / verum baptismum et eorum pueros vere baptiza-/-tos esse, nec rebaptizandos, quandoquidem / habent ipsi saltem intentionem faciendi quod / faciebat Christus et apostoli, licet contrariam / habeant intentionem ecclesiae catholicae, ut ex / pertinaci animo sentiant, non eadem sed lon-/-ge diversa ratione ab ecclesia se baptizare, et / pueros esse baptizandos. Non enim baptizanti est / necessarium ut bene sentiat de ecclesia, neque de / baptismo, aut de effectu baptismi, neque etiam de Christo / sed satis est quo ad sacramenti integritatem / tanquam opus Christi et confuse intendere tradere / sacramentum, quia Christus ipsum instituit, et imitari / Christum et Apostolos quo ad formam baptizandi nece-/-ssariam. Libet pro nostra firmanda responsio-/-ne referre sententias quasdam Beati patris [131]Augustini / in primis libro 4 contra Donatistas cap 12[132] [133]sic inquietis.

//15v/ Cum enim baptisma verbis evangelicis datur quali-/-bet ea perversitate intelligat ille per quem / datur vel ille cui datur, ipsum per se sanctum / est propter illum cuius est. /

Libro 3 cap 15[134] Sacramenta si eadem sunt (lo-/quens de substantialibus sacramentorum) ubique / integra sunt etiam si prave intelligantur, et / discordiose tractantur, sicut scriptura evange-/-lii si eadem ipsa est, ubique integra est. Ratio-/-nem huius videtur insinuare in epistola ad Vin-/-centium Sagatianum epistula 48[135] dicens: Nobiscum autem / estis in baptismo [136]in symbolo [137]et in caeteris domi-/-nicis sacramentis, in spiritu autem unitatis et / vinculo pacis, in ipsa denique ecclesia catholica no-/-biscum non estis. Haec si accipiatis non tunc aderunt / (id est quando ad catholicam ecclesiam venerint / adulti) sed tunc proderunt. Et propterea idem Divus / Augustinus Libr. 4 Contra Donatistas cap. 25[138] dicebat / Iuste igitur anathematizamus, detestamur, / abominamur perversitatem cordis hereticorum, / sacramentum autem evangelicum non ideo non ha-/-bent, quia per quod utile est non habent. / Consimiles plures possem divi Augustini sententias afferre / quibus perspicuo cuique patere posset nihil / illustri et pio illo viro fuisse abominabilius / ipsa iteratione baptismi traditi ab hereticis.

//fo. 16r/ in forma ecclesiae, esto quod de ecclesia male sentirent / vel de efficacia [139]sacramenti, aut de necessitate sa-/-cramenti, aut de natura sacramenti, si ta-/-men integrum traditum, [140]sit, quod facile colligi potest / ex iis quae docuit Lib. 6 Contra Donatistas cap. 25,[141] / quo in loco dicebat: Baptismus Christi verbis /

---

[131] *In margin:* S. Augustinus.
[132] Augustine, 'De Baptismo contra Donatistas', Lib. 4 ch. 12, *PL* 43, col. 166, M. Petschenig, ed., CSEL 51, p. 244.
[133] 'sic inquietis' *appears to be the indirect object of* referre.
[134] Augustine, 'De baptismo contra Donatistas', Book 3 ch. 15, *PL* 43, col. 148, M. Petschenig, ed., CSEL 51, p. 211.
[135] Augustine, Letter 93, *PL* 33, Caput XI, col. 344, A. Goldbacher, ed. *S. Augustini ... Epistulae* (CSEL, 34), pp. 445–496, at 488–489.
[136] *After erasure.*   [137] *Supplied between lines.*
[138] Book 4 ch. 25, *PL* 43, col. 176, M. Petschenig, ed., CSEL, 51, p. 260.
[139] *Last part of word blotted out in ms.*   [140] *Supplied between lines.*
[141] Augustine, 'De baptismo contra Donatistas', Book 6 ch. 25, *PL* 43, col. 2014.

evangelicis consecratus, ubique idem est, nec / hominum quorumlibet et qualibet perversi-/-tate potest violari. Idem contra Fulgentium cap. 3[142] / Quare ii qui defectu recte fidei de efficacia sacra-/-mentorum vel necessitate eorum reiterandum existima-/-rent esse baptismum, videntur infirmare om-/-nium catholicorum sententiam, qua mordicus tu-/-tantur simul cum beato Augustino sacramenta / ex vi operis operati conferre gratiam non po-/-nenti obicem. Ubique enim Augustinus agnoscit columbam / operantem quantumvis in ministrante adsit [143]sce-/-llus, ubique Christum et optimum maximum deum suo verbo / sanctificare, nec desunt sacri canones plurimi / decernentes hereticorum baptismum modo sit ser-/-vata forma ecclesiae non esse iterandum, ut in / Dist. 4 De consec. Ex Isidoro can. *Romanus*.[144] / De paganis baptizantibus vere , et quod heretici / si formam servent, can. [145]*Si qui*[146] et [147]*Quamvis*.[148] / Quod autem asserunt Calvinistas intentionem ecclesiae / non habere, si loquantur de [149]ecclesia catholica //16v/ profecto illis damus libenter quia ei sunt inimi-/-ci, nec eius immitationem intendunt, neque ad eu*n*-/-dem finem. Habent nihilominus alteram / partem intentionis sufficientem videlicet / baptizandi, et dispensandi baptismum Christi / et istud est satis pro pueris regenerandis / et effectu baptismi. Duplicem enim insinuant Cal-/-vinistae intentionem alteram interiorem / quia rationabiliter baptizant, alteram / exteriorem, in forma baptizandi, baptizan-/-tes in nomine Patris, Filii et Spiritus sancti, veluti docuit divus Thomas, / Par 3 qu. 64 ar. 8, dicens: et [150]haec intentio ex-/-primitur per verba que in sacramentis dicuntur[151] / puta cum dicit Ego te baptizo in nomine Patris, Filii, etc, / tam etiam [152]si deficiat specialis intentio ecclesiae, / nec intentio baptizantis feratur ad ecclesiam / quia hoc non est necessarium, [153]quin immo non desunt ex catho-/-licis, qui putent sufficere / intentionem expressam per / formam: cum ergo san-/-cta Tridentina synodus, nec non Florentina, et Catholici patres omnes asserunt [154]requiri intentionem / faciendi quod facit ecclesia, est idem ac si / dicerent intentionem faciendi id quod Christus / instituit ipsi ecclesiae et ecclesia retinet tanquam opus / et sacramentum a Christo institutum, nec video ne-/-cessitatem quod intentio feratur ad ecclesiam / sed ad illud quod ab ecclesia baptizando impri-/-mis intenditur, quomodo supra dicebamus.

[142] J.-L Maier, *Le Dossier du Donatisme*, 2 vols. (Berlin, 1987, 1989), ii, no. 111, pp. 237–285. It is not a genuine work of Augustine though a genuine Donatist work can be reconstructed from it. Cf. J. A. Hoover, *The Donatist Church in an Apocalyptic Age* (Oxford, 2018), 189–192.

[143] *Sic.*   [144] Gratian, *Decretum*, PARS III D. 4 de cons. c. 23, Friedberg, *Corpus*, i, 1368.

[145] *Cued to illegible comment in margin in the decision hand: possibly beginning* 'baptizati ab hereticis / in ?nomine Trinitatis / constitutione'.

[146] Gratian, *Decretum*, PARS III D. 4 de cons. c. 28, Friedberg, *Corpus*, i, 1369–1370.

[147] T *mark above word may be a cue to a marginal comment.*

[148] Gratian, *Decretum*, PARS III D. 4 de cons. c. 29, Friedberg, *Corpus*, i, 1370.

[149] *After deletion.*   [150] S. T. Sum *in margin.*

[151] Summa Theologica 3.64.8 'ad secundum'. *Sancti Thomae Aquinatis ... Opera Omnia*, Quaestio LXIV, Articulus VIII, p. 52.

[152] *Corr. from* sit *or* sic.

[153] quin immo ... per formam] *supplied in margin with omission mark.*

[154] *Supplied between lines.*

//17r/ quod si forte heretici gloriarentur quod eorum retine-/-mus baptismum et piis quibusdam hominibus hoc / videatur absonum, audiant divum Augustinum Contra Gau-/-dentium Libr. 3. cap. 14[155] dicentem: Nec vobis / [156]blandimini quod baptismum non rescindimus / vestrum, non est hoc vestrum sed catholicae ecclesiae / quam tenemus; nam vasa dominica etiam san-/-cta apud alienigenas permanserunt. Unde rex / qui eis contumeliose ausus est uti deo irascen-/-te punitus est. Et contra Donatistas Libr. 4 cap. / [157]ii:[158] Nos non concedimus heretico baptismum sed / illius baptismum de quo dictum est: hic est qui / baptizat in Spiritu sancto ubicunque invene-/-rimus agnoscimus.' Haec sunt quae de paupere / mea paenu ad propositam questionem obtuli, / meliori iudicio purganda, et Catholice ecclesiae censu-/rae [159]corrigenda.'

The following final document matches the one on fo. 6r–v almost exactly but gives, in the margins, the decisions of the Congregation and the pope in a proper script, not in an almost illegible form as in the version earlier in the busta.

'//fo. 116r/ Quoniam ex Concilii Tridentini decreto habetur can. / iiii° sess. septimae quod si quis dixerit baptismum qui etiam / ab haereticis datur In nomine patris et filii et spiritus sancti / cum intentione faciendi quod facit ecclesia, non esse ve-/-rum baptismum, anathema sit, maxime videtur ambigu-/-um pluribus Catholicis doctoribus an haereticorum Calvinista-/-rum modernorum baptismus sit verus, et an vere baptizant, / cum eis desit intentio [160]etiam universalis faciendi quod facit ecclesia, / nullam etenim vim [161]efficaciam, et virtutem tribuunt baptis-/-mo, asserunt, Libro iiii° Institutionis Christianae c. xiiii° et xv[162] / ex Ioanne Calvino, ubi negant baptismum [163]esse sacramentum efficax / gratiae collativum, et peccatorum remissivum in puero, quem / puerum credunt in utero materno esse iustificatum, modo / a parentibus christianis procreatur, ita quod si decedat / sine baptismo, non minus ingreditur regnum. Cum itaque in-/-tentio saltem universalis requiratur ad integritatem / baptismi, quam non habent, nec particularem, nec univer-/-salem, nec formalem, nec virtualem, heretici moder-/-ni Calvinistae, verisimile habetur quod vere non bap-/-tizant, [164][*response in left-hand margin, cued to text with letter alpha:* **'sanctissimus dominus noster etiam ex sententia / congregationis concilii censuit / eos vere baptizare'**] id quod humillime peroptant Catholici quidam / doctores plenius intelligere, et suam sanctitatem reverendissimos-/-que cardinales obnixe supplicant, super hac re decerne-/-re

---

[155] Augustine, 'Contra Gaudentium', Book 2 c. 10, *PL* 43 col. 747, M. Petschenig, ed., CSEL, 53, p. 267.

[156] *In margin:* S. August.   [157] *Error for* 11?

[158] Augustine, 'De Baptismo Contra Donatistas', Book 4 c. 11, *PL* 43 col. 165, M. Petschenig, ed., CSEL, 51, p. 242.

[159] *After deletion.*   [160] *Supplied between lines.*   [161] *Corr. from* efficcaciam.

[162] Allen, *Institutes of the Christian Religion by John Calvin*, iii, Book IV, chs. 14 and 15, pp. 298–346.

[163] *Supplied between lines.*

[164] *The decision given in margin – see passage in square brackets – is cued to the text by the letter alpha.*

/116v/ an liberum sit evangelizantibus verbum Domini do-/-cere populum
fidelem, [165]quod baptizati ab ipsis Cal-/-vinistis haereticis sint denuo baptizandi
an non? /Quia, ut iam dictum est, illis deest tertia pars baptis-/-mi integralis,
scilicet intentio.'

The decision, left-hand margin, cued to text at '... an non?': **'Sanctissimus
Dominus Noster etiam ex sententia / Congregationis Concilii censuit /
non esse iterum baptizandos.'**

*1587/8, February 19. BL Add MS 6878 (9).

*Sixtus V, 'Notification to the clergy of Funay, Japan, of provision of Sebastian
[de Moraës] to that see'.*[166] *Idris Bell noted evidence of holes for the threads
attached which would have connected the document to the leaden seal. The
elaborate decoration of the first letters of Sixtus, Dilectis, Clero, Civitatis and
Funaiensis confirms that this is in the medieval letter of grace tradition, though
there are no longer tittles or long ligatures. It was a Chancery, not a
Secretariate, product.*

'Sixtus episcopus servus servorum dei dilectis filiis clero civitatis et diocesis
Funaiensis /1// salutem et apostolicam benedictionem. Hodie ecclesie
Funaiensis in partibus insularum Iapponiarum quam nos et hodie in
cathedralem /2// ecclesiam sub invocatione beate Marie Virginis ex certis causis
de fratrum nostrorum consilio apostolica auctoritate erexi-/3//-mus et instituimus
a primeva illius erectione pastoris solatio destitute de persona dilecti filii
Sebastiani /4// electi Funaiensis nobis et fratribus ipsis ob suorum exigentiam
meritorum accepta de eorundem fratrum consilio dicta /5// auctoritate
providimus, ipsumque illi in episcopum prefecimus et pastorem curam et
administrationem ipsius /6// ecclesie sibi in spiritualibus et temporalibus
plenarie committendo prout in nostris inde confectis litteris plenius /7//
continetur, quocirca discretioni vestre per apostolica scripta mandamus
quatenus eundem Sebastianum electum /8// tanquam patrem et pastorem
animarum vestrarum grato admittentes honore ac exhibentes sibi obedientiam
et reverentiam /9// debitas ac devotas eius salubria monita et mandata suscipiatis
humiliter et efficaciter adimplere curetis, /10// alioquin sententiam quam idem
Sebastianus electus rite tulerit in rebelles ratam habebimus et faciemus /11//
auctore Domino usque ad satisfactionem condignam inviolabiliter observari.
Datum Rome apud Sanctum Petrum /12// anno incarnationis dominice
millesimo quingentesimo octuagesimo septimo, undecimo kal. Martii
pontificatus nostri anno tertio. /13//'

Cursive hand left-hand side: 'Pro reverendissimo Domino Summ^re A. Justus.'

---

[165] *Decision given in margin, cued to text by letter Beta: see end.*
[166] I. Bell, 'A List of Original Papal Bulls and Briefs in the Department of Manuscripts, British Museum', *English Historical Review*, 36 (1921), 393–418, 556–582, at p. 568, no. 352.

Same cursive hand right-hand side: 'Tho. Thom.^{s} Gualterutius.'

Dorse, middle, centre to right: 'Registrata apud Thomam Secretarium.'

*1588, August 3. BL Add Ch 12811.

'*Grant, in form of brief, at request of doge and* governatori *of Genoa, of concessions concerning fasts, celebration of mass, &c, on the Genuese fleet. ... Trace of Anulus Piscatoris*'.[167]

'   SIXTUS PAPA V /1//

Ad futuram rei memoriam. Honestis principum votis benigne annuere volentes, precibusque dilectorum filiorum nobilium virorum Ducis, et Gubernatorum Reipublicae Genuensis nobis super /2// hoc humiliter porrectis inclinati, quod quoties classis predictae republicae navigabit, omnes, et singuli christifideles super ea exeuntes quibusvis ieiuniorum ab ecclesia praescriptorum temporibus /3// prandium, quod de mane sumi solet, vespere facere possint, ientaculum vero in ipso mane capere, praeterea quod missae sacrificium, quando necessitas navigandi aderit, cena hora /4// post meridiem, et alia hora ante diem celebrari valeat: Insuper decem presbyteris super ipsa classe pro tempore existentibus ab eorum ordinariis approbatis quoscunque, quibus navigare /5// necessarium erit, in omnibus casibus etiam reservatis absolvendi facultatem impartimur: Item cum acceperimus consuetudinem esse armandi unam tendam, seu ba-/6//-raccam nuncupatam, et ibi cum uno altari portatili in omnibus locis quo triremes applicare solitae sunt, missa celebrari possit, quod idem uti solitum est, fieri valeat, /7// auctoritate apostolica tenore praesentium concedimus, et indulgemus, contrariis non obstantibus quibuscunque. Datum Romae apud Sanctum Marcum sub annulo Piscatoris, die iii /8// Augusti M. D. LXXXVIII Pontificatus Nostri Anno Quarto. /9//'

Right-hand side of page, in different hand, 'Tho. Thom.' Gualterius.'

On dorse, in Frenz position 28,[168] 'P. Navarra.'

*1618–1620. ACDF, S.O., D.B. (*De Baptismate*) 1 (1618–1698), n. 1, fo. 1v.

A Capucin Franciscan, baptised as a Calvinist, who feared that his baptism and subsequent orders were invalid, is allowed a conditional baptism and orders, but forbidden to publish his treatise against the validity of Calvinist baptism.

---

[167] Bell, 'List', no. 353, p. 568.
[168] '(rechts am unteren Rand auf dem Kopf stehend) Auskultationsvermerk (*litterae rescriptae*)'.

'Queritur an validus sit baptismus collatus a Calvinistis. / Hoc dubium excitavit P. Angelus de Raconis[169] Concionator Capuccinus, qui natus est / Basilee ex parentibus haereticis Calvinistis, et in templo Calvinistarum baptizatus fuit / adhibita iuxta morem aqua rosacea pro materia. Quod illi etiam significavit eius soror / maior nata, Clara de Sanctissimo Sacramento religiosa ordinis Carmelitarum. Petit igitur, ut saltem / baptizetur sub conditione, ac proinde denuo eidem conferantur ordines. / In hac positione adest manuscriptum eiusdem fratris Angeli de Raconis 'De septemplici Calvini-/-starum circa baptismum errore.' /

Die 25 Octobris 1620 Sanctissimus decrevit quod Fr. Angelus baptizetur in urbe sub conditione / sine praeiudicio professionis, quod ei intimetur iudicialiter. /

In Gallia non procedatur ulterius pro diligentiis faciendis circa eius baptismum, et detur eidem / licentia discedendi ab urbe. /

Liber quem exhibuit 'De septemplici Calvinistarum errore' consideretur, et referatur. /

Die 22. eiusdem Sanctissimus dispensavit, ut ordines tam minores quam sacros per eum / [170]suscipiandos, sub conditione [171]suscipiantur extra tempora, et non [172]servatis interstitiis. Prae-/-terea mandavit ei prohiberi, ne libellum 'De septemplici Calvinistarum circa baptismum errore' / ullo modo publicet, neque tractet de validitate, seu invaliditate proprii vel Calvinistarum / baptismi.'

---

[169] See entry with bibliography in the scholarly alphabetical database FRANAUT-A compiled by Maarten van der Heijden and Bert Roest: http://users.bart.nl/~roestb/franciscan/franauta.htm#AngelusdeRaconis (consulted 4 July 2022).

[170] *Final letters have been altered and are unclear.*

[171] *After* suscipiantur *deleted. Probably the intention was to correct to* 'suscipiat', *but the scribe instead repeated the word he had just deleted.*

[172] *Between lines.*

Reproductions

The text passages relating to the documents reproduced at the end of this volume can be found via the general index under MS, followed by the call number (or 'signature') of the manuscript. A majority of the small selection are from the British Library. This was not just for convenience. The British Library has a very large collection of papal letters of heterogeneous provenance, thanks to the collecting of English aristocrats in the eighteenth century and above all to the almost unlimited purchasing power and comprehensive tastes of the British Museum (as it then was) in the nineteenth century. This rich collection has been very useful! See I. Bell, 'A List of Original Papal Bulls and Briefs in the Department of Manuscripts, British Museum', *English Historical Review* 36 (1921), pp. 393–418, 556–582.

A full and representative set of reproductions would make this a different kind of book, more like Giulio Battelli's *Acta Pontificum* (Exempla Scripturarum ... Fasciculus III; 2nd edition, Vatican City, 1965) , or Bruno Katterbach's *Specimina Supplicationum ex Registris Vaticanis* (Subsidiorum Tabularii Vaticani, ii; Rome, 1927), though neither of these do, or could do, justice to the mass and range of papal records.[1] My minimalist selection aims to complement these, if only to a very modest extent. While one can get a good idea of the strange 'Roman Curiale' script by papal scribes in the early Middle Ages from Battelli, *Acta Pontificum* (see his reproduction number 1), and his selection contains excellent examples of the new aspect brought to documents from Leo IX on (e.g. numbers 5, 6, and 8), the key contrast between typical quotidian letters of grace and letters of justice in the thirteenth century and afterwards is not so easy to illustrate from his facsimiles. In the plates at the back of this volume a comparison between BL Add Ch 17857 (letter of grace) and TNA SC 7/64/40 (letter of justice) make very evident the differences, discussed in detail in the body of the book.

---

[1] There is also an excellent set of reproductions, prepared by Sergio Pagano, at the end of Frenz and Pagano, *I Documenti.*

Archivio Apostolico Vaticano, Armadio **XXXIV** 2, fo. 115r shows the rare record of behind-the-scenes discussions in the fourteenth-century papal curia – again there is nothing like this in Battelli. British Library Add MS 6878 (9) and Add Ch 12811 illustrate the contrast between a letter issued by the papal Chancery and a papal brief: see discussion in Chapter 5. These also bring us into the post-Trent period. Note that Frenz & Pagano provide some good reproductions of the often-neglected early modern papal documents.

No reproductions that I know of come up to the standard of I. Fees and F. Roberg, *Papsturkunden der zweiten Hälfte des 11. Jahrhunderts (1057–1098)* (Digitale Urkundenbilder aus dem Marburger Lichtbildarchiv älterer Originalurkunden; Leipzig, 2007). The Marburg Lichtbildarchiv from which they are taken is one example of the (still recent) accessibility of reproductions available online: see www.uni-marburg.de/de/fb06/mag/lichtbildarchiv-aelterer-originalurkunden. Many papal documents can be accessed online through the Monasterium website: www.icarus.eu/cooperation/online-portals/monasterium-net/. The Vatican Library manuscript BAV Vat. Lat. 5845, the *arenga* of which is analysed in Chapter 3, can be accessed in a brilliantly clear digitised form via the Manoscritti digitalizzati database at https://digi.vatlib.it/mss/.

Thus it is now easy to supplement the small selection of plates reproduced in the present volume.

Plates

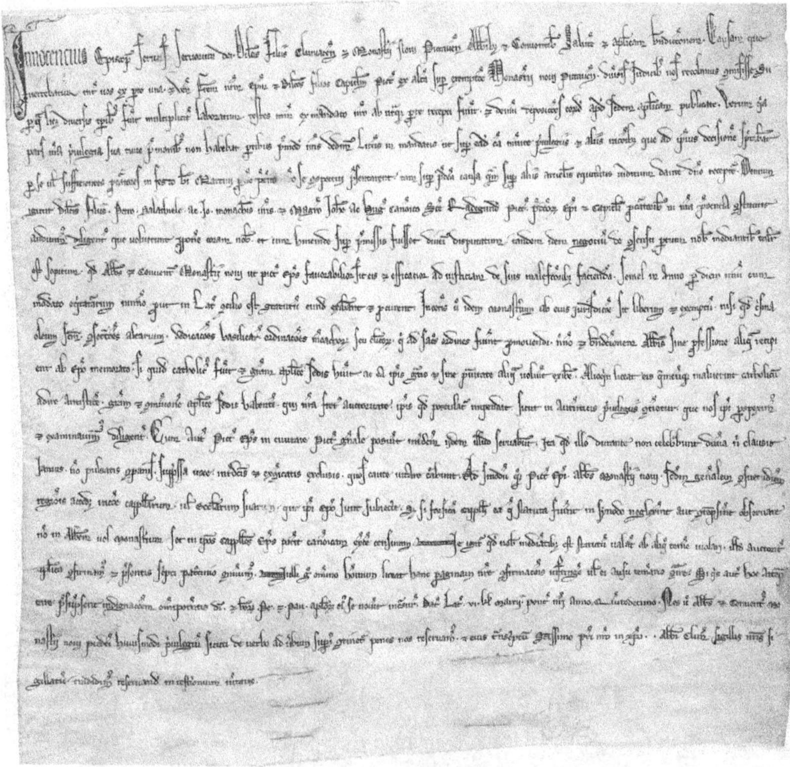

Plate 1. British Library Add Ch 1542 (1212, February 24. Innocent III); by permission of the British Library Board, all rights reserved.

233

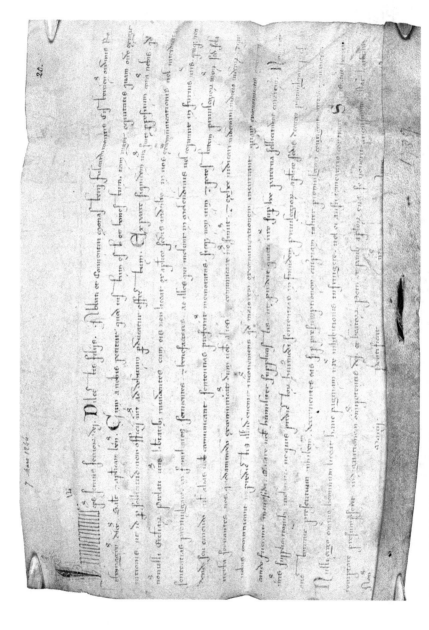

234

Plate 2. British Library Add Ch 17857 (1244, March 7. Innocent IV); by permission of the British Library Board, all rights reserved.

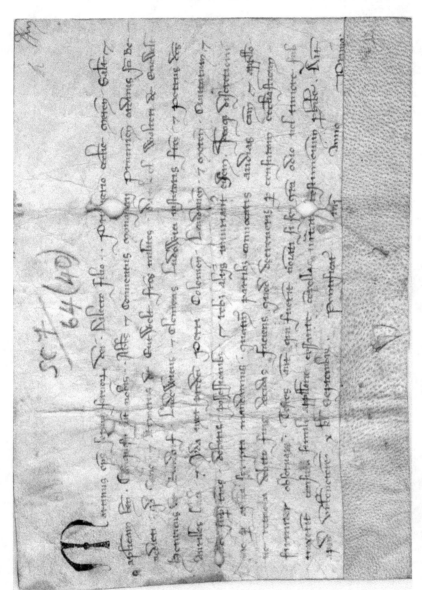

Plate 3. National Archives, Kew, England SC 7/64/40 (1281, August 23); by permission of the National Archives, all rights reserved.

235

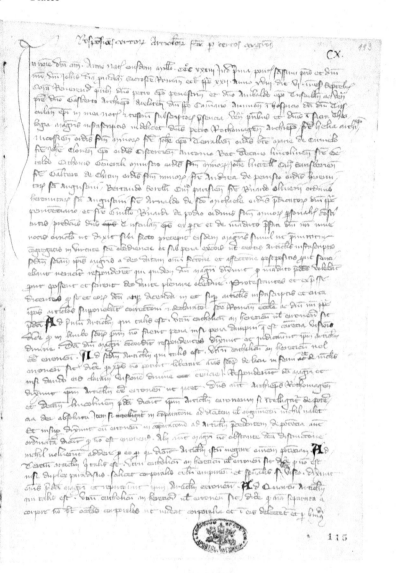

Plate 4. Archivio Apostolico Vaticano, Armadio XXXIV 2, fo. 115r
(*1333, September 6 and 7); by permission of the Prefect, Archivio
Apostolico Vaticano, all rights reserved.

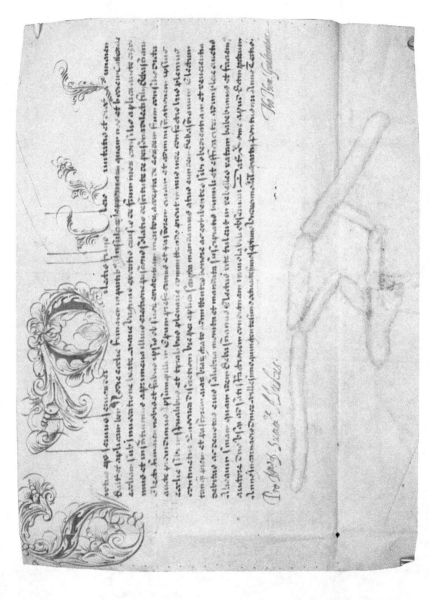

Plate 5. British Library Add MS 6878 (9) (1587/8, February 19); by permission of the British Library Board, all rights reserved.

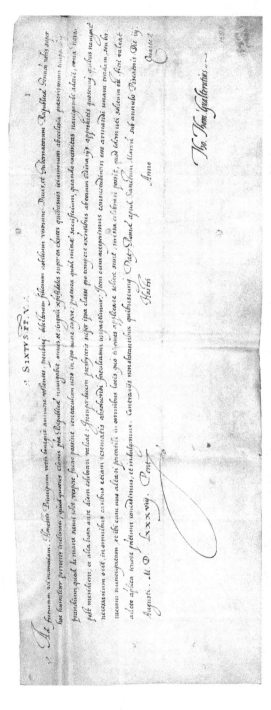

238

Plate 6. British Library, Add Ch 12811 (1588, August 3); by permission of the British Library Board, all rights reserved.

Bibliography

For manuscript sources see under 'MS' in the general index.

Alraum, C., Holndonner, A., Lehner, H.-C., Scherer, C., Schlauwitz, T., Unger, V., eds., *Zwischen Rom und Santiago. Festschrift für Klaus Herbers zum 65. Geburtstag* (Bochum, 2016).

Allen, J., ed., *Institutes of the Christian Religion by John Calvin*, iii (Philadelphia, PA, 1816).

Anderson, P., *Passages from Antiquity to Feudalism* (London, 1978).

Anton, H. H., *Studien zu den Klosterprivilegien der Päpste im frühen Mittelalter. Unter besonderer Berücksichtigung der Privilegierung von St. Maurice d'Agaune* (Beiträge zur Geschichte und Quellenkunde des Mittelalters, 4; Berlin, 1975).

Archivio Apostolico Vaticano, *Indice dei Fondi e relativi mezzi di descrizione e di ricerca dell'Archivio Apostolico Vaticano* (Vatican City, 2022) (the website is www.archivioapostolicovaticano.va/content/aav/it/patrimonio.html; pagination changes as it is updated).

Aux origines de l'état moderne. La fonctionnement administratif de la papauté d'Avignon (Collection de l'École Française de Rome, 138; Rome, 1990).

Baaken, K., and Schmidt, U., eds., *J. F. Böhmer, Regesta Imperii IV: Lothar III. und ältere Staufer, 4. Abteilung: Papstregesten 1124–1198, Teil 4: 1181–1198, Lieferung 1: 1181–1184* (Cologne, 2003).

J. F. Böhmer, Regesta Imperii IV: Lothar III. und ältere Staufer, 4. Abteilung: Papstregesten 1124–1198, Teil 4, Lieferung 2: 1184–1185 (Cologne, 2006).

Baethgen, F., 'Quellen und Untersuchungen zur Geschichte der päpstlichen Hof- und Finanzverwaltung unter Bonifaz VIII', *Quellen und Forschungen aus Italienischen Archiven und Bibliotheken*, 20 (1928–1929), 114–237.

Baier, H., *Päpstliche Provisionen für niedere Pfründen bis zum Jahre 1304* (Vorreformationsgeschichtliche Forschungen, 7; Munster i. W., 1911).

Barbiche, B., *Les actes pontificaux originaux des Archives nationales de Paris*, 3 vols. (Vatican City, 1975–1982).

'Le Censimento Bartoloni et ses premiers développements: un nouvel élan pour la diplomatique pontificale', in M. Sohn-Kronthaler and J. Verger, eds., *Europa und Memoria. Festschrift für Andreas Sohn zum 60. Geburtstag* (St. Ottilien, 2019), 227–239.

Barraclough, G., 'The Chancery Ordinance of Nicholas III. A Study of the Sources', *Quellen und Forschungen aus italienischen Archiven und Bibliotheken*, 25 (1933–1934), 192–250.

'The English Royal Chancery and the Papal Chancery in the Reign of Henry III', *Mitteilungen des Instituts für Österreichische Geschichtsforschung*, 62 (1954), 365–378.

'The Executors of Papal Provisions in the Canonical Theory of the Thirteenth and Fourteenth Centuries', in *Excerptum ex Actis Congressus Iuridici Internationalis Romae 12–17 Novembris 1934*, ed. Pontificium Institutum Utriusque Iuris, 5 vols. (1935–1937), iii, 109–153.

Papal Provisions. Aspects of Church History, Constitutional, Legal and Administrative, in the Later Middle Ages (Oxford, 1935).

Bartlett, R., *England under the Norman and Angevin Kings, 1075–1225* (Oxford, 2000).

Battelli, I., *Acta Pontificum* (Exempla Scripturarum, 3; Vatican City, 1965).

Bauer, C., 'Die Epochen der Papstfinanz: Ein Versuch', *Historische Zeitschrift*, 138 (1928), 457–503.

Bell, I., 'A List of Original Papal Bulls and Briefs in the Department of Manuscripts, British Museum', *English Historical Review*, 36 (1921), 393–418, 556–582.

Benedicti Papae XIV. Bullarium, tomus secundus, vol. 4 (Malines, 1826 edition).

Beretta, F., 'L'archivio della Congregazione del Sant'Ufficio: bilancio provvisorio della storia e natura dei fondi d'antico regime', *Rivista di Storia e Letteratura Religiosa*, 37 (2001), 29–58.

Bernard, A., and Bruel, A., eds., *Recueil des Chartes de l'abbaye de Cluny*, vi (1211–1300) (Paris, 1903).

Bliss, W. H., et al., eds., *Calendar of Entries in the Papal Registers Relating to Great Britain and Ireland, Papal Letters*, 14 vols. (London, 1893–1933).

Blouin, F. X., et al., *Vatican Archives. An Inventory and Guide to Historical Documents of the Holy See* (New York, 1998).

Blouin, F. X., Yakel, E., and Coombs, L. A., '"Vatican Archives: An Inventory and Guide to Historical Documents of the Holy See" – A Ten-Year Retrospective', *American Archivist*, 71.2 (2008), 410–432.

Boesch Gajano, S., *Gregorio Magno. Alle origini del Medioevo* (Rome, 2004).

Bombi, B., *Anglo-Papal Relations in the Early Fourteenth Century: A Study in Medieval Diplomacy* (Oxford, 2019).

Il Registro di Andrea Sapiti, procuratore alla Curia Avignonese (Rome, 2007).

Boockmann, H., 'Ablaßfälschungen im 15. Jahrhundert', in *Fälschungen im Mittelalter*, 5, *Briefe, Frömmigkeit und Fälschung, Realienfälschungen* (*MGH* Schriften, 35: 5; Hanover, 1988), 659–668.

Borgolte, M., *World History as the History of Foundations, 3000 BCE to 1500 CE* (Leiden, 2020).

Boyle, L. E., 'Diplomatics', in J. M. Powell, ed., *Medieval Studies: An Introduction* (Syracuse, NY, 1992), 82–113.

'Innocent III and Vernacular Versions of Scripture', in K. Walsh and D. Wood, eds., *The Bible in the Medieval World. Essays in Memory of Beryl Smalley* (Oxford, 1985), 97–107.

A Survey of the Vatican Archives and of its Medieval Holdings (Toronto, 1972).

Brentano, R., *York Metropolitan Jurisdiction and Papal Judges Delegate, 1279–1296* (Berkeley, CA, 1959).

Bresslau, H., *Handbuch der Urkundenlehre für Deutschland und Italien*, i (2nd edition, Leipzig, 1912); ii, first part (2nd edition, Leipzig, 1915); ii, second part, ed. H.-W. Klewitz (Berlin, 1931).

Manuale di Diplomatica per la Germania e l'Italia, transl. A. M. Voci-Rot (Rome, 1998).

Brooke, C. N. L., 'Approaches to Medieval Forgery', *Journal of the Society of Archivists*, 3 (1968), 377–386.

Broser, T., Fischer, A., and Thumser, M., eds., *Kuriale Briefkultur im späteren Mittelalter* (Forschungen zur Kaiser-und Papstgeschichte des Mittelalters. Beihefte zu J. F. Böhmer, Regesta Imperii, 37; Cologne, 2015).

Brown, E. A. R., '*Falsitas pia sive reprehensibilis*. Medieval Forgers and their Intentions', in *Fälschungen im Mittelalter*, 6 vols. (MGH Schriften, 33; Hanover, 1988–1990), i (1988), 109–119.

Caiazza, P., 'L'Archivio Storico della Sacra Congregazione del Concilio. (Primi appunti per un problema di riordinamento)', *Ricerche di Storia Sociale e Religiosa. N.S.*, 42 (1992), 7–24.

Carpenter, D. A., 'The English Royal Chancery in the Thirteenth Century', in A. Jobson, ed., *English Government in the Thirteenth Century* (Boydell, 2004), 49–69.

Chadwick, O., *Catholicism and History. The Opening of the Vatican Archives* (Cambridge, 1978).

Cheney, C. R., *A Handbook of Dates for Students of English History* (Cambridge, 1995).

Cifres, A., ed., *L'Iinquisizione Romana e I suoi Archivi. A vent'anni dall'apertura dell'ACDF* (Rome, 2018).

Cipolla, C., ed., *Codice Diplomatico des Monastero di S. Colombano di Bobbio fino all'Anno MCCVIII*, i (Rome, 1918).

Clanchy, M., *From Memory to Written Record* (3rd edition, Oxford 2012).

Clarke, P. D., 'Between Avignon and Rome: Minor Penitentiaries at the Papal Curia in the Thirteenth and Fourteenth Centuries', *Rivista di Storia della Chiesa in Italia*, 63 (2009), 455–510.

Cubitt, C., *Anglo-Saxon Church Councils c. 650–c. 850* (London, 1995).

D'Acunto, N., ed., *Papato e monachesimo 'esente' nei secoli centrali del Medioevo* (Florence, 2003).

d'Avray, D. L., 'Authentication of Marital Status: A Thirteenth-Century English Annulment Process and Late Medieval Cases from the Papal Penitentiary', *English Historical Review*, 120 (2005), 987–1013.

Dissolving Royal Marriages. A Documentary History, 860–1600 (Cambridge, 2014).

'Germany and the Papacy in the Late Middle Ages', *Journal of Ecclesiastical History*, 71 (2020), 362–367.

'Half a Century of Research on the First Papal Decretals (to c. 440)', *Bulletin of Medieval Canon Law* n.s. 35 (2018), 331–374.

Medieval Marriage. Symbolism and Society (Oxford, 2005).

Medieval Religious Rationalities. A Weberian Analysis (Cambridge, 2010).

Papacy, Monarchy and Marriage, 860–1600 (Cambridge, 2015).

Papal Jurisprudence, 385–1234. Social Origins and Medieval Reception of Canon Law (Cambridge, 2022).

Papal Jurisprudence, c. 400. Sources of the Canon Law Tradition (Cambridge, 2019).

'La Penitenzieria nel Seicento: Attività e Prassi', in K. Nykiel and U. Taraborrelli, eds., *L'Archivio della Penitenzieria Apostolica. Stato Attuale e Prospettive Future* (Vatican City, 2017), 165–172.

Rationalities in History. A Weberian Essay in Comparison (Cambridge, 2010).

Dahlhaus, J., 'Aufkommen und Bedeutung der Rota in den Urkunden des Papstes Leo IX.', *Archivum Historiae Pontificiae*, 27 (1989), 7–84.

'Rota oder Unterschrift. Zur Unterfertigung päpstlicher Urkunden durch ihre Aussteller in der zweiten Hälfte des 11. Jahrhunderts', in I. Fees, A. Hedwig and F. Roberg, eds., *Papsturkunden des frühen und hohen Mittelalters. Äußere Merkmale – Konservierung – Restaurierung* (Leipzig, 2011), 249–290 (with 'Anhang: Die Originalurkunden der Päpste von 1055–1099', 291–303).

Dale, J., *Inauguration and Liturgical Kingship in the Long Twelfth Century: Male and Female Accession Rituals in England, France and the Empire* (York, 2019).

Dannenberg, L.-A., *Das Recht der Religiosen in der Kanonistik des 12. und 13. Jahrhunderts* (Vita regularis, Abhandlungen, 39; Berlin, 2008).

de Boüard, A., *Manuel de Diplomatique française et pontificale. I, Diplomatique générale* (Paris, 1929).

de Jong, M., *Epitaph for an Era: Politics and Rhetoric in the Carolingian World* (Cambridge, 2019).

De Lasala, F., and Rabikauskas, P., *Il Documento Medievale e Moderno, Panorama Storico della Diplomatica Generale e Pontificia* (Rome, 2003).

De Luca, Johannes Baptista, *Relatio Curiae Romanae* (Cologne, 1683).

De Rosa, Thomas, *Tractatus De executoribus litterarum apostolicarum* (Venice, 1697).

Deanesly, M., *The Lollard Bible and Other Medieval Biblical Versions* (Cambridge, 1920).

Dehio, L., 'Der Übergang von Natural- zu Geldbesoldung an der Kurie', *Vierteljahrschrift für Social- und Wirtschaftsgeschichte*, 8 (1910), 56–78.

Dehoux, E., Galland, C., and Vincent, C., eds., *Des usages de la grâce. Pratiques des indulgences du Moyen Âge à l'époque contemporaine* (Villeneuve d'Ascq, 2021).

Del Col, A., 'Vent'anni di studi sull'Inquisizione romana: risultati e attese', in A. Cifres, ed., *L'Iinquisizione Romana e I suoi Archivi. A vent'anni dall'apertura dell'ACDF* (Rome, 2018), 45–80.

Diener, H., 'Die Grossen Registerserien im Vatikanischen Archiv (1378–1523)', *Quellen und Forschungen aus italienischen Archiven und Bibliotheken*, 51 (1971), 305–368.

Ditchfield, S., 'In Sarpi's Shadow: Coping with Trent the Italian Way', in *Studi in Memoria di Cesare Mozzarelli i* (Milan, 2008), 585–606.

'In Search of Local Knowledge. Rewriting Early Modern Italian Religious History', *Cristianesimo nella Storia*, 19 (1998), 255–296.

Dondorp, H., 'Review of Papal Rescripts in Canonists' Teaching', *Zeitschrift der Savigny-Stiftung für Rechtsgeschichte, Kanonistische Abteilung*, 76 (1990), 172–253.

Dorna, M., *Mabillon und andere. Die Anfänge der Diplomatik* (Wiesbaden, 2019).

Doublier, E., *Ablass, Papsttum und Bettelorden im 13. Jahrhundert* (Cologne, 2017).

Doublier, E., and Johrendt, J., eds., *Economia della Salvezza e Indulgenza nel Medioevo* (Milan, 2017).

Dubois, J., 'Esenzione Monastica', in G. Pelliccia and G. Rocca, eds., *Dizionario degli Istituti di Perfezione, iii* (Rome, 1976), cols. 1295–1306.

Duggan, A., '*De consultationibus*. The Role of Episcopal Consultation in the Shaping of Canon Law in the Twelfth Century', in B. C. Brasington and K. G. Cushing, eds., *Bishops, Texts and the Use of Canon Law around 1100. Essays in Honour of Martin Brett* (Aldershot, 2008), 191–214.

Dunbabin, J., *A Hound of God. Pierre de la Palud and the Fourteenth-Century Church* (Oxford, 1991).

Duval-Arnould, L., 'Élaboration d'un document pontifical: les travaux préparatoires à la constitution apostolique *Cum inter nonnullos* (12 novembre 1323)', in *Aux origines de l'état moderne. La fonctionnement administratif de la papauté d'Avignon* (Collection de l'École Française de Rome, 138; Rome, 1990), 385–409.

Egger, C., 'Vertraulichkeit und Geheimhaltung in der hochmittelalterlichen päpstlichen Kanzlei', *Archiv für Diplomatik, Schriftgeschichte, Siegel- und Wappenkunde*, 63 (2017), 253–271.

Engel, F., 'Päpstlicher als der Papst? Papstbriefe um das Jahr 1000', *Archiv für Diplomatik*, 66 (2020), 55–69.

Engl, H., 'Rupture radicale ou mise en oeuvre d'une conception ancienne? Le concept de "réforme grégorienne" à travers les recherches récentes sur la diplomatique pontificale en Allemagne', in T. Martine and J. Winandy, eds., *La Réforme grégorienne, une 'révolution totale'?* (Paris, 2021), 176–189.

Esch, A., *Die Lebenswelt des europäischen Spätmittelalters. Kleine Schicksale selbst erzählt in Schreiben an den Papst* (Munich, 2014).

Fagnani, P., *Commentaria in Secundam Partem Tertii Libri Decretalium* (Cologne, 1681).

Faivre, A., *Naissance d'une hiérarchie. Les premières étapes du cursus clérical* (Théologie historique, 40; Paris, 1977).

Falkenstein, L., *La papauté et les abbayes françaises au XIe et XIIe siècles. Exemption et protection apostolique* (Paris, 1997).

Fawtier, R., 'Documents négligés sur l'activité de la Chancellerie apostolique à la fin du XIIIe siècle. Le registre 46A et les comptes de la Chambre sous Boniface VIII', *Mélanges d'archéologie et d'histoire* 52 (1935), 244–272.

Fees, I., 'Diplomatik und Paläographie als Schlüssel zur Kulturgeschichte: Papsgeschichtliche Wende und Urkundengestaltung', in K. Herbers and V. Trenkle, eds., *Papstgeschichte im digitalen Zeitalter. Neue Zugangsweisen zu einer Kulturgeschichte Europas* (Cologne, 2018), 95–107.

'Rota und Siegel der Päpste in der zweiten Hälfte des 11. Jahrhunderts', in C. Alraum, A. Holndonner, H.-C. Lehner, C. Scherer, T. Schlauwitz and V. Unger, eds., *Zwischen Rom und Santiago. Festschrift für Klaus Herbers zum 65. Geburtstag* (Bochum, 2016), 285–298.

Fees, I., Hedwig, A., and Roberg, F., eds., *Papsturkunden des frühen und hohen Mittelalters. Äußere Merkmale – Konservierung – Restaurierung* (Leipzig, 2011).

Fees, I., and Roberg, F., *Papsturkunden der zweiten Hälfte des 11. Jahrhunderts (1057–1098)* (Digitale Urkundenbilder aus dem Marburger Lichtbildarchiv älterer Originalurkunden; Leipzig, 2007).

Fichtenau, H., *Arenga. Spätantike und Mittelalter im Spiegel von Urkundenformeln* (Mitteilungen des Instituts für Österreichische Geschichtsforschung, Ergänzungsband, 18; Graz, 1957).

'La situation actuelle des études de diplomatique en Autriche', *Bibliothèque de l'École des chartes*, 119 (1961), 5–20.

Fink, K. A., 'L'Origine dei Brevi Apostolici', *Annali della Scuola Speciale per Archivisti e Bibliotcari dell' Università di Roma*, 11 (1971), 75–81.

Das Vatikanische Archiv: Einführung in die Bestände und ihre Erforschung (2nd edition, Rome, 1951).

Foerster, H., ed., *Liber Diurnus Romanorum Pontificum* (Bern, 1958).

Forrest, I., *Trustworthy Men: How Inequality and Faith Made the Medieval Church* (Princeton, NJ, 2018).

Fossier, A., *Le Bureau des âmes. Écritures et pratiques administratives de la Pénitencerie apostolique (XIIIe–XIVe siècle)* (Bibliothèque des Écoles françaises d'Athènes et de Rome, 378; Rome, 2018).

Frech, K. A., *J. F. Böhmer, Regesta Imperii, III. Salisches Haus 1024–1058. 1. Lieferung: 1024–1046* (Cologne, 2006).

J. F. Böhmer, Regesta Imperii III. Salisches Haus 1024–1125. 5. Abt.: Paptregesten 1024–1058. 2 Lieferung: 1046–1058 (Cologne, 2011).

Frenz, T., www.phil.uni-passau.de/histhw/forschung/lexikon-der-papstdiploma tik/ (consulted 9 May 2022).

'Die "Computi" in der Serie der Brevia Lateranensia im Vatikanischem Archiv', *Quellen und Forschungen aus Italienischen Archiven und Bibliotheken*, 55/56 (1976), 251–275.

Die Kanzlei der Päpste der Hochrenaissance (1471–1521) (Tübingen, 1986).

Papsturkunden des Mittelalters und der Neuzeit (Stuttgart, 1986).

Frenz, T., and Pagano, S., *I Documenti Pontifici nel Medioevo e nell'Età Moderna* (Vatican City, 1998) (a revised edition of Frenz, *Die Kanzlei*).

Friedberg, A. [= Aemilius = Emil] *Corpus Iuris Canonici*, 2 vols. (Leipzig, 1922 edn.).

Fuhrmann, H., *Einfluß und Verbreitung der pseudoisidorischen Fälschungen*, 3 vols. (*MGH* Schriften, XXIV, 1–3; Stuttgart, 1972–1974).

Galland, B., 'Les publications des registres pontificaux par l'École Française de Rome', *Revue d'historie de l'Église de la France*, 217 (2000), 645–656.

Gasnault, P., 'L'élaboration des lettres secrètes des papes d'Avignon: Chambre et Chancellerie', in *Aux origines de l'état moderne. La fonctionnement administratif de la papauté d'Avignon* (Collection de l'École Française de Rome, 138; Rome, 1990), 209–222.

Gioanni, S., *Gouverner le monde par l'écrit. L'autorité pontificale en Dalmatie de l'Antiquité tardive à la réforme 'grégorienne'* (Bibliothèque des Écoles Françaises d'Athènes et de Rome, 386; Rome, 2020).

Girgensohn, D., 'Kehrs Regesta Pontificum Romanorum: Entstehung – wissenschaftlicher Ertrag – organisatorische Schwächen', in K. Herbers and J. Johrendt, eds., *Das Papsttum und das vielgestaltige Italien. Hundert Jahre*

Italia Pontificia (Abhandlungen der Akademie der Wissenschaften zu Götttingen, n.s., 5; Berlin, 2009), 215–257.

Giry, A., *Manuel de diplomatique* (1st edition, Paris, 1894).

Giusti, M., *Inventario dei Registri Vaticani* (Collectanea Archivi Vaticani, 8; Vatican City, 1981).

Studi sui Registri di Bolle Papali (Collectanea Archivi Vaticani, 1; Vatican City, 1979).

Goeller, E., *Die Päpstliche Pönitentiarie von ihrem Ursprung bis zu ihrer Umgestaltung unter Pius V* (Bibliothek des Königlich Preussischen Historischen Instituts in Rom, 3, 4, 7, 8 [4 vols. in 2]; Rome, 1907–1911).

Gorochov, N., 'Le recours aux intercesseurs. L'exemple des universitaires parisiens en quête de bénéfices ecclésiastiques (vers 1340–vers 1420)', in H. Millet, ed., *Suppliques et requêtes. Le gouvernement par la grâce en Occident (XIIᵉ–XVᵉ siècle)* (Collection de l'École Française de Rome, 310; Rome, 2003), 151–164.

Gregory I, pope, *Epistolae: MGH Epistolae (in Quart) (Epp.)*, I. Libri I–VII, ed. P. Ewald and L. Hartmann (Berlin, 1891); II Libri VIII–XIV, ed. L. Hartmann (Berlin, 1899).

Guillemain, B., *Les recettes et les dépenses de la Chambre Apostolique pour la quatrième année du pontificat de Clement V (1308–1309) (Introitus et Exitus 75)* (Rome, 1978).

Guyotjeannin, O., ed., *L'art médiéval du registre. Chancelleries royales et princières* (Études et rencontres de l'École des Chartes, 51; Paris, 2018).

Guyotjeannin, O., with Pycke, J., and Tock, B.-M., *La Diplomatique médiévale* (Turnhout, 1993).

Hack, A. T., *Codex Carolinus. Päpstliche Epistolographie im 8. Jahrhundert*, 2 vols. (Päpste und Papsttum, 35; Stuttgart, 2006–2007).

Hageneder, O., 'Päpstliche Reskripttechnik: Kanonistische Lehre und kuriale Praxis', in M. Bertram (ed.), *Stagnation oder Fortbildung? Aspekte des allgemeinen Kirchenrechts im 14. und 15. Jahrhundert* (Bibliothek des deutschen historischen Instituts zu Rome, 108; Tübingen, 2005), 180-196.

'Die päpstlichen Register des 13. und 14. Jahrhunderts', *Annali della Scuola Speciale per Archivisti e Bibliotecari dell' Università de Roma*, 12 (1972), 45–76.

'Die Rechtskraft spätmittelalterlicher Papst-und Herrscherurkunden "*ex certa scientia*", "*non obstantibus*" und "*propter importunitatem petentium*"', in P. Herde and H. Jakobs, eds., *Papsturkunde und europäisches Urkundenwesen: Studien zu ihrer formalen und rechtlichen Kohärenz vom 11. bis 15. Jahrhunderts* (Archiv für Diplomatik, Schriftgeschichte Siegel- und Wappenkunde, 7; Cologne, 1999), 401–429.

Halkin, L. E., *Les Archives de Nonciatures* (Bibliothèque de l'Institut Historique Belge de Rome, 14; Brussels, 1968).

Hallman, B. M., *Italian Cardinals, Reform, and the Church as Property* (Berkeley, CA, 1985).

Haren, M. J., ed., *Calendar of Entries in the Papal Registers Relating to Great Britain and Ireland: Papal Letters*, vol. XV: *Innocent VIII: Lateran Registers 1484–1492* (Dublin, 1978).

Calendar of Papal Letters Relating to Great Britain and Ireland, xv, Innocent VIII. Lateran Registers 1484–1492 (Dublin, 1978).

Hartmann, F., *Hadrian I. (772–795)* (Päpste und Papsttum, 34; Stuttgart, 2006).

Hartmann, F., and Orth-Müller, T. B., eds., *Codex epistolaris Carolinus. Frühmittelalterliche Papstbriefe an die Karolingerherrscher* (Darmstadt, 2017).

Hartmann, W., ed., *Das Sendhandbuch des Regino von Prüm* (Darmstadt, 2004)

Hauck, A., *Kirchengeschichte Deutschlands, ii* (9th edition, Berlin, 1958).

Hayez, A.-M., 'Les demandes de bénéfices présentées à Urbain V: une approche géographico-politique', in H. Millet, ed., *Suppliques et requêtes. Le gouvernement par la grâce en Occident (XIIe–XVe siècle)* (Collection de l'École Française de Rome, 310; Rome, 2003), 121–150.

Herbers, K., *Geschichte des Papsttums im Mittelalter* (Darmstadt, 2012).

Herbers, K., ed., J. F. Böhmer, *Regesta Imperii, I: Die Regesten des Kaiserreiches uner den Karolingern 751–918 (926/962), iv, Papstregesten 800–911, t. 2: 844–872, Lieferung 1: 844–858* (Cologne, 1999).

J. F. Böhmer, *Regesta Imperii, I: Die Regesten des Kaiserreiches uner den Karolingern 751–918 (926/962), iv, Papstregesten 800–911, t. 2: 844–872, Lief. 2: 858–867* (Vienna, 2012).

Leo IV. und das Papsttum in der Mitte des 9. Jahrhunderst. Möglichkeiten und Grenzen päpstlicher Herrschaft in der späten Karolingerzeit (Päpste und Papsttum, 27; Stuttgart, 1996).

Herbers, K., et al., eds., *Regesta Pontificum Romanorum ... edidit ... P. Jaffé*, 3rd edn., 3 vols. to date (Göttingen, 2016–), i, ed. N. Herbers, M. Schütz, et al. (2016); ii, ed. N. Herbers, W. Könighaus, T. Schlauwitz, et al. (2017); iii, ed. N. Herbers, J. Werner, and W. Könighaus (2017).

Herbers, K., and Johrendt, J., eds., *Das Papsttum und das vielgestaltige Italien. Hundert Jahre Italia Pontificia* (Abhandlungen der Akademie der Wissenschaften zu Götttingen, n.s., 5; Berlin, 2009).

Herbers, K., López Alsina, F., and Engel, F., eds., *Das begrenzte Papsttum. Spielräume päpstlichen Handelns. Legaten – delegierte Richter – Grenzen* (Abhandlungen der Akademie der Wissenschaften zu Göttingen, NS, 25; Berlin, 2013).

Herbers, K., and Simperl, M., eds., *Das Buch der Päpste – Liber pontificalis. Ein Schlüsseldokument europäischer Geschichte* (Römische Quartalschrift, Supplementband, 67; Freiburg im Breisgau, 2020).

Herbers, K., and Trenkle, V., eds., *Papstgeschichte im digitalen Zeitalter. Neue Zugangsweisen zu einer Kulturgeschichte Europas* (Cologne, 2018).

Herbers, K., and Unger, V., eds., *Papstbriefe des 9. Jahrhunderts* (Darmstadt, 2019).

Herde, P., *Audientia litterarum contradictarum: Untersuchungen über die päpstlichen Justizbriefe und die päpstliche Delegationsgerichtsbarkeit vom 13. bis zum Beginn des 16. Jahrhunderts*, 2 vols. (Bibliothek des Deutschen Historischen Instituts in Rom, 31, 32; Tübingen, 1970).

'Zur Audientia litterarum contradictarum und zur "Reskripttechnik"', *Archivalische Zeitschrift*, 69 (1973), 54–90.

Beiträge zum päpstlichen Kanzlei-und Urkndenwesen im 13. Jahrhundert (2nd edition, Kallmünz, 1967).

'Ernst Pitz, Supplikensignatur und Briefexpedition an der Römischen Kurie im Pontifikat Papst Calixts III. (Bibliothek des Deutschen Historischen Instituts in Rom 42)', *Zeitschrift der Savigny-Stiftung für Rechtsgeschichte: Kanonistische Abteilung*, 60.1 (1974), 414–424.

'Der Geschäftsgang in der päpstlichen Kanzlei des dreizehnten Jahrhunderts', in *idem, Beiträge*, 149–242 (+ 'Exkurs').

'Litterae clausae', in *idem, Beiträge*, 72–78.

'Papal Formularies for Letters of Justice (13th–16th Centuries): Their Development and Significance for Medieval Canon Law', in M. Bertram (ed.), *Stagnation oder Fortbildung? Aspecte des allgemeinen Kirchenrechts im 14. und 15. Jahrhundert* (Tübingen, 2005), 221–247.

'Zur päpstlichen Delegationsgerichtsbarkeit im Mittelalter und in der frühen Neuzeit', *Zeitschrift der Savigny Stiftung für Rechtsgeschichte*, 119, *Kanonistische Abteilung*, 88 (2002), 20–43.

'Die Urkundenarten im dreizehnten Jahrhundert', in *idem, Beiträge*, 57–71.

Herde, P., and Jakobs, H., eds., *Papsturkunde und europäisches Urkundenwesen: Studien zu ihrer formalen und rechtlichen Kohärenz vom 11. bis 15. Jahrhunderts* (Archiv für Diplomatik, Schriftgeschichte Siegel- und Wappenkunde, 7; Cologne, 1999).

Hill, F., *Excommunication in Thirteenth-Century England: Community, Politics and Publicity* (Oxford, 2022).

Hirschmann, S., *Die päpstliche Kanzlei und ihre Urkundenproduktion (1141–1159)* (Frankfurt am Main, 2001).

Hitzbleck, K., *Exekutoren: Die ausserordentliche Kollatur von Benefizien im Pontifikat Johannes' XXII.* (Tübingen, 2009).

Holmwood, J. and Stewart, A., *Explanation and Social Theory* (Basingstoke, 1991).

Holtzmann, W., *Papsturkunden in England*, i, *Bibliotheken und Archive in London* (Abhandlungen der Akademie der Wissenschaften in Göttingen, Philologisch-historische Klasse, n.s., xxv, 1; Berlin, 1930).

Hoover, J. A., *The Donatist Church in an Apocalyptic Age* (Oxford, 2018).

Hotz, B., *Litterae apostolicae. Untersuchungen zu päpstlichen Briefen und einfachen Privilegien im 11. und 12. Jahrhundert* (Münchener Beiträge zur Geschichtswissenschaft, 9; Munich, 2018).

Iberia Pontificia, VI: see Knie, C.

Ingesman, P., *Provisioner og Processer. Den romerske Rota og dens behandling auf danske sager in middelalteren* (Aarhus, 2003).

Jacobson Schutte, *see* Schutte.

Jamme, A., 'De Rome à Florence, la curie et ses banquiers aux XIIe et XIIIe siècles', in W. Maleczek, ed., *Die römische Kurie und das Geld. Von der Mitte des 12. Jahrhunderts bis zum frühen 14. Jahrhundert* (Vorträge und Forschungen, 85; Ostfildern, 2018), 167–205.

Jasper, D., and Fuhrmann, H., *Papal Letters in the Early Middle Ages* (Washington, D.C., 2001).

Jenks, S., ed., *Documents on the Papal Plenary Indulgences 1300–1517 Preached in the Regnum Teutonicum* (Later Medieval Europe, 16; Leiden, 2018).

Johrendt, J., 'Der Empfängereinfluß auf die Gestaltung der Arenga und Sanctio in den päpstlichen Privilegien (896–1046)', *Archiv für Diplomatik* 50 (2004), 1–11.

'Papsturkunden und Papstbriefe bis zu Bonifaz VIII.', *Archiv für Diplomatik*, 66 (2020), 331–356.

Papsttum und Landeskirchen im Spiegel der päpstlichen Urkunden (896–1046) (*MGH* Studien und Texte, 33; Hanover, 2004).

Johrendt, J., and Müller, H., eds., *Rom und die Regionen. Studien zur Homogenisierung der lateinischen Kirche im Hochmittelalter* (Abhandlungen der Akademie der Wissenschaften zu Göttingen, n.s., 19; Berlin, 2012).

Römisches Zentrum und kirchliche Peripherie: Das universale Papsttum als Bezugspunkt der Kirchen von den Reformpäpsten bis zu Innozenz III (Neue Abhandlungen der Akademie der Wissenschaften zu Göttingen, Philologisch-Historische Klasse, NS 2, Studien zu Papstgeschichte und Papsturkunden; Berlin, 2008).

Jones, A. H. M., *The Later Roman Empire, 284–602. A Social, Economic and Administrative Survey*, 3 vols. (with a maps volume) (Oxford, 1964).

Katterbach, B., *Referendarii utriusque Signaturae a Martino V ad Clementem IX et Praelati Signaturae Supplicationum a Martino V ad Leonem XIII, Sussidi per la Consultazione dell'Archivio Vaticano* ii (Studi e Testi, 55; Vatican City, 1931).

Specimina Supplicationum ex Registris Vaticanis (Subsidiorum Tabularii Vaticani, ii; Rome, 1927).

Kéry, L., *Canonical Collections of the Early Middle Ages (ca. 400–1140). A Bibliographical Guide to the Manuscripts and Literature* (Washington, D.C., 1999).

'Klosterfreiheit und päpstliche Organisationsgewalt. Exemtion als Herrschaftsinstrument des Papsttums?', in J. Johrendt and H. Müller, eds., *Rom und die Regionen. Studien zur Homogenisierung der lateinischen Kirche im Hochmittelalter* (Abhandlungen der Akademie der Wissenschaften zu Göttingen, n.s., 19; Berlin, 2012), 83–144.

Knie, C., Panzram, S., Livorsi, L., Selvaggi, R., and Könighaus, W., eds., *Iberia Pontificia*, VII, *Hispania Romana et Visigotha* (Göttingen, 2022).

Knowles, D., *The Monastic Order in England. A History of its Development from the Times of St Dunstan to the Fourth Lateran Council 943–1216* (Cambridge, 1940).

Kölzer, T., 'Bonifatius und Fulda. Rechtliche, diplomatische und kulturelle Aspekte', *Archiv für mittelrheinische Kirchengeschichte* 57 (2005), 25–53.

Kortüm, H.-H., *Zur päpstlichen Urkundensprache im frühen Mittelalter. Die päpstlichen Privilegien 896–1046* (Beiträge zur Geschichte und Quellenkunde des Mittelalters, 17; Sigmaringen, 1995).

Koziol, G., *The Politics of Memory and Identity in Carolingian Royal Diplomas: The West Frankish Kingdom (840–987)* (Turnhout, 2012).

Krafft, O., *Bene Valete. Entwicklung und Typologie des Monogramms in Urkunden der Päpste und anderer Austeller seit 1049* (Leipzig, 2010).

'Der monogrammatische Schlußgruß (*Bene Valete*). Über methodische Probleme, historisch-diplomatische Erkenntnis zu gewinnen', in I. Fees, A. Hedwig, and F. Roberg, eds., *Papsturkunden des frühen und hohen*

Mittelalters. Äußere Merkmale – Konservierung – Restaurierung (Leipzig, 2011), 209–247.

Lange, C. R., Müller, W. P., and Neumann, C. K., eds., *Islamische und westliche Jurisprudenz des Mittelalters im Vergleich* (Tübingen, 2018).

Lawrence, C. H., 'The English Church and its Clergy in the Thirteenth Century', in P. Linehan, J. L. Nelson, and M. Costambeys, eds., *The Medieval World* (Abingdon, 2018), 746–769. Accessed at Routledge Handbooks Online, 7 February 2023.

Le Bras, G., 'Boniface VIII, symphoniste et modérateur', in *Mélanges d'histoire du Moyen Âge, dédiés à la mémoire de Louis Halphen* (Paris, 1951), 383–394.

Lea, H. C., *A Formulary of the Papal Penitentiary in the Thirteenth Century* (Philadelphia, PA, 1892).

Lemaître, J.-L., 'Exemption', in P. Levillain, ed., *The Papacy. An Encyclopaedia*, 3 vols. (London, 2002), i, 551–554.

Lemarignier, J.-F., *Étude sur les privilèges d'exemption et de juridiction ecclésiastique des abbayes Normandes : depuis les origines jusqu'en 1140* (Paris, 1937).

Luhmann, N., *Einführung in die Systemtheorie* (Heidelberg, 2002).

Lunt, W. E., *Papal Revenues in the Middle Ages*, 2 vols (New York, 1934, 1965).

Maassen, F., *Geschichte der Quellen und der Literatur des canonischen Rechts im Abendlande bis zum Ausgange des Mittalalters, i* (Graz, 1870).

Mabille, M., Garany, M.-C., and Metman, J., under the general editorship of C. Samaran and R. Marichal, *Catalogue des manuscrits en écriture latine. Portant des indications de date, de lieu ou de copiste, tome VI [2] Planches. Bourgogne, Centre, Sud-Est et Sud-Ouest de la France* (Paris, 1968).

McKitterick, R., *Rome and the Invention of the Papacy: The Liber pontificalis* (Cambridge, 2020).

Maier, J.-L., *Le Dossier du Donatisme*, 2 vols. (Berlin, 1987, 1989).

Maitland, F. W., *Domesday Book and Beyond. Three Essays in the Early History of England* (Cambridge, 1897; reprint London, 1960).

'Canon Law in England III. William of Drogheda and the Universal Ordinary', *English Historical Review*, 12 (1897), 625–652 (reprinted in *idem, Roman Canon Law in the Church of England*, 100–131).

Roman Canon Law in the Church of England. Six Essays (London, 1928).

Maleczek, W., 'L'Edition autrichienne des registres d'Innocent III', *Mélanges de l'École Française de Rome* 112 (2000), 259–272.

'*Litterae clausae* der Päpste vom 12. bis zum frühen 14. Jahrhundert', in T. Broser, A. Fischer and M. Thumser, eds., *Kuriale Briefkultur im späteren Mittelalter* (Forschungen zur Kaiser-und Papstgeschichte des Mittelalters. Beihefte zu J. F. Böhmer, Regesta Imperii, 37; Cologne, 2015), 55–128 (followed by facsimile reproductions).

'Les registres pontificaux du XIIIᵉ siècle', in O. Guyotjeannin, ed., *L'art médiéval du registre. Chancelleries royales et princières* (Études et rencontres de l'École des Chartes, 51; Paris, 2018), 37–54.

Maleczek, W., ed., *Die römische Kurie und das Geld. Von der Mitte des 12. Jahrhunderts bis zum frühen 14 Jahrhundert* (Vorträge und Forschungen, 85; Ostfildern, 2018).

Urkunden und ihre Erforschung. Zum Gedenken an Heinrich Appelt (Veröffentlichungen des Instituts für Österreichische Geschichtsforschung, 62; Vienna, 2014).

Martine, T., and Winandy, J., eds., *La Réforme grégorienne, une 'révolution totale'?* (Paris, 2021).

Märtl, C., 'Modus expediendi litteras apostolicas: Pragmatische Schriftlichkeit und *stilus curiae* am Ende des 15. Jahrhunderts', in J. Nowak and G. Strack, eds., *Stilus – Modus – Usus. Regeln der Konflikt-und Verhandlungsführung am Papsthof des Mittelalters* (Turnhout, 2019), 335–351.

Matheus, M., 'Das Deutsche Historische Institut (DHI) in Rom und Paul Fridolin Kehrs Papsturkundenwerk', in K. Herbers and J. Johrendt, eds., *Das Papsttum und das vielgestaltige Italien. Hundert Jahre Italia Pontificia* (Abhandlungen der Akademie der Wissenschaften zu Götttingen, n.s., 5; Berlin, 2009), 3–12.

May, G., *Ego N.N. Catholicae Ecclesiae Episcopus. Entstehung, Entwicklung und Bedeutung einer Unterschriftsformel im Hinblick auf den Universalepiskopat des Papstes* (Kanonistische Studien und Texte, 43; Berlin, 1995).

Mayer, H. E., 'Ibelin versus Ibelin: The Struggle for the Regency of Jerusalem 1253–1258', *Proceedings of the American Philosophical Society* 122 (1978), 25–57.

Mayer, T. F., *The Roman Inquisition. A Papal Bureaucracy and its Laws in the Age of Galileo* (Philadelphia, PA, 2013).

Meduna, B., *Studien zum Formular der päpstlichen Justizbriefen von Alexander III. bis Innozenz III. (1159–1216): Die non obstantibus-Formel* (Vienna, 1989).

Meens, R., 'Remedies for Sins', in T. F. X. Noble and J. M. H. Smith, eds., *The Cambridge History of Christianity*, iii. *Early Medieval Christianities, c. 600–c. 1100* (Cambridge, 2008), 399–415.

Meserve, M. *Papal Bull. Print, Politics and Propaganda in Renaissance Rome* (Baltimore, MD, 2021).

Meyer, A., *Arme Kleriker auf Pfründensuche. Eine Studie über das in forma pauperum-Register Gregors XII. von 1407 und über päpstliche Anwartschaften im Spätmittelalter* (Forschungen zur kirchlichen Rechtsgeschichte und zum Kirchenrecht; Cologne, 1990).

'The Curia: The Apostolic Chancery', in K. Sisson and A. A. Larson, eds., *A Companion to the Medieval Papacy. Growth of an Ideology and Institution* (Brill Companions to the Christian Tradition, 70; Leiden, 2016), 239–258.

'Der deutsche Pfründenmarkt im Spätmittelalter', *Quellen und Forschungen aus italienischen Bibliotheken und Archiven*, 71 (1991), 266–279.

'Die päpstliche Kanzlei im Mittelalter – ein Versuch', *Archiv für Diplomatik, Schriftgeschichte, Siegel-und Wappenkunde* 61 (2015), 291–342.

'Regieren mit Urkunden im Spätmittelalter. Päpstliche Kanzlei und weltliche Kanzleien im Vergleich', in W. Maleczek (ed.), *Urkunden und ihre Erforschung. Zum Gedenken an Heinrich Appelt* (Veröffentlichungen des Instituts für Österreichische Geschichtsforschung, 62; Vienna, 2014), 71–91.

'Das spätmittelalterliche Kirchenrecht', in C. R. Lange, W. P. Müller and C. K. Neumann, eds., *Islamische und westliche Jurisprudenz des Mittelalters im Vergleich* (Tübingen, 2018), 169–181.

'Spätmittelalterliche päpstliche Kanzleiregeln', in G. Drossbach, ed., *Von der Ordnung zur Norm: Statuten in Mittelalter und Früher Neuzeit* (Paderborn, 2010), 95–108.

'Das Wiener Konkordat von 1448 – eine erfolgreiche Reform des Spätmittelalters', *Quellen und Forschungen aus italienischen Bibliotheken und Archiven*, 66 (1986), 108–152.

Zürich und Rom. Ordentliche Kollatur und päpstliche Provisionen am Frau-und Grossmünster 1316–1523 (Bibliothek des deutschen historischen Instituts in Rom, 64; Tübingen, 1986).

Meyer, A., Rendtel, C., and Wittmer-Butsch, M., eds., *Päpste, Pilger, Pönitentiarie. Festschrift für Ludwig Schmugge zum 65. Geburtstag* (Tübingen, 2004).

MGH Concilia (Conc.), 6. 1, *Die Konzilien Deutschlands und Reichsitaliens 916–1001, Teil 1 916-961*, ed. E.-D. Hehl et al. (Hanover, 1987).

MGH Epistolae (in Quart) (Epp.) Gregorii papae Registrum: see Gregory I, pope.

Millar, F., *The Emperor in the Roman World (31 BC–AD 337)* (London, 1977).

Millet, H., ed., *Suppliques et requêtes. Le gouvernement par la grâce en Occident (XIIe–XVe siècle)* (Collection de l'École Française de Rome, 310; Rome, 2003).

Minnich, N. H., 'Lateran V and the Reform of the Curia', *Bulletin of Medieval Canon Law*, 37 (2020), 135–196.

Mollat, G., and Samaran, C., *La fiscalité pontificale en France au XIV siècle (période d'Avignon et Grand Schisme d'Occident)* (Bibliothèque des Écoles Françaises d'Athènes et de Rome, 96; Paris, 1905).

Montaubin, P., 'L'administration pontificale de la grâce au XIIIe siècle: l'exemple de la politique béneficiale', in H. Millet, ed., *Suppliques et requêtes. Le gouvernement par la grâce en Occident (XIIe–XVe siècle)* (Collection de l'École Française de Rome, 310; Rome, 2003), 321–342.

Moreau, D., 'Non impar conciliorum extat auctoritas. L'origine de l'introduction des lettres pontificales dans le droit canonique', in J. Desmulliez, C. Hoët-van Cauwenberghe and J.-C. Jolivet, eds., *Étude des correspondances dans le monde Romain, de l'antiquité classique à l'antiquité tardive: permanences at mutations* (Lille, 2010), 487–506.

Morgan, S., 'The Religious Dimensions of English Cistercian Privileges' (PhD thesis, University College London, 2008).

Müller, H., 'Entscheidung auf Nachfrage: Die delegierten Richter als Verbindungsglieder zwischen Kurie und Region sowie als Gradmesser päpstlicher Autorität', in J. Johrendt and H. Müller, eds., *Römisches Zentrum und kirchliche Peripherie: Das universale Papsttum als Bezugspunkt der Kirchen von den Reformpäpsten bis zu Innozenz III* (Neue Abhandlungen der Akademie der Wissenschaften zu Göttingen, Philologisch-Historische Klasse, NS 2, Studien zu Papstgeschichte und Papsturkunden; Berlin, 2008), 109–131.

'Generalisierung, dichte Beschreibung, kontrastierende Einzelstudien? Stand und Perspektiven der Erforschung delegierter Gerichtsbarkeit des Papstes im Hochmittelalter', in J. Johrendt and H. Müller, eds., *Rom und die Regionen. Studien zur Homogenisierung der lateinischen Kirche im*

Hochmittelalter (Abhandlungen der Akademie der Wissenschaften zu Göttingen, n.s., 19; Berlin, 2012), 145–156.

'Päpste und Prozeßkosten im späten Mittelalter', in M. Bertram (ed.), *Stagnation oder Fortbildung? Aspekte des allgemeinen Kirchenrechts im 14. und 15. Jahrhundert* (Bibliothek des deutschen historischen Instituts zu Rome, 108; Tübingen, 2005), 249–270.

Päpstliche Delegationsgerichtsbarkeit in der Normandie (12. und frühes 13. Jahrhundert), 2 vols. (Studien und Dokumente zur Gallia Pontificia; 4, 1 & 2; Bonn, 1997).

Müller, W., 'Die Gebühren der päpstlichen Pönitentiarie (1338–1569)', *Quellen und Forschungen aus italienischen Bibliotheken und Archiven*, 78 (1998), 189–261.

'The Price of Papal Pardon – New Fifteenth-Century Evidence', in A. Meyer, C. Rendtel and M. Wittmer-Butsch, eds., *Päpste, Pilger, Pönitentiarie. Festschrift für Ludwig Schmugge zum 65. Geburtstag* (Tübingen, 2004), 457–481.

Nemec, J., 'L'Archivio della Congregazione per le Cause dei Santi (ex-S.Congregazione dei Riti)', in *Miscellanea in Occasione del IV Centenario della Congregazione per le Cause dei Santi (1588–1988)* (Vatican City, 1988), 339–352.

Nold, P., *John XXII and his Franciscan Cardinal: Bertrand de la Tour and the Apostolic Poverty Controversy* (Oxford, 2003).

Marriage Advice for a Pope: John XXII and the Power to Dissolve (Leiden, 2009).

Nowak, J., and Strack, G., eds., *Stilus – Modus – Usus. Regeln der Konflikt-und Verhandlungsführung am Papsthof des Mittelalters* (Turnhout, 2019).

Nykiel, K., and Taraborrelli, U., eds., *L'Archivio della Penitenzieria Apostolica. Stato Attuale e Prospettive Future* (Vatican City, 2017).

Octavianus Vestrius see Vestrius.

Omont, H., 'Bulles pontificales sur papyrus (IXe–XIe siècle)', *Bibliotèque de l'École des chartes*, 65 (1904), 575–582.

Pagano, S., 'Una Discutibile "Guida" degli Archivi Vaticani', *Archivum Historiae Pontificiae*, 37 (1999), 191–201.

'Documenti Pontifici', in B. Ardura, ed., *Lessico di Storia della Chiesa* (Rome, 2020), 261–265.

'Registri pontifici', in B. Ardura, ed., *Lessico di Storia della Chiesa* (Rome, 2020), 515–517.

Paravicini Bagliani, A., *La Cour des papes au XIII*^e *siècle* (Paris, 1995).

Il Papato nel Secolo XIII. Cent'Anni di Bibliografia (1875–2009) (Florence, 2010).

Parayre, R., *La S. Congrégation du Concile. Son Histoire – sa procédure – son autorité. Thèse présentée à la Faculté de Théologie de Lyon* (Paris, 1897).

Partner, P., *The Pope's Men. The Papal Civil Service in the Renaissance* (Oxford, 1990).

Pásztor, E., 'La Curia Romana', in *Le istituzioni ecclesiastiche della 'societas christiana' dei secoli XI–XII. Papato, cardinalato ed episcopato* (Milan, 1974), 490–504.

Pásztor, L., *Guida delle fonti per la storia dell'America Latina negli archivi della Santa Sede e negli archivi ecclesiastici d'Italia* (Collectanea Archivi Vaticani, 2; Vatican City, 1970).

Pattenden, M., *Electing the Pope in Early Modern Italy, 1450–1700* (Oxford, 2017).

Paulus, N., *Geschichte des Ablasses im Mittelalter, vom Ursprunge bis zur Mitte des 14. Jahrhunderts*, 2 vols. (Paderborn, 1922–1923).

Peter Lombard, *Magistri Petri Lombardi … Sententiae in IV Libris Distinctae* [ed. Ignatius Brady], II, Liber IV et IV (Spicilegium Bonavernturianum, V; Grottaferrata, 1981).

Pfaff, V., 'Die päpstlichen Klösterexemtionen in Italien bis zum Ende des zwölften Jahrhunderts. Versuch einer Bestandsaufnahme', *Zeitschrift der Savigny Stiftung für Rechtsgeschichte, kanonistische Abteilung*, 72 (1986), 76–114.

Pfeiffer, U., *Untersuchungen zu den Anfängen der päpstlichen Delegationsgerichtsbarkeit in 13 Jahrhundert. Edition und diplomatisch-kanonistische Auswertung zweier Vorläufersammlungen der Vulgataredaktion des Formularium Audientie Litterarum Contradictarum* (Vatican City, 2011).

Pferschy-Maleczek, B., 'Rechtsbildung durch Reskripte unter Gregor dem Großen? Zu einem neuen Buch', *Mitteilungen des Instituts für österreichische Geschichtsforschung*, 99 (1991), 505–512.

Pfurtscheller, F., *Die Privilegierung des Zisterzienserordens im Rahmen der allgemeinen Schutz- und Exemtionsgeschichte vom Anfang bis zur Bulle 'Parvus Fons' (1265). Ein Überblick unter besonderer Berücksichtigung von Schreibers Kurie und Kloster im 12. Jahrhundert* (Bern, 1972).

Pietri, C., *Roma Christiana. Recherches sur l'Église de Rome, son organisation, son politique, son idéologie de Miltiade à Sixte III, 311–440*, 2 vols. (Bibliothèque des Écoles Françaises d'Athènes et de Rome, 224; Rome, 1976).

Pitz, E., *Papstreskripte im frühen Mittelalter. Diplomatische und rechtsgeschichtliche Studien zum Brief-Corpus Gregors des Großen* (Beiträge zur Geschichte und Quellenkunde des Mittelalters, 14; Sigmaringen, 1990).

Plettenbergius, H., *Notitia Congregationum et Tribunalium Curiae Romanae* (Hildesheim, 1693) (available online).

Polancec, I., 'The Domestic Papal Court between Avignon and Rome in the Pontificate of Urban V (1362–1370)' (PhD thesis, University College London, 2008).

Poncet, O., *Les entreprises éditoriales liées aux archives du Saint-Siège. Histoire et bibliographie (1880–2000)* (Collection de l'École Française de Rome, 318; Rome, 2003).

La France et le pouvoir pontifical (1595–1661). L'Ésprit des institutions (Bibliothèque des Écoles françaises d'Athènes et de Rome, 347; Rome, 2011).

Pontificum Romanorum Diplomata Papyracea quae supersunt in tabulariis Hispaniae Italiae Germaniae (Rome, 1928).

Poole, R. L., *Lectures on the History of the Papal Chancery down to the Time of Innocent III* (Cambridge, 1915).

Powicke, F. M., *The Thirteenth Century, 1216–1307* (Oxford, 1953).

Prestwich, J., *Edward I* (London, 1988).

Prodi, P., *Il Sovrano Pontefice: un corpo e due anime: la monarchia papale nella prima età moderna* (Bologna, 1982).

Prosperi, A., 'Una Esperienza di Ricerca al S. Uffizio', in idem, *L'Inquisizione Romana. Letture e Ricerche* (Rome, 2003), 221–261.

Puza, R., 'Signatura iustitiae und commissio. Ein Beitrag zum Prozeßgang an der römischen Kurie in der Neuzeit', *Zeitschrift der Savigny Stiftung für Rechtsgeschichte, kanonistische Abteilung*, 95 (1978), 95–115.

Rabikauskas, P., 'Abbreviatori della Cancelleria Pontificia nella prima metà del secolo XIV', *Annali della Scuola Speciale per Archivisti e Bibliotecari dell' Università di Roma*, 12 (1972), 153–165.

Diplomatica pontificia. (Praelectionum lineamenta), Editio sexta emendata et aucta (ad usum auditorum) (Rome, 1998).

Die römische Kuriale in der päpstlichen Kanzlei (Miscellanea Historiae Pontificiae, 20, Collectionis no. 59; Rome, 1958).

Raimondi, M., 'Damasus and the Papal *Scrinium*', in R. L. Testa and G. Marconi, eds., *The Collectio Avellana and its Revivals* (Cambridge, 2019), 280–301.

Rathsack, M., *Die Fuldaer Fälschungen. Eine rechtshistorische analyse der päpstlichen privilegien des Klosters Fulda von 751 bis ca. 1158, i* (Stuttgart, 1989).

Regino of Prüm, *Libellus de Ecclesiasticis Disciplinis et Religione Christiana*, in *PL* 132.

Rennie, K. R., *Freedom and Protection. Monastic Exemption in France, c. 590–c. 1100* (Manchester, 2018).

Reutter, U., *Damasus, Bischof von Rom (366–384)* (Studien und Texte zu Antike und Christentum, 55; Tübingen, 2009).

Reynolds, R. E., *Clerics in the Early Middle Ages. Hierarchy and Image* (Aldershot, 1999).

Richard, P., 'Origines et développement de la Secrétairerie d'État Apostolique (1417–1823) (Suite) (1)', *Revue d'histoire ecclésiastique*, 11 (1910), 505–529.

Rollo-Koster, J., *Avignon and its Papacy, 1309–1417. Popes, Institutions and Society* (Lanham, MD, 2015).

Romita, F., 'Le Origini della S. C. del Concilio', in idem, *La Sacra Congregazione del Concilio*, 13–50.

Romita, F., ed., *La Sacra Congregazione del Concilio. Quarto Centenario della Fondazione (1564–1964)* (Vatican City, 1964).

'Lo "Studio" della Sacra Congregazione del Concilio e gli "Studi" della Curia Romana', in idem, *La Sacra Congregazione del Concilio*, 633–677.

Ronzani, R., 'Notes on the Diplomatic Aspects in the Documentation of the *Scrinium Romanae Ecclesiae*', in R. L. Testa and G. Marconi, eds., *The Collectio Avellana and its Revivals* (Cambridge, 2019), 260–279.

Rosa, M., *La Curia Romana nell'età moderna. Istituzioni, cultura, carriere* (Rome, 2013).

Rosenwein, B., *Negotiating Space: Power, Restraint and Privileges of Immunity in Early Medieval Europe* (Ithaca, NY, 1999).

Rustow, M., 'Fatimid State Documents', *Jewish History*, 32 (2019), 221–277.

Salonen, K., 'Cardinals and the Apostolic Penitentiary', in M. Hollingsworth, M. Pattenden and A. Witte, eds., *A Companion to the Early Modern Cardinal* (Leiden, 2020), 144–153.

Papal Justice in the Late Middle Ages. The Sacra Romana Rota (London, 2016).

The Penitentiary as a Well of Grace in the Later Middle Ages: The Example of the Province of Uppsala, 1448–1527 (Helsinki, 2001).

Salonen, K., and Schmugge, L., *A Sip from the 'Well of Grace'. Medieval Texts from the Papal Penitentiary* (Washington, D.C., 2009).

Sancti Thomae Aquinatis … Opera Omnia, ed. Commissio Leonina, xii (Rome, 1906).

Santifaller, L., *Liber diurnus. Studien und Forschungen*, ed. H. Zimmermann (Päpste und Papsttum, 10; Stuttgart, 1976).

Saraco, A., *La Penitenzieria Apostolica. Storia di un Tribunale di misericordia e di pietà* (Vatican City, 2011).

Saraco, A., ed., *La Penitenzieria Apostolica e il suo Archivio. Atti della Giornata di Studio … 18 novembre 2011* (Vatican City, 2012).

Savill, B., *England and the Papacy in the Early Middle Ages: Papal Privileges in European Perspective, c. 680–1073* (Oxford, in press).

'Papal Privileges in Early Medieval England, c. 680–1073' (D.Phil. thesis, University of Oxford, 2017).

Sayers, J. E., 'The Influence of Papal Documents on English Documents before 1305', in P. Herde and H. Jacobs, eds., *Papsturkunden und europäisches Urkundenwesen* (Archiv für Diplomatik, Beiheft 7; Cologne, 1999), 161–199.

Original Papal Documents in England and Wales from the Accession of Pope Innocent III to the Death of Pope Benedict XI (1198–1304) (Oxford, 1999).

Papal Judges Delegate in the Province of Canterbury, 1198–1254. A Study in Ecclesiastical Jurisdiction and Administration (London, 1971).

Schäfer, K. H., ed., *Die Ausgaben der apostolischen Kammer unter Benedikt XII., Klemens VI. und Innocenz VI. (1335–1362)* (Paderborn, 1914).

Schieffer, R., 'Die päpstlichen Register vor 1198', in K. Herbers and J. Johrendt, eds., *Das Papsttum und das vielgestaltige Italien. Hundert Jahre Italia Pontificia* (Abhandlungen der Akademie der Wissenschaften zu Götttingen, n.s., 5; Berlin, 2009), 261–273.

Schimmelpfennig, B., 'Römische Ablaßfälschungen aus der Mitte des 14. Jahrhunderts', in *Fälschungen im Mittelalter* v (*MGH* Schriften, 33, 5; Hanover, 1988), 637–658.

Schmidt, T., ed., *Libri Rationum Camerae Bonifatii Papae VIII (Archivum Secretum Vaticanum, Collect. 446 necnon Intr. et ex. 5* (Littera Antiqua, 2; Vatican City, 1984).

Schmidt, U., ed., *J. F. Böhmer, Regesta Imperii, Regesta Imperii IV. Lothar III und ältere Staufer 1125–1197. 4 Abt.: Papstregesten 1124–1198, Teil 4, Lieferung 3, 1185–1187, Urban III. und Gregor VIII* (Cologne, 2012).

J. F. Böhmer, Regesta Imperii, Regesta Imperii IV. Lothar III. und ältere Staufer 1125–1197 4. Abt.: Papstregesten 1124–1198, Teil 4, Lieferung 4: 1187–1191: Clemens III (Cologne, 2014).

J. F. Böhmer, Regesta Imperii IV. Lothar III. und ältere Staufer. 4. Abt.: Papstregesten 1124–1198, Teil 4: 1181–1198, Lieferung 5: 1191–1195, Cölestin III (Cologne, 2018).

Schmitz-Kallenberg, L., ed., *Practica Cancellariae Apostolicae saeculi XV. exeuntis* (Münster i. Westfalen, 1904).

Schmitz-Kallenberg, L., in R. Thommen and L. Schmitz-Kallenberg, *Grundriss der Geschichtswissenschaft. Urkundenlehre. II. Papsturkunden* (2nd edition, Berlin, 1913).

Schmugge, L., 'Suppliche e diritto canonico. Il caso della Penitenzieria', in H. Millet, ed., *Suppliques et requêtes. Le gouvernement par la grâce en Occident (XIIe–XVe siècle)* (Collection de l'École Française de Rome, 310; Rome, 2003), 207–231.

Schmugge, L., Hersperger, P., and Wiggenhauser, B., *Die Supplikenregister der päpstlichen Pönitentiarie aus der Zeit Pius' II. (1458–1464)* (Tübingen, 1996).

Scholz, S., *Politik – Selbstverständnis – Selbstdarstellung. Die Päpste in karolingischer und ottonischer Zeit* (Stuttgart, 2006).

Schreiber, G., *Kurie und Kloster im 12. Jahrhundert. Studien zur Privilegierung, Verfassung und besonders zum Eigenkirchenwesen der vorfranziskanishen Orden vornehmlich auf Grund der Papsturkunden von Paschalis II. bis auf Lucius III. (1099–1181)*, 2 vols. (Stuttgart, 1910).

Schutte, A. Jacobson, *By Force and Fear. Taking and Breaking Monastic Vows in Early Modern Europe* (Ithaca, NY, 2011).

Schwarz, B., 'Der Corrector litterarum apostolicarum. Entwicklung des Korrektorenamtes in der päpstlichen Kanzlei von Innozenz III. bis Martin V.', *Quellen und Forschungen aus Italienischen Archiven und Bibliotheken*, 54 (1974), 122–191.

'Die Erforschung der mittelalterlichen römischen Kurie von Ludwig Quidde bis heute', in Michael Matheus, ed., *Friedensnobelpreis und historische Grundlagenforschung* (Bibliothek des Deutschen Historischen Instituts in Rom, 124; Rome, 2012), 415–439.

Die Organisation kurialer Schreiberkollegien von ihrer Entstehung bis zur Mitte des 15. Jahrhunderts (Tübingen, 1972).

Regesten der in Niedersachsen und Bremen überlieferten Papsturkunden 1198–1503 (Hanover, 1993).

'Rolle und Rang des (Vize-)Kanzlers an der Kurie', in K. Herbers and V. Trenkle, eds., *Papstgeschichte im digitalen Zeitalter. Neue Zugangsweisen zu einer Kulturgeschichte Europas* (Cologne, 2018), 171–190.

'The Roman Curia (until about 1300)', in W. Hartmann and K. Pennington, eds., *The History of Courts and Procedure in Medieval Canon Law* (Washington, D.C., 2016), 160–228.

'Römische Kurie und Pfründenmarkt im Spätmittelalter', *Zeitschrift für historische Forschung*, 20 (1993), 129–152.

Shotwell, J. T., and Loomis, L. R., *The See of Peter* (New York, 1991) (originally published 1927).

Smith, T. W., 'The Development of Papal Provisions in Medieval Europe' *History Compass* 13 (2015), 110–121 (online resource, https://onlinelibrary.wiley.com/doi/full/10.1111/hic3.12223, accessed 21 September 2021).

'The Italian Connection Reconsidered: Papal Provisions in Thirteenth-Century England', in A. Spencer and C. Watkins, eds., *Thirteenth Century England XVII. Proceedings of the Cambridge Conference, 2017* (Woodbridge, 2021), 147–162.

'The Papacy, Petitioners and Benefices in Thirteenth-Century England', in T. W. Smith and H. Killick, eds., *Petitions and Strategies of Persuasion in the Middle Ages: The English Crown and the Church, 1200–1550* (Woodbridge, 2018), 164–184.

'Papal Executors and the Veracity of Petitions from Thirteenth-Century England', *Revue d'Histoire Ecclésiastique* 110 (2015), 662–683.

Stubbs, W., *The Constitutional History of England. Its Origin and Development, i* (Oxford, 1875).

Select Charters (Oxford, 1888).

Summerlin, D., *The Canons of the Third Lateran Council of 1179. Their Origins and Reception* (Cambridge, 2019).

Szaivert, W., 'Die Entstehung und Entwicklung der Klösterexemtion bis zum Ausgang des XI. Jahrhunderts', *Mitteilung des Instituts für Österreichische Geschichtsforschung,* 59 (1951), 265–298.

Tangl, M., ed., *Die päpstlichen Kanzleiordnungen von 1200–1500* (Innsbruck, 1894).

Tangl, M., 'Das Taxwesen der päpstlichen Kanzlei vom 13. bis zur Mitte des 15. Jahrhunderts', reprinted in *idem, Das Mittelalter in Quellenkunde und Diplomatik. Ausgewählte Schriften,* ii (Graz, 1966), 734–838.

Tardif, A., *Privilèges accordés à la couronne de France par le Saint-Siège. Publiés d'après les originaux conservés aux Archives de l'Empire et à la Bibliothèque impériale* (Paris, 1855).

Tedeschi, J., *Il Giudice e l'eretico. Studi sull'Inquisizione romana* (Milan, 1997).

Theodor van Mayden, *see* van Meyden.

Théry, J., 'Allo Scoppio del Conflitto tra Filippo il Bello di Francia e Bonifacio VIII. L'affare Saisset (1301). Primi Spunti per una rilettura', in G. Minucci (ed.), *I Poteri Universali e la Fondazione dello Studium Orbis. Il pontifice Bonifacio VIII dalla Unam sanctam allo schiaffo di Anagni* (Archivio per la storia del diritto medioevale e moderno, Miscellanee, 1; Bologna, 2008), 21–68.

Thomas de Rosa, *see* De Rosa.

Toustain, C. F., and Tassin, R. P., *Nouveau traité de Diplomatique,* 6 vols. (Paris, 1750–1765).

Trusen, W., *Anfänge des gelehrten Rechts in Deutschland. Ein Beitrag zur Geschichte der Frührezeption* (Wiesbaden, 1962).

Ullmann, W., *Growth of Papal Government in the Middle Ages* (London, 1955).

Unger, V., ed., *J. F. Böhmer, Regesta Imperii I. Die Regesten des Kaiserreichs unter den Karolingern 751–918 (926/962), 4. Papstregesten, 800–911. Tl. 3. 872–882* (Vienna, 2013).

Unger, V., *Päpstliche Schriftlichkeit im 9. Jahrhundert. Archiv, Register, Kanzlei* (Forschungen zur Kaiser-und Papstgeschichte des Mittelalters. Beihefte zu J. F. Böhmer, Regesta Imperii, 45; Vienna, 2018).

van Meyden, Theodor, *Tractatus de officio et jurisdictione Datarii, et de sylo Datarii* (Venice, 1654).

Vestrius, Octavianus, *In Romanae Aulae Actionem ... Introductio* (Venice, 1573).

Villard, F., *Recueil des documents relatifs à l'abbaye de Montierneuf de Poitiers (1076–1319)* (Archives Historiques de Poitou, LIX; Poitiers, 1973).

Violante, C., 'Il Monachesimo Cluniacense di Fronte al Mondo Politico ed Ecclesiastico. Secoli X e XI', in *idem, Studi Sulla Cristianità Medioevale. Società, Istituzioni, Spiritualità,* ed. P. Zerbi (Milan, 1975), 3–67.

von Heckel, R., 'Das päpstliche und sicilische Registerwesen in vergleichender Darstellung mit besonderer Berücksichtigung der Ursprünge', *Archiv für Urkundenforschung*, 1 (1908), 371–511, Beilage 'Der Libellus petitionum des Kardinals Guala Bichieri', 500–511.

'Studien über die Kanzleiordnung Innozenz' III', *Historisches Jahrbuch* 57 (1937), 258–289.

von Ottenthal, E., *Regulae Cancellariae Apostolicae. Die päpstlichen Kanzleiregeln von Johannes XXII. bis Nicolaus V.* (Innsbruck, 1888).

von Schulte, F., and Richter, E. L., *Canones et Decreta Concilii Tridentini ... accedunt S. Congr. Card. Conc. Trid. Interpretum Declarationes ac Resolutiones* (Leipzig, 1853).

Weber, M., *Wirtschaft und Gesellschaft*, 5th edn., 3 vols. (Tübingen, 1976).

Weckwerth, A., *Ablauf, Organisation und Selbstverständnis westlicher antiker Synoden im Spiegel ihrer Akten* (Jahrbuch für Antike und Christentum, Eränzungsband Kleine Reihe 5; Münster, 2010).

Weiß, S., *Rechnungswesen und Buchhaltung des Avignoneser Papsttums (1316–1378). Eine Quellenkunde* (*MGH* Hilfsmittel, 20; Hanover, 2003).

Werner, J., *Papsturkunden vom 9. bis ins 11. Jahrhundert. Untersuchungen zum Empfängereinfluss auf die äussere Urkundengestalt* (Berlin, 2017).

Wetzstein, T., '*Roma carpit marcas, bursas exhaurit et arcas.* Die Gier des Papstes und der Groll der Christenheit', in W. Maleczek, ed., *Die römische Kurie und das Geld. Von der Mitte des 12. Jahrhunderts bis zum frühen 14. Jahrhundert* (Vorträge und Forschungen, 85; Ostfildern, 2018), 337–372.

Wickham, C., *Medieval Rome. Stability and Crisis of a City, 900–1150* (Oxford, 2015).

Wiedemann, B., 'The Papal Camera and the Monastic Census. Evidence from Portugal, c. 1150–1190', *Zeitschrift für Kirchengeschichte*, 126 (2015), 181–196.

Wirbelauer, E., *Zwei Päpste in Rom. Der Konflikt zwischen Laurentius und Symmachus (498–514)* (Munich, 1993).

Wolfinger, L., 'König Ludwig der Heilige und die Genese fürstlicher Ablasspolitik. Beobachtungen zur Heilsökonomie weltlicher Herrschaft im Spätmittelalter', in E. Doublier and J. Johrendt, eds., *Economia della Salvezza e Indulgenza nel Medioevo* (Milan, 2017), 149–181.

Wolter, H., *Die Synoden im Reichsgebiet und in Reichsitalien von 916–1056* (Paderborn, 1988).

Zanke, S., *Johannes XXII., Avignon und Europa. Das politische Papsttum im Spiegel der kurialen Register (1316–1334)* (Leiden, 2013).

Zechiel-Eckes, K., *Die erste Decretale: Der Brief Papst Siricius' an Bischof Hmerius von Tarragona vom Jahr 385 (JK 255)* (*MGH* Studien und Texte; Hanover, 2013).

Zielinska, A., 'Territorialization, the Papacy, and the Institutions of the Polish Church, 1198–1357' (PhD thesis, University College London, 2021).

Zimmermann, H., ed., *J. F. Böhmer, Regesta Imperii II. Sächsisches Haus 919–1024. 5. Papstregesten, 911–1024* (Vienna, 1998).

Zimmermann, H., *Papsturkunden 896–1046*, 3 vols. (Österreichische Akademie der Wissenschaften, phil.-hist. Klasse, Denkschriften, 174, 177, 198; Vienna, 1984–1989).

Zutshi, P., *The Avignon Popes and their Chancery: Collected Essays* (Florence, 2021).

'Changes in the Registration of Papal Letters under the Avignon Popes (1305–1378)', in T. Broser, A. Fischer, and M. Thumser, eds., *Kuriale Briefkultur im späteren Mittelalter. Gestaltung – Überlieferung – Rezeption* (Cologne, 2015), 237–261 (reprinted in Zutshi, *The Avignon Popes and their Chancery*, 107–138).

'*Inextricabilis curie labyrinthus* – The Presentation of Petitions to the Pope in the Chancery and the Penitentiary during the Fourteenth and First Half of the Fifteenth Century', in A. Meyer, C. Rendtel and M. Wittmer-Butsch, eds., *Päpste, Pilger, Pönitentiarie. Festschrift für Ludwig Schmugge zum 65. Geburtstag* (Tübingen, 2004), 393–410.

'The Office of Notary in the Papal Chancery in the Mid-Fourteenth Century', in *idem, The Avignon Popes and their Chancery*, 155–178.

Original Papal Letters in England, 1305–1415 (Index Actorum Romanorum Pontificum / Commision internationale de diplomatique, 5; Vatican City, 1990).

'The Origins of the Registration of Petitions in the Papal Chancery in the First Half of the Fourteenth Century', in H. Millet, ed., *Suppliques et requêtes. Le gouvernement par la grâce en Occident (XIIe–XVe siècle)* (Collection de l'École Française de Rome, 310; Rome, 2003), 177–191 (reprinted in his *The Avignon Popes and their Chancery*, 69–83).

'The Papal Chancery: Avignon and Beyond', in *idem, The Avignon Popes and their Chancery. Collected Essays* (Florence, 2021), 3–24.

'The Papal Chancery and English Documents in the Fourteenth and Early Fifteenth Centuries', in P. Herde and H. Jacobs, eds., *Papsturkunden und europäisches Urkundenwesen* (Archiv für Diplomatik, Beiheft 7; Cologne, 1999), 201–217.

'Petitioners, Popes, Proctors: The Development of Curial Institutions, c. 1150–1250', in G. Andenna (ed.), *Pensiero e sperimentazioni istituzionali nella 'Societas Christiana' (1046–1250)* (Milan, 2007), 265–293.

'The Political and Administratve Correspondence of the Avignon Popes, 1305–1378: A Contribution to Papal Diplomatic', in *Aux origines de l'état moderne. La fonctionnement administratif de la papauté d'Avignon* (Collection de l'École Française de Rome, 138; Rome, 1990), 371–384.

'Unpublished Fragments of the Registers of Common Letters of Pope Urban VI (1378)', in B. Flug, M. Matheus, and A. Rehberg, eds., *Kurie und Region. Festschrift für Brigide Schwarz zum 65. Geburtstag* (Stuttgart, 2005), 41–61.

Index

Manuscripts and documents are indexed under 'MS'

celibacy, 6
census, 91
Chadwick, O., 15
Chalcedon, Council of, 44
Chancery, 2, 12, 17, 45, 64–65, 68, 79, 86,
    115, 117–118, 120, 129, 139–140,
    147–148, 150, 152, 161–162, 164,
    166–169
charisma, office, 6–7
Charlemagne, 4, 46, 48, 59, 81
charters, Anglo-Saxon, 31
Cheney, C. R., 45
Cifres, A., 174
Clanchy, M., 81, 132
Clarke, P. D., 102
clausulae, 109, 206
Clement II, 68–69
Clement V, 113
Clement VI, 100, 113
Cluniac monasteries, 92, 94, 102, 200,
    206–207
Cluny, 58
Codex Carolinus, 46, 49, 75, 81, 133
Collectio Avellana, 23, 45–46
comminatio, 20
complexity, 77, 83, 138
Congregation of the Council, 13, 25, 146,
    159, 177–181, 193, 195
Congregation of the Inquisition, 13, 25,
    174–176
constitutiones synodales, 42
corrector, 88, 116, 124, 126–127, 129, 135
    Penitentiary, 150
criminous clerics, 97
crusades, 2
Cubitt, C., 42
cursus, 11, 87

D'Acunto, N., 32, 90
Dahlhaus, J., 70–71
Dale, J., 101
Damasus I, 10, 45–46
Dannenberg, L.-A., 32
data communis, 116
Dataria, 160, 165–166, 192
de Boüard, A., 19
de Jong, M., 33
De Lasala, F., 9, 20–21, 31, 42, 49, 54,
    67–69, 78, 89, 116
De Luca, J. B., 163, 170, 182, 184
Dean, T., 107
Deanesly, M., 29
Decentius of Gubbio, 41
decretals, 88
Dehio, L., 138

Diener, H., 12
Dionysiana, 39, 46–47
diplomacy, 77
dispensations, 97, 100, 148, 161–164, 167
dispositio, 20, 29, 149
distributores, 126, 129, 134
Ditchfield, S., 174
ditio, 59
Donation of Constantine, 33, 141
Dondorp, H., 109
Dorna, M., 14
Doublier, E., 101
Dubois, J., 59
Duggan, A., 189

École des Chartes, 15, 27
École Française de Rome, 15–16, 131
Egger, C., 140
emperor, Byzantine, 45
emperor, Roman, 4, 6, 10, 36, 43, 65, 75,
    131, 188
Engel, F., 49
Engl, H., 69
English royal government, 107–108,
    111–112, 125, 130, 132, 135, 190
Epistolae ad principes, 157
Esch, A., 137
Ewald, P., 17, 50
Ewig, E., 55
ex certa scientia, 109
excommunication, 38, 77, 90, 97, 100, 103
executors, 105, 110
exemption, 31–32, 54, 56, 59, 72–73, 76,
    89–90, 92
expeditio per cameram, 139–140

Fagnani, P., 175
Faivre, A., 58
Falkenstein, L., 32, 72
Fawtier, R., 81
fees, 123–124, 144
Fees, I., 69–70, 72, 232
Fiat de speciali, 149–150
Fiat de speciali et expresso, 150
Fiat in forma, 150
Fiat ut petitur, 149
Fichtenau, H., 6, 10, 26–27, 35, 39
Ficker, J., 27
finance, papal, 2–3, 8, 86, 124, 138, 153, 191
Fink, K. A., 25, 141, 155, 157
food rents, 111, 138
forgery, 14, 32, 37
formularies, 11, 19, 54–55, 61, 64,
    102–103, 106, 113–114, 123, 132,
    135–136, 162, 209

Printed in the USA
CPSIA information can be obtained
at www.ICGtesting.com
LVHW020246300823
756703LV00005B/261